# AIRWAR

# AIRWAR

★★★ OUTRAGED SKIES

★★★★ WINGS OF FIRE

EDWARD JABLONSKI

DOUBLEDAY & COMPANY, INC., GARDEN CITY, NEW YORK

For my friends,
CLAIRE and PETER CLAY
once of the hospitable "George II,"
Luton, Bedfordshire, and now
of the "Coach and Horses," Rickmansworth,
Hertfordshire, England.

*Man, have pity on man.*
*Rain from the outraged sky*
*drowned the innocent earth*
*yet the seed did not die.*
*Flowering from that rebirth,*
*man, have pity on man*
*as you hold the fire in your hand*
*that can destroy mankind*
*and desolate every land.*
*If the power and the glory is this,*
*a flame that burns to the bone,*
*what shall be left to grow*
*when you and your fires have gone?*
*What maimed and desolate few*
*shall recover life's full span*
*from among the ashes of time?*
*Man, have pity on man.*
                    **Ursula Vaughan Williams**

# OUTRAGED SKIES

# Contents

# Preface

For many months, while the war raged in Europe—only in the air until after D-Day—the war in the Pacific seemed practically a matter of marking time. Not, of course, to those who were there, for in the exotic further reaches of the Pacific Theater of Operations, they lived a hellish existence and fought under frightful and frightening conditions.

Roosevelt and Churchill agreed at their "Arcadia" Conference held in Washington in the latter days of 1941 that the Grand Strategy would be aimed at "getting Hitler first." While the Japanese had struck an impressive blow and in time permeated a large area of the Pacific, the Arcadia agreement recognized the futility of trying to fight two wars simultaneously (as Hitler himself had so stupidly chosen to do); the Japanese were spread all over the Pacific, but Hitler was concentrated in Europe.

At the same time, however, the Japanese would have to be contained and someone would have to contain them; to a great extent, the Pacific became primarily an American problem—with, of course, the incomparable aid of Australian and New Zealand troops. To those sent to the Pacific, that was the Big War and, uninformed as they were about Grand Strategies, they found it difficult to understand why they were low men on the military totem pole. Supplies, replacements, parts, small luxuries seemed always in short supply. Planes and men literally fell apart.

All glamour was quickly stripped from the island paradises of the Pacific; the fighting ability of the Japanese soldier became a legend: He was mysterious, nearly invincible, and strangely indifferent to death. This was frightening, at first, and there were brave men who ran from this kind of fanatic warrior in the confusion of battle.

The fighting men—and this was true of both antagonists—were also, in a sense, victims of the power and personality struggles of their own leaders. This was especially marked in the Pacific, where MacArthur's headquarters seethed with intrigue and animosity; to this was added the further complication of the division of authority between the Army and the Navy. The war in the air over the Pacific was even further entangled because MacArthur's Chief of Staff simply did not like airmen. After all, they had all been kicked out of the Philippines, the Netherlands East Indies, and other points, so what good were they? They were a bunch of lighthearted kids who used up their expensive airplanes and who flouted every form of military propriety and dress; they were not "good soldiers." It took a hard little airman named Kenney to revise this attitude toward the kid fliers in his command and to teach the brass, earthbound as they were, how to make war in the air. In doing this he also taught the Japanese a thing or two.

Kenney's warring was for a time a kind of improvisation, as he used whatever he could get his hands on to keep going; when things turned against the Japanese, Kenney had himself an air force and a well-knit, disciplined army of kids. Although a great deal of bitter ground fighting occurred in New Guinea, much of the victory could be credited to Kenney's wily employment of air power.

Even after the tide had turned, the war in the Pacific was not over. The Battle of Midway took place in June of 1942, after which it was impossible for Japan ever to win the war; perhaps, but it continued for three long, life-consuming years. The first step on the road back was initiated by the Marines at Guadalcanal two months after Midway. It was called Operation Shoestring by the men who fought it, with good reason; they fought with very little, at times with aircraft that had no right to be in the sky, just as had the Air Force out of Australia and New Guinea.

The Pacific presented a unique battleground, consisting as it did of so much water; it was here that the aircraft carrier came into its own. By the time these appeared in numbers in the Pacific it was the Japanese airman who was forced to operate under terrible conditions. They too were worn out (to a greater degree than American pilots ever were) and their planes were pushed beyond normal usage. As fresh American airmen, with new planes in great numbers, appeared, tired or poorly trained Japanese pilots in used-up planes suffered. They too should not have been in the air. It was this that made a Marianas "Turkey Shoot," however unpredictable, inevitable.

This third volume in the series entitled *Airwar* attempts to present the story of the early fighting over the Pacific, to give some idea of what it was like to fight a poor man's war in an area rich in handicaps, problems, and unpredictability—not the least of which were human.

Considering the vasty distances, the Pacific war was fought on a small scale, until the war in Europe took its positive turn. It was a war of hit-and-run dogfights and, for a time, meager bombing missions; it was not at all a textbook war.

EDWARD JABLONSKI

# OUTRAGED SKIES

# BOOK I
# Kenney's Kids

*This was the type of strategy we hated most. The Americans attacked and seized, with minimum losses, a relatively weak area, constructed air fields, and then proceeded to cut supply lines to our troops in that area.*

—GENERAL MATSUIOCHI INO

*Because of the food shortage, some companies have been eating the flesh of Australian soldiers. The taste is said to be good.*

—LIEUTENANT SAKAMOTO

# I

# BUCCANEER

THE Pacific theater of operations offered an infinity of vista: great stretches of water and curving horizons, broken only by jungle-gnarled islands, coruscated atolls, and palm-fringed islets. There was more water than land and more sky than either. Clearly it was not a setting for massive land battles, such as Europe was, and distance precluded the strategic bombardment of the Japanese homeland. Instead, until air bases could be established within range of Japan, a series of contained, savage land battles must be fought, along with far-flung naval engagements and air battles. The deeper strategy lay in eliminating Japanese air power, in order to permit Allied naval and ground troops to function.

At Midway it had been revealed, to those receptive to revelation, that the war in the Pacific would be dominated, even resolved, by aircraft and not the battleship. Classic sea-borne warfare by the books was finished in the Pacific no less than land war in Europe. Those who clung to the old concepts were committed to certain defeat. Midway had proved this; but if it had proved that Japan could no longer win the Pacific war, that the end was not immediately in view was equally certain.

The United States Navy coveted all that Pacific water, and with its triumph through carrier aviation at Midway, it had raised its eyes to the heavens also. The Navy was most anxious to avenge Pearl

*General Douglas MacArthur, General Sir Thomas Blamey, commander of Australian ground forces in the Southwest Pacific, and MacArthur's Chief of Staff, Lieutenant General Richard K. Sutherland. Before Kenney could feel he rightfully commanded MacArthur's air force, he found he had to come to a proper understanding with Sutherland, who, though he brilliantly served MacArthur, liked having his finger in every pie—including Kenney's air forces. Kenney, putting his cards on the table in characteristic out-in-the-open manner, emerged as the only and full commander of the air forces in the Southwest Pacific—and remained as such for the rest of the war.*

(U. S. ARMY)

*Curtiss C-46 "Commando" of Air Transport Command flying over "the Hump" between India and China. Not only were the U.S. air forces and the RAF in-* *volved in fighting the Japanese in the air, the problem of supplies of the entire China-Burma-India theater was solved by air.* (U. S. AIR FORCE)

Harbor, hoping to assume full strategic control of the Pacific. Therein lay sufficient fuel for interservice argument, with enough remaining for international disagreements as well. The British had their hands full in the China-Burma-India theater, what with personal intrigues and a complex supply problem; in China proper Chennault continued to have to make do with what little he could get from the United States and the even less he received from Chiang Kai-shek. These theaters were preponderantly land masses and the problem of their internal politics interfered only indirectly with the Pacific.

All that stood between the U. S. Navy and full

control of the Pacific was General Douglas MacArthur. After enduring the ignominy of being booted out of the Philippines, the patrician, vain, and egocentric MacArthur found small consolation in being given half command of a second-rate war. MacArthur's share of the theater, called the Southwest Pacific Area, included, running southward, those regions in Japanese hands, the Philippines, Borneo, Celebes, New Guinea (the northern coast of which in time was overrun also), and the great subcontinent of Australia, which lay in the path of the invaders and where MacArthur languished, awaiting definition of his command.

The remainder of the Pacific "belonged" to Admiral Chester W. Nimitz, based at Pearl Harbor. A line running north and south, eventually along the 159th meridian just east of Australia cut through the Solomon Islands, skirting one of the southernmost of the group, Guadalcanal (which placed it technically under naval jurisdiction), while leaving the largest island, Bougainville (in the north) under MacArthur's jurisdiction. The definition of command became at times rather hazy, if not heated. In their respective theaters, MacArthur and Nimitz were absolute monarchs commanding all forces, naval, ground, and air. Where the battle lines merged or overlapped, the question of jurisdiction must be decided by co-operation, which was not always readily forthcoming in the scramble for supplies, men, matériel, and power.

Where MacArthur was motivated by a histrionic sense of his position in history, Nimitz was a cool professional Navy man who aimed for as much co-operation as possible. MacArthur's real naval bête noire was Admiral Ernest J. King, Chief of Naval Operations, Commander in Chief, United States Navy. King, blunt, decisive, brilliant—as was MacArthur—viewed the war from the standpoint of the United States Navy. Not only did this earn him the enmity of such men as Churchill (a navy man himself), but of a host of U. S. Army, Air Force, and Navy men as well.

MacArthur suspected King's Pacific planning was a personal vendetta out of Washington. That Europe was the favored battleground in 1942 was but another unfortunate sting, for the supplies required for MacArthur's avowed return to the Philippines were drained away. Isolated as he was in Australia, MacArthur pondered the defense of that great land mass with few troops, a worn-out and he believed a "disloyal" air force, and little hope of acquiring the means and the men to turn the losing defensive war into the offensive.

MacArthur assumed command of the Southwest Pacific Area on April 18, 1942. "None of the three elements of my command—naval, air or ground—was adequate " he said. He had left more troops in the Philippines than he had at his disposal in Australia, and these were either the remnants of the fighting which had gone before or green troops, ill-equipped and poorly trained. His small naval detachment had no carriers. His air force, commanded by Lieutenant General George H. Brett, was little more than a ragtag of P-40s, P-400s (an early export model of the Bell P-39, Airacobra), P-39s, and a few worn-out B-17s, the even more worn Douglas A-24s (the Air Force version of the Navy's Dauntless) which were joined later by a trickle of B-25s and B-26s.

Brett was not regarded by MacArthur as one of the loyal ones (primarily because Brett did not get along with MacArthur's Chief of Staff, Major General Richard K. Sutherland). As far as the entire Air Force was concerned, MacArthur was certain it would contribute little to the war. Brett and MacArthur were thoroughly estranged, and Sutherland by no means eased the situation. Sutherland, in fact, enjoyed the position of all but running the show and, as described by an old classmate of his at the Army War College, "rubbed people the wrong way. He was egotistic, like most people, but an unfortunate bit of arrogance combined with his egotism had made him almost universally disliked."

From Australia MacArthur hoped to lunge northward via New Guinea, at the great Japanese base at Rabaul, in New Britain. From Rabaul, Japanese fighters and bombers were positioned to sweep down into New Guinea to attack the major Allied base at Port Moresby, to initiate the assault upon Australia. On the other hand, the Navy had its attention drawn to the Solomons, where great activity on Guadalcanal made it obvious that the Japanese were constructing an air base there. From the Solomons, by bombing Allied bases in the New Hebrides and New Caledonia, the Japanese could eventually cut the supply lines to Australia as well as the South Pacific. From air fields in the Solomons also the Japanese could protect Rabaul, with its concentration of ships and aircraft.

Brett had much to contend with as the commander of the Allied Air Forces in the Southwest Pacific besides Sutherland. His personality, a mingling of hauteur and ego, caused trouble too. Brett could not bring himself to warm up to the Australians, particularly with its governmental representatives, members of a "radical" Labour government and therefore "left wing." The problem of replacement and supply was formidable and the morale of exhausted crews was low. Fatigued men flew long distances, much of it over water (the 49th Fighter Group, with its P-40s, for example, was based at

Darwin in northern Australia), to engage in combat with superior Japanese aircraft, or to drop a small load of bombs without appreciable results. Planes that should have been junked were patched and flown until they fell apart. Some did, and airmen resented serving in a forgotten theater, forgotten because of the "Hitler first" strategy. Deliveries of supplies arrived slowly; and crates when they finally came, were found to have been pilfered by desperate crews en route. Disgruntled by poor food, miserable living conditions, and the methods of the Australian Air Force and its part in the operations, American airmen had grown apathetic and believed that if conditions prevailed, an Allied victory was hopeless.

The sacking of Brett would not solve all of the problems, but according to the workings of the military mind he was "responsible" (momentarily and conveniently excluding the Japanese) and therefore must go. And so it was that on August 4, 1942, stubby, cocky, pugnacious, and anything but aristocratic Major General George C. Kenney succeeded Brett as air commander in the Southwest Pacific. This tough, outspoken, practical, no-nonsense fighter found himself a rather lone figure in a nest of prima donnas and debilitated warriors.

Kenney, upon arriving in Brisbane, seat of MacArthur's command, was established in the air-conditioned Lennon's Hotel and spent some time listening to Sutherland berating the Australians, various American officers, with emphasis upon the consistently unlucky Lewis H. Brereton (who had been MacArthur's air commander in the Philippines), and, of course, the obstinate Brett. The Air Force was especially vile: ". . . none of Brett's staff or senior commanders was any good, the pilots didn't know much about flying, the bombers couldn't hit anything and knew nothing about proper maintenance of their equipment or how to handle their supplies. He also thought there was some question about the kids having much stomach for fighting. . . . In fact, I heard just about everyone hauled over the coals except Douglas MacArthur and Richard K. Sutherland."

Shrewdly the canny ex-World War I fighter pilot, whose experience with aircraft maintenance, production, and manipulation went back more than two decades, said little at this point. But he thought, ". . . Sutherland was inclined to overemphasize his [own] smattering of knowledge of aviation."

*George Kenney, who ran the "air show" in MacArthur's section of the Pacific. Down to earth, pragmatic, loyal, Kenney not only won over MacArthur but also his own men, whom he called "kids," because, in the main, that was what they were.*

(U. S. AIR FORCE)

It was not until the next morning that Kenney was ushered in to meet with MacArthur, in lonely splendor, on the eighth floor of a nine-story office building in downtown Brisbane. After initial formalities, MacArthur began pacing and speaking, repeating the same criticisms of the Air Force which Sutherland had spouted the evening before. In MacArthur's view, "air personnel had gone beyond just being antagonistic to his headquarters, to the point of disloyalty. He would not stand for disloyalty."

During a pause in the outpouring of words, Kenney rose to full height (he was about a head shorter than MacArthur), deciding "it was time to lay my cards on the table."

He began by reminding MacArthur that he had come out to the Pacific because MacArthur had requested him and that "as long as he had had enough confidence in me to ask for me to be sent out to run his air show for him, I intended to do that very

B-17E, one of the few, based near Mareeba, Australia.
"A formation of five or six B-17s was regarded . . . as
. . . impressive . . ." (U. S. AIR FORCE)

thing." Kenney bluntly told the general that he could
run an "air show" better than or as well as anyone
available. The emphasis was on the fact that he—
Kenney—would run the air show. As for loyalty,
the day that Kenney no longer felt loyal to his chief,
"I would come and tell him so and at that time I
would be packed up and ready for the orders sending me back home."

MacArthur's stormy expression changed; the
fierce glint left his eyes. He studied the small man
before him, appraising him, then walked over, threw
an arm around Kenney's shoulders, and said,
"George, I think we are going to get along together
all right."

George Kenney served as air commander in the
Pacific from that day until the end of the war. If
he could pledge loyalty to MacArthur, whom he
genuinely admired, it was exceeded only by his devotion to his "kids," the young airmen who were
then fighting a great war with so little.

With characteristic promptitude, Kenney applied

himself to finding out what was wrong. He had
arrived on July 28 and would not assume command
until August 4. He found Brett's directorate system,
"with about a dozen people issuing orders in the
commander's name, . . . too complicated for me. I
decided to see how it worked first but I was afraid
I was not smart enough to figure it out. Further-
more, it looked to me as if there were too many
people in the headquarters. . . ."

In the interests of Allied co-operation, Kenney
found a rigid attempt to intermix Australian and
American throughout the organization. Obviously, it
did not always work. Despite the crowded office,
Kenney learned also that the bulk of the Allied
Air Staff, along with all personnel and supply records, was based in Melbourne about eight hundred
miles distant. But not so distant as MacArthur, only
three floors above in the same building. Brett could
never reach the commander and was forced always
to deal through Sutherland. This was not Kenney's
way of running an air show.

That same evening he borrowed Brett's Flying
Fortress, the famed *Swoose,* which enjoyed a better
press than Brett and took off for the forward bases

in Australia and in New Guinea. At Port Moresby, in southern New Guinea, Kenney found little to comfort him. The organization and procedure were "chaotic." Bombing missions, for example, were assigned out of Brett's headquarters in Brisbane. Orders were then sent to Major General Ralph Royce in Townsville to the north; Royce, in turn, notified the 19th Bombardment Group (H), based at Mareeba, about two hundred miles north of Townsville, and "the 19th Group sent the number of airplanes it had in commission to Port Moresby, where they were refueled, given their final 'briefing' on weather conditions along the route to the target and whatever data had been picked up by air reconnaissance.

"The fighter group at Port Moresby [35th Fighter Group] sat around waiting for the Japs to come over and tried to get off the ground in time to intercept them, which they seldom did, as the warning service rarely gave the fighters over five minutes' notice that the Nip planes were on the way." Those aircraft which did get off the ground seemed to operate without leadership, even on bombing missions. A formation of five or six B-17s was regarded as an impressive number then in the Pacific, although what with problems with weather or engines, it was a good mission if three aircraft found the target—Japanese shipping or the bases at Rabaul. But the meager accomplishment rarely made the effort worth it. Kenney found, too, that aircrews frequently abandoned missions when Japanese aircraft intercepted them, fearing that a single bullet would detonate either the auxiliary fuel tanks or the bomb load. No one had thought to inform them that this was not necessarily true.

If MacArthur demanded that a man be loyal, Kenney insisted that he be an "operator." Within days after his arrival and inspection of conditions, quite a number of non-operators were sent back to the States. He found the system of supply especially reprehensible, overladen with an obsession with paper formality. "An average time of one month elapsed from the time the requisition started until it was returned, generally with the notation 'Not available' or 'Improperly filled out.'" When told that desperately needed replacement parts for combat aircraft were denied to the fighting units, Kenney found it difficult to believe, "but the kids made me eat my words when they showed me a whole filing case of returned requisition forms. I

took along a handful for future reference and as evidence that some of the people in the organization were playing on the wrong team."

Immediately, too, Kenney began sending in his own team of operators. He had discussed his views on the air situation in Australia and New Guinea with MacArthur, asking for authority to send anyone home he regarded as "deadwood." MacArthur concurred and Kenney moved quickly. He found men who were genuinely tired from earlier campaigns, or ill from Australian heat or New Guinea jungle; they deserved relief, but those "who were not pulling their weight could go home and the rest would move north to take their turns eating canned food and living in grass huts on the edge of the jungle."

Kenney had been preceded to the area by two competent officers, Brigadier Generals Kenneth N. Walker, a bombardment specialist, and Ennis C. Whitehead, a fighter commander. In time Walker would head Kenny's bomber command and Whitehead, as Kenney's deputy, moved into Port Moresby to command the advanced echelon of what was to become the Fifth Air Force. With him Kenney had brought young Major William Benn, who had served as his aide when Kenney was commander of the Fourth Air Force in San Francisco. Benn, as were Walker and Whitehead, was definitely an operator. Anxious to serve in a combat unit Benn was happy to be given command of the 63rd Squadron of the 43rd Bombardment Group, which at the time of Kenney's advent was depleted—"all they had left was a flag and a couple of guys to hold it up." As soon as the 43rd Group became operational with B-17s, it would take the work load off the much abused 19th Bomb Group, then commanded by Lieutenant Colonel Richard N. Carmichael. The 19th Group had been, in Kenney's words, "kicked out of the Philippines and out of Java and kicked around ever since."

Upon his arrival Kenney had requested an inventory of aircraft strength (when he had asked Brett, the latter told him simply that he did not know). According to the books, Kenney learned in a few days that he had "in the United States part of the show, 245 fighters, 53 light bombers, 70 medium bombers, 62 heavy bombers, 36 transports, and 51 miscellaneous aircraft, or a total of 517. . . . The Australian Royal Air Force listed 22

*An Airacobra and a B-17 nestled in revetments near Port Moresby, New Guinea. The P-39 was a disad-* *vantaged contender as far as the Zero was concerned; the Fortress, the "E," with a stinger in the tail was respected by Japanese pilots.* (U. S. AIR FORCE)

squadrons, but most of these were equipped with training planes doing anti-submarine patrol off the coasts of Australia itself. Two fighter squadrons in New Guinea had a total of 40 planes, and four reconnaissance squadrons had a total of 30 aircraft."

But out of the 245 American fighters, 170 were awaiting salvage or were being overhauled, none of the light bombers were ready for operations, and "only 37 mediums were in shape or had guns and bomb racks to go to war with." Of the 62 heavy bombers only 43 were more or less fit to fly; less than half of the mixed bag of transports were flyable. As for the "miscellaneous" aircraft, none was fit for combat. A Dutch squadron, equipped with American B-25s, was training but required a good deal of time before it would be ready for combat.

"All told I had about 150 American and 70 Australian aircraft, scattered from Darwin to Port Moresby and back to Mareeba and Townsville, with which to dispute the air with the Jap." Kenney estimated that the Japanese had at least five times the number of planes he could muster, besides being in a position to replace losses within days from their homeland.

The greatest concentration of Japanese air power facing Kenney's forces was based at Rabaul, New Britain. The 25th Koku Sentai (Air Flotilla) consisting of the Tainan Kokutai (Air Corps), the 4th Kokutai, and the Yokohama Kokutai, under Rear Admiral Sadayoshi Yamada, operated from Rabaul chiefly against Port Moresby as well as Guadalcanal in the Solomons. These were land-based units, equipped with the Zero fighters; in addition there were bomber units (mediums: *Nell, Betty*) which attacked Port Moresby regularly and which gave occasional attention to Darwin and other Australian ports. In addition to the land-based planes there were also the planes of the Japanese carrier divisions to consider.

Until he could obtain better and more aircraft as well as replacements for tired crews, Kenney faced a formidable job.

By this time the Joint Chiefs of Staff had decided on a plan of operation giving priority to the Navy's proposal to move into the Solomons as against MacArthur's to move into New Guinea to seize and occupy the Buna area.

The honor, then, of making the first American offensive move in the Pacific fell to the U. S. Navy, not to MacArthur, under Vice-Admiral Robert L. Ghormley, commander of the South Pacific Area. The honor fell, more specifically and traditionally, to the 1st Marine Division, which was to assault the

Solomons. MacArthur's contribution to the offensive was to be a Kenney-mounted bombing mission against Rabaul. This small effort did not please MacArthur, nor did it comply with the image of himself as a major contributor to the offensive.

While these decisions were being made, the Japanese themselves began moving ashore at Buna on July 21, 1942. Having been thwarted in an invasion attempt at Port Moresby in the Battle of the Coral Sea, the Japanese hoped to move in on this chief Allied base by crossing over the Owen Stanley Mountains, through the Kokoda trail, to take Port Moresby from the rear. This would not only place Australia within more convenient striking distance, but would also serve as protection for Rabaul as well as the Solomons in the South Pacific.

The assault in the Solomons was scheduled for August 7, 1942, just about a week after Kenney had begun moving and shaking up his command. For his first official "show" he had promised MacAr-

*A Flying Fortress off the coast of New Guinea. About forty were operational when Kenney arrived to assume command of the air forces in the Southwest Pacific.*

*Zero pilots respected the big bomber, although many had been worn out by constant use.*

(U. S. AIR FORCE)

thur that twenty B-17s would be ready for the mission and he guaranteed that sixteen to eighteen would bomb the target. MacArthur appeared skeptical, though hopefully commenting that, if so, it would be the "heaviest bomber concentration flown so far in the Pacific war."

One of Kenney's first moves upon visiting the base of the 19th Bombardment Group at Mareeba was to order all flying suspended until the group's B-17s could be put in some sort of flying condition. On the day of his visit Kenney found that a maximum effort by the group might have gotten about four bombers into the air. Engines were sadly worn and many planes were grounded for lack of tail wheels. Rather than bother with requisition forms, Kenney reached Major General Rush B. Lincoln, in Melbourne eight hundred miles distant, by phone and simply read off a list of the supplies required by Carmichael's group.

When he checked in at Mareeba a few days later, Kenney was gratified to hear that Carmichael hoped to have twenty B-17s ready for the mission to Rabaul. So great a number of aircraft caused some concern among squadron commanders when Kenney impressed them with the importance of holding formation—they had not flown in such large numbers before. Defensive formations were important to the bombers to hold off, with their gun concentrations, attacking Japanese fighters.

On the morning of August 7, 1942, Carmichael had sixteen B-17s at Port Moresby, where they refueled after flying up from Mareeba. While the Marines were heading in for their objectives in the Solomons—Tulagi, Gavutu, Tanambogo, and Guadalcanal—Carmichael led his formation over the treacherous Owen Stanleys to Rabaul. There were now thirteen B-17s; one having crashed on takeoff and two others having been forced back with engine trouble. Proceeding on to Rabaul and the bomber base, Vunakanau, the Fortresses encountered fighters, little dancing Zeros which swarmed in around the bombers. During the attacks one Fortress, piloted by Captain Harl Pease (whose aircraft was not functioning properly) was shot down burning; it was the only B-17 lost in the attack. Bombs pirouetted down upon the parked bombers of Vunakanau, wreaking havoc and leaving smoking bombers to clutter the runway. Kenney thought eleven of the twenty Japanese fighters were de-

stroyed, but another claim amounted to seven. Whatever the claims, Japanese fighters and bombers of Rabaul had been kept busy during the Solomons landings. Kenney was also certain that the bombing had destroyed perhaps seventy-five parked aircraft, although the figure appears rather generous. Some fighters of the Tainan Kokutai had rushed down to Guadalcanal to challenge Marine and Navy fighter planes over the invasion beaches. In this battle Japanese ace Saburo Sakai accounted for four American planes before being seriously wounded himself and his Zero shot up. All but blinded by his wounds, Sakai managed to fly his damaged plane over the nearly six hundred miles from Guadalcanal back to Rabaul.

The success, though limited, of the 19th Group's Rabaul mission was good for the group's morale and for Kenney's reputation as an "operator." He quickly revealed a near-fiendish inventiveness in dealing with the air situation in the Pacific. Soon (by August 9) he could announce the formation of the Fifth Air Force and began injecting spirit into it and developing its personality in his own aggressive image.

II

Kenney, as he explained to MacArthur, visualized his primary mission as the taking out of Japanese air power "until we owned the air over New Guinea. There was no use talking about playing across the street until we got the Nips off of our front lawn."

His methods were far from conventional. During his flight from the United States to Australia, Kenney had discussed with his aide, Major William Benn, the possibilities of low-altitude bombing to knock out ships. This was not, in fact, a new concept. Earlier in the summer Benn had observed demonstrations of the idea at the Eglin Field, Florida, proving ground. Here the hope of bouncing bombs into tanks from fighters was being tested under the direction of Colonel Sargent Huff. The British had also tried minimal-altitude bombing, but had given it up. It remained for Kenney and Benn to give the idea its special significance in the Pacific. High-altitude bombing, such as had been attempted at Midway by the B-17s, proved ineffective. Since the Japanese were dependent upon "open-water defense" (that is, shipping supplies and reinforcements to their outposts in large convoys), thus counting upon the vastness of the Pacific, the ability of ships to maneuver, and their own Navy and aircraft to protect them, dealing with ships at sea presented a challenge. As they flew eastward, Kenney and Benn considered the possibilities of swooping down close to the water, much like a Navy torpedo bomber, to eject the bomb from the plane. Dropped at the correct speed, altitude (about mast-high), and distance from the ship, the bomb with delayed-action fuzes literally skipped along the water until it struck the side of the vessel. It would then, ideally, sink a little and detonate against the side of the ship. Meanwhile, the bomber would have cleared the enemy ship and hurtled away from the scene of the explosion. Shortly after their arrival in Australia, Kenney "fired" Benn as his aide and placed him in command of the 63rd Squadron (43rd Bombardment Group) so that he might test the feasibility of "skip-bombing" with the B-17.

Kenny realized that in order for his skip-bomber to be effective it must be able to overwhelm the deck defenses of Japanese ships. The skip-bomber must have plenty of firepower in the nose, a problem he turned over to a slender, tanned, raffish character, Major Paul I. Gunn. Because he was over forty, Gunn was nicknamed "Pappy" by the younger pilots and was so called even by Kenney, himself then about fifty.

When the war began in 1941, Gunn was an experienced pilot and operations manager of the new Philippine Air Lines. As a captain the second day of the war Gunn began a legendary career flying supplies, evacuating refugees, and accomplishing impossible flying feats under the eyes and guns of the Japanese. He used the Philippine Air Lines civilian Beechcrafts for his missions, frequently hugging the ground and thinking how much harm he could do to the Japanese if only he had had guns installed in the nose of the Beechcraft. This was not, of course, an original conception, for the concept of attack aviation was not in itself new (Kenney, in fact, had taught the subject in the Air Corps Tactical School for a decade). One of the Air Force units Kenney found languishing in Australia when he arrived was the 3rd Bombardment Group (Light), specialists in ground assault and equipped with the Douglas A-24 (Dauntless), the Douglas

A-20 (Havoc), and a third squadron with the North American B-25; the fourth squadron had no planes at all.

The "fortunes of war" brought together Kenney, Benn and his skip-bombing Flying Fortresses, the 3rd Group's assortment of twin-engined attack planes, and the wild-flying, resourceful Pappy Gunn.

If MacArthur had a historic mission to fulfill in his promise to return to the Philippines, Gunn had a deeper, more personal one. When the air forces were scrambled out of the Philippines after the fall of Corregidor in May of 1942, Gunn's wife and four children were imprisoned at the Santo Tomás prison camp near Manila.

Walter D. Edmonds perceptively observed ". . . Pappy Gunn governed himself as though there were two wars against Japan: the one the United States had on its hands, and his own. He fought them both."

Kenney had one other device in mind when he arrived to take over the Allied Air Forces in the Southwest Pacific. "Back in 1928," Kenney has written, "in order to drop bombs in a low-altitude attack without having the fragments hit the airplane I had put parachutes on the bombs; the parachutes opened as the bombs were released from the airplane. . . . With a supersensitive fuze, which kicked the thing off instantaneously on contact with anything—even the leaf of a bush—the bomb was a wicked little weapon. . . ." These so-called "parafrags" were small bombs, weighing about twenty-five pounds, which fragmented in more than a thousand pieces that could "go through a two-inch plank." Kenney's targets were not planks, of course, and he considered "trying them out on some Jap airdrome and wondering if those fragments would tear airplanes apart—as well as Japs, too, if they didn't get out of the way." It was while he was in Washington awaiting transportation to the Pacific and "looking around for anything that was not nailed down" that Kenney found several thousand of his parachute bombs still stored away. He had them shipped to Australia.

Another wicked weapon was named the "Kenney Cocktail"; this was a standard M-47 100-pound bomb loaded with white phosphorus which, when it burst, flung out streamers of burning incendiary material in all directions for 150 feet. Its effect upon man and machine was deadly. By the end of

*A Douglas A-20 "Havoc" demonstrating a skip-bombing on a Japanese freighter. Splashes to left of ship mark the spots at which the bombs bounced (two from the photo ship and two from the Havoc in the photograph). One of the dangers of skip-bombing was collision with the target; another was being caught in your own bomb explosion. This type of bombing required great skill.* (U. S. AIR FORCE)

1942 Kenney's name was known in Tokyo whose radio referred to him as "the Beast" and one of the "gangster leaders of a gang of gangsters from a gangster-ridden country."

Kenney held no grand strategic illusions. He wished "to own the air over New Guinea" primarily so that MacArthur's ground troops, Australian and later American, could push the Japanese over the Owen Stanley Mountains back to Buna and out of New Guinea. Co-operation with the ground forces would be essential to this design. "Tanks and heavy artillery can be reserved for the battlefields of Europe and Africa," Kenney wrote to his chief, Arnold. "They have no place in jungle warfare. The artillery in this theater flies. . . .

"In the Pacific theater we have a number of islands garrisoned by small forces. These islands are nothing more or less than aerodromes or aerodrome areas from which modern fire-power is launched."

"The Air Force is the spearhead of the Allied attack in the Southwest Pacific," Kenney believed. "Its function is to clear the air, wreck the enemy's land installations, destroy his supply system, and give close support to troops advancing on the ground.

"Clearing the air means more than air superiority; it means air control so supreme that the birds have to wear our Air Force insignia. Wrecking the enemy's ground installations does not mean just softening them up. It means taking out everything he has —aerodromes, guns, bunkers, troops. Destroying his supply system means cutting him off the vine so completely and firmly that he not only cannot undertake offensive action but, due to his inability to replenish his means to wage war, he cannot even maintain a successful defense."

In order to carry out his mission, however, Kenney was forced to improvise and get along as best he could with what little he had. One of the innovations was a converted Havoc (A-20 light bomber), the handiwork of Pappy Gunn, which instead of its meager four .30-caliber machine guns had an additional four .50 calibers in the nose. Its limited range, too, had been increased with the introduction of two 450-gallon fuel tanks in the bomb bay which would give the Havoc the additional fuel to get over the 13,000-foot barrier of the Owen Stanleys. One further modification was a fanciful bomb rack installed in the old bomb bay; this carried the parachute-fragmentation bombs which Kenney wished to try out on a Japanese airfield.

The first opportunity arrived on September 12, 1942. Captain Donald P. Hall led nine Havocs of the 89th Attack Squadron (of the 3rd Bombardment Group) in low over the Buna, New Guinea, airstrip. The first element, with Hall in the van, swooped in over the palm trees and saw to their delight a number of new enemy aircraft neatly lined up on the strip. With their forward firing guns churning up the area before them the Havocs swept over the Buna strip scattering parafrags (forty per plane) in their wake. As the light bombs gently lowered to the ground aroused Japanese guards, apparently assuming paratroopers were being dropped, rushed out to fire at them. Until the first supersensitive fuze touched something, the hapless riflemen did not realize how exposed they were to the vicious effect of the descending silken packages.

The primary objective was, however, aircraft, and Hall's bombers scattered the bombs across the airstrip and pulled away to escape the bomb blasts— as well as Japanese antiaircraft fire. The parafrags, falling about fifty yards apart, began doing their work, wrecking aircraft (claims were made for sev-

enteen of the twenty-two planes on the strip) and very quickly discouraging both the men with rifles and the antiaircraft crews. The second wave strung out its bombs with no interference from the ground. To complete the job, postholing the airstrip itself, Kenney followed the Havoc attack with B-26s and B-17s (five of the former, seven of the latter), which bombed from higher up with thousand-pounders onto the runways. Not one American plane was lost and the first parafrag mission was judged a success, for even if the claims for aircraft destroyed were exaggerated, serious damage had been done at Buna.

By this time the Japanese were dangerously near Port Moresby, pushing the Australian 7th Division before them. Upon seeing the situation firsthand, Kenney flew back to Australia, suggesting that the Australians be reinforced with Americans of the 32nd Division. Although MacArthur felt the 32nd was ill trained, he realized that unless the Japanese were stopped before reaching Moresby, Australia itself would become a battleground. He had decided to send the 32nd Division to New Guinea and put his staff to work arranging for transportation.

Kenney suggested flying the troops to Port Moresby; MacArthur's eyes lit up, but his staff demurred. After all, when a body of water intervened between the place where you wished to send troops and the place where they were at, it followed that you placed these troops on ships for transport. This was the normal way to do it. It would also take two weeks, Kenney argued. Planes would get them there in a day or two. To MacArthur's staff this just didn't seem proper and they wanted the movement to proceed "in an orderly way." But MacArthur elected to let Kenney fly the 126th Regiment of the 32nd into Moresby. By borrowing transport planes from the Australians Kenney transported the first 230 infantrymen to Port Moresby by the evening of September 15, 1942; the rest of the regiment was still waiting at the docks. Disappointed, Kenney asked to be given another regiment (the 128th Infantry), and over the protests of his staff MacArthur said all right.

Soon ground troops were arriving in Port Moresby at a rate of six hundred a day. By this time Kenney was using a dozen Australian civil transports and even had American civilians working for him. Two B-17s had arrived from the United States with ci-

*Factory-fresh Lockheed P-38 "Lightning," which re-
lieved the P-40 and P-39 in the Pacific. No dogfighter,*
*it was heavy and sturdy and carried plenty of fire-
power. Its twin engines were an added safety device.*
(ERIK MILLER/LOCKHEED-CALIFORNIA)

vilian pilots, employees of the Boeing Company. Kenney pressed them into service and soon the B-17s were ferrying troops out of Australia. The last of the 128th Infantry had been transported to Port Moresby and the remainder of the 126th Infantry was still at sea; they arrived two days later. MacArthur was elated, Kenney was "crowing," and MacArthur's staff was put out. There were dark suggestions voiced within MacArthur's hearing that Kenney was "reckless and irresponsible."

Kenney's job did not conclude with the delivery of the bulk of the 32nd Division to Port Moresby. He would have to see that they were supplied, that various Japanese airfields—Rabaul, Lae in New Guinea—were given attention, besides bombing and strafing Japanese emplacements along the Kokoda trail. Further, there were calls for assistance in the South Pacific from Admiral Ghormley and the Solomons campaign. This generally called for B-17s to bomb Rabaul during the day and Catalinas of the Royal Australian Air Force during the night.

III

The Japanese too had the problem of supply and replacement. Like MacArthur's staff, their thinking favored the "orderly way," which generally meant large convoys of ships, transports with escorts. Supply by air, though not completely ignored, was not seriously considered by the Japanese. Once the air over New Guinea was owned by Kenney, it left the Japanese convoys open to aerial attack. By the end of the year Kenney had acquired some B-24s (this was the 90th Bombardment Group), which were plagued, however with mechanical problems (cracked nosewheel collars) and out of action for a month. When new collars were specially manufactured and the group made its first missions in mid-November 1942, it demonstrated a need for further training (on the second mission—to Rabaul—the B-24 carrying Group Commander Colonel Arthur Meehan did not return, nor did one other, and the other crews had little idea of where they had been). This was a bitter development for Kenney, who had already relieved the overworked 19th Bombardment Group, which had begun flying their equally overworked B-17s back to the United States. In

time, however, the 90th Bombardment Group's B-24s—and crews—were ready. They would then join up with Kenney's then only active heavy group, the 43rd.

Also arriving in the Pacific by the end of 1942 was the Lockheed P-38 ("Lightning"), a plane which seemed unloved in Europe, but which Kenney favored for the simple reason that it flew. There were other good reasons, of course, once the kinks were ironed out of the plane (initially leakage in the intercooling system); it was a superb fighter for the Pacific theater. Its twin engines was one of its blessings, considering the distances over which it must range. A single-engined craft simply went down and out, but with its two engines, the P-38 could lose one and still return to its base. It was a great, heavy aircraft for a fighter and although it could not match the Zero in dogfighting, it proved to be the scourge of the Japanese fighter in the Pacific. The Lightning was faster than the Zero, achieving a top speed of more than four hundred miles an hour; it could outclimb and outdive the Japanese fighter, performed exceptionally well at high altitude, and carried plenty of firepower (20-mm. cannon and four .50-caliber machine guns). In addition, the P-38 came equipped with features which the Japanese hardly considered (because they added weight): self-sealing fuel tanks and armor plating to protect the pilot.

Twenty-five Lightnings had arrived in Brisbane in September but remained grounded until the various mechanical defects had been cleared up. Newly arrived pilots were forced to wait until the P-38s were ready or use the worn-out P-39s and P-40s for combat. The bugs were not eliminated from the P-38s until December; meanwhile another batch of twenty-five arrived but without feeds for the guns —these too were grounded until the feeds could be installed. Finally, by October Kenney had sixteen P-38s of the 49th Fighter Group flown up to Port Moresby. Further complications set in what with leakages discovered in the cooling system, problems with disintegrating wing tanks—and "borrowing" of the operational P-38s by the South Pacific command for the Solomons campaign.

Eventually, in December 1942, the P-38s began to operate. The first Japanese plane brought down by one was achieved in an unorthodox manner. According to General Kenney "a big good-natured New Orleans Cajun named Faurot" was flying over

*Japanese fighter pilots, who "owned the air" over New Guinea when Kenney arrived to take over the aerial operations for MacArthur. These Zero pilots, often victorious over American and Australian pilots in their P-40s and P-39s, would find the arrival of the Lightning in the Pacific a serious challenge to their superiority.* (DEFENSE DEPT., U. S. MARINE CORPS)

the Japanese air base at Lae. For days the Americans had radioed insulting messages (Japanese and Americans exchanged such insults over their radios in English), but without inciting the Zeros to come up. Faurot on this day carried, as did the others in the flight, two five-hundred-pound bombs under his plane's wing. The plan was to make holes in the runway at Lae. Finally after the by now traditional exchange of insults the Americans had succeeded in arousing one of the Japanese pilots. His Zero had begun a takeoff run when Faurot noticed him and dived. He was down to two thousand feet when he recalled that he carried a thousand pounds of bomb, which would deter him immeasurably if he and the Zero tangled. Faurot quickly released the two five-hundred-pounders, pulled back on the control column to escape the blast, and pulled around in a turn, ready to pounce on the Zero. As he watched, the two bombs fell into the water at the end of the runway, which ran right to the beach. The resultant splash caught the Japanese plane, at that moment at runway's end and lifting off the ground. The Zero lurched crazily and careened into the water, a total wreck.

"When the kids returned, I asked Faurot if he had nerve enough to claim 'the first Nip brought down in air combat in this theater by a P-38.' He grinned and asked if I was going to give him an Air Medal. I had promised one to anyone that got an official victory. I said, 'Hell, no. I want you to shoot them down, not splash water on them.'" Kenney, whose relationship with his "kids" was marked by an affectionate, bantering humor of the crusty father, awarded Faurot his Air Medal, although warning him that "he'd better keep the whole thing quiet."

With a few airplanes to his credit and some new eager kids to fly them, Kenney felt himself reasonable able to take on the "Nip" in his own back yard. Curiously this was echoed, almost in Kenney's own words, in a Japanese diary found in New Guinea. Early in December 1942 the diarist noted of Kenney's Kids that "they fly above our position as if they owned the skies."

Kenney's first great opportunity to prove himself in a spectacular manner came in March 1943. Buna on the northeast coast of New Guinea was wrested from the Japanese—after a half year of savage ground fighting—in January; Guadalcanal, in the Solomons, had been reluctantly abandoned by the Japanese, also following a half year of sanguinary land, sea, and air battles leading to the first major land defeat by the Japanese. The Nipponese tenta-

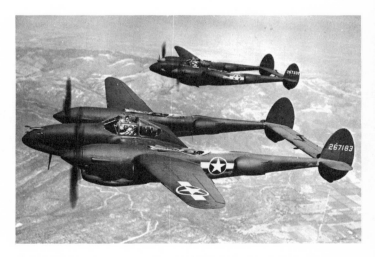

*Lightning in battle dress showing its armament: a 20-mm. cannon and three of the four .50-caliber machine guns in the nose.* (ERIK MILLER/LOCKHEED-CALIFORNIA)

cles into the Solomons and New Guinea constricted bloodily. In the Solomons the focus shifted to the northernmost island, Bougainville; in New Guinea it moved up the coast, about 150 miles from Buna to the Lae-Salamaua area in the Huon Gulf.

Having abandoned Guadalcanal and Buna the Japanese proceeded to reinforce their position at Lae. Late in February 1943 Kenney's intelligence unit had learned that a Japanese convoy, forming at Rabaul, was scheduled to arrive in Lae early in March. This would coincide with a period of bad weather predicted for the area, which would curtail air operations. Although the information was meager, Kenney sensed a large-scale troop movement in the offing. He alerted General Whitehead at Port Moresby and ordered reconnaissance aircraft to cover the area of the Bismarck Sea.

Meanwhile about five thousand troops of the Japanese 51st Infantry Division assigned to reinforce the Lae-Salamaua garrison had begun boarding seven merchant vessels in Rabaul Harbor. Eight destroyers were to serve as escort, along with an air cover of about a hundred fighters (not simultaneously, but on a schedule in order to furnish protection over a period of days, generally in groups of twenty to thirty). Special service vessel *Nojima* rounded out the convoy of sixteen ships; aboard one of the transports, the *Kembu Maru,* besides troops, was a precious cargo of aviation fuel and other supplies.

The convoy set forth under cover of darkness and stormy weather the night of February 28. The weather hindered Kenney's reconnaissance planes and it was not until the afternoon of March 1 that a B-24 crew spotted "fourteen ships with Zero escort" about 150 miles west of Rabaul. The weather closed in again, preventing further spotting as well as an attack by eight B-17s of the 43rd Group which did not locate the convoy.

The weather continued bad on March 2 and it took until midmorning before a 90th Group B-24 found the convoy and radioed its position—about fifty miles north of Cape Gloucester, New Britain, heading south for the Vitiaz Straits. As soon as possible the 43rd Group's B-17s left Port Moresby, climbed the Owen Stanleys, and began dropping thousand-pound bombs from sixty-five hundred feet. This first flight of eight Flying Fortresses made the attack without fighter protection, having missed its

rendezvous with the P-38s. Zeros closed in and in the fighting three were claimed shot down; all B-17s returned to Port Moresby claiming hits on two transports, reporting that one had split in two and sank within minutes of the initiation of the attack. This was the *Kyokusei Maru,* whose survivors, about eight hundred men, were taken aboard two destroyers and rushed to Lae during the night. The destroyers rejoined the convoy early the next morning.

A second flight of B-17s, twenty in all, followed the first to continue the bombing, claiming two hits and several near misses. Crews reported ships dead in the war, burning or sinking as well as the rescue operations of the two Japanese destroyers. Further defensive attacks by Zeros holed the B-17s but did not knock any of the bombers down; one Zero was claimed. In the early evening further bombing attacks by the 43rd Group near the northern entrance to the Vitiaz Straits claimed one vessel "left sinking" and another Zero. Enemy fighters, it was noted, were less persistent than in the earlier phases of the battle. As the sudden tropical night fell, the B-17s returned to Port Moresby while a Royal Australian Air Force PBY Catalina remained over the Japanese convoy during the night; in the morning a B-17 appeared to relieve the Catalina and found the convoy off the Huon Peninsula and within striking range of the medium bombers.

On Wednesday, March 3 at "ten o'clock the big brawl began about 50 miles southeast of Finschhafen, right where we had planned it," Kenney has written. Australian Beauforts of the RAAF 9th Operational Group carrying torpedoes opened the attack but without success; soon after, Australian Beaufighters, armed with nose cannons and machine guns in the wings, swooped in for a low-level attack. Above the Beaufighters B-17s co-ordinated a high-altitude attack and B-25s a medium-level attack with the Beaufighters. The sea churned with the explosion of bombs, the splash of cannon, and machine-gun fire whipping across the dodging Japanese ships. Thousands of feet above the carnage Zeros and P-38s fought their battles. The Battle of the Bismarck Sea had reached a climax.

Following the Beaufighter, B-17, and B-25 attack, twelve B-25Cls, newly converted into powerful strafers by the hand of Pappy Gunn and led by Major Edward Larner of the 90th Squadron (3rd

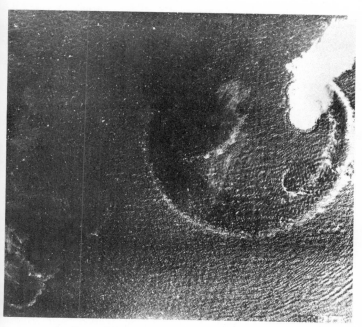

*A direct hit upon a Japanese ship in the Bismarck Sea. The wake of the evasive circle of the ship may be seen.* (U. S. AIR FORCE)

Bombardment Group), swept down to the water for the most savage attack of the battle.

Larner was one of Kenney's favorites among his kids. When Kenney first met Larner the latter was a lieutenant who had "fire, leadership, and guts." This had been demonstrated during the Buna campaign at least twice, the first time during a strafing run on Japanese artillery and machine-gun positions at Soputa, just inland from Buna. Larner, leading the 90th Squadron, blazed in on the gun positions at a low level. An antiaircraft burst under the tail of his plane, tipping its nose, flung Larner's plane through the treetops for hundreds of yards, battering the plane as well as various trees. As laconically reported by the pilot, "following this accident I was able to make only two more strafing passes before the plane became so unmanageable that I thought it best to return to base where repairs could be made."

As Kenney observed, Larner landed the B-25 at nearly 175 miles an hour because of the damages to the wing surfaces which affected the lift. The underside of the plane was grooved where a palm tree had grazed it; the wing was dented and gouged

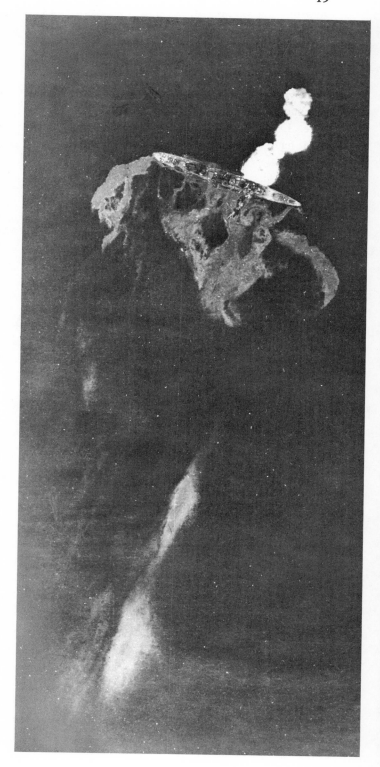

*Battle of the Bismarck Sea: Japanese destroyer in distress, burning, losing oil, and dead in the water after Kenney's Fifth Air Force bombers hit it.*

(U. S. AIR FORCE)

and one engine was stuffed with foliage and bits of branches. The plane was in a condition that would have normally suggested abandonment, but Larner brought it home instead. Kenney gave him a Silver Star and promoted him to captain.

The second incident occurred when Larner brought his B-25 down low to strafe a Japanese machine-gun position—so low that the aircraft's tail bumper had hit the ground and dragged through the sand for several yards. Larner explained that he had been forced to go so low because he had "to look in the windows of the bunker to see what to shoot at."

As he studied the scraped-up plane, Kenney stood with one of Larner's machine gunners. The sergeant sighed audibly and said, "I guess I'll have to quit this pilot of mine. He's gone nuts. He runs into trees and tears 'em down and now he thinks he's a farmer and he's started plowing up the ground with his tail bumper. . . ."

Catching the mood, Kenney replied with the suggestion that he could fix it up. "I've got a chauffeur over at my headquarters who wants to shoot a pair of fifty-caliber guns. How about swapping jobs?"

The gunner hesitated just an instant before answering. "General I'd better stick. You see, Captain Larner is so crazy he really needs me to look after him."

So it was that Major Larner lead his strafers down into the melee that had become the Battle of the Bismarck Sea. The twelve B-25s, each with eight forward-firing .50-caliber machine guns in the nose, plus two in the top turret—ten in all—razed all before them as they came in at five hundred feet. The Japanese ships broke convoy formation and scrambled in an attempt to get out of the way. The B-25s swirled and separated, selecting a target. Waiting in an 89th Squadron Havoc, Pilot Edward Chudoba heard the B-25 pilots arguing over targets as the radio sputtered, "This is my ship—go get yourself a ship!"

The machine-gun fire blasted the decks clear of return fire as Larner's squadron bore down upon the dodging Japanese ships. At the correct point of release, five-hundred-pound bombs were flung from the B-25s and skipped along the water. Of the thirty-seven released the 90th Squadron claimed seventeen as direct hits. The destroyer *Arashio* took three of them, snapped out of control, and smashed into the

already hit *Nojima*. The *Nojima* sank within minutes and the *Arashio* sank several hours later. This meant that its crew was to suffer the further attentions from the planes which followed.

Having caused frightful distress to the convoy (a cruiser and a transport sank, two destroyers and seven other ships were damaged), Larner led his B-25s back to Port Moresby. All twelve of his planes returned, although one, shot up in the attack, crashed during its landing run without serious injury to the crew.

The 89th Squadron, also of the 3rd Bombardment Group, followed the 90th, in their Havocs. "I got my first sight of the battle," Edward Chudoba later recalled, "when a ship ahead and to the left blew up, throwing flames a half mile into the air. I thought it was a destroyer, but the destroyer I had marked in that position slowly pulled away revealing a tanker [this may have been the *Kembu Maru* with its cargo of men, replacement parts, and aviation fuel] beyond it sending up flames and smoke from stem to stern. . . .

*One of "Pappy" Gunn's "commerce destroyers," a B-25 with four .50-caliber machine guns in the nose and two on either side of the fuselage just below the wing. The bombardier's compartment was removed and so was the Mitchell's lower turret. The eight forward-firing guns concentrated a withering fire in the plane's path.* (U. S. AIR FORCE)

"We were now about opposite the middle of the convoy on its port [left] side. Our two Vs of six Havocs each wheeled almost at right angles to the left to come in against it broadside. We were sliding down from about 2,000 feet now at an angle that would have us brushing the masts as we went over the enemy ships. . . .

"The time was exactly 10:03. The ships ahead were rapidly growing larger now.

"Young Charles Mayo (just turned twenty-one), my right wingman, and I were flying on the right side of our V of six ships. There was a ship ahead and two to the left. I dived and turned to the left under Captain Clark, our flight leader, and Mayo followed me. But the two planes on the left side of our V formation were going after the nearest ship on the left. I swung back and toward the big ship ahead. In spite of Captain Clark's warning not to pile up on the same ship, things were getting a bit confusing. I looked over my shoulder and there was Clark behind me. Young Mayo on my right said, 'I'm going off and get me a fat one.'

"The ship was rushing broadside at me now. I pulled the trigger on the wheel that started my machine guns spurting. I could see tracers and big stuff coming from the ship. I was pulling the bomb switch when a bullet came through the plexiglass canopy. Thirty caliber, I found later. I couldn't see a man on deck. The gun crews were well hidden. I let my two 500-pound bombs go now, just as I used to release them on calm days to skip against that old wreck at Port Moresby.

"Wham! I got it just as I passed over the ship. *Ol' Adam LaZonga* shuddered with the blow. (The plane was named for the great lover of the Li'l Abner strip and *Adam* sure could take it.) There was something wrong with the right wing and the plane wasn't flying right. I thought I had been hit with ack-ack. Captain Clark told me later that I had clipped off the top of the ship's radio mast. There was a dent on the front surface of my wing six inches deep."

The target was one of the troop-carrying transports, the *Tamei Maru,* which sank. All twelve of the 89th Squadron's Havocs returned to Port Moresby. During the battle Chudoba overheard radio conversations between the bombers and fighters, for the Zeros had begun concentrating on the B-17s in this climactic phase of the battle.

"Hey, Joe," Chudoba heard a Fortress pilot yell, "come on down. I've got three Zeros on my tail."

"Come on up," Joe said. "I have thirty of them."

The thirty or so Zero pilots must have been hard pressed to make any decision as to which planes to attack: the skip-bombing Mitchells and Havocs, the Beaufighters below, the B-25s in between, or the B-17s above. The Fortresses were the largest and appeared therefore to be the deadliest, so many Zeros attempted to get at them. One flown by Lieutenant Woodrow W. Moore was severely hit in the wing, which burst into flame. Moore ordered the bombs salvoed and the crew to jump. Seven managed to get out of the plane before it went into a steep dive and plunged into the Pacific, taking Moore with it.

As the seven chutes floated down the Zeros strafed them. Captain Robert Faurot (he who had splashed down the first Japanese plane with a P-38) left the fighting and with his two wingmen, Lieutenants Hoyt A. Eason and Fred D. Schifflet, all of the 35th Fighter Group, dived down to aid the helpless bomber crewmen. All ten men, the seven in parachutes as well as the fighter pilots, perished in the ensuing fight, although Kenney believed that the P-38 pilots took "five Japs along with them."

These four aircraft, one B-17 and three P-38s, were the only Allied planes lost in the Battle of the Bismarck Sea. Although the weather turned sour by the afternoon of March 3, a few more strikes were made by B-17s, Larner's B-25s again and RAAF Bostons of the 9th Operational Group. It was the final co-ordinated attack, for the battle was over except for such details as mopping up, sinking ships that remained above water but could not move, and picking up survivors, if any.

Five torpedo boats of the U. S. Navy's Seventh Fleet (*"MacArthur's Navy"*) slipped into the battle area after dark that night and sank one of the crippled ships, and on the morning of the next day, Thursday, March 4, bombers dispatched another stray. The battle was as good as over and high jubilation ensued in the Fifth Air Force. Kenney, about to leave for conferences in Washington, wired Whitehead: *Congratulations on that stupendous success. Air Power has written some important history in the past three days. Tell the whole gang that I am so proud of them I am about to blow a fuze.*

Historian Samuel Eliot Morison, with exceptional grace for a Navy man, called the Battle of the Bismarck Sea "the most devastating air attack on ships of the entire war, excepting only that on Pearl Harbor." At the cost of thirteen men killed, twelve wounded, and four aircraft (plus two which crash-landed), Kenney's forces had sunk every transport (probably eight, although exact figures seem never to have been determined) and four destroyers for a total of twelve of the original eighteen ships which had left Rabaul. An estimated three thousand Japanese troops went down with the transports, about half of those which had boarded the ships; of the six thousand troops intended for Lae only about eight hundred reached there. These were the survivors of the sinking of the *Kyokusei Maru,* which the B-17s had broken in half in the initial attack of the battle on March 2.

For the Japanese it was almost as shocking a defeat as Midway. But in addition to the loss of men, ships, and aircraft (claims were made for twenty), it meant something even more costly: the end of large-scale supply and reinforcement runs to northeastern New Guinea. The beleaguered Japanese troops must subsist from that day on on what little could be brought in by barge, submarine, and other small craft.

The ultimate effect upon the development of the situation in New Guinea was far-reaching indeed. It meant that MacArthur could seriously consider moving up the carapace of the turtle-shaped island and toward the Philippines.

# 2

# "CLEARING THE AIR"

THE Battle of the Bismarck Sea had been unique; the Japanese would never again place so many men and ships within the range of land-based aircraft. But if the sea was less a threat, there still remained along the line of MacArthur's projected advance in New Guinea several Japanese air bases at Lae (including those at nearby Salamaua and Nadzab) and at Wewak (a complex of fields including those at But, Dagua, and Boram). At the same time there was also the target at Rabaul, New Britain, with its inviting Simpson Harbour and several air bases: Vunakanau, Keravat, Lakunai, Rapopo, and Tobera. From Rabaul the Japanese were capable of interfering with MacArthur's plans in New Guinea as well as those of Vice-Admiral William F. Halsey (who had relieved Ghormley as commander) in the South Pacific.

Kenney therefore unleashed the devastating fury of his Pappy Gunn gadgetry upon Japanese shipping and air power along the route of the proposed Allied advance. He hoped to "clear the air" with everything he had until the Japanese had nothing.

With the Buna area secured, it was possible to establish airstrips at nearby Dobodura; thus the fighters, especially, were spared the high haul over the Owen Stanleys. MacArthur had his strategic eye next upon the Huon Peninsula, particularly Lae and Salamaua. But these targets lay nearly two hundred miles west of Dobodura, which meant that although

within fighter range, the time possible over the target was so brief for the fighters that they could give little protection to the bombers. Consequently, Kenney sent out Lieutenant Everette E. Frazier, an aviation engineer attached to the Fifth Air Force, to scout out the location for an advance airdrome within flying distance of Lae and the Wewak complex of Japanese airdromes.

Frazier, by air and by foot in the jungle, covered hundreds of square miles of New Guinea until he found a likely spot, all but under the very noses of the Japanese in the vicinity of Marilinan, more specifically at the village of Tsili-Tsili, within sixty miles of the Japanese at Lae. Kenney preferred calling the location Marilinan—"it was a pretty name" —in case "the Nips should take us out, somebody might throw that Tsili-Tsili thing back at me." While the base was being built Kenney decoyed the Japanese to another position, which was made to look like an active installation. The Japanese bombed the decoy spot and somehow did not find the Marilinan base until it was completed and operating. By mid-August more than three thousand troops were based in the area, including the 2nd Air Task Force, commanded by Lieutenant Colonel Malcolm A. Moore and later by Colonel David W. Hutchison.

The Japanese bombed the forward base for the first time on August 15, 1943, when a dozen Sallys escorted by a dozen Zeros swooped down by sur-

*A C-47 (the civilian Douglas DC-3) of the 6th Troop Carrier Squadron, with P-39 escort, flying over New Guinea.* (U. S. AIR FORCE)

amounted to one Thunderbolt. After these two costly attempts, the Japanese chose to leave Marilinan reasonably unmolested.

On the next day, August 17, 1943, Kenney opened up his campaign upon the Wewak airdromes. Reconnaissance photos revealed more than two hundred aircraft distributed among the installations at But, Boram, Dagua, and Wewak. It was after midnight that B-17s and B-24s from Port Moresby began dropping bombs on the various targets. Although Japanese night fighters attempted interception, anti-aircraft fire and searchlights proved to be the most formidable, resulting in the loss of three heavy bombers. Early morning photographs accounted for "at least 18 unserviceable" aircraft left on the Japanese airdromes, in addition to the damage to the strips which two hundred tons of bombs could do. But this was only the curtain raiser designed to foul the strips in order to interfere with Japanese aerial efforts during the next act.

At dawn the B-25 "Strafers," with P-38 escort, slashed across the tops of the palm trees in the Wewak area for the climax of "the show." Lieutenant Colonel Donald P. Hall, who had first experimented with the parafrag bomb during the early days of the Buna campaign, led the 8th and 13th Squadrons (3rd Bombardment Group) down upon the strips at Boram. It was, as Kenney observed, a "sight to gladden the heart of a strafer." Japanese bombers, perhaps sixty or more, lined up on both sides of the runway with engines warming up in preparation for

prise and shot down a C-47 carrying men of the ground echelons of the 35th Fighter Group, stationed at Marilinan; another transport crashed into the jungle and was never found. Escorting P-39s tangled with the bombers and fighters while the other C-47s sought refuge in the treetops and flew back to the comparative safety of Port Moresby. Four P-39s (but only one pilot) were lost and claims were made for eleven Japanese bombers and three fighters in the battle.

Realizing now that American planes were based in their back yard, the Japanese followed with a strafing raid on the following day. They were met not only by P-38s but also by the new P-47 Republic Thunderbolt, flown by the 348th Fighter Group led by Colonel Neel Kearby. The Japanese lost nine fighters (of the approximate fifteen dispatched) and five bombers (of sixteen). American losses

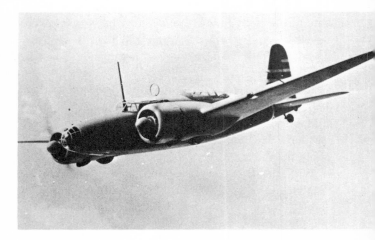

*Japanese Mitsubishi, Type 97, "Sally," heavy bomber which occasionally operated as a fighter.*

(U. S. AIR FORCE)

*A Sally taking off during a Fifth Air Force attack on a Japanese base in New Guinea. Shortly after it was* destroyed by another bomber, a B-25 Mitchell.

takeoff. No doubt the Japanese planned to avenge the midnight bombings by the B-17s and B-24s. Half a hundred fighters, the escort, also lined up on other runways getting ready to take off. The lead bomber had begun its run down the strip when Hall roared in with his potent Mitchells.

A shattering burst from his nose guns caught the Japanese bomber still on the runway. Enveloped in flame, it crashed to the ground and rendered the runway inoperable for any further takeoffs. The 8th and 13th Squadrons, seventeen planes altogether, led by Hall, in the words of Kenney, "swept over the field like a giant scythe," blasting at the lined-up bombers and fighters with their nose guns and drop-

ping parafrags in their wake. The bombs wafted down among the smoking, burning wreckage, further detonating aircraft and ripping up planes. Fuel drums burst into flame, adding their liquid propulsion to the holocaust. Those antiaircraft positions missed by the strafers were deracinated by the parafrags. In just minutes, the airdrome at Boram was left a burning, wreckage-strewn charnel house. Men of the 8th Squadron believed that they had left fifteen of the sixty or so planes they had counted on the strips totally destroyed and over twenty-five burning. The 13th Squadron was more expansive, claiming that of eighty or so aircraft it had counted all had been destroyed or severely damaged.

*Parafrags falling on a Japanese airstrip at Boram, New Guinea. Earlier attacks have already decapitated palm trees and burned up bombers (lower left); at* *upper right a fuel truck about to service a Zero will be the victim of the floating bombs.*

(U. S. AIR FORCE)

At the same time, twelve B-25s of the 90th Squadron (3rd Bombardment Group) were attending to Wewak proper. The surprise attack caught a number of Japanese fighters on the ground and left half of them, about fifteen, destroyed or damaged. Those Oscars (the Nakajima Ki.43) which got off the ground were driven off by the gunners in the Mitchells, leaving nothing to be done by the escorting P-38s, of which there were no less than eighty-five hovering around waiting for something to do.

Of the twenty-six B-25s which had taken off from Port Moresby that morning, assigned targets at Dagua and But, only three managed to rendezvous, because of bad weather. These three continued on to Dagua (But was not hit at all) and, despite their small number, created a burning shambles with guns and more than a hundred parafrags. Gunners shot down one intercepting Oscar, but at least seventeen lay in burning junk heaps on the ground when the Mitchells returned to Port Moresby.

Precise damage could not of course be estimated, but following what the Japanese came to call "The Black Day of August 17," there was little of the Japanese Air Force remaining in the Wewak area. But that did not mean it no longer existed, as was revealed on the following day, when similar strikes were made on Wewak. The weather spoiled the efforts of the heavy bombers to some extent; of the

*Japanese antiaircraft gunners seek shelter from the bombing-strafing Fifth Air Force Mitchells as a parafrag drifts toward their gun position.* (U. S. AIR FORCE)

*A "sight to gladden the heart of a strafer": Mitchells seeding the airbase at Dagua, New Guinea; smoke from a burning "Helen" bomber fills the air as three neatly lined-up "Tony" fighters await their turn.*

(U. S. AIR FORCE)

forty-nine which took off only twenty-six succeeded in bombing Wewak and Boram. The 3rd Bombardment Group followed with another low-level strafing and parafrag attack. The airdrome appearing to be pretty well taken care of, the 3rd swung out to sea, struck at some cargo vessels anchored off Wewak, and then blazed supply dumps at Boram.

The 38th Bombardment Group had been assigned Dagua. Major Ralph Cheli of the 405th Squadron led the attack, which was intercepted by about a dozen Japanese fighters, Zekes and Oscars, several miles out of Dagua. The fighters furiously attacked the low-flying Mitchells, concentrating on Major Cheli's flight. Within seconds, one of the B-25s was forced to pull away because of damage and fluttered back to base. An Oscar which had attacked this plane swung into Major Cheli's also and sent a burst along the right wing and engine. Flame erupted from the Mitchell as Cheli continued leading the

*Though the tide was turning, the air war over Boram, Wewak, and Dagua was not one-sided. Here is a Mitchell down in the water off New Guinea.*

(HENRY W. UHLIG/U. S. AIR FORCE)

B-25s toward Dagua, still two miles away. Rather than pull up, Cheli remained in place at the head of the squadron leading the attack. His leaving the formation at this critical point might easily have upset the strike; he chose to remain near the ground (too low to take to parachutes) with himself and his crew in the burning Mitchell.

The plane spouted flame as Cheli swept in over Dagua, strafing and dropping parafrags. This completed, Cheli instructed his wingman to take over the formation for the return flight, saying that he would attempt to bring the burning plane down into the sea. He turned and made for the water, reached it in fact, but it was too late. The flames had reached

a fuel tank and the explosion ripped a wing off the B-25, which crashed into the Pacific. Ralph Cheli was awarded the Medal of Honor for his action that day.

These two days of low-level attacks had succeeded in seriously crippling the Japanese aerial potential in New Guinea. By the end of the month it was estimated that more than two hundred aircraft had been destroyed on the ground alone (the revised, more precise figure was 175, which is still impres-

*Troops of the 503rd Parachute Infantry float down upon Nadzab, New Guinea, in MacArthur's move to eliminate the Japanese stronghold at Lae.*

(U. S. AIR FORCE)

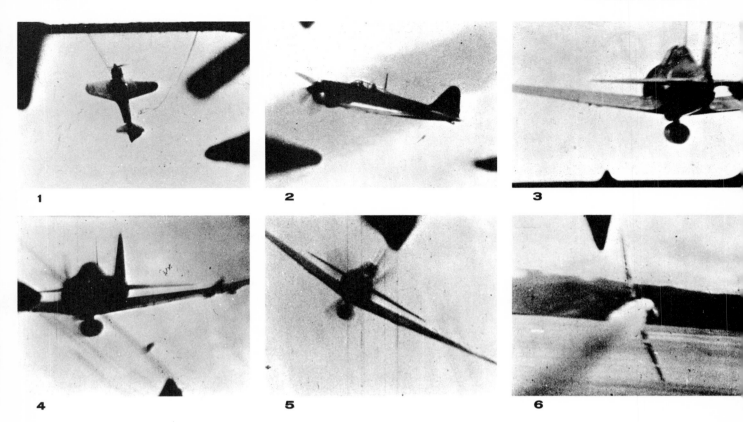

*The death of a Zero over Salamaua south of Nadzab and Lae about a week before the latter fell to MacArthur's forces.* (U. S. AIR FORCE)

sive). Claims were made for 126 Japanese aircraft accounted for in combat against the loss of five Mitchells, four B-24s, and thirteen fighters in combat and by accident during the month of August.

Marilinan, from which attacks could be mounted, served also as an emergency field and refueling depot for the fighters. Kenney concluded the field "had already paid for itself."

By late August MacArthur was confident that his forces could strike at another Japanese stronghold up the spine of New Guinea—Lae in the Huon Gulf. Amphibious troops, both Australian and American, went ashore near the village of Hopoi to set up a beachhead about fourteen miles east of Lae on the morning of September 4, 1943. This was preceded by naval and air bombardment of the landing area as well as concentrated bombing of Japanese positions in New Guinea and Rabaul. Even so, some Japanese aerial activity interfered slightly with the Lae landing, although at heavy cost, for Kenney's P-38s and P-47s swarmed around for in-

terceptions. Within four hours of the opening of the operation some 7800 troops had been put ashore along with their weapons and supplies.

The next morning the C-47s of the 54th Troop Carrier Wing lifted off the strips at Port Moresby carrying Australian troops and the men of the U. S. 503rd Paratroop Regiment. The unarmed transports, seventy-nine C-47s carrying about seventeen hundred men, were met by their first escorts over Thirty-Mile airdrome. As the armada proceeded, the escort eventually rose to a hundred fighters. Over Marilinan, just southwest of Lae, the C-47s formed into drop formation and flew to Nadzab, which flanked Lae to the west. What followed was one of the finest, most precise airdrops of the war, as, according to Kenney, MacArthur in his command B-17 observed "the show . . . jumping up and down like a kid." The paratroopers landed without meeting any resistance, and their C-47s returned to Port Moresby without the loss of a single plane. The Americans soon joined with the Australians and the area belonged to the Allies. Almost immediately construction of an air base was begun at Nadzab; Lae itself fell on September 16, 1943, and Kenney became proprietor of yet another major base.

Another way station like that at Marilinan was an airdrome constructed on Kiriwina, one of the Trobriand Islands, which lay almost directly east of Dobodura, New Guinea, and about 325 miles from Rabaul to the north. From the strips on Kiriwina, built by Royal Australian Air Force engineers, it would be possible for the B-25s to "stage" (refuel, etc.) before heading for Rabaul with weighty bomb loads. Fighters, primarily P-38s, were able to escort the bombers to Rabaul and not concern their pilots too much with fuel problems, for even if the Mitchells returned to New Guinea, the fighters could always land at Kiriwina. The heavy bombers could use Dobodura as their staging area. By October Kenney was ready to launch an offensive upon Rabaul similar in intensity to those with which he had been afflicting the Japanese along the northern coast of New Guinea.

*Reconnaissance photograph of Vunakanau, one of the major Japanese air bases at Rabaul, New Britain (an island group east of New Guinea). This strip had already been visited by the Fifth Air Force as evidenced by wreckage.* (U. S. AIR FORCE)

Rabaul had long been a prime target area, what with its several airdromes (two of which, at Lakunai, had been built by the Australians before the war), its harbor facilities, and warehouses in the city itself. As an important Japanese base, feeding men and matériel into New Guinea and the Solomons, Rabaul was also heavily protected: the estimate by early October 1943 was about 145 fighters, 124 bombers, and over 350 antiaircraft guns. The Japanese Navy had also installed quite efficient early warning radar systems. From Rabaul, too, bombing missions to New Guinea and to the Solomons were dispatched. In co-operation with the forces of Halsey's South Pacific units, and to assist in taking some of the pressure off the Allied Bougainville offensive in the Solomons, Kenney was determined to "take out Rabaul."

II

He had begun this task shortly after his arrival in the Pacific with the August 7, 1942, strike, which had consisted of thirteen 19th Bombardment Group Flying Fortresses. Rabaul had been under intermittent attack and regular reconnaissance since the previous January, in fact. From time to time Kenney would send a force of bombers to hit the shipping

or airfields in the area; but it was a costly target. During the Buna campaign Kenney and his Bomber Command chief, Brigadier General Walker, agreed that striking at Rabaul's shipping would confute Japanese plans to send reinforcements to New Guinea. On one of these strikes, that of January 5, 1943, Walker disobeyed Kenney's orders and flew in one of the dozen bombers sent to bomb Rabaul Harbor. Although Kenney had ordered a dawn attack, Walker believed a noon attack would achieve higher accuracy. While this may have been true—for claims for no less than ten ships sunk or burning were made—the antiaircraft fire was murderous and attacks by defending Japanese fighters profuse, if not expert. However, two American bombers were lost, one of them carrying Walker. Apparently hit by flak, the B-17, with engine burning, lost altitude and attracted two Zeros, which followed the plane away from the main battle. That was the last seen of Walker's B-17 by those ten crews which returned to Port Moresby.

When it came time to intensify the Fifth Air Force's attention on Rabaul, a campaign scheduled to open the middle of October 1943, Kenney was able finally to plan a sizable attack. There were no dozen or so patched up B-17s now, but several squadrons each of Mitchells, P-38s, and B-24s—nearly 350 aircraft. This too was a tribute to the resourcefulness of Kenney, who, by whatever means, had built up his air force. He fought with MacArthur's staff, he fought with Arnold's staff in far-off Washington, he demanded, "squawked," to use his term, and simply took what he could. This affected supplies, matériel of all types from planes to food for his "kids." If Service of Supply, bogged down with red tape, would not issue fresh food to his front-line fliers, Kenney arranged for a fleet of aircraft to smuggle it in from Australia. While this infringed on rules and regulations, it made a great deal of difference to the men who fought in terms of health and morale. Kenney even blinked when refrigerators were flown into New Guinea labeled as aircraft engines; if anything, he no doubt initiated the shipment of contraband.

He regularly had to defend his men. When Service of Supply officers in Sydney complained of the behavior of Kenney's airmen on leave, indicating that it was time "these brats grew up and behaved themselves," Kenney lashed out at the complainants, in-dicating that he didn't want his kids to get "old, fat, bald-headed and respectable like some people present because I was quite sure that, if they did they would no longer shoot down Nip planes and sink Nip boats."

In so many words, Kenney told the by now red-faced rear echeloners that since leave was granted to men who had been fighting the war, it was just too bad that their cavortings disturbed the slumber of the SOS. So far as he was concerned they could . . .

Just then MacArthur appeared in the doorway.

Kenney stopped talking to say, "Good morning, General."

MacArthur studied the group for just a moment, then said, "Leave Kenney's Kids alone. I don't want to see them grow up either." Chuckling, but with great dignity, he left.

MacArthur enjoyed Kenney's at times gauche style, his bluntness, his unconventional handling of supply and command problems. It was as if the austere, limelighted MacArthur could unbend through Kenney. Soon he came to call Kenney "Buccaneer," in recognition of the airman's freewheeling, productive manner of operating. On the other hand, Kenney was popular also with his men, who admired his informal swashbuckling manner—and the fact that he never failed to go out on a limb for them, if necessary.

They, in turn, willingly went out on a limb for Kenney. Taking out Rabaul was one of those limbs. On the eve of the opening of the intensive campaign, Kenney wrote to Arnold, "This is the beginning of what I believe is the most decisive action initiated so far in this theater. We are out not only to gain control of the air over New Britain and New Ireland but to make Rabaul untenable for Jap shipping and to set up an air blockade of all the Jap forces in that area."

Because of the oncoming monsoon predicted by his weathermen, Kenney unleashed his bombers on October 12, 1943, three days ahead of the agreed-upon date of the official top-level meetings. The early morning phase of the attack was led by Lieutenant Colonel Clinton U. True, commanding officer of the 345th Bombardment Group, at the vanguard of more than a hundred strafer Mitchells. Flying low over the water to elude radar, the Mitchells crossed the Solomon Sea to Kiriwina (where the

*The Fifth Air Force delivers parafrags to Vunakanau bomber revetments in Kenney's offensive on Rabaul.*
(U. S. AIR FORCE)

P-38 escort was picked up) and swung around to approach Rabaul. As they came in at treetop level, the formations split: the forty Mitchells of the 3rd Group veered sharply to port, streaking for the airdrome at Rapopo, and the sixty-seven aircraft of the 38th and 345th Groups turned slightly, to pounce upon Vunakanau. The attacks followed the pattern of those at Wewak and Lae. The 3rd Group, for example, swept in in a succession of shallow Vs, about a dozen Mitchells across, with the Vs about a mile apart. Spraying the target area with their eight nose guns, the Mitchells roared over the airfields dropping their parafrags into revetments (con-

structed to protect aircraft from horizontal bomb blasts) and over the general dispersal area.

Surprise having apparently been achieved, the Mitchells encountered remarkably little opposition. Antiaircraft fire was neither persistent nor accurate. Fighters, however, attempted interception and in a battle over Vunakanau with Zekes (the more modern Zero) the Mitchell piloted by Lieutenant Sidney W. Crews, with engine aflame, crashed into the waters of St. George Channel. It was the only Mitchell lost in the attack.

As soon as the Mitchells had cleared the area, a dozen Australian Beaufighters of No. 30 Squadron swooped down to work over Rapopo and Tobera. One of these aircraft was knocked down by ground fire.

*A Japanese bomber burns after a parafrag has alighted near it.* (U. S. AIR FORCE)

Shortly after noon the B-24s of the 90th Bombardment Group came in high over Simpson Harbour to drop thousand-pound bombs on the shipping in the harbor. Zekes quickly rose to challenge the Liberators, and in the ensuing battle, which lasted for more than a half hour, two B-24s were lost, with gunners in the bombers claiming ten of the forty Zekes and Zeros attacking. The Liberators of the 43rd Group followed the 90th Group's planes (which drew off most of the Japanese fighters) and strung their bombs across the harbor. Crewmen reported burning ships and much confusion in Simpson Harbour and heavy but inaccurate antiaircraft fire. Escorting P-38s claimed twenty-six Japanese fighters shot down; the strafer-bombers estimated that no less than a hundred Japanese planes had been destroyed on the ground with another fifty badly damaged. The heavies claimed over a hundred ships of various sizes, function, and tonnages sunk or destroyed—rather optimistic claims, as revealed in later photoreconnaissance. Exact damages could not be known, in fact, because of the speed of the action and the smoke left in the target areas by the Mitchells. But the claims were not as critical as the fact that the big campaign on Rabaul had begun with a decided success and with a reasonably small loss.

Despite intermittent bad weather, which either canceled out strikes or interfered with missions, the Fifth Air Force continued pounding away at Rabaul. Unless Kenney maintained a constant assault the Japanese were able to repair damage and replace lost aircraft. Meanwhile, too, Japanese strikes were mounted upon Allied positions in New Guinea, to upset any plans for what appeared to the Japanese to be a softening-up prelude for an invasion of Rabaul. This clearly near-suicidal effort was never attempted, however. It was the fate of Rabaul to be bypassed, isolated, as were so many other Japanese strong points on the way to Tokyo.

The ships in Simpson Harbour were as important as targets as were the aircraft on the five major airdromes of Rabaul. When the weather grounded planes, the ships continued to bring in supplies and troops. It devolved upon the 8th Photo Squadron, flying converted P-38s (the F-5), to keep an eye on the weather as well as the installations at Rabaul. Reconnaissance had revealed a concentration of ships in Simpson Harbour toward the end of October, making an attack from low level (always more effective than high-altitude bombing against ships) next on the Fifth Air Force agenda.

The weather caused the scrubbing of several missions to Simpson Harbour at the end of October. November came and the bad weather seemed fated to continue; the missions of the first and second were also canceled. But then, P-38s in the Rabaul area reported, after the morning mission of November 2, 1943, had been scrubbed, that not only was the weather over Rabaul promising, but that Simpson Harbour was filled with ships: a destroyer, a tender, and about twenty assorted transports. The mission was on again.

Because of the sudden shift in plans, not many Fifth Air Force aircraft were dispatched from New Guinea and the base at Kiriwina. According to Kenney there were seventy-five (Air Force historians say eighty) B-25 strafers and fifty-seven P-38s (historians claim eighty). The actual numbers assume a certain importance because of the intensity

*The attack on Rabaul's Simpson Harbour, November 2, 1943. As shore installations burn in the background, a skip-bombing Mitchell sweeps across the harbor as ship burns.* (U. S. AIR FORCE)

*Rabaul goes up in smoke after the November 2 mission to Simpson Harbour.* (U. S. AIR FORCE)

of the battle which ensued. It is likely that Kenney's are closest to the actual figures because the squadrons participating were not up to full strength.

Nine B-25 squadrons took part in the attack: the 8th, 13th, and 90th (of the 3rd Bombardment Group); the 71st and 405th (38th Bombardment Group); and the 498th, 499th, 500th, and 501st of the 345th Bombardment Group. Furnishing fighter cover for the strafers were six fighter squadrons: the 9th (49th Fighter Group); the 39th (35th Fighter Group); the 80th (8th Fighter Group); and the 431st, 432nd, and 433rd of the 475th Fighter Group.

By 11 A.M. the force was air-borne and headed for Rabaul. The P-38s of the 39th and 80th Squadrons opened the attack by swooping in upon the harbor to shoot up the antiaircraft installations there. Major Benjamin Fridge followed with the four B-25 squadrons of the 345th Group to strafe the gun emplacements around the harbor, drop Kenney Cocktails (the phosphorus bombs), and sweep over to

Lakunai airdrome and do the same there. The Kenney Cocktails laid a screen of smoke over the landbased guns and ignited Rabaul itself.

But unlike the earlier squadrons, the planes of the 345th ran into tough interception and intense antiaircraft fire. Several Mitchells were shot up during the attack and three were lost. The initial attack, however, prepared the way for the remaining five squadrons of B-25s, led by Major John P. Henebry, which had time to circle over Rabaul (impossible normally because of the harbor guns) for an effective run on the shipping in the harbor.

As Henebry dropped down upon Simpson Harbour, two Japanese destroyers which lay in the mouth of a river opened up on the forty-one Mitchells. This plus the smoke of the already burning ships disturbed, to some degree, the plan of attack. Despite this the strafers, breaking up into small units, poured fire in upon the ships in the harbor. Some of the Japanese ships shot directly into the water in the path of the approaching American planes, geysering water into the very cockpits of the B-25s. At the same time, especially aggressive Zeros pounced upon Henebry's squadrons. These fighters proved more effective than any encountered by the Fifth Air Force in quite some time. They were veteran Japanese Imperial Navy pilots of the 1st Koku Sentai (Carrier Division) from old Admiral Nagumo's carriers *Shokaku, Zuikaku,* and *Zuiho.* It had been a long time since the Fifth Air Force men had seen so many Zeros in the air at one time.

Kenney, who called this battle "the toughest, hardest-fought engagement of the war" for his air force, estimated that the Japanese put up "between 125 and 150 fighters" that day. Their numbers, and skill as pilots, enabled the Japanese to break through the P-38 escort to get at the Mitchells bombing the harbor. Despite the persistent Zeros and the ground fire, the Mitchells slashed at the ships, striking more than forty, of which twenty-four were hit by bombs and seventeen strafed.

In the melee, six B-25s and one P-38 were knocked down into Simpson Harbour. Henebry's plane was so badly shot up that when he left the battle area, his B-25 was full of holes and one engine was gone. With extraordinary airmanship, Henebry skimmed and yawed away from Rabaul until the Mitchell fell into the Pacific just short of Kiriwina. Henebry and his crew were rescued shortly after.

One of Henebry's squadron commanders, Major Raymond H. Wilkins, did not get away from Rabaul. Leading the 8th Squadron, the last to attack, Wilkins flew on the formation's left flank, which brought him under fire from cruisers near the shore. The area by this time, actually only twelve minutes after the initial attack, was a turmoil of smoke, machine-gun tracers, water spray, and concentrated antiaircraft fire.

"Smoke from bombs dropped by preceding aircraft necessitated a last-second revision of tactics on his part," Wilkins' Medal of Honor citation reads, "which still enabled his squadron to strike at vital shipping targets but forced it to approach through concentrated fire, and increased the danger of Major Wilkins' left-flank position.

"His airplane was hit almost immediately, the right wing damaged, and control rendered extremely difficult. Although he could have withdrawn he held fast and led his squadron in to the attack."

Wilkins' forward-firing eight-gun battery roared to life as he "strafed a group of small harbor vessels, and then, at low-level, attacked an enemy destroyer. His thousand-pound bomb struck squarely amidships, causing the vessel to explode. Although antiaircraft fire from this vessel had seriously damaged his left vertical stabilizer, he refused to deviate from his course. From below mast-head height he attacked a transport of some nine thousand tons, scoring a hit which engulfed the ship in flames. Bombs expended he began to withdraw his squadron.

"A heavy cruiser barred the path. Unhesitatingly, to neutralize the cruiser's guns and attract their fire, he went in for a strafing run. His damaged stabilizer was completely shot off." With his directional control all but gone, Wilkins might easily have flown into the path of the Mitchells flying alongside him. He rolled the plane slightly, with what little aileron control he still had, to avoid colliding with his wing mates. In doing this he exposed the belly and full wing surfaces to the heavy fire erupting from "those damned cruisers." In an instant the Mitchell's left wing crumpled and the bomber smashed into the sea.

Wilkins and his crew were among the forty-five men lost in the attack: one of the heaviest tolls suffered by the Fifth Air Force. Eight bombers and nine fighters were lost (although four of the pilots of the latter were found and crews of three bombers, such as that of Henebry, were picked up). A Mitchell and three P-38s, badly damaged in the fighting, cracked up while landing at Dobodura. It had been an expensive "show."

Simpson Harbour had been left a smoking shambles when the last Mitchell of the 8th Squadron passed through its hail of fire. But any accurate assessment of the damage would have been questionable. The first official communiqué claimed fifteen Japanese vessels, of various types, sunk and an additional thirteen damaged (after the war the Japanese admitted to three merchant vessels, a minesweeper, and two small ships sunk and damage to a ten-thousand-ton tanker). Whatever the differences, the attack proved costly to the Japanese also.

Besides the damage to shipping in the harbor (and tankers were an especially precious commodity at the time), the town of Rabaul was also set aflame, which accounted for the destruction of supplies. In

*As the fighting progressed all around Rabaul and Simpson Harbour, Kenney Cocktails fanned over Lakunai gun positions (center and right bottom), scourging the hapless gun crews.* (U. S. AIR FORCE)

the air fighting, bombers and fighters claimed sixty-eight Japanese planes shot down; the strafers claimed an additional sixteen destroyed on the ground at Lakunai plus ten float planes which were left burning in the harbor. So, if the battle had been hard on the Fifth Air Force, it was also a definite blow to the Japanese.

By the end of November, with Halsey's carriers closing in on Rabaul, Kenney relinquished the further "neutralization of Rabaul" to the South Pacific forces, which included the recently formed Thirteenth Air Force besides the Marine and Navy pilots. Although Rabaul was never invaded, any such attempt would have been costly in the extreme, it was not completely taken out either. But the incessant attacks upon it eventually forced the withdrawal of air units stationed there by February 20, 1944. Left behind were nearly 100,000 ground

troops, who waited in 350 miles of tunnels and caves. It was one of the good fortunes of war that the Joint Chiefs did not order an invasion of Rabaul. Had they, "Tarawa, Iwo Jima and Okinawa would have faded to pale pink in comparison with the blood that would have flowed" in an attempted assault on Rabaul, in the opinion of Samuel Eliot Morison. Even so, the blood continued to flow until the end.

Meanwhile, Kenney gave his attention to MacAr-

*A low-flying Mitchell, of the 345th Bomb Group, Thirteenth Air Force, catches a Japanese "frigate" (destroyer escort) off the coast of China. In moments the B-25s of the group, known as the "Air Apaches," finish off the ship which capsizes.* (U. S. AIR FORCE)

thur's advance up the coast of New Guinea, employing the methods used upon Rabaul as he went.

### III

The attacks by strafers, the deliverers of Kenney Cocktails, parafrags, and the heavy bombs, were protected whenever possible by fighters. Kenney's fighter pilots were among the most colorful of the war, and the so-called "Ace of Aces" of all American wars was one of Kenney's Kids. Richard Ira Bong, "a blond, blue-eyed cherub" from Madison, Wisconsin, first came to Kenney's attention in San Francisco. Kenney was then commanding the Fourth Air Force when word came to his office that one of his pilots "had been looping the loop around the center span of the Golden Gate Bridge in a P-38 fighter plane and waving to the stenographic help in the office buildings as he flew along Market Street."

From nearby Oakland a lady complained of having her washing blown off the line by a low-flying aircraft. Though angry and a bit embarrassed over the performance of one of his pilots, Kenney was also delighted. Kenney himself had nearly been dismissed from the Air Service in the summer of 1917 for flying under the bridges of New York's East River.

Kenney laced into the youthful pilot, a "boy about five feet six, with a round, pink baby face and the bluest, most innocent eyes," affecting his harshest voice and sternest expression. He reminded Bong of the trouble he had caused, which would make it necessary for Kenney to talk with everyone, from the governor on down to the lady with the washing.

Then Kenney's curiosity got the better of him. "By the way," he said to Bong, "wasn't the air pretty rough down in the street around the second-story level?"

The innocence vanished from Bong's eyes. "Yes, sir, it was kind of rough, but it was easy to control the plane." He then launched into a speech on the excellent aileron control of the P-38 before realizing that he was in his commanding general's office for an entirely different reason.

Kenney rather dramatically began tearing up the pile of complaints that had accumulated on his desk thanks to this cherubic "airplane jockey." Threatening the by now incredulous Bong with in-

*Richard Bong, P-38 fighter pilot, New Guinea, 1943. Bong would become the American "ace of aces" with a total of forty confirmed air-to-air victories.*

(U. S. AIR FORCE)

stant dismissal from the Air Force should he ever repeat his performance, Kenney added further reprimand: Bong was ordered to report to the lady near Oakland.

And "if that woman has any washing to be hung out on the line, you do it for her. Then you hang around being useful—mowing a lawn or something—and when the clothes are dry, take them off the line and bring them into the house. And don't drop any of them on the ground or you will have to wash them over again."

Almost immediately after the incident, Kenney was on his way to the Pacific and when he placed a request with Arnold for fifty P-38 pilots, he specifically requested that Bong be among them.

In Kenney's professional eye, Bong (who was then twenty-two) combined those several qualities which add up to a superb fighter pilot. Quick reflexes, good physical condition, a sense of joy in the very idea of flight, an understanding of aircraft and its limitations, as well as his own. Aggressiveness too was an important psychophysiological component. Along with this must be a self-confidence bordering on an overwhelming sense of invincibility. The hesitant, too cerebral fighter pilot did not generally survive. Swooping down for a screaming attack, most often as not upon an unaware enemy—for in reality, for all of the scorekeeping, combat aviation was no clean sport—the fighter was too preoccupied with air speed, angle of attack, getting a bead on the enemy aircraft to consider the outcome of this attack as less than fatal for the enemy.

Like so many other American fighter pilots, Bong was not, in the beginning at least, a very good shot. He actually completed his first tour of missions, with more than twenty "kills" to his credit, before he attended a school for training in aerial gunnery. The bulk of Bong's forty official victories can be attributed to his courage (another term for aggressiveness or self-confidence), his skill with the P-38, and a willingness to work as part of a team.

Early in the Pacific war it became obvious that the dogfighting tactics of the First World War were suicidal with the Zero, which could dance circles around the heavier American fighters. "Defense against Jap fighters is resolved around the superior speed of our fighters," Bong pointed out, and it was that difference between the machines, his and the Japanese, that he exploited, not individual flying abilities. The Japanese were better pilots—and had much sharper vision than early Allied propaganda intimated. So were their aircraft better under certain conditions; because they were less ruggedly constructed, weight and speed were important in battle. As Bong observed, "An indicated airspeed never less than 250 miles per hour in combat is good life insurance."

Even so, there were sudden unknowns confronting even an experienced pilot—and it was these too which often saved him. One of these incidents occurred to Bong even after he had already achieved acedom. He and his wingman intercepted a Japanese bomber formation, escorted by Zeros, over the Buna area of New Guinea. The bombers seemed beautifully set up for a quick, slashing attack. "Any number of Nips," he once wrote, "can be safely attacked from above. Dive on the group, pick a definite plane as your target, and concentrate on him. . . ."

As he concentrated on his bomber, Bong, with the fighter pilot's instinct for searching the air around him, came to a sudden shocking realization. On his wing was not a twin-boomed P-38, but a Zero with a large red circle on its side. In seconds it could slip behind him and begin firing with its cannon.

Chopping the throttle of one of his engines, Bong suddenly flipped away in a careening dive. Checking his rear-view mirror, and not seeing a Zero, he leveled out at five thousand feet. Suddenly, there it was again, pulling up behind him, but too distant for accurate shooting. Bong flipped the P-38 once again and dived for the water. The Zero could not follow him there—it might plunge into the Pacific if it did, or else pull apart in the high-speed dive.

*Japanese bombers ("Sally") in the gun camera of an American pilot. While thus occupied once Richard Bong acquired himself a Zero for a wingman.*

(U. S. AIR FORCE)

Bong opened the throttles and raced over the water, glancing again into the mirror. He had left the Zero way behind; maybe now he could deal with the persistent Japanese. He snapped the plane into a tight turn and found himself in the middle of a nine-plane Japanese formation he had not seen until that instant.

There was nothing in the books to cover this situation. Bong relied on instinct as he yanked the great plane's nose into the path of the lead Japanese aircraft. A short burst from Bong's gun blew the Zero out of his way. This apparently had shaken the remaining eight Zeros, for their fire was not accurate. Bong ripped the P-38 through the scattering Japanese formation and shot and detonated another Zero. Ramming his engines at full throttle, he climbed for altitude, loosing another burst at a passing Zero. The Japanese plane paused, emitted smoke, and fluttered away from the battle.

By this time Bong was far from the dispersed Japanese planes and heading for home base.

Despite the preoccupation with keeping score of kills, the true function of the fighters was, of course, protecting the bombers during the attacks upon shipping or such bases as Rabaul, Lae, Wewak, and the other steps toward the Philippines. Lone-eagle fighting generally ended in the death of the eagle.

The system of fighting in pairs may have denied a wingman his share of "credits" (and there were those pilots who resented it), but it did preserve life. But not forever.

Once the American pilots began adding up kills it was inevitable that a certain rivalry would grow among the pilots. It was a good-natured, locker-room kind of competitiveness, this obsession with kills, except that instead of touchdowns men's lives were at stake.

When Bong passed the score of First World War ace Captain Eddie Rickenbacker, the latter sent the young ace a case of scotch with which to celebrate. This resulted in quite a tempest in a scotch glass, for a flood of complaints and criticism deluged Kenney for permitting this (in fact, Bong himself did not drink and was more delighted with a gift of Coca-Cola from Generals Arnold and MacArthur). The back-home do-gooders could not reconcile themselves to the fact of the "boys'" drinking, although they readily accepted the fact that they were out killing their fellow man. Wartime provides

the setting for any number of moral incongruities, with the most pietistic leading the pack.

When Bong arrived in New Guinea to embark upon his legendary career as a fighter pilot, the top-scoring ace of the time was Boyd David Wagner, who was best known as "Buzz," with a score of eight. A veteran of the early Pacific fighting, Wagner returned to the United States only to die in an accidental crash during a takeoff at Eglin Air Force Base.

Bong's rival during his initial tour was another youngster, Captain Thomas J. Lynch of Catasauqua, Pennsylvania. Lynch had led the first P-38 mission (December 27, 1942), twelve in all, from the Laloki airstrip near Port Moresby. Intercepting a Japanese bomber and fighter formation over Dobodura, the P-38 pilots returned from the battle claiming no less than fifteen Japanese planes. Bong, Lynch, and another future ace, Lieutenant Kenneth C. Sparks, claimed two apiece. Although the green fighters committed any number of tactical errors—firing from too great a distance, attempting to dogfight with a Zero—their initiation into battle had been exciting and without loss. Kenney, in reporting the battle debut of the P-38 to Arnold, noted that "morale in that squadron [the 9th of the 49th Fighter Group] is so high it almost scares you."

Another group, the 348th, had arrived in New Guinea around the end of June 1943. The commander, Colonel Neel E. Kearby, looked to Kenney "like money in the bank." The 348th was equipped with the Republic P-47 ("Thunderbolt," or "Jug") and Kearby was anxious to prove what the as yet unpopular aircraft could do. The P-47 was a hulk of an aircraft, the largest single-engine one-man fighter of the war. It did not have the range of the P-38 (until fitted with belly tanks), was difficult to maneuver, had a weak landing gear, and could, in a power dive, freeze the controls so that the pilot could not pull out. Or if he did, the action could tear the tail section away. Despite these drawbacks, the P-47 properly manned became one of the outstanding fighters of the war.

Kearby, one of its earliest exponents, was anxious to show what the plane, his group, and he himself could do. He had barely met Kenney before he asked about "scores," the implication being, Kenney believed, that he "wanted to know who he had to beat." It was not until August that the 348th

*Neel E. Kearby, who commanded the 348th Fighter Group, and who proved that the P-47 "Thunderbolt" was a formidable aircraft in the Pacific.*

(U. S. AIR FORCE)

Fighter Group's Thunderbolts were ready for action. Then in September, during the air fighting over Lea and the subsequent (September 5, 1943) taking of Nadzab by American paratroopers, Kearby got his chance. With a wingman as company Kearby dived on two Japanese planes, a bomber and a fighter. With his wingman following, Kearby dropped the Thunderbolt upon the enemy planes about four thousand feet below. The two planes were flying along rather close together, the bomber in the lead with the Zero following. Kearby squinted in the sight and shot off a long, exploratory burst as his wingman held his fire and twisted his neck looking for other Japanese fighters.

To the surprise of both wingman and Kearby a wing ripped off the fighter and the bomber ex-ploded before their eyes. By the end of September Kerby's score had grown to eight, one half of Bong's score at the time.

Multiple victories seemed to be a Kearby specialty, for on October 11 he gave an amazing demonstration which won him the Medal of Honor. During a fighter sweep over the Wewak area in company with three others, Major Raymond K. Gallagher, Captain John T. Moore, and Captain William D. Dunham, Kearby sighted a single Japanese plane below them.

Kearby led his flight down upon the lone Zero and in seconds sent it down burning (the eight .50-caliber guns of the P-47 literally tore the flimsy plane apart). Then as the four Thunderbolts pulled up out of their dive they saw ahead of them a large formation of Japanese fighters and bombers, about forty-five planes in all.

Kearby plunged into the formation in an instant, the three others following. The heavy P-47 lumbered through the astonished Japanese spouting fire: three enemy planes burst into flame within minutes. Then, kicking rudder, Kearby turned to see that two Zeros had got onto the tail of one of his flight. He roared in and with two bursts sent the two Japanese down burning. Instinctively he scanned the air around him and saw that a Zero had begun a dive upon another P-47. Kearby whipped the guns into the enemy plane, which collapsed, falling like a bird with a broken spine.

Realizing that they were getting low on fuel, Kearby called his men in—all were safe. Besides Kearby's seven victories, two more had been accounted for by other members of the flight and another had been seen leaving the battle on fire. Because it had not been seen to crash this was claimed as a "probable." Discounting this one, it meant that the Japanese had lost nine planes to the four Thunderbolts in a single action.

But there was an additional hitch. Kearby's gun camera had run out of film in mid-attack on the seventh plane and there was no "official" evidence, the three other pilots then being occupied themselves, that the seventh plane had been destroyed. So Kearby was credited with an official six victories in a single battle (the record to that date was the Navy's Lieutenant Edward "Butch" O'Hare, who had shot down five Japanese bombers in a single action). For his feat, Kearby received the Medal of

44

Honor and his score stood at fourteen, only three less than Bong's.

Shortly after, Bong was sent home for a rest (with a score then of twenty-one), and while he was away Kearby's total rose to twenty. At this time Bong's other rival, Thomas Lynch, had a score of sixteen (he too had been sent back home for a rest), so that the rivalry of these three aces now became intense.

When all three were in operation their individual scores were watched daily; by the beginning of March 1944 Bong and Kearby were tied (with twenty-two) and Lynch trailed with nineteen.

Whether or not the desire to be top ace blunted Kearby's customary vigilance, or whether it was a simple matter of running out of luck, would be difficult to ascertain. On March 4, 1944, Kearby was again leading a four-plane flight (Major Samuel Blair, Captain William Dunham, and Captain William Banks), this time over Wewak, New Guinea. Sighting a fifteen-plane Japanese formation, Kearby ordered an attack, the first assault of which sent one enemy plane down under his guns. He had broken the tie.

*Thomas J. Lynch, one of Richard Bong's friendly rivals and battle companions.* (U. S. AIR FORCE)

Turning, he rammed back into the battle and with a long shot, knocked another Zero down. Kearby was now official Ace of Aces. Then three Zeros converged upon his Thunderbolt. Dunham and Banks swept in with guns firing, each taking one of the Zeros off Kearby's tail. But the third from close up fired a burst of cannon directly into the cockpit of the P-47. It tipped on its nose and fell directly into the jungle; no parachute was seen. Obviously Neel Kerby was dead in the plane.

Ironically, on that same day Bong had destroyed two enemy aircraft; the score was still tied. Lynch with nineteen victories was now Bong's closest rival.

At this stage, Lynch—a lieutenant colonel—and Bong—a captain—had teamed up. They had been taken out of their regular squadrons and placed upon the staff of General Paul Wurtsmith, commander of Kenney's Fighter Command. Lynch was nominally Wurtsmith's operations officer and Bong his assistant. Thus it was hoped to keep the two fighters out of combat as much as possible and preserve their experience, which could be transferred to the new pilots coming into the Pacific.

This worked on paper, but it was difficult to keep the two men out of battle. They either went off together, or attached themselves to other squadrons and continued to add to their scores. They remained, as they did at the time of Kearby's death, Bong: twenty-four, Lynch: nineteen.

Just five days after Kearby's last fight, Bong and Lynch took off on one of their two-man hunts. Over Tadji, New Guinea, they surprised another two-man combat team and each took out one. There being no other Japanese aircraft in the sky, they pointed their P-38s down toward the water, where they spotted a Japanese ship, a corvette obviously headed for Hollandia. It was the best they could find, so they swept down upon the vessel. Raking the deck with .50-caliber bullets, the P-38s dived and pulled away, dived and pulled away as the guns on the ship's deck traded fire with them.

Suddenly Bong noticed that Lynch had turned away and headed for shore; an engine trailed smoke. Even more suddenly one of the propellers tore away, and as Bong watched in horror, he saw Lynch struggling out of the cockpit, ready to jump. Before he and his chute were free of the plane, the P-38 detonated. If Lynch had had a chance, the

*Despite the superiority of American air power over New Guinea, attacking Japanese strongholds was not without hazard. In this series of photographs a Fifth*

*Air Force Havoc attacking Kokas, New Guinea, is hit by antiaircraft fire and plunges into the water.*

(U. S. AIR FORCE)

flame of the explosion canceled that—the chute certainly burned and Lynch, if not already dead, fell to his death. Bong circled the area for signs of life (something he realized was futile), but there were no indications that Lynch had survived. He returned to his base and Kenney, concerned with Bong's morale, sent him to Australia, ostensibly to ferry a newly arrived P-38 back to New Guinea. But Kenney saw to it that the depot commander would not have one ready for two weeks.

By early April Bong had returned, and by the twelfth, upon adding two more kills to his credit in a battle over Hollandia, he had passed the score of Rickenbacker, making him the American Ace of Aces of both world wars. Kenney quickly took him out of combat, partly because there was some concern from Washington over the recent deaths of Kearby and Lynch and the loss of their "invaluable

services." Bong was returned to the United States at this point to be reunited with his family, his fiancée, Army public relations officers—and to study gunnery. He was to return to the Pacific as an instructor upon completion of this course.

Meanwhile, a new rival had arisen: Major Thomas Buchanan McGuire, Jr. When he arrived in the Pacific, in the spring of 1943, McGuire was assigned to Bong's own unit, the 49th Fighter Group. Bong's score was then eight. In time McGuire was reassigned to the 475th Fighter Group to serve in the 431st Squadron. A fine pilot, McGuire quickly revealed himself as one of the outstanding air fighters in the Pacific.

But it seemed to be his fate that he always remained eight victories behind Bong. Even when Bong was away from combat, McGuire himself was also out of things with various jungle illnesses. "I'll

*Thomas B. McGuire, Jr. (here an air cadet), one of Kenney's most aggressive "kids," who risked his life—and lost it—trying to aid a fellow pilot.*

(U. S. AIR FORCE)

bet," he once told Kenney, "when this war is over, they'll call me Eight Behind McGuire."

In time McGuire became commander of the 431st Squadron and his victory score mounted rapidly. "A fighter pilot must be aggressive," he believed. "The enemy on the defensive gives you the advantage, as he is trying to evade you, and not shoot you down. Never break your formation into less than two-ship elements. A man by himself is a liability. . . . On the defensive, keep up your speed.

"Go in close, and then when you think you are too close, go in closer."

McGuire was an excellent teacher and conscientious in looking after green pilots. All through Bong's combat career, McGuire trailed his victory tally, but it was obvious that he might eventually overtake the top ace, for the word went out that Bong must be taken out of combat. Following Bong's return from the United States he was supposed to instruct, not fight—except in self-defense. By late December 1944, when MacArthur had indeed returned to the Philippines, Bong's score had grown into the thirties. If the Japanese air forces had

petered out over New Guinea, there was still fight left in them over the Philippines. Bong therefore had to "defend" himself rather frequently, even if he only went along to observe how a squadron he had trained in gunnery performed on a routine patrol.

Within hours of arriving at Tacloban, Bong was "forced to defend himself," in the words of Kenney's report to Arnold, and shot down his thirty-first Japanese plane. The following day, while on a reconnaissance mission to find possible sites for airfields in the Tacloban vicinity, he accounted for two more Japanese aircraft within view of the Allied airdrome.

Arnold wired Kenney: "Major Bong's excuses in matter of shooting down three more Nips noted with happy skepticism by this headquarters. Subject officer incorrigible. In Judge Advocate's opinion, he is liable under Articles of War 122." This referred to willful or negligent damage to enemy equipment or personnel.

Tacloban was a busy place indeed, for when McGuire arrived there in early October (1943), it was just in time for a tangle with a Japanese fighter formation. The twenty P-38s, warned by radio of the approaching ten Japanese fighters, shot down six and drove the rest off. One of the victims was McGuire's twenty-third victory. Elated upon landing, McGuire said, "This is the kind of place I like, where you have to shoot 'em down so you can land on your own airdrome! Say, how many has Bong got now?"

The slender, little major learned he was now ten behind. With Bong himself in the area, McGuire jokingly kept an eye on him, muttering words about taking off "to protect his interests." The two men were good friends and teamed up to go "Nip hunting." Now and then McGuire "permitted" Bong to accompany his squadron on regular patrols during which each shared in the kills.

When Bong's official score reached forty (his actual score was probably much higher), Kenney decided to take him out of combat. He had flown 146 combat missions and had nearly 400 hours of combat time. He had lived a charmed life and Kenney felt it was time to stop tempting fate. Bong was reluctant, hoping to bring his score to an even fifty, but Kenney was unyielding.

Bong would be sent home to rest, to marry the girl back home, and to get into an entirely new concept in aviation, the jet plane. In order not to spoil his stateside reception, Kenney grounded McGuire, who had finally broken his "eight behind" jinx.

"You look tired to me," Kenney told McGuire.

"General, I never felt better in my life. I've gained five pounds in the last month. Besides, I'm only two behind—"

"That's just it," Kenney told McGuire. "You are tired and you won't be rested enough to fly again until I hear that Bong is back in the United States and has been greeted as the top-scoring ace of the war." Kenney explained that he did not want Bong to arrive in San Francisco to be greeted with "Hello, Number Two, how's the war going?"

McGuire laughed and understood Kenney's point,

saying he certainly did not want to spoil anything for Bong. He promised to take a few days off to rest, although he seemed quite anxious for Bong to be on his way. Kenney promised that he would personally place Bong on a transport in a day or two.

On this last day Bong, perhaps for the first time, learned a fact of war. Bong in his P-38 and Kenney in his B-17 proceeded to an airdrome at San Jose, Mindoro. Just as they landed and taxied to a parking area the sirens sounded. Colonel Gerald Richard Johnson, Bong's old group commander, led some P-38s to the attack.

When the Lightnings intercepted the Japanese formation, Johnson fired at the leader. The plane burst into flame instantly as Johnson turned away

". . . the formation was bounced by a single 'Hamp' . . ." *a later model of the Zero, the so-called clipped-wing variant of the maneuverable fighter. Also called* the "Hap," *the name was changed after General Henry* "Hap" *Arnold learned of this designation.*

(U. S. AIR FORCE)

to tackle another enemy aircraft. The action occurred almost directly over the field, so that Kenney and Bong watched in fascination.

As they watched, the Japanese pilot, unable to stand the flames, jumped from his plane. "The Jap pilot hit flat on the steel plank surface of the airdrome about a hundred feet from where Dick and I were standing. It was not a pretty sight. I watched for Bong's reaction. I had predicted a long while ago that if he ever found out that he was not shooting clay pigeons, I would have to take him out of combat. . . . He walked over to some bushes at the edge of the field and for the next five minutes was violently ill."

Kenney was certain more than ever that he was correct in taking Bong out of combat. McGuire, however, returned to the battle as soon as he knew that Bong had received his hero's welcome. Word came in on January 6, 1945; on the seventh McGuire was in the air again.

In the morning he took off in company with another experienced P-38 pilot (a Major Rittmayer of the Thirteenth Air Force) and two new pilots. To familiarize the green pilots, McGuire intended to make a quick sweep over a Japanese field on Negros Island, west of Leyte. The morning promised to be quiet, for as they flew along at about two thousand feet there seemed to be no Japanese air activity.

Unexpectedly the formation was bounced by a single "Hamp" (a late variant, the A6M3, of the Zero), which fastened itself to Rittmayer's tail, pouring fire into the P-38. McGuire reacted immediately and characteristically—he swept in to the rescue of the pilot in distress. To do this, however, he was forced to violate several of his own precepts for air combat. He had to turn the heavy P-38 tightly, and he had to do this at extremely low altitude—and with two heavy auxiliary fuel tanks attached to his wings.

McGuire apparently forgot about the wing tanks in the urgency of the moment, as he tipped the P-38 in a vertical bank to go to Rittmayer's aid. Ordinarily, since he was so skilled a pilot, he might have succeeded, but with the extra weight and resistance of the wing tanks it was not possible. In the tight turn the P-38 shuddered in mid-air for a moment, stalled, and then dropped straight to the ground. A massive explosion ripped out of the jungle. Meanwhile, the Hamp pilot persisted on the

other P-38, and in moments, Rittmayer joined McGuire in death. The Japanese pilot then slipped down among the hills of Los Negros and blended into the jungle and out of sight. The two new pilots returned to Leyte with the grim news.

The courageous Japanese pilot who single-handedly attacked the four-plane formation was, according to recent research, probably Shoichi Sugita, whose own victory tally placed him, by war's end, in the position of Japan's number two ace; he was therefore McGuire's Japanese counterpart. Sugita's score, however, was eighty, just twice that of Bong's.

Japanese aces, unlike those of the Allies and Germany, were not publicized; they were, in fact, as little known to their own countrymen as to the enemy. Partly this was because it was simply expected of them to serve the Emperor and if in so doing they shot down many enemy aircraft, so be it. Another reason for their scanty fame was simply class consciousness. Only the high officer class received due recognition; the non-commissioned officer or the skilled fighter who had come from the lower classes was not mentioned.

Nor were they looked after as in the fatherly manner of Kenney, "buccaneer" though he was supposed to be. Japanese pilots were expected to go until they died or dropped. Many flew in an exhausted, run-down state; many flew although seriously ill with malaria, dysentery, and other tropical diseases, or diseases caused by poor diet and fatigue.

One such remarkable pilot was Hiroyoshi Nishizawa, who, before he was killed while piloting a transport rather late in the war, shot down more than a hundred Allied planes. Nishizawa was Japan's top-scoring fighter pilot, although his name was not known during the war except to fellow pilots, who called him "the Devil." Sugita was second; the famed Saburo Sakai was third, with sixty-four victories. Other outstanding Japanese fighter pilots were Waturo Nakamichi (fifty-five victories), Naoshi Kanno (fifty-two), Yasuhiki Kuroe (fifty-one). Temei Akamatsu was one of the most fascinating airmen, for he was so totally un-Japanese in outlook. Like a throwback to the First World War, Akamatsu was an undisciplined advocate of wine and women and possibly song. His total score was fifty (he survived the war), which he shared with Kinsuke Muto and Toshio Ota.

These men fought under conditions of abuse and

*A Japanese Nakajima L2D ("Tabby"), an obvious copy of the Douglas DC-3, such as carried Japanese ace Hiroyoshi Nishizawa to his death in the latter months of the war. (This Tabby was actually destroyed by Sergeant W. Tackett of Los Angeles from the top turret of a B-24 piloted by Captain Augustus V. Connery, East Providence, Rhode Island, while on a bombing mission over the Celebes.)*

(U. S. AIR FORCE)

hardship which their commanders expected them to endure, in addition to being overwhelmed by a steady flow of fresh young pilots which the enemy sent against them. And these pilots flew better aircraft than the Japanese did toward the conclusion of the war.

But Bong was safely out of all that and happy in a new life; he had married Marjorie Vattendahl, the girl from Wisconsin, and he was working at the Lockheed plant in California, testing a new jet fighter, the P-80. Bong was still the American Ace of Aces; McGuire's score had been thirty-eight—and these would remain the two highest victory scores of the war.

Bong had made it, he had survived, a rare thing with top-scoring fighter pilots. But he could not elude the irony of endings; on the front page of the New York *Times* dated Tuesday, August 7, 1945, which carried the headline beginning "FIRST ATOMIC BOMB DROPPED ON JAPAN," there was another news item.

Just the day before, August 6, 1945, Richard Bong, aged twenty-five, died when the "Shooting Star" jet he was testing crashed and burned at Lockheed airport at Burbank. The concurrence of the two events, merging the atomic bomb and the jet aircraft, ended forever the kind of war that Richard Bong—and Neel Kearby, and Thomas Lynch, and Thomas McGuire, and, for that matter, George C. Kenney—had fought. History assured Bong his special place: he would be the American Ace of Aces forever and there would be no more rivals.

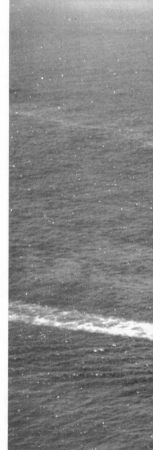

*Approaching Guadalcanal, summer of 1942; in the foreground the* Enterprise *and in the distance the* Saratoga. *Above, a Dauntless, with arrester hook down, is about to make a landing on the* Enterprise.
(NAVY DEPT., NATIONAL ARCHIVES)

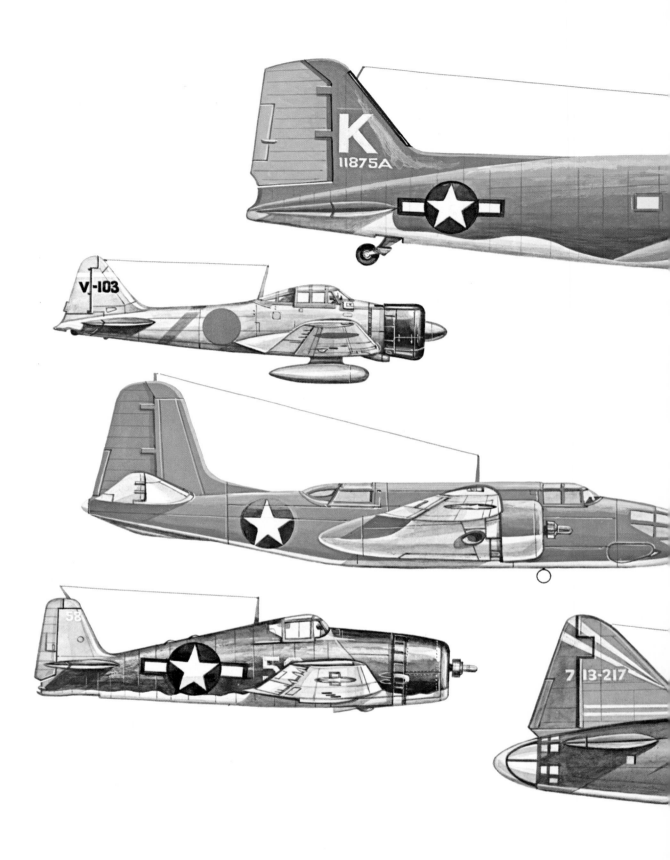

Chief aerial contenders in the critical phase of the war in the Pacific. Straddling the center fold near top, is the Douglas C-47 (the DC-3 of civil life), in battle dress, which served in all war theaters as a freighter and troop transport and was used to transport 7,000 Allied troops across the Owen Stanley Mountains in New Guinea. Continuing counterclockwise: a Mitsubishi A6M2 "Zero" fighter in the markings of Saburo Sakai, based at Lae, New Guinea, in the summer of 1942; Douglas A-20 *Havoc* which was widely used as a deadly skip-bomber by Kenney's Fifth Air

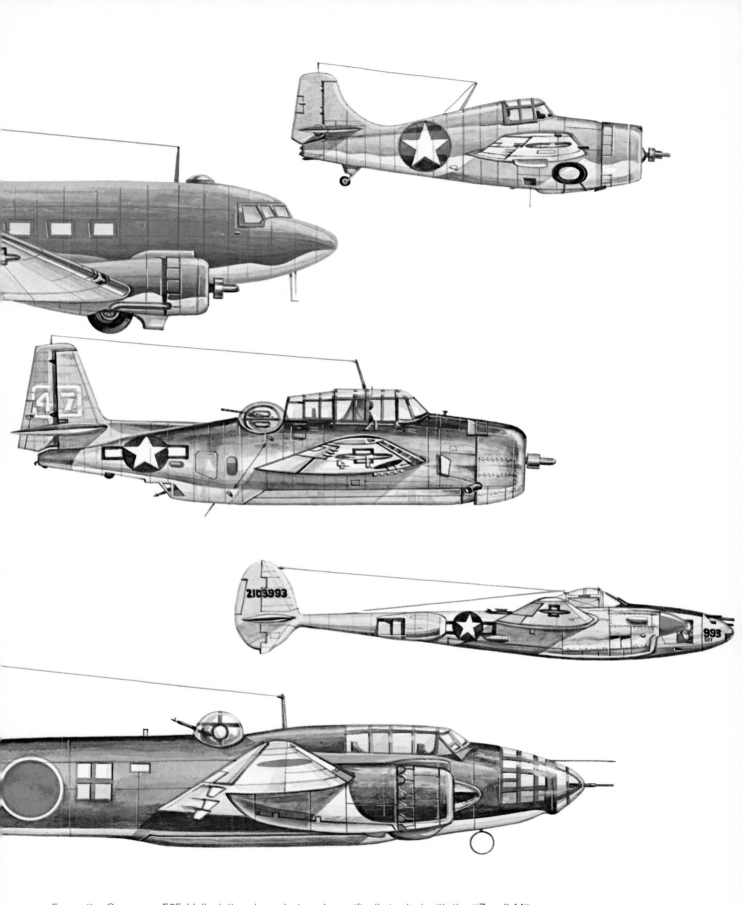

Force; the Grumman F6F *Hellcat,* the plane designed specifically to deal with the "Zero;" Mitsubishi G4M "Betty," land-based Navy medium bomber, which ranged over the Pacific; Lockheed
P-38J *Lightning* as flown by Richard Bong of the 49th Fighter Group, Fifth Air Force; Grumman
TBF (actually an Eastern Aircraft TBM, manufactured by General Motors) *Avenger,* which fared
so badly at the Battle of Midway but exceedingly well in the later battles; Grumman F4F *Wildcat,*
the standard Navy fighter at the war's opening.

*Joseph A. Phelan*

# BOOK II
# Some Sailors—and a Few Marines

# 3

# THE ISLAND

THE military High Thinkers, with their penchant for simple but at the same time grandiloquent catchwords, called it Operation Watchtower. The directive, issued by the Joint Chiefs and dated July 2, 1942, ordered the South Pacific Force (Vice-Admiral Robert L. Ghormley commanding) to seize and occupy the "Santa Cruz Islands, Tulagi and adjacent positions" in the Solomon Islands chain. One of the "adjacent positions," not even mentioned in the directive, was an island named Guadalcanal.

The United States Marines, who took, held, and died on this pestilential island, coined their own word for the operation: Shoestring.

"Shoestring" was less grand than "Watchtower," but closer to the realities of the situation. Partially, the problem lay in the simple fact of inexperience in what was the first real offensive move in the war, and the first American amphibious operation since 1898. And it was made with less than adequate planning and equipment plus mixed emotions at high level. Ghormley was not too certain as to what his objectives were: Were we beginning on the road to Tokyo or merely stopping the Japanese before they became too well entrenched in the Solomons?

The entire operation had been conceived and set under way—inspired by the burgeoning airfield on Guadalcanal—in so great a hurry that Ghormley had little time to prepare for whatever it was he was supposed to accomplish. He was pessimistic, indeed, when he first began working on the project: there were no maps of the area, his amphibious forces had not yet arrived in the Pacific, and there was little intelligence on the disposition of the Japanese in the area. If Ghormley harbored doubts, Vice-Admiral Frank J. Fletcher, to whom he had delegated execution of the operation, did not like it at all—and said so. Fletcher as carrier commander was loath to expose his three precious carriers (the *Enterprise, Saratoga,* and *Wasp*) in an undertaking which he "opposed" and which he felt "sure . . . would be a failure."

He made it clear, in fact, at a meeting (not attended by Ghormley) before the assault, that he would not leave the carriers exposed while the Marines were being put ashore for more than two days. It was estimated that it would take five to complete the job. This would, of course, in turn, expose the Marines to attack by the Japanese. Fletcher's attitude, no doubt, could be attributed to the fact of his not seeing any point to the entire operation, and more subtly, to the fact that two carriers (the *Yorktown* and *Lexington*) had gone down under him; he did not wish to court further disasters.

But King, despite the objections of the Joint Chiefs, had initiated Watchtower, and it would go, as ordered, early in August 1942.

*Bridge conference on the* Wasp *with Dauntlesses spotted on flight deck. Hatless Commander D. F. Smith and steel-helmeted Captain Forrest Sherman, skipper of the* *carrier, attend while Rear Admiral Leigh Noyes receives report from Lieutenant Commander W. N. Beakley (back to camera). Operation Watchtower is under way.* (NAVY DEPT., NATIONAL ARCHIVES)

## II

Guadalcanal stank—literally.

It was the effluvium of green decay that first told the sleepless Marines of the amphibious force in the early morning of August 7, 1942, that they had arrived off Red Beach. The smell of the place was evil and the consensus was best expressed by the Marine who was supposed to have said before the invasion began, "What do we want with a place nobody ever heard of before?" He was not alone,

for Ghormley back in Auckland at South Pacific Force headquarters and Fletcher aboard the *Saratoga,* a hundred miles south of Guadalcanal, struggled with the same question.

The initial aerial operations, following the pre-invasion softening up of the Guadalcanal-Tulagi-Gavutu area by the B-17s of Kenny's 11th Bombardment Group during the last week in July and early August, were the attacks by carrier planes upon the various proposed landing areas. Taking off from the *Enterprise, Wasp,* and *Saratoga* before sunrise, the Wildcats and Dauntlesses assembled in the still darkened sky about thirty miles west of Guadalcanal.

It was delicate, if nerve-racking work. In the darkness, although navigation lights were permitted, the usual mix-ups occurred. Fighters and bombers formed up, or squadrons intermixed as pilots mindful of collision gingerly tried to assemble with their own units. What unity had been achieved was suddenly dispersed when a sudden bright flash and explosion erupted under the rendezvous area. Scattering pilots were certain that two unfortunate planes had come together in the dark. Actually one of the Dauntless pilots had accidently dropped his bomb, which blew up on striking the water. By the time the fighters and scout bombers convened again, the invasion beaches—to the utter surprise of the Japanese—came under heavy fire from American naval big guns.

With the coming of first light, as the Marines clambered out of transports into landing craft offshore, the Wildcats and Dauntlesses swept over Beach Red (Guadalcanal) and Beach Blue (Tulagi, about twenty miles northeast of Florida Island). With very little opposition the carrier planes bombed and strafed the two landing areas, blasting buildings, vehicles, warehouses, gun emplacements, and, near Tulagi, a number of float planes moored offshore.

Shortly after 9 A.M. the Marines of the 1st Division began moving in—the landing at Guadalcanal proceeding "with the precision of a peacetime drill." It was not quite so in the vicinity of Beach Blue, where fifteen hundred Japanese fought, and most died, before the little islands of Tulagi, Gavutu, and Tanambogo could be declared secured.

The major problem on Guadalcanal at first seemed to be the accumulation of supplies on the beach. The Japanese troops (six hundred, not five thousand as Allied intelligence had assumed) fled inland, abandoning much of their own supplies. The laborers, who had been constructing the airstrip, inland and to the west of Beach Red, also faded into the jungle. Brigadier General Alexander A. Vandegrift, commanding the Marines, could not stop unloading troops in order to clear Guadalcanal's beaches of the clutter. By noon he realized that "smoothness" and "precision" were gone.

At twelve-thirty the first bombers from Rabaul arrived. Forty-five planes, bombers with fighter escort, of the 25th Koku Sentai opened up the Japanese counterattack. Navy F4Fs caught the initial wave over Florida Island, after Lieutenant Vincent DePoix of the *Enterprise* spotted them and led three other Wildcats into the attack.

Within minutes smoking Bettys dropped from the neat formations and Zeros whipped into the Wildcats. At the same time on the beaches, all unloading of transports was stopped and ships scurried about to afford as poor targets as possible for the bombers. Antiaircraft too came into action. The guns and the Navy fighters distracted the bombers, so there were no hits on the shipping as bombs dropped uselessly into Sealark Channel—a body of water between Florida and Guadalcanal which would become better known as "Iron Bottom Bay." During the early minutes of the first aerial battle over Guadalcanal Navy pilots deposited the initial metal into the bay in the form of Bettys and Zeros.

The first attack had been expected, thanks to an enterprising Australian coast watcher, the ex-planter Paul Mason, who saw the Bettys and Zeros flying over Buin on Bougainville, three hundred miles to the north of Guadalcanal. HQ radioed the message to Brisbane, which relayed it to Pearl Harbor, from which it was sent to the Solomons. But later in the afternoon another attack, this time by dive bombers, came in without advance warnings, and despite the Navy planes on combat air patrol, managed to strike the destroyer *Mugford*. While the ship did not sink, twenty-two men died in the bombing. *Saratoga* Wildcats all but annihilated the attackers, but the harm had been done.

The Japanese planes were as persistent as gnats, despite losses. (Of the fifty or so planes sent from Rabaul that day, about thirty were lost. It was in this first battle over Guadalcanal that Saburo Sakai was badly wounded and somehow managed to return to Rabaul in his Zero.) Some of the losses were those Vals which ran out of fuel on the way back. But a simple fact had emerged: the Japanese could be expected to fight hard for the "place nobody ever heard of before."

The reason lay in an unfinished airstrip on Guadalcanal. If the Japanese had expected to use it to strike at New Zealand and Australia-bound shipping, the Allies could employ it to hammer away at Rabaul.

*D-Day, Guadalcanal, August 7, 1942. Bettys from Ra-* *tom Bay) as antiaircraft bursts attempt to put them*
*baul skim the surface of Sealark Channel (Iron Bot-* *into the bay.* (DEFENSE DEPT., MARINE CORPS)

While Guadalcanal remained quiet, the heavy fighting progressed across Sealark Channel. It was savage and bitter fighting, which, on land, gave the Americans the first shocking, acrid taste of the Japanese soldiers' lethal fighting style. For the time being, the Marines on Guadalcanal were spared this introduction. They gathered souvenirs abandoned by the Japanese, cursed the heat and the insects, and moved farther inland.

The aerial assault, despite the previous day's losses, continued on August 8. Early warning came via coast watcher Jack E. Read on Bougainville, who counted "Forty bombers heading yours." While the Navy Wildcats sought the expected attackers over Savo Island, in the channel between Guadalcanal and Florida, the Bettys dropped down to the water, skimmed in over Florida, and made for the ships.

As the Wildcats tangled with the Zeros overhead, the Bettys were met by a wall of antiaircraft from the ships in the channel. The bombers bore down upon the American ships, then flared one by one, cartwheeling in a pattern of flame before sinking into Iron Bottom Bay. At least a dozen Bettys

went down in the wall of fire from the ships, but one released a torpedo, which struck the destroyer *Jarvis*. The *Jarvis* was caught by Japanese torpedo planes the following day as it made for Nouméa, New Caledonia, and sunk with all hands.

Another stricken Betty flew directly into the transport *George F. Elliott*. Although the troops had already left the ship, the supplies still in the hold burned and the *Elliott* was beyond salvation. The fire went out of control and the *Elliott* was scuttled at twilight—the first American contribution to the debris of Iron Bottom Bay.

The next morning there was much more. Vice-Admiral Gunichi Mikawa, after hastily assembling ships from Rabaul and Kavieng, raced to the Solomons to deal with the enemy. His orders opened with these words: "We will penetrate south of Savo Island and torpedo the enemy main force at Guadalcanal." And as he led his force of seven cruisers and a destroyer toward the island he wired the ships that "In the finest tradition of the Imperial Navy we shall engage the enemy in night battle. Every man is expected to do his best."

The weather and a series of American blunders

were with Mikawa. Fletcher, fearful lest his carriers be struck by Japanese planes or submarines, but using as an excuse that he was low on fuel (this was not true), withdrew the three carriers from Guadalcanal. This also withdrew Navy reconnaissance planes as well as the bombers and fighters which had been countering the Japanese. Although a search plane had spotted Mikawa's ships near Guadalcanal, its warning was neither properly understood nor distributed.

Early in the morning of August 9, 1942, Mikawa's cruisers began firing their deadly "Long Lance" torpedoes at the unsuspecting Allied ships. No one expected the Japanese, who all Americans were told and believed suffered from poor eyesight and could not see at night, to attack after one-thirty in the morning. Following a terrible night battle, the in-famous battle of Savo Island, the morning light found four heavy cruisers and a destroyer at the bottom of Iron Bottom Bay. More than a thousand men were dead and seven hundred wounded. Mikawa, unaware of his advantage, had slipped away before he did all the damage he might have done, but he had done enough.

By noon Rear Admiral Richmond Kelly Turner, who was in command of the ships of the amphibious force, withdrew his transports from the danger zone. With Fletcher gone and Turner gone, that left only sixteen thousand of Vandegrift's Marines, with only half their supplies, to wonder what the Japanese would try next. They had been furious in their air attacks, had wreaked havoc in the Battle of Savo Island. What would they try now?

The answer came with the initial run of the

*The Ichiki detachment, transported to Guadalcanal by the newly instituted "Tokyo Express," has a rendez-vous with death and the U. S. Marines on the Tenaru* *River. Their major objective had been the airfield on Guadalcanal, which had fallen into American hands.*
(DEFENSE DEPT., MARINE CORPS)

"Tokyo Express." The American ships having left Guadalcanal, the Japanese planes took to bombing the airfield being readied by the Marines. Submarines surfaced during the day to lob shells into it and destroyers stood offshore at night. Almost nightly "Washing Machine Charlie" flew down from Rabaul to keep the Marines from sleeping. The Japanese, certain there were only three thousand Americans on Guadalcanal (the actual number was closer to nineteen thousand), dispatched the Ichiki detachment to "quickly attack and destroy the enemy in the Solomons" in co-operation with the Japanese Imperial Navy.

The Ichiki detachment, commanded by Colonel Kiyanao Ichiki, was brought from Guam, to which it had been taken after the Midway fiasco. Instead of sailing home, as the detachment had been promised, it went instead to Truk, and by August 18, having been brought there by the Tokyo Express, began going ashore on Guadalcanal. Within two days the Ichiki detachment was ripped to pieces in a swift series of horrible battles. As Vandegrift reported, ". . . I have never heard or read of this kind of fighting. These people refuse to surrender. The wounded will wait until men come up to examine them . . . and blow themselves and the other fellow to pieces with a hand grenade."

*Reinforcements for the "Cactus Air Force," Marine Wildcats at Henderson Field, Guadalcanal.*

(DEFENSE DEPT., MARINE CORPS)

Having lost about eight hundred of his men in heedless slaughter (charging automatic weapons with bayonets), Ichiki had no other recourse but to join the honorable dead. After ripping his regimental colors to shreds, inundating them with oil, and setting them afire, Ichiki blew out his brains.

The pattern was established: if the Marines operated on a shoestring, the Japanese chose to use small rubber bands. From Rabaul the bands stretched dangerously; the Tokyo Express would bring in small, inadequate detachments under cover of night and the Imperial Navy would venture forth from time to time. But although they coveted Guadalcanal—especially its airfield—the Japanese High Command, with eyes elsewhere (New Guinea) was unwilling to pursue its course in the Solomons except fragmentally. In the ensuing hard six months, the Japanese and the Americans would learn a good deal about each other.

### III

The day before the Battle of Tenaru River, which wiped out the Ichiki detachment, the first elements of what was called the "Cactus Air Force" landed upon Guadalcanal. On August 17, 1942, the Japanese field, taken over and completed by the Americans, was named Henderson Field, for the Marine

dive bomber commander Major Lofton Henderson, who died at Midway. Cactus was the code name for Guadalcanal.

On August 20 the first Wildcats of Marine Aircraft Group (MAG) 23 began alighting on the strip at Lunga Point. These were nineteen new Grumman F4F-4s of Marine Fighter Squadron (VMF) 223, led by a lean Oklahoman, Captain John L. Smith. Along with the Wildcats came a dozen SBD-3s of Major Richard C. Mangrum's VMSB-232 (Marine Scout Bomber Squadron). The arrival of this tiny air force was greeted by the cheering Marines, who pitched in to change the hard-rubber tail wheels (for carrier deck landing) to pneumatic tires.

The next day Smith of Fighting 23 took four Wildcats out to strafe the remnants of the Ichiki detachment. While on patrol over Savo Island Smith sighted several Zeros and led his men in to the attack. The Zeros had the advantage of perhaps two thousand feet of altitude on the Wildcats, so Smith could do little else but turn the more rugged planes into the aggressors. A Zero flashed by without hitting Smith's plane; then another came in and Smith rolled and found the belly of the Zero in his sights. His mouth went dry, he later remembered, and his heart beat heavily as he squeezed the button. For an instant he watched the stitching of his guns travel along the underside of the Zero, which burst open and flamed. As Smith watched, the Japanese plane fell to the beach of Savo. He had killed his first enemy (the first of nineteen).

Turning back to the battle, Smith unhappily noticed that one Wildcat was missing. Searching, he led the two remaining planes to a formation of strangely gyrating and performing aircraft—but they were all Zeros. Why they insisted upon performing like so many Sunday afternoon pilots at an air show, Smith could not fathom. Perhaps they knew that the Wildcat could not dogfight with the Zero; at the same time they wasted the precious fuel for the long return flight to Rabaul—if they ever got there.

Smith led the two pilots back to Henderson, where they saw the fourth Wildcat. Technical Sergeant John D. Lindley's F4F had been hit in the Zero attack and he made for the landing strip, where he crash-landed. Emerging oil-soaked from the cockpit, Lindley collapsed to the ground. He was not

*John L. Smith, USMC, commander of the first squadron of fighters to arrive at Guadalcanal. Smith survived the months of hard fighting over the Solomons (for which he received the Medal of Honor), later became an instructor.* (DEFENSE DEPT., MARINE CORPS)

seriously hurt and eventually returned to the battle. But his plane was out for the time being.

Fighting 23 had had its first encounter with the dreaded Zero, and although they lost a plane, they had not lost a man. And Captain Smith had actually scored against a Zero. The myth of the invincible Zero was nearing its bitter end.

But the little Cactus Air Force grew slightly. On August 22 the 67th Fighter Squadron, commanded by Captain Dale Brannon, flew up with five Army P-400s (the inferior export P-39, which pilots called "Klunkers"). Two days later an unexpected increment, eleven SBDs, orphans on the wing, flew from the stricken *Enterprise*. These were the Dauntlesses of "Flight 300" led by Lieutenant Turner Caldwell, which, unable to land on the thrice-hit deck of the *Enterprise* during the Battle of the Eastern Solomons, were forced to seek haven at Henderson Field. Immediately drafted into the

*Bell P-39s, which in its export version was designated P-400 (originally intended for Britain but repossessed by the Army after Pearl Harbor). Although disparagingly called "Klunkers" by Air Force pilots, the planes served with distinction in the Cactus Air Force. Here they are mud-mired on Henderson.*

(U. S. AIR FORCE)

Cactus Air Force, these strays from the *Enterprise* would spend the next month on Guadalcanal.

Thus the battle for Guadalcanal took on its own peculiar forms: on land, at sea, and in the air, with Henderson Field at the focus of action. Emphasis might shift from one aspect of the fighting to the other when the fighting on land erupted bloodily; and then it might shift to the sea (such as the ill-starred Battle of Savo Island). The aerial fighting was generally on a small scale because both forces operated under their individual handicaps—the Marines and their small units, lack of spare parts, minimal fuel supply, and the problem of the weather and climate.

The Japanese had access to a supply of replacement aircraft (which were brought into Rabaul from the homeland, Tinian, Truk, and other outposts). These planes and the new pilots were then tossed away in piecemeal, wasteful attempts. Both aircraft and men were pressed beyond endurance and both were consumed with abandon.

When both sea and air battle combined, the results were more decisive than the prodigal thrusts from Rabaul. Such was the Battle of the Eastern

Solomons (August 24–25, 1942). In this engagement, primarily a battle of carrier forces, land-based Marine aircraft participated in their first major air battle in the Solomons.

Yamamoto had assigned a formidable armada of carriers, battleships, and cruisers to protect four transports of the Tokyo Express carrying fifteen hundred troops to Guadalcanal. The striking force, under Nagumo, somewhat recovered from Midway, was based upon the heavy carriers *Shokaku* and *Zuikaku;* the light carrier *Ryujo* was assigned to a diversionary group under Rear Admiral Chuichi Hara, whose task it was to draw American attention away from Rear Admiral Raizo Tanaka's transports and the big carriers.

When word came in from coast watchers and reconnaissance planes of the presence of large Japanese naval forces proceeding toward Guadalcanal, Admiral Ghormley ordered Fletcher's three carriers north to cover the sea approaches to Guadalcanal. Ever since Fletcher had pulled away from Guadalcanal he had patrolled in the seas to the south of the Solomons. By dawn of August 23 the *Enterprise, Saratoga,* and *Wasp* lay east of Malaita Island (about 150 miles east of Henderson Field).

August 22 and 23 the two fleets feinted gingerly in unfavorable weather (unfavorable, that is, for search planes), neither actually finding the other although both Japanese and Americans knew of

*A Marine Wildcat takes off to meet an oncoming Japanese bomber force. Henderson was either soaked in mud or choked with dust, neither of which was salutary for engines or aircraft.*

(DEFENSE DEPT., MARINE CORPS)

one another's presence. Fletcher, misinformed by his intelligence that the Japanese fleet still lay far to the north and thus not expecting action, sent the *Wasp,* with its screen, off to refuel. This left the *Saratoga* and *Enterprise* aircraft plus the tatterdemalions of the Cactus Air Force to take on Yamamoto's forces.

As the *Wasp* pulled away to the south, Yamamoto ordered Vice-Admiral Nobutake Kondo, commanding the Guadalcanal supporting force, to press on with the attack.

Shortly after nine o'clock on the morning of August 24 an American Catalina on patrol spotted a Japanese carrier, just about 200 miles north of Malaita—and about 280 miles from Fletcher's remaining carriers. It was the *Ryujo* on its mission of diverting Fletcher away from the other two Japanese carriers and the landing forces approaching Guadalcanal.

While the ruse worked—Fletcher dispatched bombers and torpedo planes from the *Saratoga* and *Enterprise*—the cost was rather excessive for the inconsiderable *Ryujo.* After dodging the *Enterprise* Avengers and Dauntlesses, it was struck by planes from the *Saratoga* and sunk. Meanwhile, the fifteen bombers and dozen fighters which the *Ryujo* had launched earlier had tangled with Smith's Fighting 23 on the way to attack Henderson Field.

Not one of the Japanese planes reached Guadalcanal. The Wildcats intercepted the Japanese formation and destroyed sixteen enemy aircraft—six of which were Zeros. One of Smith's few veterans of VMF-223—a veteran, in fact, of Midway—Captain Marion Carl knocked down two Kates and a Zero himself. Other Fighting 23 members, Lieutenants Zennith A. Pond and Kenneth D. Frazier and Gunner Henry B. Hamilton, each shot down two of the attackers. The surviving Kates and Zeros, driven off by the Wildcats, returned to the *Ryujo,* only to find a crazily listing, careening, and burning carrier. The planes were ordered to fly on to the Japanese field at Buka near Bougainville to the north.

The Marines of Fighting 23 chipped away further at the myth of the Zero in the opening fight of the Battle of the Eastern Solomons. But not without cost to them, for the squadron suffered its first serious losses that day. Fred Gutt, noted for his sardonic humor, was seriously wounded; Roy Corry,

*The Zero, specifically the "Zeke 52," the mythical fighter of the early months of the Pacific war, but which the Marines, especially of Smith's "Fighting 23," found vulnerable. A beautifully designed, nimble aircraft, the Zero was susceptible to the heavy-gunned American planes. Its pilots were unprotected by armored cockpits and it burned easily.*

(U. S. AIR FORCE)

the gunnery officer—also, like Carl, a Midway veteran and who had given Smith cause for concern on the ship coming over because he brooded about his chances of death in the air—was lost. The last seen of him was when he dived into a swarm of Zeros. The first to go, however, had been a youngster named Bailey who had married just the day before he joined VMF-223. His Wildcat was last seen afire as it splashed into the sea.

The *Ryujo* and its aircraft having been attended to, there still remained the *Shokaku* and *Zuikaku,* whose special targets were the American carriers. Almost simultaneously the two carrier captains, Fletcher and Nagumo, became aware of each other's presence when their respective search planes came upon carriers. This was Nagumo's desired moment; he ordered the aircraft launched, the first wave, consisting of sixty-seven planes led by Lieutenant Commander Mamoru Seki, which raced for the spot where an American carrier had been sighted. A second wave, launched less than an hour later and consisting of forty-eight planes, was led astray by a navigational error and never found the American carriers.

Seki's Kates, Vals, and Zeros, however, found the *Enterprise*. As soon as "bogies" were discovered on the radarscopes of the two American carriers, now about ten miles apart, the air above them filled with more than fifty Wildcats. Lieutenant A. O. Vorse, leading a section of four F4Fs from the *Saratoga,* was the first to sight the Japanese planes —two groups of bombers, shepherded above and below by fighters.

With a shout of "Tally Ho!" Vorse pointed the four Wildcats at the bombers, still about ten thousand feet higher than the American planes. Zeros dropped down to intercept, but the Wildcats, straining at full throttle, continued to climb above the Zero's top altitude. Now with the advantage of altitude, Vorse led a screaming attack upon the Japanese bombers. But again the Zeros darted in to disrupt the run on the bombers, and in the ensuing dogfight three Zeros and what appeared to be an Me-109 fell burning into the sea. Out of ammunition and low on fuel, the four Wildcats returned to the *Saratoga,* except for Vorse, who had to land in the water—he did not have enough fuel to make it all the way. A destroyer swept by to pick him up.

But the bombers continued coming in. Some had dropped very low to avoid radar, but four Wildcats, the section of Ensign G. W. Brooks, had been dispatched by the fighter director of the *Enterprise* to investigate a curious echo on the radarscope. Sixty miles from the carrier Brooks and his section found eleven bombers, Vals and Kates—but without Zeros —heading for the *Enterprise*. Brooks's first burst destroyed a Val, and as he turned away, a Kate came into his sights. Another quick burst and the bomber splashed wing over wing across the water. Within minutes four other bombers, victims of the other members of Brooks's section, fell into the sea, three of them shot down. One Val, its pilot rattled by the attack, simply flew into the water. The five survivors turned tail and fled.

Above the *Enterprise,* too, the battle raged, and burning aircraft—American as well as Japanese— fell into the Pacific. With all its fighters air-borne and its bombers aloft, the *Enterprise* waited. Men on deck squinted into the sunny yet cloud-flecked sky, smeared by the smoke of falling aircraft. Crews at their battle stations manned their 20-millimeters. About twenty-five miles away from the *Enterprise,* Seki fired a signal flare. The Zeros had climbed to

engage the Wildcats, the Kates descended to near water level for torpedo attacks, and the Vals, dividing into small groups, prepared for dive attacks.

Around twelve minutes after five in the afternoon, the first Val tipped on its nose and dropped toward the *Enterprise*. Even while it was still out of range a nervous 20-millimeter gunner indicated its approach with his tracers. In seconds other guns, from the carrier itself and from its escort, the *North Carolina,* joined in on the Val. Soon other bombers followed the Val; the Japanese pilots felt that they were diving into "a wall of fire."

But they came on nonetheless, despite the heavy antiaircraft fire and the Wildcats. Within two minutes of the opening of the attack the *Enterprise* took its first bomb of the war. It struck the aft elevator and cut through three decks before detonating. The explosion whipped the *Enterprise,* throwing men in the forward section to the deck, blasting men from their gun positions, tossing them like rag dolls across the decks. Below, where the bomb had burst, more than thirty men lay dead.

Within seconds a second bomb burst, five yards from where the first had hit. In a searing flash, men suddenly vanished from the earth. The great carrier, spouting black smoke, listed; a quarter of its guns were out of action and more than seventy men dead. But repair parties went to work immediately attending to dozens of injured, and began to clear the damaged area and to contain the fires.

Even while this went on a third bomb fell onto the flight deck. Less effective than the first two bombs, the third, however, ripped a ten-foot hole out of the flight deck and knocked an elevator out of operation.

Suddenly, after about four minutes of concentrated havoc, the last of Seki's bombers, a Val, hugging the water raced for its own carrier.

The listing, burning *Enterprise,* though in serious trouble, was not in danger. Even while the damage-repair crews worked, the great ship continued to make speed and even informed the concerned men aboard the *North Carolina* that it "required no assistance." Within an hour after the last bomb had struck, the *Enterprise* was able to turn into the wind to land its aircraft, all except Turner Caldwell's fuel-depleted Flight 300, which landed at Henderson Field (to join the Cactus Air Force).

The *Saratoga* escaped attack, and although two

*The third bomb striking the* Enterprise, *putting the elevator out of operation and killing Navy photographer*

*Robert Frederick Read. Following the Battle of the Eastern Solomons, the* Enterprise *was under repair for two months.* (NAVY DEPT., NATIONAL ARCHIVES)

heavy Japanese carriers were found, they too escaped serious damage (the *Zuikaku* received one bomb on the flight deck). Returning Japanese pilots gleefully reported sinking the *Hornet,* Doolittle's "Shangri-La," and thus avenging the insult to the Emperor. It was, of course, the *Enterprise,* not the *Hornet,* and it was not sunk, but would be out of battle for two months while being repaired at Pearl Harbor.

The carrier battle was over on the first day; both Fletcher and Nagumo gingerly husbanded their carrier strength. As the day came to a close, five Avengers and two Dauntlesses, led by Lieutenant

Harold Larsen of the *Saratoga,* were sent out to do something about Kondo's advance force heading for Guadalcanal. The handful of planes attacked and sent the seaplane carrier *Chitose* back to Truk with a thirty-degree list, the loss of the port engine, a fire aboard, and casualties. Kondo continued looking for Fletcher, but by midnight gave up the search.

But "Tenacious" Tanaka, the brilliant overseer of the Tokyo Express, continued on for Guadalcanal with his troop-laden transports. While the carriers and fighting ships had been battling to the east of the Solomons, Tanaka had been coming in from the north. On the morning of August 25, Tanaka's ships

*"You never had it so good"—Marine camp on Guadalcanal during the rainy season.*

(DEFENSE DEPT., MARINE CORPS)

were discovered and Mangrum's Dauntlesses of VMSB-232 and the mixed bag of strays of the *Enterprise*, Flight 300, took off to stop the Japanese.

Before they had found the ships, however, Smith had to turn back his protective Wildcats, at the end of their fuel for the trip out. The Henderson Field bombers, meanwhile, continued their search. Suddenly, as if they had materialized out of the mist, there were the ships: the cruiser *Jintsu*, Tanaka's flagship, plus eight destroyers and the transports.

The Marine and Navy bombers struck. Lieutenant Lawrence Baldinus, of VMSB-232, neatly placed a bomb on the deck of the *Jintsu*, just forward of the bridge and between the two forward turrets. In a

reverberating flash, the ship leaped in the water. Tanaka was knocked unconscious as plates buckled, bulkheads were sprung, communications went out, and the forward ammunition lockers flooded. Tanaka, when he came to, realized his flagship was finished as a warship for the time being. He transferred his flag to the destroyer *Kagero* and ordered the *Jintsu* to return to Truk.

Having barely taken up his new post, Tanaka saw Ensign Christian Fink of Flight 300 place a thousand-pound bomb into the heavily loaded transport *Kinryu Maru*. He immediately ordered the destroyers *Mutsuki* and *Yayoi* to run alongside the stricken transport, glowing with heat, to take off survivors.

The American dive bombers, having expended their bombs, circled the scene of damage—the *Jintsu* limping away and the *Kinryu Maru* (which was later sunk) burning furiously—and returned to Henderson. Tanaka then felt he could apply himself better to the problems at hand. But no sooner had the Dauntlesses become specks in the south than high overhead appeared a formation of eight Flying Fortresses. This was not so distressing to Tanaka; as the antiaircraft batteries opened up on these planes, from Colonel LaVerne Saunder's 11th Bombardment Group based in the New Hebrides, Tanaka took some consolation in the fact that the high-flying heavy bombers had never hit a ship, despite American claims to the contrary.

A pattern of five-hundred-pound bombs tumbled from the open bomb bays and before Tanaka's horrified eyes the *Mutsuki* erupted in a series of three flashes and sank. Shortly after, around noon August 25, 1942, Tanaka was ordered to retire to the Shortland Islands, one of the smaller Solomon groups, south of Bougainville. The first major attempt by the Japanese to reinforce Guadalcanal had failed; it had cost them the *Ryujo*, ninety aircraft, and hundreds of men. American losses amounted to seventeen planes and the services of the injured *Enterprise* for several weeks. If the battle of the carriers had not been truly decisive, at least the full contingent of reinforcements had not been landed on Guadalcanal.

IV

That Marine and Navy morale was high could not be attributed to conditions at Henderson Field. For all its blood-soaked significance, Henderson was no pleasure drome. "Henderson Field," Robert Sherrod wrote, "was a bowl of black dust which fouled airplane engines or it was a quagmire of black mud. . . ." Maintenance of the few aircraft was formidable because of the dust and mud; then too there was the humidity. The oil that prevented gun barrels from rusting on the ground caused them to freeze up at fighting altitude.

Ground crews therefore had as tough a time as the airmen. All shared the miseries of climate and the shortage of fresh food (captured Japanese rice was eaten, but only after the careful removal of worms). Malaria and dysentery were common and

so was nagging fatigue. There was no rest at night thanks to "Washing Machine Charlie" or "Louie the Louse," who either dropped random bombs or lighted up the Marine areas with flares so that Tanaka's ships could shell the field and the Marine positions around it.

Yet there was a dash to the style of the pilots of the Cactus Air Force. They became familiar, when photographs came out of the Solomons, in their informal flight clothes all but invariably topped with a blue baseball cap—popular because the visor protected the eyes from the blinding sun. But living and fighting operations took their toll and the problem of reinforcement and supply became critical.

During the day supplies could be brought in by American ships—provided they eluded Japanese submarines and planes. When night fell the big ships raced away from Guadalcanal and the smaller vessels slipped into Tulagi; the land-based Marines dug in. All awaited the arrival of the Tokyo Express, which arrived to land reinforcements and to bring in supplies while its destroyer escort shelled the American positions. Thus, piecemeal, each side kept the fighting going but neither was able to swing the balance.

But piece by piece the American buildup continued at what seemed a piddling pace to those Marines on Guadalcanal. Clearly the Japanese intended to take back Henderson Field, and so it became essential to hold the island. At the end of August the rest of MAG-23 joined its forward echelons—these were Major Robert E. Galer's VMF-224 (with nineteen Wildcats) and Major Leo R. Smith's VMSB-231 (twelve Dauntlesses). At the same time, however, almost twice as many planes were flown in to reinforce Rabaul. The situation remained generally as before: shoestring and rubber band. But standing resolutely between the proper reinforcement by the Japanese of the Guadalcanal forces were the shoestring Marines, the bombers and fighters of Kenney's Fifth Air Force, and the few B-17s and P-39s of those groups that would one day be unified into the Thirteenth Air Force.

Vice-Admiral John S. McCain, commander of all air operations in the South Pacific, stated the facts when he informed Nimitz that "Guadalcanal can be consolidated, expanded and exploited to the enemy's mortal hurt, the reverse is true if we lose Guadalcanal and if reinforcement required is not available Guadalcanal cannot be supplied and cannot be held."

Plenty of action soon blooded the newly arrived Fighting 24 and squadron commander Galer himself opened his string of victories with a double. The veterans of Fighting 23 joined with the new men on missions in order to give them the benefit of their experience.

John Smith continued as his squadron's leading ace with his closest competitor for that position being Marion Carl. But even the veterans could lose a battle, and on September 14, 1942 (while on land the Marines fought at Bloody Ridge to hold Henderson from a heavy attack) Carl's Wildcat was shot into the sea. Carl checked his parachute and took to the air himself. Landing in the water, he swam to shore, where he met one Corporal Eroni, one of the local scouts in the service of Martin Clemens, the Australian coast watcher.

It took Carl and Eroni five days to return to Henderson Field, during which time the colorful and likable pilot was mourned by his squadron mates. He arrived a gaunt, unshaven tall man in dirty khakis at the headquarters of the commander of the 1st Marine Air Wing (1st MAW), Brigadier General Roy S. Geiger. The latter had only recently arrived in Guadalcanal himself to organize operations. His headquarters had been established only two weeks previously in a wooden shack, called "the Pagoda" by the men, about two hundred yards from the Henderson runway—called "the Bull's-eye."

When Carl reported to Geiger the latter was visibly pleased that the man given up for lost had returned. So was Smith, who happened to be in the Pagoda. After relating his adventures with Eroni and the wheezy little launch that had brought him back, Carl—as had the aces in New Guinea—wondered about his score as compared with Smith's.

"Well," Geiger told him, "Smitty has run his score up to fourteen during the five days you were away. That puts you only three behind. What can we do about it?"

"Goddammit, General," Carl retorted, "ground him for five days!"

Thus did the double-edged sword of attrition oscillate from one crisis to the other. Three days before Marion Carl went temporarily missing Cactus Air Force received an unexpected reinforcement: twenty-four Wildcats of VF-5 (Lieutenant Com-

*Robert E. Galer, commander of Marine Fighting 24 of Guadalcanal, thirteenth-scoring ace of the Marine Corps and Medal of Honor recipient.*

(DEFENSE DEPT., MARINE CORPS)

mander Leroy C. Simpler commanding), rendered homeless after the torpedoing of the *Saratoga* by Japanese submarine I-26. While the carrier put into Pearl Harbor, joining the *Enterprise,* there also undergoing repair, its airmen spent nearly ten days twiddling their thumbs at Espiritu Santo in the New Hebrides. By September 11, 1942, they had arrived at Henderson in time for the heavy battling around the airfield.

Although Admiral Ghormley had consistently refused to permit carrier-based aircraft to operate from Guadalcanal (except the *Enterprise*'s Flight 300, which had no other place to go), he dispatched Simpler's Wildcats to Henderson's attrition center. Obviously something was brewing—and it was, for the Japanese were determined to seize Henderson Field.

The operational toll at Henderson because of primitive repair facilities and fatigued pilots was

*Marion E. Carl of Hubbard, Oregon, and a top-scoring ace of Fighting 23.* (DEFENSE DEPT., MARINE CORPS)

high. On one day in September, for example, eight planes crashed during takeoff. Two were put together again but the remaining half dozen were dragged off to the plane bone yard to be cannibalized for parts. One fighter pilot, it was reported, looked at the growing junk heap and said to another, "At this rate we can whip ourselves without any assistance from the Japs."

Bombing attacks were intensified, Japanese destroyers shelled Marine positions, and Major General Kiyotaki Kawaguchi arrived, via the Tokyo Express, in the evening of the same day the *Saratoga* had been hit, to organize the taking of Henderson. These plans were most thorough, for they embraced even the surrender ceremonies in which the Americans were expected to participate in the role of the vanquished.

Meanwhile, with the pickup in the activity of the Tokyo Express, a concentration of naval forces at Truk-Palau, and additional aircraft flown into Rabaul noted, all efforts were made to reinforce the Marines at Guadalcanal. When Kawaguchi struck on September 12 one battalion, led by Lieutenant Colonel Kusukichi Watanabe, was expected "to dash through to the airfield." The Marines, expecting something, took a different view. Like the Ichiki detachment, Kawaguchi's force, which fought furiously, was chopped to pieces by the Marines. Further, Kawaguchi's men came under various air attacks, one of the worst being the noonday (September 12) visit by more than two dozen Bettys with Zero escort, which mistakenly bombed and strafed Kawaguchi's rear echelon at Tasimboko on the north coast.

Even the Klunkers, the three remaining airworthy 67th Squadron P-400s, came in low during the final phase of the Battle of Bloody Ridge to end all Japanese hopes of making the dash to Henderson Field.

The fighting was hard and the Marines suffered 59 dead (to the Japanese toll of 708), but despite the clear-cut victory on land, there was a disaster at sea.

On September 15, the day following the Battle of Bloody Ridge, the *Hornet* and *Wasp*, the two remaining carriers in the Pacific, had been called to escort six transports carrying the 7th Marines to Guadalcanal. While moving into the waters of the Coral Sea known as "Torpedo Junction" (between Espiritu Santo and Guadalcanal), the carriers came under submarine attack. The battleship *North Carolina* was hit by a torpedo; so was the destroyer *O'Brien*. Although the *North Carolina* remained afloat and returned to Espiritu Santo, the *O'Brien*, after making temporary repairs, split in two on its way to the United States.

The *Hornet* eluded the Japanese "fish" but three twenty-one-inch torpedoes ripped into the *Wasp* and it sank, a burning mass of junk. That left only the *Hornet* against Nagumo's large carriers, the *Shokaku* and *Zuikaku*, and the light carriers *Zuiho* and *Junyo*. This was an unhealthy imbalance of naval power in the Pacific and it did not bode well for the Marines and Navy and Army men on Guadalcanal.

The only slight brightness was the additional Navy aircraft that, deckless because of the loss of carriers, bolstered up the always tattered Cactus Air Force. "What saved Guadalcanal," Brigadier General Ross

*The* Wasp, *torpedoed en route to Guadalcanal, before it sank on September 15, 1942.*

(NAVY DEPT., NATIONAL ARCHIVES)

E. Rowell, commander of the Marine Pacific Air Wings, commented, "was the loss of so many carriers." On October 1, 1942, General Geiger had a total of fifty-eight operational aircraft (Wildcats, Dauntlesses, Avengers, and the usual three Klunkers) on Guadalcanal. But at Rabaul the Japanese had about three times this number.

And the Japanese remained resolute in their plans to take Guadalcanal. Lieutenant General Harukichi Hyakutake, commander of the Seventeenth Army at Rabaul, had his own timetable to keep. His major project was the taking of Port Moresby, but before that he wished to recapture Guadalcanal by October 21. After the disasters of the Ichiki detachment and the Kawaguchi force,

however inexplicable, Hyakutake proposed to lead the recapture himself. As additional insurance he built his force around two tough divisions, veterans of the fighting in the Philippines, Java, and other conquered areas. These units, the 2nd (Sendei) and 38th Divisions, were equipped with heavy artillery and tanks, neither of which Ichiki nor Kawaguchi had had. At the same time the aircraft strength at Rabaul was raised to 180; a bomber base was established at Buka in the northern Solomons and fighters could be accommodated at Buin on Bougainville. Even the generally unsympathetic Imperial Navy co-operated with the promise of such great battleships as the *Haruna, Kongo, Hiei,* and *Kirishima.* The Tokyo Express was in fine shape.

By the time Hyakutake himself arrived by the nightly express he had around twenty thousand (perhaps several thousands more; precise figures were not maintained during these tense days) troops awaiting the word to go. On this October 9 Hyakutake, the soul of efficiency, had a good idea of which spot was to be selected for the surrender of General Vandegrift.

On this same day twenty Wildcats of MAG-14 arrived (making the total forty-six fighters); the planes were led in by Major Leonard K. Davis. These were the aircraft of VMF-121, a squadron whose executive officer was Captain Joseph J. Foss. Smith's veteran VMF-223 had by this time become depleted with six pilots killed and six wounded. Eight, among them Smith himself, survived. Smith, with a score of 19, was the squadron's ace, and Marion Carl was second with a total of 16. But the contribution of Fighting 23 did not lay in numbers (the squadron total was 111½), but in the day-to-day fighting against odds for nearly two months. For his part John L. Smith was awarded the Medal of Honor and returned to the United States to train future Marine fighter pilots.

Richard Mangrum, who led the first of the Dauntless squadrons (VMSB-232), like Smith, survived although the squadron had suffered eleven killed (seven of whom were pilots) and five wounded (four of these being pilots); the rest of the squadron had to be evacuated by air for hospitalization. Only Mangrum was able to leave under his own power.

Flight 300 of the *Enterprise* had been used up in the battling and its last crew members were shipped out to return to their carrier by late September. The weight of the bombing effort out of Henderson devolved upon Major Gordon A. Bell's VMSB-141, which began arriving on September 23 and which by October 6 could muster twenty-one pilots, and upon Leo Smith's depleted VMSB-231 and other strays which had come in from the south.

Joseph Foss got his first Zero on October 13, 1942, during an afternoon raid by Japanese bombers and Zeros. It was this day which the Japanese selected to open their final seizure of Guadalcanal, which Hyakutake told his troops would "truly decided the fate of the entire Pacific."

The first of the Japanese bombers, coming over just after noon, holed the runway at Henderson and a nearby strip, Fighter 1. Even more irreparable harm was done when five thousand gallons of aviation fuel went up in smoke. More bombers came over about an hour later and again Henderson was worked over. Because both raids had come without advance warning there was little opportunity for interception, except for a couple of Zeros, one of them shot down by Foss.

Just before these raids the first Army troops, the "Americal Division" (164th Infantry Regiment), had debarked to be treated to the typical atmosphere of Guadalcanal. Nighttime brought even more of the same. To the Marines' surprise, just after six o'clock in the evening shells began falling on Henderson. There were no Japanese ships offshore. This was "Pistol Pete," one of the heavy artillery guns which had been brought in on the Tokyo Express only two nights before.

But that was only the preliminary to the evening's diversion. From time to time Pistol Pete would lob one over, just to keep everyone on their toes, and nerves' edge, and then in the middle of the night Louie the Louse flew over and planted three flares across Henderson Field, a red one at one end, white in the middle, and blue at the other end. For the next hour and a half the *Haruna* and the *Kongo*

*Marines extinguish a burning Wildcat at Henderson Field after a Japanese bombing raid.*

(DEFENSE DEPT., MARINE CORPS)

laid more than nine hundred fourteen-inch shells into the Henderson area, ripping up the steel matting of the runways, damaging planes, and killing men. It was a nightmare, literally, of flame, explosion, and terror. As Tanaka observed he found that "the whole spectacle [made] the Ryogoku fireworks display seem like mere child's play. The night's pitch dark was transformed by fire into the brightness of day. Spontaneous cries and shouts of excitement ran throughout our ships."

This exhilaration was not echoed ashore. When the Marines and soldiers finally crawled from their foxholes, the destruction their bleary eyes took in was disheartening. To begin with, forty-one men were dead, five of them pilots; one of the latter was Major Gordon Bell, only recently arrived with his replacement Dauntlesses. General Geiger, who had dived into shelter knowing he had thirty-nine Dauntlesses to dispatch against the Japanese, found upon emerging that only four were still flyable. Sixteen of his forty Wildcats were wrecks and all of the remaining ones required repairs. Two Flying Fortresses, of eight which had arrived from Espiritu Santo, were destroyed. The surviving six got away from Henderson as soon as possible, some on less than full power.

About the only damage that no one regretted was

a direct hit upon a ration dump which deposited bits and pieces of Spam in every direction for a half mile. And since the airfield was the center of attention, General Geiger's Pagoda was also hit. This structure, which afforded the Japanese a good aiming point, was bulldozed to the ground, and the Marine aviation commander moved his headquarters to the eastern end of Henderson Field.

And so it went on: savage fighting in the jungle around Henderson, bombardment by night and day, as each contender attempted to reinforce their forces on the island. This made for what Samuel Eliot Morison called "a curious tactical situation . . . : a virtual exchange of sea mastery every twelve hours." It was like some mad changing of the guard, with the Japanese in control at night and the Americans by day. But Hyakutake, with the aid of Yamamoto, hoped to change all that once and for all.

The night following "the Night," as the Marines called it, the Japanese ships returned, this time in the form of a couple of cruisers, which laced the Henderson area with nearly eight hundred eight-inch shells to cover the landing of more reinforcements. By dawn of the next day, October 15, the Japanese believed that Henderson had been pretty well taken care of—and they were not far from wrong. In the morning an American search plane came upon five Japanese transports, standing off Tassafaronga (about ten miles west of Henderson on the north coast of Guadalcanal) rather discon-

*Bombed-up Dauntlesses over Guadalcanal head for their targets—ships of the Tokyo Express.*
(DEFENSE DEPT., MARINE CORPS)

*A Consolidated PBY "Catalina," a patrol bomber that Marine Major "Mad Jack" Cram converted (for one battle) into a dive bomber.*

(CONVAIR/GENERAL DYNAMICS)

certingly unloading troops and supplies in broad daylight.

Geiger found he had little with which to contest this affront. Only three Dauntlesses were in condition to get off the ground, and only one actually did. The other two cracked up while attempting to get off the pocked Henderson runway. But single attacks could accomplish very little, especially when the Zeros could come down from Bougainville to circle over the transports. But as the day progressed, ground crew men patched up the aircraft and found some long-forgotten supplies of fuel hidden in the swamps around the airfield; they siphoned this fuel into whatever planes could be mustered for disputing with the Japanese their bold attempt to take over during the American daylight period of sea mastery.

By ten in the morning, three hours after the first single-plane attacks, a dozen Dauntlesses were ready to fly. Wildcats, Klunkers (P-400s), and even a single Catalina went out to raze the transports' rendezvous area. Major Jack Cram, the pilot of the Catalina, *Blue Goose,* General Geiger's personal aircraft, took off with two two-thousand-pound torpedoes slung under the Catalina's wing. He had arrived from Espiritu Santo with the torpedoes, but found there were no Avengers in condition to deliver them. Although no PBY had ever made a daylight torpedo run before, Cram, by dint of vocal power, obtained permission to drop the fish. Cram, who earned the nickname of "Mad Jack" on this mission, took off in company with a mixed flight of Dauntlesses and Wildcats. Counting his slow Catalina, the American formation consisted of twenty-one planes. Over the Japanese transports milled about thirty Zeros.

As the Dauntlesses raced in for their attacks, Cram set the Catalina on its own, near-dawdling bomb run. The big plane soon came under anti-aircraft fire from the ships (one hit sheared off the plane's navigation hatch). Cram bore down on one of the transports and released the torpedoes, both of which tore into the side of one of the transports, ripping it open.

Mad Jack Cram, though successful in his unorthodox mission, was now in plenty of trouble. Several Zeros, upon realizing what the pilot of the Catalina had been up to, peeled out of the fighting above and began devoting full attention to the *Blue Goose*. Having already dived the Catalina beyond its normal safe speed, Cram tested the groaning airframe and wing even more in attempting to evade the Zeros. Although he managed to keep his crew and himself from being holed with his crazy aerobatics, the Catalina itself was punctured half a hundred times on the way to Henderson Field. Coming in low to pull in to the field, Cram found he still had one angry Zero on his tail. His airspeed was also too high for a landing, so Cram continued on to the satellite field, Fighter 1.

His luck improved over Fighter 1, for as he waddled onto the strip one of the fighter pilots, VMF-121's Lieutenant Roger Haberman, forced out of the fighting with a smoking Wildcat, also came in to the field. Seeing the Catalina under attack, Haberman eased his Wildcat, its wheels already lowered for landing, onto the Zero pilot's tail and shot the Zero out of the air.

When Geiger saw what remained of his command plane he threatened Mad Jack Cram with a court-martial for "deliberate destruction of government property," and then awarded him the Navy Cross.

By the day's end the Japanese had lost three transports, which burned and had to be beached, with much destruction to their cargoes. This included

*Major Jack R. Cram, aide and pilot for Marine Major General Roy S. Geiger.*

supplies, artillery ammunition, and, of course, troops. Even B-17s had come up from the New Hebrides to sink one of the ships. Fighters, in addition to mixing with the Zeros, also strafed the transports and the beaches, inflicting a terrible toll on the Japanese troops. American losses were three Dauntlesses and four Wildcats, but those Japanese ships which had not been destroyed pulled away from Tassafaronga.

Still, nearly five thousand troops had been landed and the night was again rendered hideous by shelling from cruisers. On October 15 Geiger had only thirty-four aircraft (nine Wildcats) to stand off any Japanese attempt to retake Guadalcanal. The truth was that all was not at all well in the Solomons. While the word was not released to the American public, the words of Admiral Nimitz were arresting:

*Harold W. Bauer (in an early photograph), who earned a Medal of Honor on the day he arrived at Henderson Field, and was lost in combat before he could be decorated.* (DEFENSE DEPT., MARINE CORPS)

"It now appears that we are unable to control the sea in the Guadalcanal area. Thus our supply of our positions will only be done at great expense to us. The situation is not hopeless, but it is certainly critical."

General Vandegrift was far less reticent when he informed Ghormley that it was "Urgently necessary that this force [i.e., Vandegrift's command on Guadalcanal] receive maximum support of air and surface units."

Ghormley was able to send additional Wildcats of VMF-212 (some of whose pilots were already at Henderson), under Lieutenant Colonel Harold W. Bauer. This put Geiger's fighter strength up to twenty-eight; also arriving with Bauer's flight were seven Dauntlesses which had accompanied them up from Efate (New Hebrides). As the formation set-

tled down for a landing late in the afternoon they found they had arrived in the middle of a dive-bombing attack. Nine Vals were working over the U.S.S. *McFarland,* which had just delivered a cargo of aviation fuel and was preparing to pull out of the Solomons with medical evacuees aboard.

Seeing this, and despite nearly empty fuel tanks after the long flight north, Bauer singlehandedly took after the Vals. He dived into the squadron of Japanese bombers and slashed through with his guns hammering; in minutes four Vals fell away burning. Bauer, now dangerously low on fuel, had to pull away and land at Henderson Field. He was to receive a Medal of Honor for this attack, but he did not survive to accept it.

v

The date of Bauer's Medal of Honor fight was October 16, 1942. On this same day Ghormley received word of great activity by the Japanese fleet in the vicinity of the Santa Cruz Islands, south and east of the Solomons. Ghormley recognized the situation as more than critical, wired Nimitz that his "forces [were] totally inadequate to meet" the impending threat. In two days, on October 18, 1942, Ghormley was out. He was replaced by a "more aggressive commander" (the words are Nimitz's) in the person of Vice-Admiral William F. Halsey. When word was released in the Pacific it was greeted by cheers from the men, who had been discouraged over the stalemate at Guadalcanal.

General Hyakutake, meanwhile, had formulated his plan of attack upon the Henderson perimeter; there would be three simultaneous assaults at widely separated points. The main push would come up from the south under Lieutenant General Masao Maruyama. A keen sense of history motivated the general, for he instructed his engineers to construct a trail through the swamp and jungle leading to Henderson Field, which he, free of false modesty, decided to name "the Maruyama Road." The total plan was elaborate, therefore complex, and like so many grand military enterprises, appeared fine on paper and sounded beautiful in high-level discussion, but proved to be much different when attempted "on the ground" and with live men instead of symbols.

Timed to coincide with Hyakutake's seizure of

Henderson Field, Yamamoto at Truk had impressive plans for the Combined Fleet. He assembled four carriers, five battleships, fourteen cruisers, and forty-four destroyers for an all-out effort which, it was planned, would settle the bothersome Solomons question once and for all. Yamamoto was emboldened by the knowledge that with the *Wasp* sunk and the *Saratoga* undergoing repairs, his only carrier opposition would come from the *Hornet*. He did not know, however, that the *Enterprise* had recovered from the three bomb hits taken in the Battle of the Eastern Solomons and was ready for action.

The land battle opened first, when Hyakutake's three-pronged attack got off to an unco-ordinated start on October 23. Communications being what they were in Guadalcanal's jungles, the neatly laid plans went quite readily awry. To soften up the American positions for Hyakutake's grand blow a large force of Japanese bombers with fighter escort came down from Rabaul and Buin. These were met by two dozen Marine and Navy Wildcats.

Climbing to meet the Japanese, Joseph Foss counted sixteen bombers and perhaps twenty-five Zeros. As he led his flight in an attack upon five Zeros, Foss found himself about to be victimized by twenty, which dived out of the sun. The Wildcats snapped into a fast dive to accumulate the speed to escape the enemy fighters. As he zoomed out of the way Foss caught a glimpse of a Wildcat on the tail of a Zero. Another Zero was attached to the Wildcat. Foss reacted immediately and the second Zero quickly, under his guns, disintegrated in mid-air. Foss, who witnessed several such explosions, described the process: "The motor goes off in a crazy, lopsided whirl. The pilot pops out of his cockpit like a pea that has been pressed from a pod. The air is filled with dust and little pieces, as if someone has emptied a huge vacuum cleaner bag in the sky. The wing section, burning where it had joined the fuselage, takes a long time to fall. It goes down like a leaf—sailing, then almost stopping as it attacks the air, sailing again, and attacking the air again." Foss was forced to turn sharply to avoid "the falling junk" as he whirled into another Zero. Before he was forced out of the fighting with a badly smoking engine, the result of a head-on attack by a Zero, which he also shot out of the sky, Foss had shot down four of the day's tally of twenty Zeros and four bombers.

*Joseph J. Foss, USMC, who shot down twenty-six Japanese planes over the Solomons (twenty-three of them over Guadalcanal during the period October 9–November 19, 1942) to earn himself the Medal of Honor and the accolade of America's ace of aces until Richard Bong's score began accumulating over New Guinea.* (DEFENSE DEPT., MARINE CORPS)

Rain on the next day discouraged all activity except for the Japanese troops slithering through the jungle over the prematurely named Maruyama Road. The day after, October 25, 1942, went down in Marine history as "Dugout Sunday." Thanks to the mud, most U.S. aircraft were immobilized when the Japanese planes came over in the morning and gave the Marine positions a severe mauling. Japanese land, sea, and air traffic picked up; the big final push was on.

American aircraft were unable to get off the airstrips until later in the day, but once they did they dealt severely with the Japanese. Once again Foss scored copiously, five Zeros in a single combat —bringing his total up to sixteen (his final score would be twenty-six). Dugout Sunday, which had begun so propitiously for the Japanese airmen, closed with a loss of twenty-two aircraft to fighters and four to antiaircraft guns.

Three hundred miles to the east of Guadalcanal, meanwhile, Yamamoto's Guadalcanal support force, the Third Fleet (Nagumo), and the Second Fleet (Kondo) waited. This powerful force was assigned the task of intercepting American attempts to reinforce the Guadalcanal garrison, presumably being torn to ribbons by Hyakutake's troops on the island, and also to prevent the survivors from escaping. Aware of the presence of the large Japanese naval forces to the north of the Santa Cruz Islands, Halsey ordered Task Force 61 (the *Enterprise*) and TF 17 (the *Hornet*), the only carrier forces available, to a rendezvous point north of the New Hebrides. To this was also added TF 64 (built around the battleship *Washington*). These forces were under the tactical command of Rear Admiral Thomas C. Kinkaid of the *Enterprise*.

The odds were far from even. Nagumo with his 4 carriers could count on 212 aircraft; Kinkaid had 171. There was but 1 American battleship to stand against 4 Japanese (as it eventuated, Task Force 64 did not participate in the battle, which left only the *South Dakota* of TF 61). To round out the picture: there were 12 Japanese cruisers versus 6 American, and 24 destroyers against 14. Nagumo exuded confidence for the first time since Midway, even more so, for he was not aware of the fact that the *Enterprise* had returned to active duty.

Still, Nagumo was uneasy. He awaited word of Vandegrift's surrender to Hyakutake, but it did not come. In fact, because of some confusion (and poor communications between the three broad arrows pointing toward Henderson Field on his field map), Hyakutake had been forced to postpone the concerted assault. Nagumo fretted and wired Hyakutake to get on with the American defeat, for the ships were running low on fuel. Then good word came from the island: Kawaguchi, of the ill-fated earlier fighting at Bloody Ridge, in an excess of hope was certain he saw some of his men overrun Henderson Field. A naval liaison officer with the ground troops sent the message, "Airfield taken." It was a premature conclusion, as it turned out, but it was enough for anxious Nagumo. He refueled and turned toward Guadalcanal, not knowing the Marines were blunting the land attack.

After midnight, October 25, 1942—Dugout Sunday on Guadalcanal—a Catalina out of Espiritu Santo found the Japanese fleet. The message sent was laconic: "Sighted enemy task force Lat. 'a' Long. 'b' course 'c' speed 'd' x-ray. Please notify next of kin." The Catalina, after dropping flares upon the Japanese force, shadowed the carriers for a time, attempting to collect more information. Then the big flying boat, low on fuel, turned away.

So did Nagumo, who reversed course. When Dauntlesses, Avengers, and Wildcats, launched from the *Enterprise* later in the day, fanned out searching for Japanese ships, Nagumo had slipped into the darkness and no enemy ships were found. The same frustration attended Nagumo. He was aware of the Americans and the increase of aerial and radio activity, but he had no real idea where their carriers were.

On October 26 all mystery was dispelled when a search plane from the *Shokaku* sighted the American forces bearing northwest. A search mission from the *Enterprise* also spotted Nagumo's carriers. There were no longer any military secrets as men began preparing for attacks upon the carriers in what came to be called the Battle of Santa Cruz.

Two Dauntlesses, one piloted by Lieutenant Stockton B. Strong and the other by Ensign Charles Irvine, came upon the big *Shokaku* and the small *Zuiho;* the *Zuikaku* was hidden under cloud some miles away. Strong signaled to Irvine that they would attack the nearest carrier, the *Zuiho,* so Irvine moved in closer, though behind Strong's Dauntless. So far so good, for they had moved into attack position without antiaircraft or Zero interference.

Strong rolled over, put his flaps in dive position, and with an eye on his aiming scope, plummeted toward the slender yellow deck of the *Zuiho.* Three hundred yards behind, Irvine followed. The Dauntlesses screamed down out of the sun until each reached a point about fifteen hundred feet above the *Zuiho,* which, Strong noted, carried no aircraft on its decks. Evidently a strike had already been launched by Nagumo. Strong released his five-hundred-pound bomb and seconds later Irvine's arched away from the belly of his Dauntless also. Both struck the *Zuiho* in the after section of the flight deck, ripping the deck open, toppling antiaircraft guns, and ending the *Zuiho* as an effective carrier for the rest of the battle. Although it would have been possible to launch aircraft, which he had already done, Captain Sueo Obayashi reported to Nagumo that the *Zuiho* would not be able to land any aircraft. The *Zuiho,* vulnerable and all but helpless, must leave the scene of combat.

Strong and Irvine, meanwhile, had pulled out of their dives, then sought the safety of near-water flight to escape the antiaircraft fire and the attacks by Zeros. While their rear gunners fought off the Zeros that came in too close, Strong radioed the location of the *Zuiho* and the amount of damage he estimated he and Irvine had done to it. Irvine's Dauntless had taken some hits in the wing and tail, which slowed him up a bit, as the two Navy planes strained at full speed for the *Enterprise.* The question was: Where would the *Enterprise* be? If it had come under observation, the ship would have certainly shifted course; if the Japanese planes, absent from the *Zuiho's* flight deck, had found it, the situation could even be worse.

Finally, after a forty-five-mile chase, close to the waves and then dodging through puffs of cloud,

the Zeros gave up after losing two of their number to the Dauntless gunners. With practically no fuel the two Dauntlesses settled down upon the deck of the *Enterprise.* The time was ten twenty-six; the Dauntlesses had been air-borne since six that morning. They had done a good morning's work—and the *Enterprise,* thanks to a sudden local rain squall, had momentarily escaped attack.

At 5:15 A.M. Nagumo had launched the first attack group, under the command of Lieutenant Commander Mamoru Seki, from the *Shokaku* and the *Zuikaku.* For this strike the *Shokaku* had provided twenty-two Vals and twenty-seven Zeros; the *Zuikaku* put up eighteen Kates. Thus the strike was composed of dive bombers, torpedo bombers, and fighters. As the formation proceeded toward the American carriers they passed another group of aircraft going in the opposite direction. These were Dauntlesses from the *Hornet* on their way hoping to do hurt to the Japanese carriers. For some reason Lieutenant Commander Hideki Shingo, leading the *Shokaku's* Zeros high above the bombers,

*An Avenger of Air Group 10 prepares to take off from the* Enterprise *at Santa Cruz. Hand-held signs give aircrews last-minute information; sign directly* *under the cowling reads: "Jap CV [carrier] Speed 25 at 8:30" and, directly over wheel, "Proceed without Hornet."* (NAVY DEPT., NATIONAL ARCHIVES)

*A Kate passes over a cruiser, its target a carrier; Battle of Santa Cruz.*

did not see the *Hornet* formation, or did not recognize the planes as those of the enemy, so no attack was ordered. For this oversight Shingo's home ship would suffer. It was a ludicrous fraction of a moment as the bomber pilots, brothers under the skin though enemies, passed each other on similar errands. The good luck of the men of the *Hornet*'s first strike force would last until it found the Japanese ships.

Not so, however, for the men of the first *Enterprise* team. Eight Avengers, three Dauntlesses, and an escort of eight Wildcats took off early and headed for the presumed position of the Japanese carriers. Barely a half hour out from the *Enterprise* the formation suffered a sudden attack from above by Zeros. Almost simultaneously two Avengers, one of them flown by Lieutenant Commander John A. Collet, commander of Torpedo 10, spiraled burning into the ocean four thousand feet down. In the slashing attack by fighters from the already burning *Zuiho,* the *Enterprise* force was cut in half. The Wildcats, at a disadvantage at low altitude, were handicapped; three went down into the ocean and another, smoking, turned back for the *Enterprise,*

only about fifty miles away. When the survivors reassembled only four Avengers remained with the three Dauntlesses to make the attack and there were only four Wildcats to protect them.

But they did not find the carriers and dropped their bombs and torpedoes into what was believed to be "a *Kongo*-type" battleship. While the *Kongo* and the *Haruna* were units in Vice-Admiral Kondo's advance force, they were not hit that day. This was probably the *Chikuma*, a cruiser in Nagumo's striking force. Though struck and damaged rather heavily, the *Chikuma* continued to function despite casualties.

Though deprived of the Zero escort, which turned back after it had attacked the *Enterprise* force (because of fuel consumed in the fighting), Lieutenant Commander Seki led his Vals and Kates toward the *Hornet.* As combat air patrol Wildcats swept in to attack, Seki dived toward the *Hornet.* Heavy antiaircraft fire rose to hammer him and shortly after he had given his command for the attack, Seki was hit several times. His plane rolled over on its back, flame streaming behind, and continued toward the *Hornet.* Bombs were flung into the carrier

The Battle of Santa Cruz, October 26, 1942. The air filled with antiaircraft fire, the sea churning with the movement of heavy ships and plunging aircraft—and the Enterprise (left) dodging a bomb or Japanese plane.

from the Vals. A stricken Val, probably Seki's, came in upon the *Hornet,* careened off the stack, smashed through the flight deck, and burst with the detonation of its own bombs. And then the Kates came in, low on the water, to jab torpedoes into the carrier's sides. Two fish cut into the engineering spaces and the *Hornet,* spouting steam, flame, and gouts of black smoke, lurched to the starboard. During the torpedo attack another suicidal run was made on the *Hornet,* portent of things to come, when a Kate, which may have been that of Lieutenant Jiichiro Imajuku, ran in upon the *Hornet* from dead ahead (seemingly under control), smashed a gun gallery, rolled into a ball of flaming metal, and exploded near the forward elevator shaft.

The U.S.S. *Hornet,* Doolittle's "Shangri-La," was finished and truly could the Japanese at long last claim vengeance for the Tokyo raid. But for those who believe wars can be fought on vengeance, the *Hornet* would, before it sank into the Pacific, have its small share. Led by Lieutenant James E. Vose, the *Hornet*'s dive bombers located the *Shokaku* and broke through the screen of antiaircraft fire and Zeros. Bombs splashed across the deck of the *Shokaku,* Nagumo's flagship, splintering great holes in the deck and producing violent flames, twisting hot gun barrels out of action and starting fierce blazes below decks. Although the *Shokaku* was to escape the final fate of the *Hornet,* it was no longer capable of either taking or launching planes and its communications were out. Nagumo was forced to leave the battle. He turned over the command to Rear Admiral Kakuji Kakuda aboard the unharmed *Zuikaku* and fled northward for Truk. The *Shokaku* would be out of the war for nine months.

But the *Zuikaku* and the *Junyo* (the latter of

Kondo's advance force) were still very much in the battle. Vals and Kates from both these carriers found the *Enterprise,* and though the Japanese planes were badly mauled by fighters and heavy antiaircraft fire, three bombs struck the *Enterprise,* causing terrible fires and damage and resulting in the death of forty-four men. The Kates too added to the misery of the day, but skillful dodging under the cool command of Captain Osborne B. Hardison saved the *Enterprise* from further damage. Gunners of the *South Dakota,* a battleship armed with heavy AA batteries, destroyed Japanese planes attempting to hit the *Enterprise* also. The *South Dakota,* however, suffered a hit from one of the *Junyo* bombers. So did the cruiser *San Juan.* The destroyer *Smith* was crashed by a Kate, which set the ship aflame. And as it drew into the vicinity of the *Hornet* to take men from the burning carrier, the

destroyer *Porter* was torpedoed by Japanese submarine I-21. The *Porter* sank, taking fifteen men trapped in the firerooms, and later the *Hornet,* "a flaming mass," was sunk by the Japanese destroyers *Makikumo* and *Akigumo.*

The *Hornet* and *Porter* were the only ships, both American, which were lost in the Battle of Santa Cruz. Truly could the Imperial fleet make claims for a great victory in what they called "the Battle of the South Pacific." Despite the damages to the *Shokaku* and *Zuiho,* it could be said that Yamamoto had won the battle, but there was a subtle perplexity to consider. No Japanese ships had gone down, it was true, and the only carrier which sizzled under the sea was American, but under that sea also were sixty-nine Japanese aircraft totally lost, with an additional two dozen forced down into the sea. Some of the pilots from the latter were saved, but all the aircrews of the sixty-nine bombers and fighters, the few remaining veterans of Pearl Harbor, the Indian Ocean, and the Coral Sea, were lost.

*To reduce the hazard of fire, a damaged Dauntless is pushed off the deck of the* Enterprise *into the waters off Santa Cruz.* (NAVY DEPT., NATIONAL ARCHIVES)

*Lieutenant Stanley W. "Swede" Vejtasa of VF-10, the* Enterprise, *climbing into the cockpit of his Wildcat.* (NAVY DEPT., NATIONAL ARCHIVES)

If the Battle of Santa Cruz was frustrating in its lack of a clean-cut victory it was also obvious that American "carrier strength in the Pacific was now dangerously low," in the words of King. Even so, the Japanese had lost their last major attempt at taking back Guadalcanal. But the loss of so many experienced pilots, who might have trained more "sea eagles" for Nippon, was a heavy price to pay for the *Hornet* and the *Porter* and seventy-four U.S. planes.

Typical of the aerial action which marked the ferocity of the Santa Cruz battle was that engaged in by Lieutenant Stanley W. "Swede" Vejtasa. Leading three other members of VF-10 (the famed Lieutenant Commander James Flatley's "Grim Reapers" of the *Enterprise*) Vejtasa spent more than nine hours in the air on October 26, 1942. Shortly after Captain Hardison all but oscillated his

massive *Enterprise* out of the attack of five torpedo planes, Vejtasa and his four Wildcats were vectored to investigate more unidentified, incoming aircraft.

It had been an active flight, for Vejtasa had already destroyed two dive-bombing Vals, and upon reaching the new point, he saw no less than eleven Kates streaking for the *Enterprise*. If the Kates split up, as was customary, Hardison would have had to make the *Enterprise* dance to elude all of them. With his wingman, Lieutenant Leroy Harris, Vejtasa approached the stepped-up column of three Vs plus two Kates trailing. The other two men in his flight, Lieutenant Stanley E. Ruehlow and Ensign W. H. Leder, teamed up to attack. While Ruehlow and Leder were busy with a pair of Zeros, Vejtasa and Harris came in below and astern of the Kates. As soon as they were within range both men began firing and each took out one Kate, the two trailing the three V-formations. They pushed throttle to overtake the nine remaining Kates and just as they did entered a great cumulus cloud.

Vejtasa no longer saw Harris, but ahead of him, dimly, he could make out some Kates. He moved in, aimed at the left-hand member of the formation, and opened with his six .50-calibers. The Kate exploded and fell away. The next plane lost its rudder and then burst into flame and fell too. Alerted, the third Kate attempted to turn, but the faster Wildcat turned more sharply and Vejtasa opened up on the Japanese bomber. It had exposed its length to the spray of Vejtasa's guns and the last plane of the V splashed into the sea.

Low on ammunition, Vejtasa spotted another Kate, but it had pulled well away from him and he elected to leave it to the antiaircraft fire which awaited it. As he circled the arena of battling ships Vejtasa saw another Kate, obviously free of its torpedo, fleeing the scene. The Wildcat dived upon the bomber, and with his last few rounds Vejtasa knocked down his seventh enemy plane of the day. The four VF-10 Wildcats had so disrupted the Kate attack that three of the survivors jettisoned their torpedoes and fled. Two others did not even drop theirs, although the one Vejtasa had left for the ship's antiaircraft batteries may have been the Kate that crashed into the *Smith*.

The Battle of Santa Cruz ended, a tactical victory for the Japanese. The *Hornet* was gone and the *Enterprise* had been hit and crippled; this left only

". . . and the last plane . . . splashed into the sea."
*The Battle of Santa Cruz, though it cost the Ameri-* cans the Hornet *and crippled the* Enterprise, *cost the Japanese heavily in aircraft and experienced pilots.*
(NAVY DEPT., NATIONAL ARCHIVES)

two carriers in the Pacific, the *Enterprise* and the *Saratoga,* which was also crippled and undergoing repair. Wisely, Kinkaid pulled away to the south out of reach of Kondo's big ships and Kakuda's remaining aircraft. The *Zuikaku* and *Junyo* were still capable of dispatching bombers which might have spelled the end of the *Enterprise.* Nor could

Kinkaid risk the possibility of a night engagement for the simple reason that the Japanese were better at it at the time than the Americans. It was a frustrating engagement all around: the Japanese had won, but they had lost too many experienced pilots. The battle ashore, which the naval battle had been designed to cover, had failed.

# 4

# DERAILING THE TOKYO EXPRESS

GUADALCANAL remained in American hands. General Hyakutake's beautifully reasoned plan of attack and his formal, very proper surrender ceremony never came off. By October 28, with more than three thousand Japanese dead on Guadalcanal and sixty-nine irreplaceable pilots deep in the sea off Santa Cruz, it was obvious that another Japanese attempt to take the miserable island had miscarried. The island took on a significance beyond its strategic importance (which militarists eventually realized was secondary). The Allies were determined to keep it and the Japanese were resolved to take it back. It became for both sides as much a matter of "face" as military consequence.

But to the men garrisoned on "the Canal" it was much less a matter of face than skin. Keeping alive was the major preoccupation, of course—and scrounging simple comforts (like keeping dry). Even these basic pursuits became monotonous in day-after-day operations. But when the fighting came again, monotony was regarded with nostalgia. Between battles the Marines engaged in the art of bitching, their most colorfully profane antipathy being reserved for "Dugout Doug" MacArthur. The average line Marine was sure that only MacArthur's grabbing and holding of equipment, such as the P-38 for example, was responsible for the shoestring

operation on Guadalcanal. General Arnold of the Air Force was placed a few degrees above MacArthur, and almost on an equal level was General Marshall. At this time, actually, supplies that might have gone to the Pacific were being sent instead to Europe for the projected invasion of North Africa. But the so-called "Big Picture" was of little concern to the Marine who believed himself all but marooned on 'Canal.

Yamamoto, on Truk, was unhappy also. Despite all his attempts to co-ordinate the operations of the Imperial fleet with those of the Army, the Army had not yet taken back Guadalcanal. And this failure by the Army cost the Imperial Navy heavily in men, ships, and aircraft. The Army, on the other hand, could not understand that the Navy was unable to maintain its ships indefinitely at sea "consuming valuable fuel" while the Army fought out its inconclusive land battles.

As always, the solution must devolve upon the Imperial Navy. Obviously Hyakutake's error lay in attempting to take Henderson Field by land. Just as obviously—at least it appeared so to Yamamoto—Henderson must be taken from the sea by very heavy bombardment. This would ground the planes and keep the men in their foxholes while reinforcements were brought in. With Henderson pulverized, it would be no problem for Hyakutake's starving, ill-equipped, sick, and dying troops (plus reinforcements, of course, not so hungry and better equipped) to end the protracted, embarrassing wretchedness of Guadalcanal.

The plan, as outlined to Hyakutake by Captain Toshikazu Ohmae, Chief of Staff, Southeastern Fleet, seemed to make sense. While Tanaka's Tokyo Express brought reinforcements (the 38th Division) to Guadalcanal in eleven transports down The Slot (the channel between New Georgia and Santa Isabel islands northwest of Guadalcanal), a large force of battleships, a cruiser, and destroyers from Admiral Kondo's Second Fleet would subject Henderson Field and environs to a tremendous shelling. At the same time another force of Kondo's fleet would lay to the north of Savo Island to furnish distant cover. Close in, Vice-Admiral Gunichi Mikawa, with cruisers and destroyers, would provide close support for the landings of the 38th Division.

During the night of November 12/13, 1942, what has come to be known as the Battle of Guadalcanal erupted when the Japanese raiding force, under Vice-Admiral Hiroaki Abe, on its way to open the shelling upon Henderson, ran up against a handful of American ships under the command of Rear Admiral Daniel J. Callaghan. With his five cruisers and eight destroyers Callaghan took on Abe's two battleships (the *Hiei* and *Kirishima*), the cruiser *Nagara,* and fourteen destroyers.

For the next twenty-four deadly, confused minutes "one of the most furious sea battles ever fought," according to Admiral King, illuminated the dark night sky and rocked the air with savage gunfire. At close quarters the two fleets fought to a near standstill, with the heaviest loss on the American side. Four American destroyers and two cruisers were lost. The Japanese lost only two destroyers, but the battleship *Hiei* had been hit many times, which prevented the planned heavy bombardment of Henderson Field (for this failure Abe was relieved of his command). Callaghan paid the full price for this frustration, for he and nearly all of his staff aboard the *San Francisco* were killed when the bridge of the ship was struck. More than seven hundred American lives were lost in the nightmarish battle. But Abe had run and Henderson had been spared.

Also frustrated was "Tenacious" Tanaka, who

*An Avenger on a takeoff run from the flight deck of the* Enterprise. *Aircraft of this unit (CV-6) sank the first Japanese battleship of the war, the* Hiei *(with the aid of other Navy and Marine planes from Guadalcanal).* (NAVY DEPT., NATIONAL ARCHIVES)

was ordered to turn back from his Express run and await further word. While he fumed on his way back to the Shortland Islands, dawn came to Guadalcanal. Marine pilots in Dauntlesses and Avengers found the crippled *Hiei* just ten miles north of Savo Island. Though in trouble, the Japanese ship, screened by five destroyers, could still put up anti-aircraft fire. But under the attack of the first ten planes, two torpedoes went into the side of the battleship. More Dauntlesses came shortly after and further harassed the stricken ship.

Meanwhile, as the damaged but operational *Enterprise* plowed northward for Guadalcanal, nine Avengers escorted by six Wildcats were dispatched

*Dauntless on morning patrol in the Pacific.*
(NAVY DEPT., NATIONAL ARCHIVES)

to the island. As they came into Guadalcanal the *Enterprise* pilots spotted the *Hiei*. While the Wildcats discouraged the lurking Zeros the Avengers, led by Lieutenant Albert P. Coffin, swooped down upon the Japanese battleship and put three more torpedoes into it. This continued for most of the day as Marine and Navy aircraft ran a bomb shuttle between the *Hiei* and Guadalcanal. In the fighting eight Zeros were destroyed. They too had failed in this mission, for by night the ship, abandoned and scuttled by its crew, sank into the Pacific—the first Japanese battleship to be sunk by American forces.

Despite this upset, Yamamoto's plan proceeded. The following night (November 13/14) was torn by a thousand eight-inch shells lobbed into Henderson from cruisers sent from Rabaul. No great damage was done, though two Wildcats were completely destroyed and fifteen others pocked by shell fragments. These, along with a holed Dauntless, were repaired and ready to fly by the next day. None of the eight P-38s sent down by MacArthur only the day before suffered any damage, however. The holes in Fighter 1 were quickly filled. The Japanese ships had proved

less destructive than previously, partly because they had been harassed during their bombardment by little PT boats from Tulagi, which had flitted distractingly around them.

On November 14, 1942, Tanaka, all but certain that Henderson Field had really been put out of commission by the night naval bombardments, raced his Express down The Slot with the largest number of reinforcements to date (three thousand men of a combined naval landing force and eleven thousand troops of Lieutenant General Tadayoshi Sano's 38th Division). The eleven transports were screened by a dozen destroyers and a small umbrella of Zeros from the light carrier *Hiyo*.

At 9:49 A.M. Lieutenant Doan Carmody, flying a search Dauntless from the *Enterprise,* now closer to Guadalcanal, found the transports in The Slot. The ships were 120 miles from Guadalcanal, making fourteen knots; the Express was due to arrive at the island around seven in the evening. After radioing this information to the *Enterprise,* Carmody, in company with another Dauntless (pilot: Lieutenant W. E. Johnson), dived upon the Japanese ship formation in The Slot. Both missed with their bombs, however, because of heavy antiaircraft fire and the quick action of seven Zeros of Tanaka's air cover. Johnson's SBD fell into the sea and two Zeros swooped down to spray the splash point and the debris. During the next few hours, this depredation would be heavily avenged.

If ever there was a hell on earth, it was carried on Tanaka's eleven transports that November 14. With merciless desperation, fed by the knowledge that more Japanese reinforcements on Guadalcanal could be fatal, Marine and Navy aircraft assaulted the Tokyo Express. All afternoon every flyable plane on Guadalcanal, plus others from the *Enterprise,* fully loaded with bombs or torpedoes, raced to The Slot. Despite the whirring Zeros, of which there were only a few thanks to the hesitant Kondo 150 miles to the north, who sent small numbers from time to time from his two carriers, the Dauntlesses and Avengers ripped into the Japanese ships. Thousand-pound bombs rained onto the decks of the transports and torpedoes slashed into their sides. Even the Wildcats, when they ran out of Zeros, dived to water level to strafe the crowded decks.

The first attack, made by eighteen Marine Dauntlesses led by Major Joseph Sailer, Jr. (VMSB-132)

*A beached, burned-out Japanese troop transport the morning after the "Buzzard Patrol," which literally slaughtered the men and ships of the Tokyo Express November 13–14, 1942.*

(DEFENSE DEPT., MARINE CORPS)

and Major Robert Richard (VMSB-142), plus seven Avengers led by Lieutenant Albert P. Coffin of the *Enterprise*'s VT-10, scored hits on three transports and a cruiser. More *Enterprise* pilots, under Lieutenant Commander James R. Lee, joined in what became by midday virtual slaughter.

But true to his nickname, Tanaka tenaciously pressed on, leaving a transport here and there en route in his bloody wake. Transports lay dead in the water burning, some split open spilling men, dead and injured into the churning water, as destroyers circled in an attempt to rescue men as well as fight off the attacking American planes. The carnage on the Japanese transports, inhumanly overcrowded to begin with, was ineffably obscene. For the packed though human cargo of the transports the hours, for those who had hours, between about twelve-thirty and nightfall were one shattering crescendo of terror, pain, and death. And there was no place to hide.

Some American fighter pilots, who had come in close enough to see the butchery on the transports as well as the encrimsoned waters around them,

were literally sickened by the sight. Some vomited in their cockpits. But they machine-gunned the thousands of bobbing heads in the water, the helpless near-drowned clinging to debris and wreckage. By 4:45 P.M., when the final strike took off from Henderson—led by Glen Estes of the *Enterprise*'s VS-10: four Dauntlesses (three of which were Marine) and fighter cover—seven Japanese transports had been sunk or were sinking or burning or both. Estes dropped the last bomb of the day, made a direct hit and returned to Henderson.

The four surviving transports were in bad shape also, but Tanaka proceeded to Guadalcanal. Sometime after midnight he arrived, quite depleted, at his destination. There was nothing to do but beach the crippled transports. About 3000 troops were landed with a mere 260 cases of ammunition and 1500 bags of rice. The rest of their supplies and perhaps another 3000 of their comrades lay at the bottom of The Slot, dead or missing. Of those who had escaped the slaughter of what the Americans came to call the "Buzzard Patrol," less than 2000 were picked up out of the water. Exact figures may

*The forward deck of one of the beached Japanese transports after attacks by American planes and ships.* (DEFENSE DEPT., NATIONAL ARCHIVES)

never be determined, but Tanaka's determination— and the determination of the Buzzard Patrol—had wiped out about half of the largest attempt by the Tokyo Express. Every transport was lost, for the four beached ships were worked over the following day by aircraft, the destroyer *Meade,* and artillery.

The cost to the Americans was comparatively light: six Dauntlesses and two Wildcats. One of the latter was that of Lieutenant Colonel Joseph Bauer (VMF-212), who had gone out to escort the bombers. In company with Joseph Foss, Bauer had strafed a transport, after which both pilots were attacked by Zeros. Bauer shot one out of the air and Foss took off after the other. Antiaircraft fire from a Japanese destroyer spoiled the chase for Foss, who returned to the spot where he had last seen Bauer. Circling low over the water, Foss found pieces of the fallen Zero. About two miles away, swimming near an oil slick, Foss spotted Bauer in the water.

Circling, Foss attempted to eject his rubber boat, but found he was unable to because it was jammed. He circled again, lower, and realized that Bauer, bouncing and gesticulating in the water, was ordering him to return to base. Foss also found he could not radio for assistance, so he throttled back to

Henderson to organize a rescue party. Despite an intensive search Bauer was never found.

## II

The closing phase of the Battle of Guadalcanal, which had opened so disastrously for the Americans but which developed into a Japanese tragedy, was another nighttime surface battleship brawl. Vice-Admiral Kondo approached Guadalcanal to shell the airfield to cover the landings of Tanaka's "sorry remnant" (Tanaka's phrase) with the battleship *Kirishima* (sister ship of the *Hiei,* lost the day before), five cruisers, and nine destroyers.

Kondo ran into an American naval group (battleships *Washington* and *South Dakota* and four destroyers), under the capable command of Rear Admiral Willis Augustus Lee, in the vicinity of Iron Bottom Bay. Though in the battle which opened before midnight of November 14 Lee had lost three destroyers and the *South Dakota* was damaged, Kondo lost one destroyer and, most importantly, the *Kirishima* (so badly damaged that it was scuttled). The great battleship sank in waters close to the *Hiei,* and with it went Kondo's brilliant career. He had failed once again to ravage Henderson Field.

The common soldier behind Japanese lines by late December was certain that he had been abandoned. "Have not seen one of our planes in ages," one confided to his diary, "but every day enemy planes dance in the sky. . . ." It was a dance of death, for the strafing, dive-bombing, and bombing cut off supplies, reinforcements, and medical necessities.

While great men, irresolute yet unyielding, grappling with ego rather than conscience, sought a face-saving solution, little men died in mass, faceless numbers. At last, after weeks of acrid argument, two men called at the Imperial Palace on the final day of 1942. They were an admiral, Osami Nagano, Chief of the Naval Staff, and a general, Hajime Sugiyama, the Army's Chief of Staff. They had arrived unsmiling and they left unsmiling, but when they did leave it was with grim permission from Hirohito himself. The Japanese would abandon Guadalcanal.

Sometime during the first week of February 1943 the Tokyo Express was scheduled to run in reverse. This odious operation was a carefully guarded secret; even officers (except of exalted rank) on Guadalcanal had no idea of what was happening. New troops were even brought in to conceal the true plan. All of the activity appeared to the watchful Americans like the beginnings of a real push on Guadalcanal. "Until the last moment it appeared that the Japanese were attempting a major reinforcement effort," Admiral Nimitz wrote in retrospect. "Only skill in keeping their plans disguised and bold celerity in carrying them out enabled the Japanese to withdraw the remnants of the Guadalcanal garrison."

By February 8, 1943, after six months of appalling fighting, Guadalcanal was taken over by the Americans. Like Midway, it marked a turn in the tide from the defensive to the offensive and it was the first defeat on land experienced by the victory-drunk Japanese Army. At the same time, although he fought ferociously and often as not to an existential, sacrificial death, the Japanese soldier had proved not to be a jungle superman. The myth was over for the Japanese soldier just as it was for the Zero, the super fighter plane.

*Jefferson J. DeBlanc, one of the "few Marines," with Medal of Honor awarded for leading his flight into a large Japanese fighter formation before it could interfere with American Dauntlesses and Avengers.*
(DEFENSE DEPT., MARINE CORPS)

### III

Although the Japanese were out of Guadalcanal, it did not mean that the Solomons were entirely abandoned by them. Late in November 1942 preparations for constructing an airfield on Munda Point, New Georgia, were noted by Allied reconnaissance planes; so was construction on some of the smaller islands of the New Georgia group, Kolombangara and Vella Lavella. An airfield on Munda Point, however, meant only a 175-mile flight to Henderson Field, which placed it within easy reach of the Zero. And at the top of the Solomons there was Bougainville, with no less than five airfields, the largest of which was Kahili, near the southern tip of the island. If the Americans had paid heavily for Henderson Field, the Japanese had full intentions of exacting a high and bloody interest on it.

Attempts were made to discourage the building up of the new Japanese positions, now the new terminals for the Tokyo Express. Between the hard days of October, when the Americans might have been pushed out of Guadalcanal, and the nearly

magical spiriting away of the Japanese in February, there were times when the fighting became as intense as in the shoestring days. On one mission, January 31, 1943, a young Marine lieutenant, Jefferson Joseph DeBlanc, a section leader in VMF-112, was assigned to escort Dauntlesses and Avengers to bomb enemy shipping in Vella Gulf. The target area lay less than fifty miles east and slightly north of the Japanese air base on Kolombangara Island.

Upon arriving at Vella Gulf the Marine formation was met by a large number of enemy fighters. DeBlanc led his six Wildcats into the mass of Zeros at fourteen thousand feet, hoping to keep them away from the bombers while they worked over the shipping. As the battle developed, it broke up into single Wildcats against several Zeros. DeBlanc dived down to the altitude at which the dive bombers were trying to operate only to find he had swept into a large formation of float planes (probably the Mitsubishi A6M2-N, an adaptation of the Zero and called the "Rufe" by the Allies). Slashing into the Rufes, DeBlanc quickly sent three of them down burning, thus breaking up their concentration on the Dauntlesses, which proceeded to harass the Japanese surface ships in the gulf.

In the fighting DeBlanc's Wildcat had been hit and he was low on fuel. He realized he would have to return to Guadalcanal, so he climbed to get his bearings and as much height as he could. As he nursed the Wildcat up to the high clouds, DeBlanc, twisting his neck in the traditional fighter pilot fashion, spotted two Zeros closing from behind. He was now alone, for the other Wildcats were spread across the sky in their own private battles and the Dauntlesses and Avengers were engaged in bombing the Japanese ships.

DeBlanc would have to fight it out, though a stricken Wildcat was a poor match for a Zero. Timing his rudder kick for the precise moment, DeBlanc jerked the Wildcat into the path of the attacking Zeros. A good hit sent one rocketing across the sky as the other flashed by, turned, and came back at the Wildcat. DeBlanc felt the Grumman shuddering under the strain of his maneuvers and the impact of enemy slugs. As the Zero raced in, its guns twinkling maliciously, DeBlanc turned sharply again and shattered the frail Japanese plane with all four of his guns. The Zero fluttered down to the sea.

Safe now, DeBlanc found himself in other peril. The Wildcat was now in such poor condition that he knew he would never make it back to Guadalcanal. Smoking and with engine heaving badly, the plane started down for the water. DeBlanc fought with the plane to keep it from plowing into the ocean as he straightened out practically at treetop height over Kolombangara. Clearing the Japanese-held island, DeBlanc steadied the Wildcat out to sea and at a dangerously low altitude took to his chute. Upon landing in the water he found that he had been wounded in the back, arms, and legs. Supported by his lifejacket, DeBlanc spent about six hours making his way back to the beach at Kolombangara. Luckily he was not found by the Japanese but, after subsisting for two days on coconuts, was found instead by friendly islanders, who turned him over to the local coastwatcher. In about two weeks a Catalina arrived off Kolombangara to

pick up DeBlanc as well as Staff Sergeant James A. Feliton, who had parachuted during the same battle as had DeBlanc. The latter was immediately sent to a hospital to recuperate and was awarded the Medal of Honor.

On the same day that Lieutenant DeBlanc and Sergeant Feliton were taken off Kolombangara and only six days after the last living Japanese soldier had been evacuated from Guadalcanal, a curious incident occurred over Bougainville.

Navy PB4Ys (the Army's B-24, Liberator) had taken off to bomb targets on Bougainville—no mean round trip of six hundred miles—with an escort of new fighters.

As the American bombers and fighters approached Bougainville, a lone Zero pilot ignored the war momentarily in order to fly alongside the new fighters to study them with peacetime inquisitiveness. Before he was driven off the Japanese pilot saw a strange-looking plane, half beautiful and half ugly. It was deep blue in color with a pale blue, almost white underside. The pilot sat way back on the fuselage under a bubblelike canopy; a great stretch of nose projected before him, ending in a wide cowling under which roared a massive eighteen-cylinder Pratt and Whitney "Twin Wasp" engine. Its most curious feature was the graceful inverted gull wing which jutted down and then up and away from the fuselage. Once seen, this aircraft was not mistaken for any other: it was the Chance Vought F4U-1, the "Corsair." American ground troops called it "the Bent Winged Bird" in time.

The Corsair, which had arrived at Henderson Field on February 12 flown by VMF-124, had originally been designed as a carrier fighter. Problems developed during carrier landing tests, because of the plane's long nose, which interfered with the pilot's vision. It also had a tendency to bounce upon touching the deck and had other bugs, which discouraged the Navy from stationing the plane on carriers for a time. Meanwhile, it was turned over to the Marines, in whose hands, and later also the Navy's, the Corsair proved to be one of the outstanding fighters of the war. Some Japanese pilots, in fact, regarded it as the most formidable American fighter of the war. It was faster than any Japanese plane, besides which it could climb much faster (about three thousand feet a minute) and had a greater range capability than any single-engined

*Newly arrived Corsairs at Guadalcanal being prepared for combat. The plane in the foreground is having its guns bore-sighted with a homemade device.*
(C. L. SMITH/DEFENSE DEPT., MARINE CORPS)

fighter operating in the Pacific at the time. And it was rugged, which suited the hardened Marines perfectly.

But it would take time to learn how to use the Corsair's capabilities fully. This was demonstrated on the day following the incident with the curious Zero pilot in what became known as "the Saint Valentine's Day Massacre." Navy Liberators, on a bombing mission to Kahili airfield, Bougainville, were escorted by P-40s (low cover), P-38s (high cover), and Corsairs of VMF-124, staggered in between. This became the standard pattern for missions at this time, with the bombers at around twenty thousand feet and the P-38s and Corsairs above them. On this day, however, the system did not function too well, for as the formation approached Kahili it was bounced by perhaps fifty Zeros (almost certainly alerted and waiting). Two Liberators went down, as did two P-40s, two Corsairs, and, worse, the entire top cover of four P-38s. Japanese losses came to three or four Zeros, one as result of a collision with a Corsair.

This action, generally used to reveal how the Corsair nearly failed in its first test of real combat, is actually a better exemplification of the not yet (or ever, for that matter) dampened zeal of the Japanese fighter pilot. And, too, the "Zeke," as the Zero by this time was coming to be called, was still a formidable plane in a melee. But in the Corsair the Zeke had met its nemesis; it would only take a little time, a little experience, and a few Marines to establish this.

*Allied fighter pilot's view of a "Zeke," on the tail.*
(U. S. AIR FORCE)

But the problem of the inexperienced pilot was becoming even more serious for the Japanese, whose first-line veterans had been lost at Midway and Guadalcanal and whose new pilots were poorly trained for lack of experienced pilots to teach them. The American situation was differently handled, for when it was possible (and if they survived) veteran pilots were taken out of combat and given assignments training young fighter pilots. This is what happened with John Smith, Marion Carl, and Joseph Foss after they had left Guadalcanal. When Smith attempted to return to combat duty he was emphatically told, "Not until you have trained a hundred and fifty John Smiths." When he did return, almost two years later, Smith flew a Corsair.

IV

The Marines and their Corsairs owned the air over the Solomons and Kenney's Kids had begun "to play in the back yard of the Nip" in New Guinea; it was an ignominious situation to stomach in Tokyo. With the loss of Guadalcanal and then,

within a month, the Battle of the Bismarck Sea, Imperial headquarters burned with a hard, brittle flame of revenge. Yamamoto himself took full command of this vengeance operation, called *I-go Sakusen* ("Operation A"), a newly devised plan directly generated by the turn of fortune in the Pacific. *I-go Sakusen* was to wipe out, once and for all, the total American air power from the Solomons and New Guinea.

Planning *I-go Sakusen* for early April 1943, Yamamoto established his headquarters at Rabaul, major target of Kenney's forces in New Guinea and the major goal of Halsey's forces, climbing up the bloody Solomons ladder. Loath to expose his few remaining carriers to American aircraft, Yamamoto nonetheless stripped all carrier planes from their respective ships. Those from the 1st Carrier Division (the *Zuikaku* and *Zuiho*) went to Rabaul under command of Vice-Admiral Jisaburo Ozawa (who since November 16, 1942, had replaced Nagumo as commander of the Third Fleet). The aircraft of the 2nd Carrier Division (the *Junyo* and *Hiyo*) were flown to the base at Ballale, just south of Bougainville. The 21st Koku Sentai was to operate from Kavieng at the northern tip of New Ireland under Rear Admiral Toshinosuka Ichimaru (although the main body was stationed at Rabaul under command of Ozawa). The 26th Koku Sentai (Rear Admiral Kanae Kozaka) would strike from Kahili. In all, Yamamoto amassed about 350 warplanes for his strikes, Zekes, Nells, Bettys, Kates, and a few Vals. He was decidedly out for blood.

The first large assault came shortly after noon on April 7, 1943, when coast watchers and radar operators reported massive formations of enemy aircraft heading for Guadalcanal. There were, in fact, no less than 67 Vals escorted by 110 Zekes. The warning went out to ships in the harbor and to the men at Henderson, "Condition *very* Red."

The attack was met by all possible flyable fighters, seventy-six, Army, Navy, and Marine: P-38s, P-39s, Corsairs, and Wildcats. In the heavy fighting which followed, some of the Vals broke through the American fighter defenses and sank several ships in Tulagi Harbor and off Guadalcanal (the tanker *Kanawha,* the destroyer *Aaron Ward,* and the Australian corvette *Moa*).

First Lieutenant James E. Swett, of Marine VMF-221, on his first combat mission, ran into some of

*James E. Swett, USMC, who broke up a Japanese dive bomber attack (for which he received the Medal of Honor) and became an ace on his first combat mission.* (DEFENSE DEPT., MARINE CORPS)

the Japanese attackers. Leading a division of four Wildcats toward Tulagi, Swett spotted a large formation of Vals within minutes of arriving. There were between fifteen and twenty Japanese planes headed for Tulagi Harbor; shouting "Tally Ho!" Swett dived into the Vals. But even before he could begin shooting—for the first time in combat—he heard more shouting in his earphones. Someone else in his division had spotted Zekes diving from above. Already in a steep dive aimed at the dive bombers, Swett concentrated on the immediate menace and, as his Medal of Honor citation was to read, "during his dive personally exploded three hostile planes in mid-air with accurate and deadly fire."

Separated from the rest of his division, Swett was forced to do the best he could, what with the heavy concentration of "friendly" antiaircraft fire bursting around him—and six additional Vals, which bore onward toward the ships. One of his guns, too, was inoperative, so he had but five 50s with which to contend with the enemy formations. Racing in behind the Vals, Swett soon learned that the five guns worked well on the Vals, and the fourth plane swept away burning and trailing bits and pieces.

And so it went on until he shot down two more Vals, making his total for the battle seven—he had become an ace in his first combat. But as he closed in on the last of his victims Swett's Wildcat was hit by the fire of the Val's rear gunner. As his canopy shattered, blood covered his face, but Swett continued firing until his guns no longer responded: he had exhausted his ammunition. But before he did, he saw that the gunner in the rear cockpit of the Val had slumped over and smoke had begun to wisp out of the Val.

Swett's own problems were too many for him to worry about making certain that his eighth victim crashed into the waters of Iron Bottom Bay (his official score stood then at seven). He himself was injured by the flying bits of the canopy, and with his engine temperature in the red, Swett realized that the Japanese gunner had hit his Wildcat's lubricating system. The Pratt and Whitney growled and thumped, grew hot, and finally fused, and the propeller froze.

Too low now to take to his chute, Swett prepared to ditch off Florida Island. As he brought the Wildcat down near the water he suffered further consideration from "friendly" AA. Then the Wildcat splashed into Iron Bottom Bay, bounced and smacked into the water again. Swett, though held in his seat by straps, was thrown forward, smashing his nose against the gun sight. It took some time, after this stunning impact, for the pilot to place all things into focus. He knew he must get out of the swiftly sinking Wildcat. But he could not, for with a muddled, pain-racked head, he was not thinking clearly. As the plane sank Swett found that his chute harness had caught on a small handle in the cockpit.

As the Wildcat swirled down to the bottom, Swett continued to struggle until the strap loosened from the handle, which at the same time ejected the life raft stored in the plane. Suffocating, Swett finally surfaced with the help of a hastily inflated "Mae West," although encumbered by parachute, flying clothes, and the uninflated life raft. More struggling freed him and he inflated the raft and crawled, hurting and bleeding, into it. In a short time he was picked up by a small boat, whose passengers carried rifles as a precaution. Japanese pilots had demonstrated a deadly aversion to rescue, often attempting to kill their would-be Samaritans.

*Yamamoto's revenge operation* I-go Sakusen *was a simultaneous series of fruitless (but not always completely) strikes upon Guadalcanal and New Guinea. On April 12, 1943, more than a hundred Japanese aircraft struck the Fifth Air Force base at Port Moresby,* *New Guinea, setting an oil dump aflame with heavy loss of fuel and lubricants. Yamamoto's "Operation A" was his final contribution to Japan's war effort before he was shot down. He died believing the operation had been successful, which, in fact, it had not been.* (U. S. AIR FORCE)

"Are you an American?" someone shouted from the boat to Swett in his dinghy.

"You're damn right I am," he answered.

"It's OK," the voice was heard to say, according to legend; "he's another one of those loud-mouthed Marines."

Yamamoto's first big blow of *I-go Sakusen* had proved rather expensive, for claims were put in that day for a hundred planes by pilots and AA gunners. The actual number was closer to thirty-nine (twelve

Vals and twenty-seven Zekes; Japanese postwar figures admit to the loss of twelve Vals but only nine Zekes). American losses for the day amounted to seven aircraft but only one pilot, Major Walden Williams of the 70th Fighter Squadron.

Yamamoto's other big raids were aimed at New Guinea, and he believed that by April 14, according to the claims of his pilots, Operation A had fulfilled its function. Four days later Yamamoto crashed in a burning Betty after being intercepted

*Kenneth Walsh, USMC, first to achieve acedom in a Corsair.* (DEFENSE DEPT., MARINE CORPS)

by P-38s over Kahili. Yamamoto's successor, Admiral Mineichi Koga, although not as brilliant a man, continued to practice the great man's philosophy—perhaps with less intensity—and did all he could to bloody the rungs of the Solomons ladder.

By the close of April more Corsairs had come into Guadalcanal, and by May 13, 1943, the first Corsair ace was brought to the fore. He was Lieutenant Kenneth Walsh of VMF-124, born in Brooklyn and who began his military career as a flying private in the Marines. During one of the preliminary phases of Yamamoto's Operation A, on April 1, 1943, Walsh shot down his first three Zekes. On the day of Yamamoto's big blow, Walsh, like Swett, was shot down but was pulled out of the water unhurt and was soon back flying a new Corsair. On May 13 in mixed company of Marine and Army fighters, Walsh encountered twenty-five Zekes escorting a Japanese photo plane. Admiral Koga was bringing more and more planes into Rabaul and he was most anxious to know all about the aviation facilities on Guadalcanal. There were, in fact, four airfields by this time.

During the battle with the Japanese formation, Walsh shot down three Zekes; he was officially an ace. The Japanese lost sixteen fighters, although the

photo plane escaped. Three Corsairs were lost in the fighting, one of them flown by Walsh's squadron commander, Major William Gise.

Meanwhile, American troops began taking and occupying other islands in the Solomons, each step bringing them closer to Bougainville, gateway to Rabaul. The Russell Islands were occupied in February; next in line came Munda (New Georgia), the battle for which opened on June 21. Soon it was possible for the Marines to operate from a forward base on Munda for the strike on Vella Lavella, next step up the ladder. In doing this, Halsey elected to bypass Kolombangara (garrisoned by ten thousand Japanese troops), which would place American planes within ninety miles of Kahili on Bougainville.

The Vella Lavella landings took place on August 15; although the action on the beaches was reasonably normal, Japanese aerial activity was furious. Bombers and fighters came down from Kahili, Ballale, and Buin (in spite of American bombings aimed at grounding the Japanese planes during the landings) to harass the ships and troops on the beachhead. That day Kenneth Walsh was leading a division of five Corsairs of VMF-124; his score by this time had risen to ten enemy aircraft.

Fresh from a recreation tour in Sydney, Australia, Walsh was unexpectedly surprised by five Zekes at ten thousand feet. The fight became generally confused and Walsh soon found himself alone chasing a Zeke away from the battle. The powerful Corsair caught up with the Japanese fighter after a five-mile chase and with one quick blast Walsh knocked the plane down. Turning back for the beachhead, Walsh inadvertently flew into a formation of nine Vals, on their way to bomb the beach. Coming from under the Vals, Walsh quickly lessened their number by two. But he was now in a tough spot: Vals, with their rear gunners, below him and Zekes above. His Corsair became the center of destructive attention. Diving Zekes put two large 20-mm. holes through his right wing, more peppering knocked out his hydraulic system, shreds of his horizontal stabilizer flew off into the slipstream, and, still unknown to Walsh, the right tire was holed.

With his superior speed capability, Walsh rapidly pulled away from the shooting gallery. Other pilots took over the fighting (in addition to the three Japanese planes shot down by Walsh, fourteen others

*Munda Point airfield, New Georgia. Trees show effects of bombing and artillery fire—American and Japanese.*
(DEFENSE DEPT., MARINE CORPS)

fell in the day's fighting) as Walsh guided his tattered Corsair home. He brought it in to Munda Field (which was just one day old) and as anxious Marines observed, landed the Corsair with hardly a bump, even compensating for the flat right tire. When Walsh stood in the cockpit he was cheered by the troops for bringing in so badly mauled an aircraft. The plane, in fact, was junked.

Fifteen days later Walsh returned to Guadalcanal and took part in a bombing mission to Kahili. The plan was to take off from Fighter 2, fly to the Russell Islands air base, take on plenty of fuel for the expected battle over Kahili, and join up with the Liberators. Then the two dozen bombers with two squadrons of Corsairs as well as the usual low-cover P-39s and P-40s would press on to Bougainville. All went well for Walsh until after he had

taken off from the Russells. To his dismay his engine lost power and he could not keep up with the formation. Signaling to his wingman, Lieutenant W. P. Spencer, that he would have to drop out, Walsh, instead of attempting to return to the Russells or Fighter 2, guided his Corsair toward New Georgia with its advance base at Munda. Pushing his Corsair into a dive, Walsh brought the wheezing Corsair down onto the strip at Munda. There he was met by Captain James Neefus, commanding VMF-221, to whom he explained his problem and asked for another plane. Without recourse to red tape, Neefus permitted Walsh to requisition a ready, fueled, and armed Corsair on stand-by. Walsh jumped out of his plane and into the other; within

*Corsairs on Munda—the Marine fighters arrived within a week after the airstrip was taken from the Japanese.* (CHESTER L. SMITH/DEFENSE DEPT., MARINE CORPS)

minutes he raced down the runway and after the large Kahili-bound formation.

Walsh pushed the throttle in order to rejoin the bombers and at the same time he pulled the Corsair up as high as it could go—about thirty thousand feet before he spotted aircraft ahead. Happy that he had caught up, he gunned his engine and found he had caught up, instead, with a formation of from forty to fifty Zekes. Soon after, he also saw the Liberators, some distance beyond the large formation of enemy fighters, under attack by Zekes and anti-aircraft. A great air battle developed over Kahili as fighters from Kahili, Ballale, and Buin took to the air. Walsh, still undetected by the Japanese intent upon the bombers, pulled in behind the Zekes. He

was able to knock down only two before the others realized that a lone Corsair was pecking away at their formation.

The battle became a confused melee as Zekes turned on Walsh, who dived through the Liberator formation, shouting warnings on his radio. With the large number of planes in the air it became difficult to sight on any one of them and be certain he was an enemy. The sky became crisscrossed with tracers and, from time to time, a burning Liberator falling, for the Zekes were especially aggressive. The bombing run completed, the bombers turned away for the flight back to Henderson. During this phase of the battle Walsh destroyed two more Zekes, but he had had just about all the luck possible for the day. As he followed his fourth victim down to observe its fiery splash, Walsh, in turn, was trailed by four Zekes. They boxed him in, and with the advantage of altitude (and the fact that Walsh had just about expended his ammunition), they began working him over with cannon and machine-gun fire.

Smoke streamed from under the Corsair's cowling, fuel pressure dropped, the engine churned. The only other sound was that of Japanese lead pounding away at the tough Corsair. Walsh was about ready to resign to fate when a P-40 and a few Corsairs came in to take the Zekes off his back. But, though spared the final blow, Walsh knew he could not make it to any base. He must ditch off Vella Lavella. With consummate grace Walsh bounced the gull-winged craft into the Pacific a mile off Barakoma Point, where American Seabees, working on a new airstrip, observed the smoking plane.

The great plane splashed in, leaving a foamy wake, bumped up, and splashed again, then stopped and began to settle. Walsh had hardly been shaken and quickly left the Corsair and dropped into the water. Within half an hour a Seabee boat came out to pick him up and by the next day Walsh was returned to Guadalcanal. When he was ordered back to the United States in November 1943 Walsh, a Medal of Honor recipient, had destroyed twenty enemy aircraft (his twenty-first was scored during his second tour of duty in 1945).

With Vella Lavella in American hands and Kolombangara all but ignored (the Japanese evacuated the island in September–October), the next prize was to be Bougainville. This was the largest and northernmost island of the Solomons—with Rabaul but 210 miles away. With the experience of Guadalcanal behind them it was decided by the South Pacific planners that to take all of Bougainville, with its garrison of about 40,000 Japanese in the northern tip, near Buka airfield, and the southern tip, near Kahili, would be exceptionally violent and costly. So it was that Halsey elected to send the Marines in near the island's center, at Empress Augusta Bay, beat out a beachhead, and then establish a perimeter inside which airfields could be constructed.

Bougainville, like Guadalcanal, was a tropical pesthole, and the vicious land fighting was as brutal as that on the Island. If anything, the climate—wet—and the mud—glutinous—were worse. And the Japanese soldier fought to the death.

On November 1, 1943, while troops of the 3rd

*Under the cover of Marine Avengers, the Marines head for the beaches of Bougainville, Solomon Islands, November 1, 1943.* (DEFENSE DEPT., MARINE CORPS)

Marine Division and the 2nd Raider Regiment splashed ashore at Cape Torokina on Empress Augusta Bay, Avengers and Dauntlesses swooped in low to strafe and bomb the beachhead. Navy and Marine planes patrolled over the area in anticipation of the reaction from the several nearby Japanese air bases. This came minutes before the first barge ground upon the beach. About thirty Zekes and bombers converged upon Torokina to be challenged by the P-40s of the New Zealand Royal Air Force's No. 18 Squadron, the P-38s of the U. S. Air Force's 18th Fighter Group, as well as Navy and Marine Wildcats and Corsairs. In the first skirmish Captain James E. Swett, returned to VMF-221 after his dip in the sea, shot down two Vals besides sending a Tony (the Kawasaki Ki. 61 *Hien*), one of the newer Japanese fighters, smoking away from the beachhead and off the tail of one of the New Zealand P-40s.

In this initial encounter with the Japanese opposition to the Bougainville landings, seven of their aircraft were lost, with no losses by the Allies.

In the early afternoon, during the patrol of VMF-215—five Corsairs led by Lieutenant Colonel Her-

*Bougainville-based Avenger takes off the island's air-strip on a bombing mission. Avengers were used by* *Marines as torpedo and regular bombers.*
(DOUGLAS WHITE/DEFENSE DEPT., MARINE CORPS)

bert H. Williamson—a large formation of Japanese bombers and fighters came in to strike the ships and troops now cluttering up the shore line of the beaches at Torokina. Williamson led his Corsairs down upon the enemy bombers and a confused battle developed.

Flying with VMF-215 was one of the most colorful Marine pilots of the war, Lieutenant Robert M. Hanson, son of Methodist missionaries from Massachusetts. Hanson had been born in India in 1920 and had been a Marine flyer since February 1943. In the battle of the afternoon of the Bougainville landings, Hanson singlehandedly attacked six Kates with such ferocity that several jettisoned their bombs before reaching Torokina. Three others fell in flames under Hanson's guns (two others were knocked down by other men of VMF-215). But a rear gunner in one of the Kates shot down Hanson.

Setting his Corsair down on the water, Hanson broke out his dinghy and sat in it awaiting further developments. For nearly six hours Hanson waited until he saw the destroyer *Sigourney,* on its way back to Vella Lavella to pick up more passengers

for Torokina. Alternately waving and paddling, Hanson set out for the *Sigourney* cheering himself with the Cole Porter song "You'd Be So Nice to Come Home To." The American ship veered slightly from course, picked up the redoubtable Marine, and continued on to Vella Lavella.

Upon returning to VMF-215 Hanson continued with his nonchalant spree of destruction. In one period of seventeen days he shot down twenty enemy aircraft, which earned him the nickname of "Butcher Bob." Four of these victories were achieved on January 30, 1944, during an Avenger strike on Rabaul. Hanson flew with the escort and during the battle over the great Japanese base, now within easy reach of the base at Torokina, shot down four of the twenty-one Japanese planes destroyed during the mission. This brought his total of Japanese planes destroyed up to twenty-five.

Three days later, on February 3, the day before Hanson's twenty-fourth birthday and a week before he was scheduled to return to the United States, Hanson volunteered for a strafing mission in the Rabaul area, upon Cape Saint George, New Ireland. On this point, across the channel from New

*Robert M. Hanson, whose way with a Japanese plane earned him the name of "Butcher Bob" at Bougainville.* (DOUGLAS WHITE/DEFENSE DEPT., MARINE CORPS)

*Gregory "Pappy" Boyington, "AWOL" Flying Tiger and leader of the Marine's raffish "Black Sheep" (VMF-214).* (DEFENSE DEPT., MARINE CORPS)

Britain, stood a lighthouse which afforded the Japanese a fine lookout. Though never actually destroyed, it was a bothersome, challenging target. Hanson came in low over the cape and never came out of his run. Apparently hit by antiaircraft guns, Hanson crashed into the sea ending one of the most meteoric fighter pilot careers in the Pacific.

Until he was killed, it appeared that Hanson would equal or even surpass the score of another doughty Marine, Major Gregory Boyington, who had himself been splashed into the Pacific over Rabaul a month before Hanson was lost. Boyington's record (which included his Flying Tiger tally also) stood at twenty-eight (two reported after the war) enemy planes when he went down on January 3, 1944. After an extensive search Boyington was listed as "missing in action."

This, like his "desertion" and subsequent dishonorable discharge from the Flying Tigers, was an exaggeration. Although his wingman, Captain George

M. Ashmun, had been killed during the bitter fighting over Rabaul, Boyington had succeeded in parachuting from his burning Corsair. He dropped into Saint George Channel, off Rabaul, and was worked over for about a quarter of an hour by four strafing Zekes. Although unhit, Boyington was taken prisoner by a submarine which surfaced near him and he spent the rest of the war as a celebrity prisoner, although not an especially well-treated one.

A stanch individualist, Boyington (called "Pappy" by his men because of his advanced age of thirtyone) had returned to the Marines after he had bid a not too fond farewell to the Flying Tigers. While he rankled under discipline and adhering to the book, he was a born flyer and a unique leader. He may not have fitted into the organization of a squadron, but he could lead one. In recognition of this he was given permission to organize his own unit of misfits, appropriately dubbed "the Black Sheep" but more formally Marine Fighter Squadron 214

*Tending his flock: Boyington briefs his Black Sheep before a fighter sweep over Rabaul; Boyington was* *listed as Missing in Action after one of these sweeps and remained a prisoner of war for the duration.*

(MARINE CORPS)

(VMF-214). This occurred after a couple of fairly uneventful tours by Boyington in the Solomons.

When Bougainville's airstrips were sufficiently secure, Major General Ralph J. Mitchell, Marine commander of the aerial operations in the Solomons, instituted the first harassing fighter sweeps over Rabaul. The first of these—December 17, 1943—in which Boyington participated consisted of no less than seventy-six planes (twenty-three New Zealand P-40s of Nos. 14 and 16 Squadrons, twenty-two of the new Grumman F6F "Hellcat," and thirty-one Corsairs). With this formidable array of air power, the Japanese were not anxious to take off despite Boyington's profane invitations to "come up and fight."

"Come on down, sucker," was the Japanese answer. And the only fighting occurred at the P-40 level, which cost three of these, including that of New Zealand Wing Commander Freeman; however, the New Zealanders got five Japanese planes and

the Americans two. But it was not worth the effort, and upon his return Boyington argued that such a mixed bag of aircraft (all with different performances) and so unwieldy a number simply did not work.

Boyington believed in smaller, more flexible, and better-matched formations—which he got for future fighter sweeps upon Rabaul, as well as for escort missions with bombers. This was found to be more efficient, and Boyington's Black Sheep scored heavily against the Zekes. Between the first strike of December 17 and the first of the New Year, fighter sweeps over Rabaul claimed nearly 150 Japanese planes shot out of the air (after the war the Japanese admitted to 64).

Rabaul by early 1944 was in serious trouble. As new airstrips were completed on Bougainville, even short-range medium bombers could make the round trip to Rabaul. Before long, too, Thirteenth Air Force Mitchells based on Stirling Island (in the

Treasury group south of Bougainville) were reaching the beleaguered base. It was by no means out, as General Kenney rather prematurely claimed in early November 1942, but it was becoming more and more untenable for both shipping and aircraft.

Hoping to hold off the inevitable (which the Japanese believed meant an American invasion of Rabaul), Koga sent the air groups of the 2nd Koku Sentai (Carrier Division), under Rear Admiral Takaji Jojima, to bolster up the 26th Koku Sentai (in this instance, Air Flotilla—that is, land-based Navy planes). Late in January 1944 about 130 aircraft arrived from Truk to bring the total of planes at Rabaul up to the 300 mark. But it was to no avail as the massive American air power grew. Japanese pilots, long stationed at Rabaul, were worn, tired, and dispirited. It seemed that American planes came over almost at will, not only to bomb but to strafe the gun positions.

Just such a mission fell to the Bougainville-based Navy squadron, VF-17, which had arrived on January 24, the day before the planes of the 2nd Koku Sentai landed at Rabaul. On February 19, after several days of grueling operations, VF-17 was scheduled for an early morning strafing attack upon gun positions around Rabaul. Of the twenty Corsairs assigned to the job, sixteen were to concentrate upon the AA installations and the newly arrived Zekes and Tonys at Lakunai airfield. The four other Corsairs were assigned top cover, which was led by Lieutenant Merle Davenport.

The twenty Corsairs rose into a beautifully clear, sunlit sky. Climbing to about seventeen thousand feet, the Navy planes pushed onward toward New Britain. As the outline of the island emerged sharply from the glittering sea, Lieutenant Ira C. Kepford noticed that something appeared to be wrong with the Corsair of his wingman, Ensign Donald McQueen. It flew erratically and spouted puffs of smoke from the cowling. Closing in he saw that McQueen was having engine trouble—a common malady, thanks to the fine coral dust which abounded on Bougainville. McQueen must turn back, and so must Kepford, for without a wingman he could not participate in the raid on Rabaul. But Lieutenant Commander Roger Hedrick, commander of VF-17, ordered McQueen back to base and granted Kepford permission to continue with the formation until they arrived over Rabaul. There

*Ira C. Kepford, Corsair pilot of Navy Squadron VF-17, based at Bougainville.*
(NAVY DEPT., NATIONAL ARCHIVES)

seemed little possibility of McQueen's being attacked on his flight back to Bougainville.

Scanning the sky and convinced that it was clear, Kepford pulled up alongside Davenport's plane and, dipping the Corsair's gull wings, blew a kiss to Davenport and his wingman and made a wide turn for the flight back to base. Reluctant to leave, Kepford deliberately made a ranging turn as he studied the Japanese positions below. Suddenly he saw a black object in the sky approaching him. As it came closer he recognized it as a float plane (a Rufe) and swept in for the kill. The Rufe pilot, unaware of the presence of the lone Corsair, soon was sent down into the water.

Having followed the Japanese plane to make certain it had crashed, Kepford again climbed to resume his flight back to Bougainville. In the distance, high above and closer to Rabaul, Kepford spotted more dots—as he counted them he realized they were Zekes, more than fifty, waiting to pounce on Davenport and the Corsairs at seventeen thousand feet. Kepford radioed the information to Davenport, hoping that he had not yet been seen by the Japanese planes. He hugged the waves and hoped, but not for long. Four fighters, two Zekes and two of the new Tojos, dived out of the big formation to take care of the lone stray.

When they came within range the enemy fighters opened up on the Corsair. Thinking fast, Kepford suddenly "popped his flaps," which caused the Corsair to slow down abruptly, and the lead Zeke overran him. As it pulled up to turn, Kepford shot away most of its tail surfaces and the Zeke pilot, discouraged, left the battle. The two Tojos (the fast Nakajima Ki. 44 *Shoki*) came in from the right and the remaining Zeke closed in from the left. Apparently the Japanese pilots were trying to force Kepford to head north instead of south. His Corsair had just been equipped with an emergency water-injection system which, when applied, charged the engine with a great surge of power for a limited time.

This, Kepford reasoned, was an emergency: all but boxed in by three enemy fighters far from home base. He rammed in full throttle and activated the water injection and began to outstrip the Zeke and even the faster Tojos. The Corsair ran out of energy over the western shore of New Ireland—the enemy planes had driven Kepford to the north—and he was still far from home. In desperation he eased back on the throttle and injected water again. Once again the Corsair responded and the plane shot ahead. Though the three planes continued to pursue him, they were not putting any holes in him.

The chase continued at close to four hundred miles an hour, very near the surface of the sea. Kepford saw that his fuel was getting low and his emergency spurts had been consumed; the engine complained after the injection. He must move quickly. The Zeke was still close behind him. Kepford suddenly kicked left rudder and the Corsair whipped quickly to the left as Kepford's blood drained in the turn. His vision faded under the pres-

*The battle-scarred Corsair of Ira Kepford; "Skull and Crossbones" was squadron insignia.*

(NAVY DEPT., NATIONAL ARCHIVES)

*A Corsair comes in for a landing on the Bougainville strip, constructed of linked steel matting over sand.*

*A C-47 is ready for takeoff. In the distance, below Corsair, a barrage balloon floats limply.*
(P. SCHEER/DEFENSE DEPT., MARINE CORPS)

sure of the turn, but he managed to keep from blacking out completely.

The Zeke had followed with terrifying persistence and as Kepford's vision returned he saw the guns sparkling in the wing of the enemy plane. But at the same time the Zeke had attempted to turn more sharply, inside the Corsair's turn. As a wing dipped in the turn, the Zeke's wing tip brushed the water. There was a small splash, and then a series of big ones as the Japanese fighter cartwheeled across the surface of the water until its wings ripped off and it sank into the sea.

Anxiously Kepford looked back to see what became of the Tojos, but they had been lost in the turn and no longer continued the chase.

Despite the great consumption of fuel during the emergency use of the water-injection system, Kepford, though shaken, managed to return to Bougainville. He emerged from his shot-up Corsair bathed in perspiration, shaking with shock and with tears streaming down his face. A shot of brandy and nearly twenty-four hours of sleep restored the future Navy ace (with a total of seventeen victories he was the fifth-ranking ace in the U. S. Navy). The water-injection emergency system was widely

adopted and undoubtedly, as it did Kepford's, saved many an American airman's life.

On February 20, the day following Kepford's encounter, Rabaul was all but abandoned by the Imperial Navy. The 2nd Koku Sentai was pulled out and what remained of it returned to Truk, now the main Japanese base in the Pacific. Within days Allied bombers flew over the once hazardous area without escort. Rabaul, the formidable, became a milk run.

By March 6, 1944, the Green Islands, north of Bougainville and only 115 miles east of Rabaul, were occupied U. S. Marines and New Zealand troops. MacArthur's forces had already taken Cape Gloucester on New Britain itself. When Emirau Island, ninety miles north of the chief Japanese air base at Kavieng in New Ireland, was taken in April of 1944, it bottled up Rabaul completely. Invasion of Rabaul was unnecessary. Those Japanese troops stranded there were not going to do anything, nor were they going anywhere. Isolated, the Japanese troops remained there until the war ended, harassed continually by bombardment and the demoralizing realization that they wasted away ineffectually on another worthless island.

*The ring closing in around Rabaul; Thirteenth Air Force Mitchells have just bombed a supply dump at Rataval. Simpson Harbour and Rabaul lie in the distance.* (U. S. AIR FORCE)

*Rabaul checkmate: as surface ships carry troops to occupy Green Island, B-25s head for Rabaul to occupy Japanese air power during the beachhead landings. The taking of Green Island neutralized Rabaul. No invasion was necessary.* (U. S. AIR FORCE)

# 5
# TURKEY SHOOT

Far to the north of the steaming, fevered Solomons lay another island chain of questionable worth. Though still in the Pacific, the string of islands called the Aleutians was in another world. The contrast between the Solomons and the Aleutians could hardly have been more extreme if, indeed, they had been on different planets. Many who served in each frequently wished they were.

The Japanese had invaded the Aleutians, setting troops ashore at two of the westernmost islands, Attu and Kiska, as a subsidiary action of the ill-fated Battle of Midway. They had lost the great naval-aerial battle in exchange for two tiny, inhospitable, wind-swept rocks. They also lost an almost intact Zero on one of the Aleutians close to the American base at Dutch Harbor. The sequel to this single mishap, in the form of the Grumman F6F "Hellcat" fighter in the summer of 1943, rendered the taking of Attu and Kiska extremely costly.

The proximity of these two islands to Alaska, and therefore to the North American mainland, made it imperative that the Japanese be driven off. On the other hand, the Japanese saw the Aleutians "pointing like a dagger at the heart of Japan," so that the islands—on a map in the hands of an armchair strategist, at least—took on great strategic significance. Depending on which side pushed the hardest, it appeared that the islands formed stepping-stones into the back yard of the other. This was true, of course, provided the terrain and the weather could be nicely disregarded.

But to those who were there it was impossible. Admiral King stated the problem in his report to the Secretary of the Navy: "Since the Aleutian Islands constitute an aerial highway between the North American continent and the Far East, their strategic value is obvious. On the other hand, that chain of islands provides as rugged a theater for warfare as any in the world. Not only are the islands moun-

*A snowbound Alaska-based Airacobra; with the Japanese in the Aleutians, the North Pacific became one of the most uncomfortable theaters of war and especially inimical to aerial operations.* (U. S. AIR FORCE)

*A P-40 based on Umnak Island (Aleutians); "Flying Tiger" markings are a tribute to the father of the pilot, Major John Chennault.* (U. S. AIR FORCE)

tainous and rocky, but the weather in the western part of the islands is continually bad. The fogs are almost continuous, and thick. Violent winds (known locally as 'williwaws') with accompanying heavy seas make any kind of operation in that vicinity difficult and uncertain."

This was, as was characteristic of the cool King, true though understated. However, to the men of the Eleventh Air Force and the Navy's Patrol Wing 4 the Aleutians were no "aerial highway."

Nor were they an attractive spot for ships. As wryly put by Major General Simon B. Buckner, Jr., in charge of the Alaska Defense Command (which in turn, actually came under the command of the Navy in the person of Rear Admiral Robert A. Theobold), "the naval officer had an instinctive dread of Alaskan waters, feeling that they were a jumping-off place between Scylla and Charybdis and inhabited by a ferocious monster that was forever breathing fogs and coughing up 'williwaws' that would blow the unfortunate mariner into uncharted rocks and forever destroy his chances of becoming an admiral."

All operations in the Aleutians were circumscribed and dictated by nature, not man. Consequently assignment to the theater was more like being relegated to a frigid purgatory than to war. But operations did take place, whenever possible, as the Navy flew reconnaissance missions and the Air Force bombed the Japanese holdings at Attu and Kiska. "During April and May," an Air Force historian noted, "the weather for air operations is bad, during the rest of the year it is worse." Distance was another factor, for to reach Kiska, for example, the heavy bombers had to make a trip of twelve hundred miles from their base at Umnak. Bomb load would have to be sacrificed to fuel. Weather fore-

*Mud, cold, fog—the conditions under which men and machines operated in the Aleutians. These Eleventh*

*Air Force Liberators have just returned from a bombing mission in the soup.* (U. S. AIR FORCE)

casts were meaningless, for in an instant a target was fogged over. The Aleutians war was one primarily of waste and frustration.

The Japanese shared these frustrations with the Americans, for air operations for them were equally difficult. The problem of supply was acute. In time, the Americans had hacked out bases on Adak and Amchitka islands, which were much closer to the Japanese-held islands than Umnak or Dutch Harbor. By March of 1943, although still a forgotten theater, the Japanese found that attempting to supply their garrisons in the Aleutians was hazardous. Naval ships and planes, Army Air Force bombers and fighters (the P-38s of the 54th Fighter Squadron and the P-40s of the 18th Fighter Squadron) made supply runs by Japanese surface ships nearly hopeless. Even so, they remained.

Although not wishing to transform the northern Pacific into a major theater of operations and therefore complicating the priorities for the other theaters, notably North Africa and the warmer reaches of the Pacific, the Joint Chiefs of Staff agreed that the Japanese should be knocked out of Attu. At the same time Kiska, which was more heavily occupied, could be bypassed and cut off from the Japanese bases in the Kurile Islands. This idea, put forward by Admiral Kinkaid, in command of the North Pacific Force, seemed feasible and was put into operation.

The two Japanese garrisons were bombed as frequently as weather permitted, by the Eleventh Air Force B-24s as well as by P-38 and P-40 fighter bombers. Finally, in May 1943, the 7th Infantry Division went in to take Attu from the Japanese. This is a simple statement, but taking Attu was no

*Mission's end: after bombing Japanese positions in the Aleutians, this B-24 found its own home base socked in with fog and had to find a soft landing spot nearby in a smooth tundra.* (U. S. AIR FORCE)

*The new* Yorktown *in the Pacific. The great carrier's keel was laid six days before Pearl Harbor and it was launched on January 21, 1943. Commissioned in April, the* Yorktown (*named for the ship that went down at Midway*) *began operations in the Pacific by August. The earliest combat experience was gained by strikes upon Japanese-held islands such as Marcus, Wake, the Gilberts, Kwajalein.*

(NAVY DEPT., NATIONAL ARCHIVES)

simple task. From May 11 through the thirtieth, besides contending with the cold (the division had been trained with typical military wisdom in California) and the weather, the men of the 7th Division fought an outnumbered but ferocious enemy. The fighting came to a horrible close with a shrieking banzai attack, and when that failed, the survivors committed suicide by putting hand grenades to their heads.

From Attu it was possible to bomb Japanese bases in the Kuriles, at the northern extremity of the Japanese home islands. Also it was possible to pound Kiska. The loss of Attu and the bombing of Kiska,

plus good common sense, eventually decided the issue. Even as American plans were under way to invade Kiska, the Japanese under cover of a period of heavy fog evacuated all of their troops from that unfriendly island. When the landings were finally made, the American and Canadian infantrymen found an eerie welcome: no Japanese; only three yellow dogs.

When troops entered what had been the Japanese command hut at Kiska they found a message scrawled on the wall: "We shall come again and kill out separately Yanki jokers." But they did not come again and the "Yanki jokers" were left with the world's worst weather, tundra, muskeg, and fog.

## II

The Central Pacific, after the Battle of Midway, lay in a deceptive tranquillity for more than a year. While the fighting raged to the south and west (and later in the north), the forces and materials were slowly accumulated for the Central Pacific sweep toward Japan. What resources—men and matériel—could be spared from the European theater, where by the summer of 1943 the Allies had invaded Italy, went into the planning for the Central Pacific offensive.

Thus a great fleet, the Fifth, was organized under command of Vice-Admiral Raymond A. Spruance to spearhead the assault. The steel point of this head was no less than eleven carriers, including the new *Yorktown* and *Lexington*, both heavy carriers, replacing the older carriers. Also recently commissioned were the *Essex* and the *Bunker Hill*. Added to these were the veteran *Saratoga* and *Enterprise*. Five light carriers, all recently launched, were the *Independence, Princeton, Belleau Wood, Monterey*, and *Cowpens*. These were not all. For also to be employed in the operation ahead were eight escort carriers (the CVEs), smaller than the light carriers and designed to participate in close support of amphibious landings. In all, the Fifth Fleet had about nine hundred planes under its control for its assault into the Gilberts, Marshalls, and Marianas.

Preliminary strikes were made upon Tarawa and Makin (in the Gilberts) by carrier planes beginning on November 13, 1943; diversionary attacks were also made upon Wake and Marcus islands to the north. That this succeeded in confusing the Japanese as to where the next American assault would come was obvious. Admiral Koga sent Ozawa's Third Air Fleet (Koku Kantai) and Kurita's Second Air Fleet to the Marshalls, expecting the first heavy blow to fall there. When that did not come, he had nothing else to do (besides wonder) but return the planes to Rabaul.

The B-24s of the Seventh Air Force—originally based in Hawaii—began flying long-distance bombing missions to the Gilberts and Marshalls. The Seventh Air Force opened up its chapter in the Central Pacific offensive when on November 13, 1943, nine Liberators of its 431st Squadron (which was based on Funafuti in the Ellice Islands, south of the Gilberts) bombed Tarawa Atoll. Other units of the Seventh were based upon several other islands: Nanomea and Nukufetau (also in the Ellices) and Canton in the Phoenix Islands. Besides two B-24 squadrons at Canton, there were also two fighter squadrons, one of P-40s and the other of P-39s. These were stationed alongside the A-24s of the 531st Fighter Bomber Squadron. Another fighter squadron was stationed at Baker Island, a forward base, east of the Gilberts and north of the Ellices. This was to function as a staging area for fighters and a port in a storm for crippled bombers.

The Seventh Air Force, as can be seen, was dispersed over, in its own phrase, "one damned island after another."

This might very well have summed up the emotions of Admiral Mineichi Koga as he tried to decide, during the spring of 1943, where the next full-scale allied assault would fall. His head must have swirled under the widespread attacks; only strikes to begin with, but an indication of what was in the offing. His predecessor, Yamamoto, had been right. Given time, the great American productive potential would uncoil like a massive spring. Soon it would be reaching for the big base at Truk.

All doubts were cleared up when troops of the American 27th Infantry Division began coming ashore at Makin in the Gilberts on November 20, 1943. The next day Marines of the 2nd Division stormed the beaches of Tarawa. By November 24 the Army commander could claim small literary immortality by announcing "Makin taken"; but the Marines on Tarawa were destined to fight one of their most savage battles over the same period of

time. Makin was lightly held, but Tarawa was not. The Air Force and carrier plane bombings had not softened up the Japanese positions. And although the pre-invasion naval bombardment was hoped to finish the job (it was more massive than aerial bombings), it did not penetrate the coconut log, concrete, and coral sand emplacements. The Navy, experiencing its first large-scale amphibious operation, miscalculated the degree of bombardment these Japanese fortifications could withstand. The prize of Tarawa was the airfield on Betio Island.

Rear Admiral Keiji Shibasaki with 4836 picked troops of Imperial Marines under his command, and the knowledge that fifteen months of burrowing and building had gone into the island's defenses, boasted that "a million Americans could never take the island in a thousand years."

He was, of course, wrong, for a considerably lesser number secured the island in about three days. The cost was high: nearly 1000 Marines died (of a total of 3301 casualties) and nearly all of Shibasaki's crack troops were wiped out (4690 killed out of a force of 4836). The admiral himself was buried, possibly still alive, in one of his nearly impregnable bombproof shelters by Marine bulldozers. Gasoline, poured into air vents, and hand grenades did the rest.

Aerial operations during the Gilberts battle were shared among the various groups of Task Force 50, commanded by Rear Admiral Charles A. Pownall. (Land-based aircraft were assigned to Task Force 57, but these too came ultimately under Navy control.) Task Group 50.1 (built around the *Yorktown, Lexington,* and *Cowpens*) operated in the area between the Marshalls and the Gilberts to interfere with any attempt by the Japanese to reinforce the Gilberts during the operations there. Carrier planes were engaged principally in attacks upon Japanese airfields on Mili and Jaluit in the Marshalls.

Task Group 50.2 (the *Enterprise, Belleau Wood,* and *Monterey*) was assigned to the Northern Assault Force, which took Makin. Task Group 50.3 (the *Essex, Bunker Hill,* and *Independence*) supported the Betio landings. Another group, 50.4 (the *Saratoga* and *Princeton*), after attending to the airfield on Nauru Island, west of the Gilberts, operated later to the southwest of Tarawa as a relief group.

At first Japanese air reaction was light. The Solomons campaign had taken a heavy toll of the carrier-

Carrier strike on Wake Island as the Fifth Fleet ranged through the Central Pacific freely, confuting the Japanese. Wake, which had fallen on Christmas Eve 1941, a symbol of American defeat in the Pacific, was struck repeatedly by carrier planes although not invaded.

Isolated, its original strategic importance dwindled. As the Dauntless pilot prepares to make his bomb run, smoke may be seen rising from what had been Camp Two (center, across lagoon) on Wake itself.

(NAVY DEPT., NATIONAL ARCHIVES)

A Seventh Air Force Liberator begins the softening up for the projected Marshalls campaign. The B-24 is

about to turn on its bomb run for Wotje. Other islands in the group: Kwajalein and Eniwetok.

(U. S. AIR FORCE)

*Deck landing accident aboard the* Enterprise *en route to the Marshalls, November 1943. The Hellcat has veered off the flight deck and caught fire. Catapult* *officer, Lieutenant Walter Chewning, with one foot on the belly tank, climbs onto the wing to assist the pilot.* (NAVY DEPT., NATIONAL ARCHIVES)

based aircraft; so had the battling in the New Guinea area. The Betio airfield was secured before Japanese air attacks materialized on the night of November 25.

That the Japanese were planning counterattacks was demonstrated early in the morning of the twenty-fifth. A submarine had slipped into the ship concentration and put a torpedo into the escort carrier, *Liscombe Bay,* some twenty miles off Makin. The first inkling of this was noted by the men aboard the other ships when they heard an explosion and then "a few seconds after the first explosion, a second explosion which appeared to come from inside the *Liscombe Bay* burst upward, hurling fragments and clearly discernible planes two hundred feet or more in the air [burning bits of metal and other debris fell on the decks of a destroyer five thousand yards away]. The entire ship seemed to explode and almost at the same instant the interior of the ship . . . glowed with flame like a furnace." In twenty minutes the *Liscombe Bay,* the first of its type to be lost, sank, taking 644 of its crew, including Rear Admiral H. M. Mullinnix and Captain I. D. Wiltsie, with it.

Search planes and torpedo planes immediately launched from the *Enterprise* found no trace of submarine I-175 which had sunk the little carrier.

That night the air hummed overhead with the sound of engines as Japanese "snooper" planes sought the American ships. A flare blossomed over the ships as radar-directed guns scanned skyward. It was near daylight on the ships, but the sky, except for the radarscopes, was screened in night. This was a prelude, as it had been at Guadalcanal: snoopers illuminated the target area with flares and the bombers followed. But no bombs came that first night, perhaps because the radar-controlled guns of the *North Carolina* discouraged the bombers, or because no real attack had been planned.

Something was afoot, obviously, for the next day snoopers poked around the edges of radar screens as soon as the sun dipped. Aboard the *Enterprise* counterplans were being discussed to deal with the clearly impending night attack.

Newly arrived aboard the *Enterprise* to command its Air Group 6 fighters was Lieutenant Commander Edward H. O'Hare, Medal of Honor recipient. Butch O'Hare had singlehandedly saved the *Lexing-*

*Edward "Butch" O'Hare, Medal of Honor winner, who had singlehandedly saved the* Lexington *by destroying or driving off nine Japanese bombers.*

(NAVY DEPT., NATIONAL ARCHIVES)

*ton* off Bougainville in February 1942 by breaking up an attack by nine Japanese bombers. At that time O'Hare flew the F4F Wildcat; his new aircraft aboard the *Enterprise* was the F6F Hellcat, the plane specifically designed to fight the Zero. It was the plane which the lost Zero of the Aleutians had inspired. The Hellcat was tougher, faster, and a better high-altitude fighter than the Zeke. The lighter Japanese plane continued to be more maneuverable, but it paid for it by flaming all too readily, by lack of armor protection for the pilot, and by a comparatively flimsy construction which under the six 50s of the Hellcat all but disintegrated.

The Hellcat had been in action since August 31, 1943, when VF-5 of the *Yorktown* flew it in a carrier strike on Japanese installations on Marcus Island; VF-9 of the *Essex* was also equipped with the

*An F6F "Hellcat," the aircraft specifically designed to vanquish the Zero, taking off from the deck of a carrier. This is one of the hundreds of fine Navy photographs* *taken by, or under the supervision of, photographer Edward Steichen (a Navy captain during the war).*

(NAVY DEPT., NATIONAL ARCHIVES)

*The toughness of the Hellcat is revealed in this photograph of one which has returned to its carrier after combat. Flames inside the fuselage have shriveled the* *skin; fire pours out of the flaps. Soon after, the pilot was rescued by shipmates and, though burned, survived the incident.* (NAVY DEPT., NATIONAL ARCHIVES)

*Poised on the flight deck, this Avenger gets the flag for takeoff.* (U. S. NAVY)

*A rocket-armed Avenger springs into the air. Rockets were used in the Atlantic against German submarines and in the Pacific against Japanese shipping.*

(U. S. NAVY)

Hellcat and participated in this strike. But it was during the Gilbert campaign that the Hellcat saw its first real action.

The planners of the *Enterprise,* however, had something else in mind for the coming night. If a radar-equipped Avenger could lead a Hellcat into the proximity of a Japanese bomber, the Hellcat could do the rest. That evening at dusk O'Hare took off with his wingman, Ensign Warren Skon, in their Hellcats. They were followed by an Avenger piloted by Lieutenant Commander John Phillips, *Enterprise* bomber leader. In the Avenger were also radar operator Lieutenant Hazen Rand and gunner A. B. Kernan. At the same time the large radar set in the Combat Information Center would track both the friendlies and the bogies.

The bogies came and went but little happened until Phillips was directed from the *Enterprise* toward enemy aircraft. O'Hare and Skon could not find the Avenger in the dark, let alone an enemy plane. Phillips meanwhile had the bogie on his own screen and with Rand guiding him came upon a Betty heading for the ships.

Three miles away O'Hare and Skon were startled to see a sudden flare in the sky. It fell burning into the water, forming a burning lake in the blackness. Other Bettys in the Japanese formation, surprised by the unexpected attack, began firing wildly at one another.

If that was where the action was, O'Hare and Skon turned and raced to the scene. Phillips meanwhile had been vectored onto another Betty. As he approached he heard O'Hare request that he turn on the navigation lights of the Avenger so that he and Skon could find him. Reluctantly Phillips flicked on the lights, which, as he had expected, alerted the Betty. But soon that bomber too went burning into the sea. Moments later, Kernan fired at a dark form passing near the Avenger's tail.

Under orders from the *Enterprise* all three American planes turned on their navigation lights to enable them to assemble. If there were enemy aircraft nearby this would of course place the Avenger and Hellcats in jeopardy. The two fighters moved in closer to the Avenger. Soon the two Hellcats overtook the Avenger, to their left. To better cover the larger plane, Skon throttled back, swooped under the tail, and took a position off the left wing of the Avenger. O'Hare slid back toward the right wing.

Suddenly Kernan's ball turret came to life, firing, according to his report, between the two Hellcats at a darkened plane approaching from the stern. The .50-calibers lighted up the night and then again there was darkness. O'Hare's Hellcat, with navigation lights still on, veered to the left and down. Skon, certain that O'Hare was attacking, followed, but the veer became a dive and the Hellcat disappeared into the night. All Skon's attempts to call his leader were fruitless, as were the searches made the next day by other aircraft. Butch O'Hare was gone. Although he may have been hit by a Japanese plane, it was more than likely that Kernan had hit him by mistake. It was a tragedy for Kernan (though not absolute, for there will always be the chance that a Japanese gunner shot O'Hare down) and the men of the *Enterprise.*

But then tragedy and error are the very ingredients of war. Six hundred men had died, too, in the *Liscombe Bay;* a thousand Marines lay dead on Tarawa alongside four times that number of Japanese. The death of one more airman increased the figure by a single digit. But it did not diminish the tragedy.

Tragedy multiplied becomes history, eliminating thus biography; and great numbers simply become symbols which stir the blood but only afflict the heart individually. Whatever the cost, Tarawa, Makin, and Abemama—the Gilberts—belonged to the Americans. The lessons learned there at so great a price would not be wasted.

### III

The next step in the Central as well as South Pacific was defined at the so-called Sextant Conference in Cairo on December 3, 1943 (attended by Churchill, Roosevelt, and Chiang Kai-shek). Admiral King opposed the idea of relinquishing the Pacific war to MacArthur, submitting his own plan to the Allied Combined Chiefs of Staff for a dual approach in the Pacific. The Combined Chiefs concurred and issued their directive stating that the "advance along the New Guinea-Netherlands East Indies-Philippine axis will proceed concurrently with operations for the capture of the Mandated Islands. A strategic bombing force will be established in Guam, Tinian, and Saipan for strategic bombing of Japan proper." For this final phase a new bomber, the Boeing B-29 Superfortress, was being delivered to combat-training units in the United States.

The step between the Marianas (Guam, Saipan, and Tinian) was the Marshalls campaign. It proved to be one of the most successfully handled of the early combined operations, "characterized," in the words of Admiral King, "by excellent planning and by almost perfect timing in the execution of those plans." The experience gained in the Gilberts was not lost in the planning of the Marshalls invasions. As soon as the Seventh Air Force could begin launching bombing missions from new bases in the Gilberts the initial softening up of the targets began. With D-Day set for January 31, 1944, the carriers moved in two days before to strike at Majuro, Roi, and Kwajalein (in the Kwajalein Atoll), Taroa and Wotje. In concert with the Navy attacks, the Seventh Air Force sent over its B-24s and B-25s to harass the Japanese and to keep them off balance.

Japanese antiaircraft guns took their toll, but fighter defenses were weak because so many planes had previously been destroyed on the ground. Snoopers seemed even more timid than in the Gilberts. Then around dusk of January 29 the sudden appearance of nine planes low on the water electrified the fleet. The planes were quickly identified as twin-ruddered Nells and became the focus of destroyer antiaircraft guns. Combat air patrol Hellcats dropped down to attack the intruders also.

A trail of smoke came from one of the bombers before it splashed into the water. Loudspeakers on the American ships about then began booming, "Cease firing! Cease firing!" The planes that had been identified as Nells were, in fact, Mitchells of

Flaming Kate *stopped by the gunners of the* Yorktown *off Kwajalein, Marshall Islands, December 3, 1943.*
(NAVY DEPT., NATIONAL ARCHIVES)

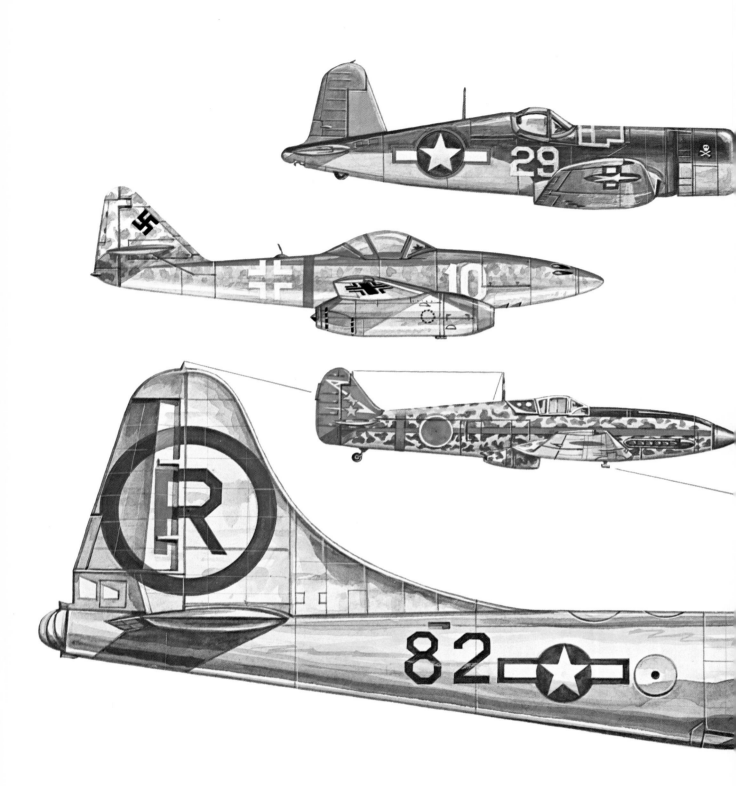

Aircraft involved in the final, devastating, air fighting of the Second World War: beginning in the right panel top (and proceeding downward) are a Focke-Wulf 190A in the markings of JG 300, a Home Defense unit that contended with the massive Allied bomber assault; next, a team-mate of the FW, the older design, a Messerschmitt 109G of JG 3 ("Udet"), based in Holland to intercept enemy bomber streams practically the moment they passed over the North Sea; the Republic P-47 "Thunderbolt" is decorated in the markings of Francis S. Gabreski, 56th Fighter Group; below that is one of the outstanding fighters of the war, the North American P-51 "Mustang" as flown by young "ace," Ernest Shipman of the 307th Squadron, 31st Fighter Group, 15th Air Force. Directly to the left of Shipman's P-51 is a Kawasaki Ki-61 (*Hien*—the "Swallow" in Japanese;

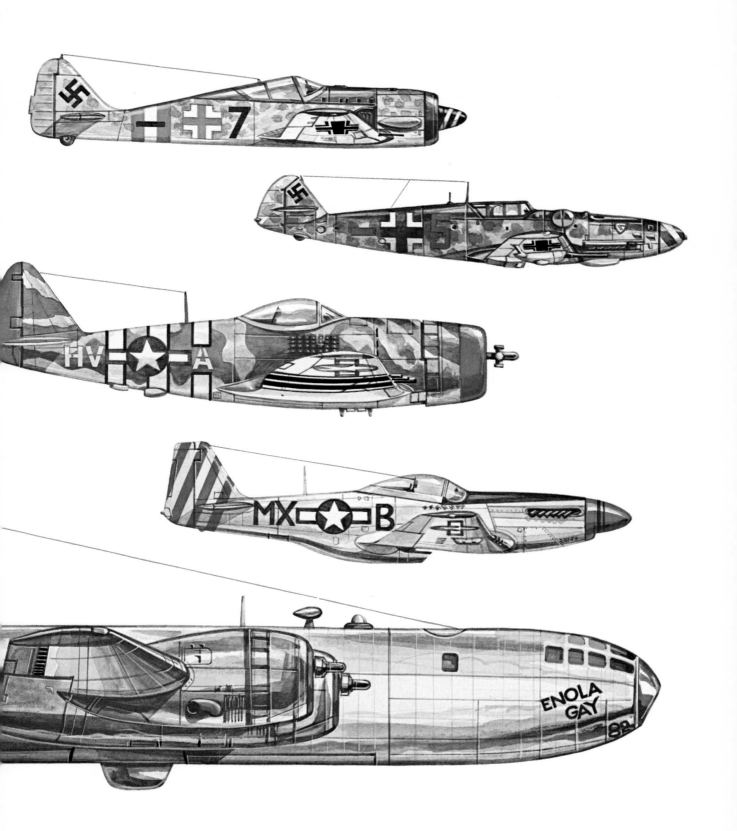

Americans dubbed it the "Tony" because of its resemblence to an Italian plane); the "Tony" is from the 244th *Sentei* based near Tokyo which was fated to intercept the war's most formidable heavy bomber. Above the "Tony" is the Messerschmitt 262, the most widely used jet fighter of the war; had its function not been grossly perverted by Hitler it might have had a devastating impact upon Allied bomber formations over Germany; the markings are those of JG 7 ("Nowotny"). Above the Me-262 is Ira Kepford's Vought "Corsair" of the U.S. Navy's VF-17; this was one of the deadliest fighters in the Pacific. Finally, dominating the lower portion of both panels, is Boeing's B-29 "Superfortress," the *Enola Gay* which ushered in the Atomic Age over Hiroshima. (Note: To show victory markings on P-47 and P-51 Artist Phelan has reversed lettering on fuselage sides.)

*Joseph A. Phelan*

the 820th Squadron (41st Bomb Group). The Mitchells had been on a mission to Wotje, where they were to have bombed shipping and shore installations. Coming in low over the water to avoid Japanese radar they had approached the unalerted Navy ships looking like torpedo bombers. The error cost the life of one man, injured five, and destroyed one Mitchell. Two others, seriously damaged, managed to return to Tarawa.

One by one, with almost clockwork precision, the islands fell: Majuro on January 31, Roi and Namur on February 2—but Kwajalein, the largest and strongest-held, took longer. Heavy shelling, much heavier than that which preceded the Tarawa landing, pounded the island for two days, almost up to

the moment that the troops were put ashore. At nine-thirty in the morning of February 1, 1944, the Army's 7th Division (which had fought on Attu) began moving in. Like Tarawa, Kwajalein was ingeniously fortified and cluttered with tank traps, pillboxes, snarls of barbed wire, and trenches. The survivors of the weeks of bombing and the hours of shelling had to be rooted out, and, as before, the Japanese fought fanatically, almost heedlessly to the death. When the fighting ended all but the 35 Japanese who had surrendered were annihilated—close to 5000 men. The total cost of taking all of the Kwajalein Atoll was 372 soldiers and Marines; the Japanese lost 7870 men of 8675 which had garrisoned that atoll.

*Eniwetok, Marshall Islands, under carrier plane attack. U. S. Marines take shelter in a shell hole as others* *set up machine guns (upper center); a burned out twin-engined Japanese bomber lies at bottom left.*

(U. S. NAVY)

*Navy Corsairs of the* Intrepid *ready for a strike on Truk. Originally not regarded as suitable for carriers, the Corsair proved otherwise. These F4U-2s are equipped with "radomes" near starboard wingtip for night operations. The Japanese hated this plane and called it "Whistling Death."*

(NAVY DEPT., NATIONAL ARCHIVES)

When the taking of Majuro and Kwajalein had come off so smoothly, it was decided that one more of the Marshalls, Eniwetok Atoll, might be taken even earlier than had been originally planned. Set for May 10, D-Day on Eniwetok was moved up to February 17. This atoll lay about 325 miles west and north of Kwajalein and about 1000 miles from the Marianas. The pattern of softening up, bombardment, and assault was repeated, and by February 20 Eniwetok fell to American forces and the Marshall Islands belonged to the United States. Several of them—Jaluit, Mili, Maloelap, and Wotje (as was Nauru in the Gilberts)—were not invaded at all. They harbored Japanese troops, held air bases, but with the other positions in American hands these atolls were isolated from everything but American air and surface attacks.

During the Eniwetok assault, Truk, the vaunted "Gibraltar of the Pacific," Japan's most formidable base outside the home islands, was rendered almost neutral by the carrier planes of Rear Admiral Marc A. Mitscher's Fast Carrier Force. On the morning of February 17, after a surprisingly uneventful trip from Majuro in the Marshalls, a fighter sweep of seventy-two Hellcats pounced upon the air base at Truk. Fighting in the air cost four Navy planes, but the Japanese lost more than fifty in the air and even more on the ground. Avengers followed the fighters, planting incendiaries on the base, leaving behind less than a hundred operational planes with which the Japanese might contend the Eniwetok landings. Dive bombers destroyed the ships in the harbor, so that by February 18 Truk was no longer any kind of Gibraltar—and, in fact, was no longer even

*Free riders: several Navy pilots came to grief near Truk during a carrier strike (April 30, 1944) due to Japanese antiaircraft or mechanical failures. This King-fisher was sent to retrieve the dunked pilots and picked up so many—six from the* Enterprise *and one from the* Langley—*that pilot John A. Burns could not take off.* (NAVY DEPT., NATIONAL ARCHIVES)

Truk. As "a formidable bastion" it was no more impressive, or potent, than any other bypassed island in the Pacific.

The Marshalls campaign closed with a carrier strike in the Marianas. Not since the fall of Guam (the largest and southernmost of the Marianas) in December 1941 had American planes passed over these islands. The purpose of the carrier raid was double: to cover the Eniwetok landings and to begin reconnaissance photography of Saipan, Tinian, Rota, and Guam for the proposed seizure of these islands for future bases. For the first time since the early Gilberts assaults, the Japanese attempted to fight back vigorously. As the carriers approached the Marianas the evening of February 21 was marked by heavy fighting.

Three attempts by bombers to stop the American ships were made by an estimated forty Japanese ships. Intense antiaircraft fire either shot them down

or drove them off, and the armada, undamaged though zigzagging, continued westward to the morning's launch point. As at Truk, Hellcats swept in over the Japanese bases, strafing and burning. Aerial opposition by Japanese fighters, many already burned on the ground, was sporadic, tentative, and lacking in characteristic Japanese fatal determination. At the same time small ships in and around Saipan, Tinian, and Guam were strafed and bombed.

Japan's inner defense line, which ran through the Marianas, had been pierced. There was consternation in Tokyo and Admiral Koga, after ordering the fleet to evacuate Truk, hurried home to confer with the Imperial General Staff. The principal Japanese naval base was moved farther westward to Palau, practically on the doorstep of the Philippines. The defensive line was drawn from the Kuriles in the north, down past the home islands, through the Bonins, southerly through the Marianas, and westward to Palau. This line, Koga stated, must be held to the death. Palau lay across the path of Mac-Arthur's forces hopping up the northern coast of New Guinea, as well as in the seas through which Halsey's ships moved toward Japan. And the Marianas, just to the northeast in the Philippine Sea, were also within reach.

American aircraft carriers became the main objective of Koga's plan, Order 73. He was fated never to know of the failure of this order, for on March 31,

*The fighting in the Central Pacific intensifies; the American carriers have moved in close to Saipan, Mariana Islands, for a strike before the coming invasion.* (NAVY DEPT., NATIONAL ARCHIVES)

*Last moments of a Japanese "Jill" (Nakajima B6N) torpedo bomber during an attempt at American ships off Truk.* (NAVY DEPT., NATIONAL ARCHIVES)

1944, Koga was lost in a storm while flying from Saipan to Davao in the Philippines. He was succeeded by Admiral Soemu Toyoda, who like Yamamoto had opposed Japan's entry into war and was a realist besides, and, in the words of Samuel Eliot Morison, "a much more aggressive character," compared to Koga.

When he became Commander in Chief, Combined Fleet, Toyoda rather bluntly said, "The war is approaching areas vital to our national security. Our situation is one of unprecedented gravity. There is only one way of deciding this struggle in our favor."

The Americans must be stopped, once and for all, in the Marianas.

IV

As the Imperial Navy made preparations for an all-out effort to stop the enemy, Minister of the Army and Prime Minister General Hideki Tojo criticized the Navy's efforts as "hysterical" and refused to permit the use of Army aircraft in the Marianas. Toyoda could do nothing, then, but alert and deploy his naval forces. He would co-ordinate his carrier force, under command of Vice-Admiral Jisaburo Ozawa, with the land-based forces of Vice-Admiral Kakuji Kakuda. Kakuda's headquarters were on Tinian and his planes were deployed through the Marianas, the Carolines, Iwo Jima, and Truk—a total of about a thousand.

The Palau anchorage having been rendered unwholesome by the marauding American carriers, Ozawa awaited developments at Tawitawi, in the Sulu Sea, just west of the southern Philippines. Under Ozawa's command was the largest fleet assembled since the attack on Pearl Harbor: seventy-three ships, including nine carriers, among them the new heavy carrier Taiho. Never before in Japanese naval history had such a heavy concentration of battle planes been assembled. There were nearly 450 planes—Zekes, Kates, Vals, and the newer Nakajima Tenzen ("Jill") torpedo bomber and the not quite so new Yokosuka Suisei ("Judy") dive bomber. The latter two planes were designed to replace the aged Kate and Val.

To meet the rampaging American forces, Ozawa

had divided his aerial forces into three carrier divisions. The 1st, under his command, consisted of the three heavy carriers Taiho (the flagship), Shokaku, and Zuikaku (the two surviving veterans of the Pearl Harbor attack). Stationed aboard these carriers were the pilots of the 601st Kokutai (Air Corps). Rear Admiral Takaji Jojima commanded the 2nd Carrier Division: the light carriers Hiyo, Junyo, and Ryuho, carrying the 652nd Kokutai. The 3rd Carrier Division (Rear Admiral Sueo Obayashi) was assigned to the main body, which consisted also of battleships and cruisers which were to deal with the American fleet. Obayashi commanded the light carriers Chiyoda, Chitose, and Zuiho (653rd Kokutai). With so vast an accumulation of air power plus the assistance which might be expected from Kakuda's land-based planes, Japanese naval officers anticipated a great aerial slaughter of the Americans. This was planned to be finished by the battleships of Vice-Admiral Takeo Kurita's force, which included the great Yamato and Musashi, two of the world's most modern battleships. An exhilarating excitement gripped the young pilots as they waited impatiently for the word to leave Tawitawi.

Even these young, untried, inexperienced, and ill-trained warriors were inclined to a touch of "victory fever."

Only the veterans awaited the coming battle with reservations. The training of the pilots aboard the nine carriers, excepting a handful of experienced leaders, was tragically inadequate, ranging from as little as two months to a maximum of six. But lack of experience began at the top, for Ozawa had never taken part in a carrier battle. He was to oppose Rear Admiral Raymond A. Spruance, who had proved himself at Midway. Directly opposing Ozawa was Vice-Admiral Marc A. Mitscher's formidable Task Force 58. Mitscher not only had quality—better-trained men, better aircraft, his own battle shrewdness—on his side, he also had overwhelming, American-made quantity, as Yamamoto had foreseen.

Early in June 1944 Task Force 58 began its approach upon the southern Marianas. Only clichés could do it justice: "massive array of sea-air power," "the greatest armada ever assembled," for as "far as the eye could see"—and beyond—great, warlike ships churned through the Pacific. There were seven heavy carriers (the Hornet, Yorktown, Bunker Hill,

*Task Force 58* "... the greatest armada ever as-sembled ..." *in the summer of 1944 poised to move into the Marianas.* (NAVY DEPT., NATIONAL ARCHIVES)

*Wasp, Enterprise, Lexington,* and *Essex*), eight light carriers (the *Bataan, Belleau Wood, Monterey, Cabot, San Jacinto, Princeton, Cowpens,* and *Langley*), seven new battleships, eight heavy cruisers, thirteen light cruisers, and sixty-nine destroyers. This does not include those ships directly assigned to Vice-Admiral Richmond K. Turner's amphibious forces, which would invade Saipan, then Guam, and then Tinian. Among the ships of Turner's force were several old battleships which had been dam-aged at Pearl Harbor, besides eight of the smaller escort carriers.

But before the landings could be made Mitscher's planes must begin clearing away Japanese aerial potential in and around Saipan. Leaving Majuro anchorage on June 6, 1944 (the same date but because of the International Date Line the day be-fore the Normandy landings in Europe), Mitscher

put to sea. His carriers transported about double the number of aircraft Ozawa had on his carriers—over 890 planes, the bulk being Hellcats, plus Avengers, Dauntlesses, and the new Curtiss SB2-C "Helldiver." Pilots, incidentally, disdained the pub-lic relations name of the plane and preferred calling it simply the "2C."

According to plans, the amphibious forces, Ma-rine and Army, would go ashore on Saipan on June 15. Three days before, Mitscher's carrier planes were to sweep over the Marianas airfields, bringing up the curtain on the operation. However, on the tenth Japanese air patrols spotted the approaching carriers; Toyoda, long suspecting, at last knew. Com-mander in Chief, Combined Fleet, had formulated his own plan: he hoped to lure the American fleet into the waters off the western Carolines (southwest of Guam). There, roughly in the vicinity of the Palau Islands and other Japanese bases (Yap and Woleai), with his vast aerial force he would an-nihilate the American carriers. Toyoda expected the

*Island and flight deck of the* Lexington *before Saipan.*
(NAVY DEPT., NATIONAL ARCHIVES)

landings at Palau and tended to regard any Marianas operations as diversions masking MacArthur's New Guinea moves.

But Mitscher's main task was to prepare the way for and cover the landings in the Marianas; it would be difficult, however alluring, to entice him into the western Carolines. In fact, as soon as he realized that Japanese reconnaissance planes had found Task Force 58, Mitscher put on speed and steamed ahead for the Marianas. By the afternoon of June 11, though still about two hundred miles east of the Marianas, Mitscher launched his first fighter sweep —the Hellcats being guided to the targets by the better-equipped (in terms of navigational instruments) Avengers.

Although the Japanese had been aware of TF 58's presence, they were apparently preparing for the customary dawn attack for the next day. Also, undoubtedly, they were preparing for a snooper attack on the carriers that very evening. About two hundred Hellcats swarmed down upon Saipan, Tinian, and Guam, destroying planes on the ground and in the air. About 150 Japanese planes were erased from Kakuda's ground-based air forces in the Marianas, crippling all possible strong air retaliation. The first night off Saipan was free of Japanese attack.

The next day American destruction of airfields and other installations continued, and on the thir-

teenth the battleships started pounding the landing beaches. On this day, also, the Japanese fleet left Tawitawi and proceeded northward. Obviously the Americans intended to invade the Marianas (which had been the prediction of Commander Chikataka Nakajima of the Naval Intelligence Staff) and not Palau (as the Staff, in general, believed). Immediately canceled was Operation *Kon* (a plan to retake the importantly strategic island of Biak, off the northwest coast of New Guinea, which had fallen to MacArthur's forces), and Toyoda ordered Ozawa to proceed at full speed for Saipan—about two thousand miles away. At the same time Kakuda's land-based planes were ordered to hold off the Americans until Ozawa's forces arrived.

By this time about five hundred planes had been destroyed and with the remaining handful there was little resistance forthcoming, at least not from the air. On June 15 Marines and Army infantrymen (2nd and 4th Marine Divisions; 27th Infantry Division) struck the beaches of Saipan. They had been properly cautioned by Navy manuals and talks. The troops were warned to beware of sea life ringing the island: "sharks, barracuda, sea snakes, anemones, razor-sharp coral, polluted waters, poison fish and giant clams that shut on a man like a bear trap."

An officer read off, according to regulations, the joys of life ashore: leprosy, typhus, filariasis, yaws, typhoid, dengue fever, dysentery, saber grass, insects, snakes, and giant lizards.

"Eat nothing growing on the island," he continued reading; "don't drink its waters and don't approach the inhabitants." The End.

"Any questions?"

A hand was raised.

The officer nodded.

"Why don't we let them keep the island?"

Unlike Japanese Naval Intelligence, the young American Marine had never heard of the B-29. On Saipan, northernmost of the islands coveted by the Americans, the Japanese had constructed Aslito Field. At the northern end of the island—that is, opposite to the end on which Aslito lay—another airstrip was being set up. It was because of these air bases, primarily, that the Americans did not want the Japanese to keep the island, and for which the invading troops were expected to risk the nearly countless hazards of life in and around Saipan.

*The invasion of Saipan, with carrier plane cover, begins; June 15, 1944. A Japanese ship burns near the shore.* (NAVY DEPT., NATIONAL ARCHIVES)

Besides these natural perils there were Lieutenant General Yoshitsugo Saito's thirty thousand troops. Also on Saipan as Commander in Chief, Pacific Fleet, in command of all Japanese Marine and naval units in the area, was Vice-Admiral Chuichi Nagumo, the reluctant hero of Pearl Harbor. Nagumo agreed with others in the Japanese High Command: the Americans were aiming for Palau. Meanwhile Saito, grumbling because the Navy had lost supply ships and troop ships to American submarines, did the best he could to prepare "to destroy the enemy at the water's edge."

The day before the landings began Nagumo, having witnessed the aerial strikes of the previous four days, hedgingly proffered a prediction and a definition. "The Marianas are the first line of defense of our homeland. It is certain that the Americans will land in the Marianas group either this month or the next." They landed, of course, the next day.

*During the Saipan invasion carrier sweeps over Guam to the south held down Japanese aerial intervention. On his mission Ensign A. P. Morner, Ironwood, Michigan, encountered six Zekes, shot down three, but was wounded himself and his Hellcat damaged—which resulted in this crash landing on Morner's home carrier.* (U. S. NAVY)

*Stowaways: Air Force Thunderbolts of the 318th Fighter Group (73rd Squadron) aboard the carrier* Manila Bay. *Japanese Vals from Saipan contributed the splashes to port.* (U. S. AIR FORCE)

"Where are our planes?" lamented tank man Tokuzo Matsuya in a characteristic query. "Are they letting us die without making any effort to save us? If it were for the security of the Empire we would not hesitate to lay down our lives, but wouldn't it be a great loss to the Land of the Gods for us all to die on this island? It would be easy for me to die, but for the sake of the future I feel obligated to stay alive."

Marine Lieutenant General Holland M. Smith, in command of the ground troops for the invasion, found that "Saito met us at the beaches at Saipan in approved Japanese fashion, and our hopes of quickly expanding our beachhead were somewhat dampened. . . . The long twenty-five-day continuous attack against strongly entrenched and fiercely resisting troops on Saipan proved the most bitter battle in the Pacific up to that time." Intense mortar and artillery fire, plus suicidal, screaming night attacks by the Japanese, made life ashore dreadful and, for many, short. By June 18, however, Aslito Field fell to the Army's 27th Division. On June 22 Thunderbolts of the 19th and 73rd Squadrons of the 318th Fighter Group, catapulted from the es-

*Thunderbolt of 73rd Squadron leaves deck of* Manila Bay *for Aslito Field (renamed Isley Field), Saipan.* (U. S. AIR FORCE)

cort carriers *Manila Bay* and *Natoma Bay,* landed at Aslito to join the Navy planes already there. By this time the field was renamed Isley Field, in honor of Commander Robert H. Isley, commander of the *Lexington*'s torpedo planes. Two days before the Saipan landings Isley's Avenger was hit by antiaircraft fire over Aslito and crashed in flames onto the field itself. From Isley Field the Seventh Air

*Aslito Field, Saipan, showing the ravages of American carrier plane attacks. Intact aircraft parked among the wrecks are U. S. Navy and Air Force planes.*

(U. S. NAVY)

Force Thunderbolts engaged in close-support operations, blasting away at Japanese positions in front of Marine and Army troops. Once established in the still beleagered airfield, the P-47s, when not engaged in sporadic air battles, bombed and strafed Japanese positions on Saipan and Tinian. By July, when the fighting on Saipan ended, the Thunderbolts of the 318th Fighter Group were armed with yet another weapon, at first popularly called the "fire bomb." These were the first of the frightfully effective napalm, diesel oil, and gasoline mixtures (later napalm and gasoline), which when dropped in wing and belly tanks from about fifty feet upon Japanese strong points (particularly caves) created a havoc of flame.

Meanwhile, even as American troops went ashore on Saipan, word was flashed from the submarine *Flying Fish* that a large Japanese carrier force had been sighted in San Bernardino Strait, headed for

*Marc Andrew Mitscher, USN, an early Navy air pioneer, canny air leader during Solomons campaign and commander of carrier force in the Central Pacific for the Marianas assault.*

(NAVY DEPT., NATIONAL ARCHIVES)

the Marianas. The next day, June 16, *Seahorse,* another submarine, sighted more ships off Surigao Strait. Spruance knew then that the Combined Fleet was coming out in full force. He immediately canceled the proposed June 18 landing on Guam (although not the June 16 air strikes upon Iwo Jima in the Volcano Islands and Chichi Jima in the Bonins, south of the Japanese homeland).

American submarines, which were to play an important role in the impending "decisive battle," tracked the Japanese fleet, waiting for the moment when they might launch their fish. Spruance positioned his carriers by June 18 about 160 miles west of Tinian. On this same day—the day that Aslito Field fell—Ozawa's forces had arrived at a position about 500 miles west of Saipan. The opposing fleets by June 19 were about four hundred miles apart.

Ozawa, therefore, had the advantage. His planes, thanks to the lack of armor plating and the lack of the heavy self-sealing fuel tanks, enjoyed a greater range than the American carrier fighters. Even before his carriers came within range of the American

carriers—Ozawa's major targets—he could launch his planes, which, after combat, could land on the Marianas airfields (excepting, of course, Aslito). Japanese search planes, meanwhile, sought out the American fleet as the Japanese carriers made preparations to hurl total destruction upon Spruance's carriers.

June 19 dawned clear over the American carriers. The night before, the pilots had been disappointed because Spruance would not authorize Mitscher, in tactical command of the carriers, to speed westward to intercept the Japanese. Spruance had in mind that the primary mission of Task Force 58 was to cover the Saipan invasion. If the carriers were too far west, there was always a possibility of Japanese ships coming in to pound the Americans from the sea. Aboard the *Lexington,* his flagship, Mitscher was reported to have stalked into his sea cabin to blow off steam in private. On the *Enterprise* Captain Matthias B. Gardner, complying, said nothing but is reported to have "hurled down his hat and stomped on it." (Spruance was later criticized for holding his carriers near Saipan and not taking the offensive on June 18. Critics, however, ex post facto as usual, possessed certain vital information which at the time the Japanese were not bestowing upon Spruance.)

Mitscher's eager pilots, however, would not lack for action on the nineteenth. An early morning strike on Orote Field on Guam was mounted to keep that base neutralized in the event that the impending battle materialized. About thirty Wildcats pounced on the already beaten-up field; a rather surprising antlike activity seemed in progress as Japanese planes were pushed out of revetments and put into the air with frantic resolution. The Wildcats began the morning's decimation, shattering the Japanese planes, barely air-borne, out of the bright morning sky.

In about an hour and a half of fighting, the American combat air patrol shot down thirty-five of Kakuda's land-based planes, which had up to that morning escaped previous attacks. Meanwhile, tension aboard the carriers mounted as Mitscher wondered about the location of the Japanese carriers.

Ozawa had begun launching his planes at dawn, search planes and bombers (a total of seventy-three), which fanned out into a squally sky to look for the American fleet. The imperfect weather over

*Hellcats of VFN-76 on the* Lexington *near Saipan; radomes converted these planes into night fighters that* *dealt with Japanese night "snoopers," reconnaissance planes and bombers.*

the Japanese ships, stretching nearly to the American dispositions, was a disadvantage to the inexperienced Japanese pilots. Animated with patriotism and little else, they were led like strangely pugnacious sheep to slaughter. Ozawa's first raid, led by Lieutenant Commander Masayuki Yamagami, began taking off at daybreak and vanished into murky eastern sky. Then Ozawa waited. He could afford to, for his ships were still beyond the range of Mitscher's carrier planes.

He was determined to make a thorough job of the Americans, so even as the planes of the first raid were taking off the van carriers of the 3rd Carrier Division, the planes of the 1st Carrier Division began launching also. Forty-eight Zekes, fifty-four Judys, and twenty-seven Jills took off from the *Zuikaku, Shokaku,* and *Taiho.* From the bridge of the latter, Japan's great new carrier, Ozawa observed the air swarming with planes. The *Taiho* was a gigantic vessel of more than sixty-four thousand tons. Launched just three months before (April 4, 1944), the *Taiho* was considered unsinkable.

As the last plane left the deck of the flagship a torpedo track was discovered knifing through the water at the *Taiho.* Warrant Officer Sakio Komatsu, whose plane was in the last wave, saw the churning line in the water and died believing he had saved the flagship by diving into the torpedo, detonating it. But that was not the only "fish" which had been ejected from the torpedo tubes of the *Albacore,* an American submarine in the area (under command of J. W. Blanchard), and despite attempts to turn the *Taiho,* it was struck. The blow jammed an elevator and fuel piping ruptured, filling the hangar space below decks with fumes. A single spark did the rest, for within six hours the *Taiho* was ripped by a splintering explosion. A mass of flames from stem to stern, the *Taiho* turned over and sank.

Admiral Ozawa in the meantime had moved to another ship, the heavy cruiser *Haguro.* He was an unhappy man, for even while the *Taiho* reeked with impending doom yet another carrier was attacked—this time the *Skokaku,* which became the victim of Lieutenant Commander H. J. Kossler's submarine *Cavalla.* The *Shokaku* sank even before the *Taiho.*

Before these misfortunes, however, Ozawa had launched about four hundred planes in four attack waves. The first of these was detected by American

*A Japanese plane shot aflame by antiaircraft fire from American ships attempts to crash into flight deck of escort carrier* Sangamon, *Marianas.*

(NAVY DEPT., NATIONAL ARCHIVES)

*A twin-engined Japanese bomber goes down near the* Kitkun Bay *near Saipan on the eve of the Marianas "Turkey Shoot."* (NAVY DEPT., NATIONAL ARCHIVES)

radar when they were almost 150 miles away, at Guam. When the first blips of aircraft apparently approaching from the open sea appeared on the radar screens, it was Mitscher himself who took the microphone of the TBS (Talk Between Ships) and initiated what would come to be called the "Marianas Turkey Shoot."

"Hey, Rube!" echoed through the fleet, alerting

pilots to scramble and antiaircraft gunners to prepare their guns. Great rings of destroyers and cruisers, guns pointing skyward, had been formed around the carriers in four large groups spread over hundreds of square miles to the west of the Marianas.

The old American circus battle cry activated the carriers, and the Wildcats that had been over Guam turned about and raced out to sea. They would intercept the oncoming Japanese, but Guam continued to suffer under bombers and torpedo bombers. At 10:07 A.M. the ticker tape on the *Lexington* read: "Unidentified planes have been picked up bearing 333°, 45 miles away." Hellcats from the *Essex, Cowpens, Bunker Hill,* and *Princeton* vectored in upon the oncoming planes—the scouts and scout bombers of the Japanese 3rd Carrier Division. In the first skirmish, well to the west of the American carriers, about twenty-five Japanese planes (of seventy-three) were splashed into the sea. The survivors continued on resolutely, only to be met head on by another formation of Hellcats—sixteen more Japanese planes fell into the sea. Those still flying (about thirty) broke through the battle line (the battleships and destroyers that stood fifteen miles in the vanguard of the carrier formations). One of the bombers scored a direct hit upon the *South Dakota,* but not one Japanese plane reached the carriers. Of the original seventy-three only twenty-four survived for the time being. Some crash-landed on Guam and others returned to their own carriers.

The first large attack wave, the 129 fighters, bombers, and torpedo bombers of the 1st Carrier Division, were intercepted about an hour after the battle had begun. The Japanese planes ran head on into a mass of Hellcats, which shattered the formations—about a hundred planes fell before the carriers were reached. And the six of these which actually broke through were destroyed by savage antiaircraft fire or the combat air patrol planes circling the carriers.

Commander Ernest M. Snowden, of the *Lexington,* recalls how "We could see vapor trails of planes coming in with tiny black specks at the head. It was just like the skywriting we all used to see before the war. The sky was a white overcast and for some reason the planes were making vapor trails at a much lower altitude than usual. That made it easier for our boys to find the incoming Japs."

There were plenty of Japanese to go around, apparently. One young pilot, Ensign Bradford Hagie, found action even during a simple ferry flight. He had been forced to land on another carrier the previous day with engine trouble. Anxious to return to the *Lexington,* about three thousand yards away, he took off the next morning during what turned out to be the attack by the first wave. Hearing the radio chatter about the approaching unidentified aircraft, he remained air-borne for a while and on his way to the *Lexington* shot down three planes.

When the second, larger wave approached another young pilot sat gloomily in his Hellcat off to one side of the battle, circling out of the way because his engine was giving him trouble. He was Lieutenant Alexander Vraicu, and with his windscreen smeared with oil and his engine incapable of pulling at full power, he and five other "orphans" (planes with assorted problems but still flyable) orbited over the carriers. The decks had to be kept clear for takeoffs for the fighters.

Disappointed, Vraicu, who had gained much experience as a wingman of Butch O'Hare's, listened to the sounds of battle to the west on his radio. He heard the voice of the fighter director of the *Lexington* calling out vectors of approach.

"Vector 265." Vraicu turned the Hellcat in that direction, sharply squinting his eyes until he saw three forms in the sky coming his way. They proved to be the first of perhaps fifty planes, Zekes, Judys, and Jills. Other Hellcats began to race for the formation also. The air armadas met, converged, and then sprang apart into twisting individual air battles. Vraicu had forgotten about his engine trouble; the Japanese planes had ventured too close to the American carriers. Vraicu dived into the formation of Japanese bombers, opening up on the first plane in sight—a Judy. Within five seconds his voice was heard over the radio, "Scratch one Judy!"

Over the next few minutes Vraicu's guns sliced through one Judy after another, until his score for the single battle amounted to six. To the youthful pilot it seemed that there were simply too many planes to be taken care of, and that some came in dangerously close to the American ships. To his dismay he saw one lone Judy heading for a battleship, and he kicked his Hellcat around hoping to head off the bomber. But antiaircraft bursts came up and the Judy flew through the puffs for a few moments

*Japanese ships dodging attacks from American carrier
planes, June 19, 1944, the day of the "Turkey Shoot."*
(NAVY DEPT., NATIONAL ARCHIVES)

and then flashed apart a thousand feet in the air.

Low on fuel, Vraicu returned to the *Lexington.*
For some reason the gunners began shooting at him
and Vraicu voiced his views on the ship's gunners
as he circled and came in again for a landing.
When his plane stopped, Vraicu stood up in the
cockpit and held up six fingers. In eight minutes he
had brought his total score up to nineteen.

A third Japanese raid was led astray by a faulty
compass reading and missed most of the fighting.
About a dozen of the forty-seven planes of the 2nd
Carrier Division ran into Hellcats, which shot down
seven. The remaining forty returned to their carriers.

When the fourth raid was launched, some of the
spared pilots of the third raid joined it to make up
a force of about eighty aircraft. This force too was
led astray, but instead of returning to the carriers,
the planes turned north, toward Guam, and ran into
the Hellcats of the *Cabot, Wasp, Monterey,* and
*Bunker Hill.* The day's slaughter continued in a
whirl of dogfights—Japanese bombers attempting
to get at the carriers were shot out of the air.
Eighteen, met by Hellcats, were soon cut in half.
The scattered survivors of the raid, forty-nine in all,
were jumped over Guam as they attempted to find
haven there. Thirty planes flared and fell; the remaining nineteen that finally landed, in various
stages of distress, either crashed or were strafed into
junk. Of the eighty planes which had left on the
strike, nine returned to their home bases. The last

*"Turkey Shoot" victor Alexander Vraicu of the* Lexington *indicates his score during one battle in a Hellcat with a bad engine.*

of the survivors of the day's battle fled for their carriers around six forty-five in the evening. The final battle of the Turkey Shoot occurred over Guam when four Hellcats, led by Lieutenant Commander C. W. Brewer over Orote Field, pounced a limping Jill attempting to land. Brewer's forces were in turn jumped by a large number of land-based Zekes, which had somehow eluded the day's bombings and strafings. Brewer was killed in this last battle of the day as darkness fell on the great battle arena.

The coming of night brought little comfort to Ozawa; he had no decisive victory to report. Two of his largest carriers were deep under the sea and 346 of his planes simply did not return to the carriers. And not one American plane had approached the Japanese carriers during the entire day. Toyoda, at Combined Fleet headquarters at Hiroshima, ordered Ozawa to withdraw before the Americans found his other carriers. Bitterly, Ozawa complied. He planned to refuel his ships and strike back with all he had on the next day.

Spruance then unleashed the straining Mitscher, who set off westward with three carrier groups, leaving one in the vicinity of the Marianas to continue creating a hell on earth on Guam and Rota. At

one o'clock on June 20, 1944, Ozawa transferred to the carrier *Zuikaku* (now the sole surviving veteran of the Hawaii Operation); he planned to strike again on the twenty-first. It appeared that he might have his way, for there was no sign of the American fleet. Search planes launched by Mitscher had not found the Japanese fleet either.

At one-thirty in the afternoon Lieutenant R. S. Nelson had taken off in an Avenger and set off on his search pattern. Two hours and ten minutes later, when he was about at the end of his tether, Nelson found what no one had yet found in the past several days: the Japanese fleet. He began sending a message back to the *Lexington,* but distance and weather garbled it and, although alerted, Mitscher was unable to make a decision. And in less than four hours he knew the sun would go down suddenly, as it did in the Pacific.

As Nelson continued sending messages they were picked up by the Japanese cruiser *Atago* nearby. They could only mean that the Americans had found the Japanese fleet. Ozawa was immediately notified and he ordered all refueling stopped and the ships away at twenty-four knots.

It took nearly fifteen minutes of sending before Nelson's contact report finally made any sense. Mitscher had already begun to make his plans, however. When Nelson's final, corrected position and disposition report came in at 4:05 P.M., Mitscher was prepared to launch his aircraft. But not without risk, for it was already late in the day and the Japanese ships were 275 miles away. It meant a long flight for them, then the battle and a long flight back.

"Taking advantage of this opportunity to destroy the Japanese fleet was going to cost us a great deal in planes and pilots because we were launching at the maximum range of our aircraft at such a time that it would be necessary to recover them after dark," Mitscher realized. "This meant that all carriers would be recovering daylight-trained air groups at night, with consequent loss of some pilots who were not familiar with night landings and who would be fatigued at the end of an extremely hazardous and long mission."

At four forty-one the carriers turned into the wind and ten minutes later no less than 216 planes were air-borne, 85 of them Hellcats. Two hours of flying brought them within sight of the Japanese ships.

*Avenger pilot Lieutenant Ronald Gift of Marlette, Michigan, after a successful strike upon Japanese ships that had fled the shambles of the "Turkey Shoot." Gift's was one of the planes that was able to land in the dark when Mitscher canceled blackout regulations. The chalked message over Gift's head was the motto of Navy bomber pilots.*

(NAVY DEPT., NATIONAL ARCHIVES)

Six oilers, left astern after Ozawa had ordered the ships away, were the first to come under attack. Dive bombers swept down and disabled two—*Genyo Maru* and *Seiyo Maru*—so thoroughly that they were abandoned and scuttled by evening.

One of the last messages the American pilots had seen as they raced from their ready rooms was chalked on the blackboards, "Get the CARRIERS." worthy targets, the carriers were the prime objectives so far as most pilots were concerned. Leaving the transports burning and scattered, the carrier pilots continued their search for the Japanese carriers. Soon they came into view.

Lieutenant George B. Brown, Avenger pilot from the *Belleau Wood,* led seven other Avengers (four of them from the *Yorktown*), circled around the Japanese ships, and then selected the *Hiyo* to the port. The *Yorktown* Avengers split away and headed

to the starboard for the larger *Zuikaku* (now Ozawa's flagship), and the four *Belleau Wood* Avengers headed for the *Hiyo*. Antiaircraft fire was desperately heavy and Brown's Avenger was hit as he ran the plane in. He had not yet dropped his torpedo when a fragment of his left wing ripped away and flames filled the cockpit of the Avenger.

*The Marianas prizes: in this reconnaissance photograph which spans a distance of twenty-six miles in a southwesterly direction, Saipan lies in the foreground. The airstrip near Marpi Point, Saipan's northernmost tip, is at the bottom of the photo. Aslito airfield is hidden under a cloud near top left of the picture. Across Saipan Channel lies Tinian with one of its two airstrips visible. With the conquest of the Marianas a new phase in the Pacific war would follow: B-29 operations from Saipan, Tinian, and Guam.* (U. S. AIR FORCE)

*The hazards of landing on a carrier deck under poor lighting conditions after combat. A Wildcat has come in, the pilot has misjudged his speed, or his arresting hook has not caught, and his plane does not stop until it ends up in the Pacific. Nor before it damages all other objects in its path. Mitscher's decision to turn on carrier landing lights helped to diminish the number of such landings.* (NAVY DEPT., NATIONAL ARCHIVES)

The radioman and gunner bailed out, but Brown, who had said before taking off that he would get a carrier "at any cost," continued the run. The fire had burned itself out and Brown dropped his torpedo; his wingman, Lieutenant Benjamin Tate, dropped too but did not claim a hit. Lieutenant Warren Omark, however, placed a torpedo into the *Hiyo.*

Tate, harassed by two Zekes and with one gun shot out, ducked into a cloud and lost the Japanese fighters. He then joined up with Brown's badly shot-up Avenger. The plane moved erratically and Brown appeared to be bleeding badly. Then Tate lost sight of Brown. Omark, having eluded a Zeke and a couple of Vals, caught up with Brown and tried to guide him back to the American carrier positions. Brown finally disappeared in a cloud and was never seen again. His two crewmen, who had parachuted, were rescued the following day, safely floating in their life jackets. They had witnessed the death throes of the *Hiyo,* which sank about two hours after Brown and Omark had placed their torpedoes into the carrier.

There was fighting aloft too, for Ozawa had scraped together about seventy-five planes to meet the Hellcats, Avengers, and Helldivers. As the Hellcats fought off the Zekes, the bombers attacked and strafed other ships, among them the *Zuikaku,* which though badly hit was not sunk, the *Junyo, Ryuho,* and *Chiyoda* (all light carriers). In the heavy fighting sixty-five Japanese planes went down; American losses reached twenty, victims of fighters and antiaircraft.

When the day ended Ozawa's log noted the tragedy of the two days' fighting of what was officially known as the Battle of the Philippine Sea. "Surviving carrier air power," it was written, "35 aircraft operational." Though he wished to continue the battle, Ozawa canceled the order for a surface battle and ordered the ships back to Okinawa.

About 190 American planes turned away from the battle and headed for their home carriers. Many were shot up, most were low on fuel—and night had fallen an hour before the first plane appeared over the American carriers. Task Force 58 turned into the wind and the hard-bitten Mitscher made another vital decision that day. Earlier in the day he had risked his pilots and planes on a long-range strike and now he believed he owed them something. In defiance of all regulations, caution, and possible Japanese snoopers and submarines, he turned to Captain Arleigh Burke, his chief of staff, and said, "Turn on the lights."

"We had almost reached the force when we saw the lights come on," Lieutenant E. J. Lawton of the *Enterprise* recalled in describing the homecoming of the planes. "It is clear that the task force did all in its power to make it easier for us to get home. Lieutenant [V. Van] Eason led us in over the *Enterprise* but her deck was fouled for some time. We circled for a few minutes, watching the lights of the planes below fan out in the pattern of a landing circle. But there had been too much strain in the last five hours to reduce things to a pattern now; and inevitably, landing circles became crowded, intervals were lost and deck crashes occurred. Many planes—too many—announced that their gas was gone and they were going into the water. Others were caught short in the groove.

*Japanese air power in the Marianas: a Marine grins down from a "meatball" on a Zeke wingtip at Aslito, Saipan.* (U. S. NAVY)

"Seen from above, it was a weird kaleidoscope of fast-moving lights forming intricate trails in the darkness, punctuated now and then by tracers shooting through the night as someone landed with his gun switches on, and again by suddenly brilliant exhaust flames as each plane took a cut, or someone's turtleback light getting lower and lower until blacked out by the waves closing over it."

About 80 planes crashed or splashed into the water during the landing attempts. Rescue ships picked up 59 men; in all, 49 were lost, either in battle or because they sank in their aircraft before they could be rescued. The two days' total loss to the American fleet was 130 planes (compared to Ozawa's 480—this number includes both carrier- and land-base aircraft). Seventy-six American airmen perished in the Battle of the Philippine Sea, a fair trade, in the arithmetic of war, for hundreds of Japanese pilots and planes and three carriers.

The trade for the Marianas as future air bases

*Guam secured: an 11th Bomb Group (Seventh Air Force) plane takes off for a mission from the Marianas* *for strikes on the Bonins and Carolines.*

(U. S. AIR FORCE)

and harbors for ships and submarines was also worthwhile. Guam and Tinian fell by August 10 and the Marianas were officially declared "secure," although thousands of enemy troops in hiding had to be killed before the islands were completely free of fighting.

Political repercussions in Japan were nearly as drastic as the military defeat. General Tojo, who had scoffed at the thought of a Marianas invasion by the Americans, declared upon the fall of Saipan that "Japan is threatened by a national crisis with-

out precedent." When the fall of Saipan was officially announced to the bewildered people of Japan, so was the fall of Tojo's cabinet. The Emperor, urged on by the *jushin* (elder statesmen without power who advised him), accepted the resignation of Tojo on July 18, 1944.

The Greater East Asia Co-Prosperity Sphere, which had swollen under Tojo's bellicose domination like some bloated balloon, had begun its inexorable collapse. The arrogant samurai had been diminished into just another turkey.

# WINGS OF
# FIRE

# Contents

# Preface

In THIS closing volume of *Airwar* the final evolution of the true meaning and consequences of air power is traced through the last months of the Second World War. Merely to state that there was a century of difference between Pearl Harbor and Hiroshima and between a Stuka attack upon a small bridge in Poland and the massive bombings of Hamburg, Berlin and Dresden practically says it all.

Except that he who plotted the attack on Pearl Harbor and the modest Stuka attack never in his wildest imagination considered the consequences, and the forms they would take. That is an interesting fact about war, no one really can predict how it will all come out—and when you do know, it is too late.

The airwar did not simply mean bombs bursting in air as techniques evolved and were refined. The bomb's detonations were understandable, expected and to a great extent possible to elude. But the results of great concentrations of bombs in a city, where fire fed on fire creating an inescapable holocaust, this was difficult for the human mind to grasp; this was not a "classic" kind of war at all. It destroyed all and everything before it, it was total, absolute and brutal. It was the Real War of the Twentieth Century. Its impact was not caused by explosives and steel, but flame.

It achieved its "classic" expression at Hiroshima and Nagasaki. But even before that, flame, caused by conventional bombs, gutted dozens of Japanese cities, including Tokyo itself. A point to consider is that the early fire-storms in Germany were accidental, the later razings in Japan were deliberate. This represents a philosophic change as well as a change in weaponry.

Changes, nuances, developments, "improvements" —these crept in subtly during the course of the war. The object was to win, at whatever cost, especially to the enemy. The little refinements to the "art of war" were born: jet aircraft, rocketry, the atomic bomb, until the arsenal at the End was hardly recognizable if compared with the weapons of the Beginning.

Tragically, as the winning side became more sophisticated in its weapons, the losing sides frantically attempted to stop it by the desperate measures of another time. Goering's Big Blow was right out of the First World War; it was grand, it was romantic and it was criminally pointless. The Japanese dependence on *Kamikaze* tactics was equally unreasonable and a terrible waste of lives to no purpose. It was a cruel weapon with certain death awaiting the pilot and a fiery death, or a lifetime of mutilation, to American seamen. In retrospect, it is obvious that all these deaths and mutilations accomplished nothing.

It is a poignant reminder of what the human mind is capable of under stress such as war provides. While the concept of the suicide pilot may be attributed to certain Japanese cultural traits (and thus dismissed as an Oriental quirk), it might be remembered that such suicide tactics were considered in Germany also.

The significance of Hiroshima and Nagasaki is these days muddied over in controversy. It is easy, now, to insist that these bombs should not have been dropped—or one should have been dropped on an open, unpopulated area. But if this last really makes sense, why was it necessary to drop yet a second bomb on a city? And even if that provided the proper face saving device for certain Japanese leaders, there were others fanatically willing to disrupt the surrender ceremonies and to continue the war despite Hiroshima and Nagasaki.

What these meant to the civilians in uniform at the time was that the war was over; to those poised for the projected invasion of Japan it meant the difference between life and death. Had this invasion come off it is highly likely that Japanese casualties would have been much higher than those so tragically accumulated at Hiroshima and Nagasaki.

The deeper significance of the "flame that burns to the bone" which seared these two helpless Japanese cities, and more importantly the people who lived (and died) there—for cities can be rebuilt, but every human life is unique—the deeper significance is that such a flame can now be dispatched to practically any city on earth. The argument over the rightness or the wrongness of Hiroshima is now really academic; it happened and no amount of argument can make it unhappen. The argument is now whether man is willing to let it happen again, knowing as he should what this weapon did (and refinements can do even more) and how wars really never end as they began.

The only constants are death, tragedy, devastation —and waste.

*New York, N.Y.*                                              E.J.

# WINGS OF
# FIRE

# BOOK **I**
# Target Germany

*Give me four years and I promise you, you won't recognize your towns!*

—ADOLF HITLER

# I

# BLUE MEDITERRANEAN SKIES

ALL roads theoretically led to Berlin—even those that seemed to lead to Rome.

The low road would run painfully and erratically through north Africa, bridge the Mediterranean into Sicily, and cross the three-mile Strait of Messina onto the toe of Italy. The high road would traverse the hostile sky from Britain's Bomber Command and Eighth Air Force bases in East Anglia. With bases in Italy, the reasoning went, it would be possible to strike at Germany from two directions along the high road. To many, strategists and non-combatants alike, the skirmishing in the Mediterranean appeared to be a roundabout route to Berlin, even by air.

It was the bumbling Mussolini who inadvertently brought attention to the Mediterranean theater with an ill-advised invasion of Greece on October 28, 1940. Three weeks before, Hitler himself revealed an Axis interest in the Balkan-Mediterranean area when he unilaterally moved German troops into Rumanian oil fields to assure the German war machine a source of fuel and lubricants. At the same time he flanked his other ally, Russia, the invasion plans of which were already in progress. This establishment of a *Festung* (fortress) Ploesti was smoothly accomplished because of an "understand-

ing" with Rumanian dictator General Ion Antonescu, a devout Nazi.

Mussolini, envious of Hitler's run of victories, longed for one of his own. With Italian-dominated Albania as a springboard he had hoped to occupy Greece, making a triumphal entry as Hitler had into Czechoslovakia before the war. Also, Mussolini wished to bring off his triumph alone, without any aid from Hitler. With the Rumanian take-over fresh in his mind, Mussolini ordered his troops across the Albanian border into Greece. There was no puppetlike Antonescu to smooth the way, and the Italian legions, met by stiff Greek resistance, barely made it across the border. This was bad enough, but worse followed: Mussolini's bungle had triggered British intervention in Greece. Hitler did not wish to have British bomber bases within range of the Ploesti oil fields. By the turn of the year, with Italian troops pushed back into Albania, Hitler realized he would have to strike. This brought the spotlight to the Balkans and the Mediterranean, diffusing the German forces further.

Italy's belated, rather reluctant entry into the war had also activated a vast, sprawling battleground across north and northeast Africa. The first six months, following Italy's declaration of war upon

*General Ion Antonescu, dictator of Rumania and a Hitler puppet, greets General Kurt Pflugbeil, chief of Luftflotte 1. The Luftwaffe had come to Rumania to protect the Ploesti airfields from the British and Hitler's "ally," Russia.* (H. J. NOWARRA)

*In the foreground Mussolini beams down upon marching Italian soldiers in Greece in the spring of 1941; in the background is the reason for the smile, Hitler, who had to send German troops into Greece to win the war for Mussolini there.* (NATIONAL ARCHIVES)

Britain and the Free French, the fighting in north Africa was sporadic and tentative. But led by Marshal Rodolfo Graziani, Italian forces moved eastward out of the Italian colony of Libya into Egypt on September 13, 1940, clearly with the Suez Canal as the objective. Although Graziani's troops outnumbered Lieutenant General Sir Archibald Wavell's forces by about five to one, the Italians advanced only sixty miles into Egypt, established defensive positions, and waited. The British were sorely disappointed that Graziani had not doubled the thrust, for awaiting him near Mersa Matruh was the Western Desert Force's 7th Armored Force, eager to strike.

While Graziani waited to see what Wavell would do, Mussolini began stirring up the Mediterranean with his vain Grecian misadventure. British troops were sent from Egypt to occupy Crete in the eastern Mediterranean and Lemnos in the Aegean Sea off the Dardanelles, as well as the Greek mainland around Athens. These latter sites served as bases for the Gladiator and Blenheim squadrons (Nos. 30, 80, 84, and 211 Squadrons) also shifted from Africa. Handicapped by weather and terrain, the pilots of these squadrons operated in close co-operation with the Greek forces over the battle lines, besides bombing Italian air bases in Albania.

From Malta, too, came aid to the Greeks and discomfort for the Italians. When war came to the Mediterranean Malta, strategically centered in the sea, could hardly be regarded as a hornet's nest of air power. Its total force consisted of five aged Fairey "Swordfish" (which crews affectionately called "the Stringbag") and even more ancient de Havilland "Queen Bees" (a variant of the Tiger Moth) and four Gladiators. One of the latter was soon damaged beyond repair and the three remaining Gladiators operated against the Regia Aeronautica (Italian Air Force) for several weeks so effectively that their estimated number was thought to be twenty-five. The Gladiators became celebrated on Malta under the names of *Faith, Hope,* and *Charity.*

Also operating out of Malta was the carrier *Illustrious,* equipped with "Stringbags" of Fleet Air Arm. On the night of November 11, 1940, the Swordfish of the *Illustrious* swooped down upon the Italian fleet in anchor at Taranto and dropped their torpedoes despite a high concentration of antiaircraft fire and a balloon barrage. In a few moments the

*Fairey "Swordfish" of Fleet Air Arm; Swordfish of the British carrier* Illustrious *crippled the Italian fleet at Taranto and demonstrated to the Japanese the possibility of destroying ships in a shallow harbor—Pearl Harbor, to be specific. The "Stringbag" was a lumbering but well-loved aircraft whose pilots harassed Italian and German ships from British bases in Malta.*

(U. S. AIR FORCE)

balance of naval power in the central Mediterranean shifted as half the battleship strength of the Italian fleet was knocked out of action for a half year. (It was this performance by aircraft upon ships in port that inspired the Japanese tactics at Pearl Harbor).

A month later Graziani in Egypt learned what the British planned to do. On December 9 Wavell launched an offensive which drove the Italians out of Egypt, across northern Libya into Bedafomm (south of Benghazi), where by February 7, 1941, the remnants of the Italian Tenth Army were rounded up. More than 130,000 prisoners were taken, along with hundreds of tanks and guns as well as other spoils. With advance outposts established deeper into Libya at El Agheila, the British planned to drive on to the port of Tripoli and perhaps complete the elimination of Italian forces in north Africa, but this was upset when British troops were withdrawn for the fighting in Greece (where Hitler had finally decided to intervene on January 19). Even so, the Italians were in deep trouble in Africa too.

Hitler again provided succor, this time in the person of Lieutenant General Erwin Rommel and the troops of the Afrika Korps. To accomplish his mis-

*The popular "Desert Fox," Erwin Rommel, visiting front-line Afrika Korps troops in March 1941, around* *the time he began to push the British back across north Africa into Egypt.* (H. J. NOWARRA)

sion Rommel could draw upon Fliegerkorps X, based on Sicily and commanded by General Hans Ferdinand Geisler. Rallying the remnants of the Italian forces, which were bolstered by German panzer troops and motorized divisions, Rommel began pushing the British out of Libya and back toward Cairo and, beyond that, the Suez Canal.

Rommel had arrived in Tripoli on February 12, 1941, and was ready to open his offensive by March 24. Thus began an oscillatory warfare that shifted back and forth across the deserts of Libya and Egypt and in which Rommel impressed the world, and particularly the British, with his wily generalship. The desert war was primarily one of armored vehicles, of tanks and movement. Rommel very quickly proved himself to be a master tactician, skilled in the art of thrust, parry, and surprise; his skill encompassed also the ability to improvise, to

exploit the situation as it developed in the field. He was often seen either in the vanguard of his panzers, which endeared him to his own men as well as to his enemies, or reconnoitering the wasted battleground in his Storch observation plane.

When Rommel sprang into action neither he nor the British were very strong in the air. Mussolini could take the blame for the one and credit for the other: the British stripped much of their air power in north Africa for the diversion in Greece and Fliegerkorps X was expected to assist in the Balkans as well as in Africa. One of its prime functions was to harass the British on Malta in order to keep the supply routes into Tripoli open. So it was that Air Marshal Sir Arthur M. Longmore, Commander, RAF, Middle East, could muster only four squadrons (and two of these of about half strength). Two were fighter squadrons: No. 3 Royal

Australian Air Force Squadron, equipped with Gladiators and later with Hurricanes; No. 73 Squadron (Cobber Kain's old unit), with its Hurricanes. No. 6 Squadron with its Lysanders was to be employed in reconnaissance, and No. 55 Squadron with its Blenheims would double in reconnaissance and bombardment.

Geisler dispatched planes to Africa for Rommel's use; they numbered a little over a hundred, mainly Ju-87 Stukas, with about thirty Me-110s and an equal number of Me-109Es of Jagdgeschwader 27. A few Ju-88s rounded out the force, under the command of Fliegerführer Afrika, Generalmajor Stephan Frölich. Considering the distances and the conditions under which aircraft were operated in the desert, it was a modest force, and Rommel was forced to depend upon his own genius for improvisation.

Beginning with Rommel's attack in late March of 1941, the desert war swayed across north Africa like a giant scythe: striking at Wavell's positions, Rommel pushed to the point at which Graziana had left off in 1940. Then Wavell was relieved by General Sir Claude J. E. Auchinleck. When he was ready for his counteroffensive, the Western Desert Force was redesignated the Eighth Army. Auchinleck, in turn, pushed Rommel back into Libya by December 1941. The pendulum made another swing when the Afrika Korps went over to the offensive

again on January 21, 1942; by the end of June Rommel was positioned at El Alamein, less than a hundred miles from Alexandria. His troops, like the British, were exhausted; supply lines were overextended and reinforcements were not forthcoming because Hitler needed them desperately in Russia, where brutal fighting had been in progress for a year.

Despite the precarious condition of the weakened Afrika Korps, Rommel, now a field marshal, was determined to press on. Mussolini, it was rumored, had already made plans for an entry into Cairo on a white horse. While neither Mussolini nor his white charger concerned him, Rommel believed he had the British "on the run" and he hoped to run them into Cairo in ten more days of fighting. But his own troops had already endured a month of heavy combat without rest and the British, though beaten and weary also, dug in at El Alamein. They took comfort in the proximity of their sources of supply and the RAF bases in Egypt. At this juncture General Sir Harold Alexander replaced Auchinleck as Commander in Chief, Middle East, and Lieutenant General Bernard Law Montgomery assumed command of the Eighth Army.

Summoning up the characteristic magisterial courage of the man who is given life-or-death decisions over the lives of others, Montgomery, self-centered, self-sufficient, and self-assured, announced, "Give

*A desert Stuka; the north African campaign gave the Ju-87 another chance after its failure in the Battle of Britain. It proved to be an excellent tank buster if not a worthy opponent of the Spitfire or Hurricane.*

(U. S. AIR FORCE)

*A desert Messerschmitt 109E. This plane, though fitted with shackles for a drop tank, is not yet equipped with a tropical filter.* (H. J. NOWARRA)

*Desert life: ground crew plays cards, with the JG 27 Messerschmitt in desert camouflage in the background. The plane has the longer special desert filter attached to the fuselage near the nose.* (H. J. NOWARRA)

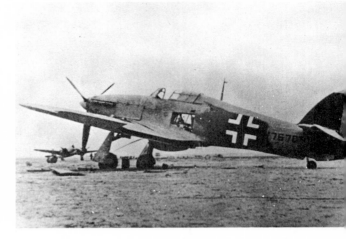

*Prize of the desert war: a captured Hurricane taken when Rommel's Afrika Korps overran a British airdrome. It was, in turn, taken back when the British took back Gambut in Cyrenaica, east of Tobruk.* (H. J. NOWARRA)

me three weeks and I can defeat the Boche. Give me a month and I can chase him out of Africa." Whereupon he took two months just getting prepared to drive Rommel out of Africa—and then he would not do it alone.

Stubbornly the British held the Alamein line, and the Germans were halted in their push toward Alexandria. During the stalemate Rommel flew to Germany, where he reported to Hitler. He said that the bombers of the RAF's Western Desert Air Force were ripping up his panzers with 40-mm., American-made shells.

"Impossible," Göring interjected. "Nothing but latrine rumors. All the Americans can make are razor blades and refrigerators."

"I only wish, Herr Reichsmarschall," Rommel answered, "that we were issued similar razor blades."

More substantial than razor blades, although not yet in any real numbers, were the American men and planes which had been arriving piecemeal and at times pell-mell in the Middle East. Following the Japanese attack on Pearl Harbor and Hitler's subsequent declaration of war on the United States, that aid which had been coming into Britain and the Mediterranean through Lend-Lease was, in theory at least, stepped up.

The first Americans to arrive manned the Liberators of Colonel Harry Halverson's "Project No. 63," en route to China bases from which it was planned

they would bomb Tokyo itself. While in Khartoum, the Sudan, Halverson learned that their intended base in China had been overrun by the Japanese, and upon the official declaration of war upon Rumania on June 5, 1942, it was decided to divert Halverson's Liberators to bomb Ploesti. The mission, the first time any American aircraft bombed enemy targets in Europe, took place on June 11-12. A dozen B-24s (of thirteen dispatched) succeeded in bombing the oil fields, although without doing much damage. No men were lost, although four Liberators had landed in Turkey (the crews were interned) and another was crash-landed. Those B-24s which had survived the mission and the desert maintenance problems (about seventeen of the original twenty-three) were pressed into service bombing Italian supply ships in the Mediterranean as well as enemy-held ports.

Additional American units began to trickle into Africa. Major General Lewis H. Brereton arrived on June 28 in Fayid, Egypt, with seven Flying Fortresses (survivors of the 7th Bombardment Group's 9th Squadron and orphans of the Japanese storm in the Pacific). Brereton had been ordered out of India, where he had commanded the Tenth Air Force, and placed in command of the United States Army Middle East Air Force; later it would be designated the Ninth Air Force.

Additional reinforcements arrived: the 98th Bombardment Group (H) with B-24s, the 12th Bombardment Group (M) with B-25s, and the 57th Fighter Group with P-40Fs. Before the green American units went into combat they were given full benefit of the accumulated experience of the men of the Desert Air Force. Fortunately, too, Brereton and the Air Commander in Chief, Middle East (replacing Air Chief Marshal Sir Arthur Longmore), Air Marshal Sir Arthur Tedder, were advocates of inter-Allied co-operation. Reflecting the attitudes of the chiefs, the British and American units blended remarkably.

"The Americans work in very well with our squadrons," Tedder wrote to Chief of Air Staff Sir Charles Portal. "They now [October 21, 1942] have their own fighter wing with two squadrons, [64th and 15th] who have already shown up well in combat. Their third fighter squadron [66th] which has had more experience and which we can make reasonably mobile, is in one of our own fighter wings [No. 239] and will go forward. They are learning from us and we are learning from them. . . ."

When Montgomery was finally ready to pounce, just two days after Tedder had written to Portal—on October 23, 1942—he believed he had the manpower and that his men were trained to use their equipment. His postponement, despite Churchill's goading from time to time, had not been in vain. The Eighth Army enjoyed about a two to one superiority in manpower over Rommel; Montgomery also had more tanks, guns, and aircraft.

That Hitler finally realized that north Africa was more than a side show was revealed when he withdrew Field Marshal Albert Kesselring from the

*The war in the desert was characterized by the absence of front lines, by movement and position. An Me-110 crew prepares for a reconnaissance mission over British positions in Cyrenaica.* (H. J. NOWARRA)

*Night-fighting Hurricanes near Suez. Equipped with 40-mm. cannon the Hurricane proved a formidable enemy of Rommel's tanks.*

(IMPERIAL WAR MUSEUM, LONDON)

Russian Front to command the Mediterranean. Kesselring had commanded Luftflotte 2 during the Battle of Britain. Also drained away from Russia were the staff and remnants of Fliegerkorps II (commanded by Göring's old World War I comrade, Bruno Lörzer). By this time Fliegerkorps X had been withdrawn from Sicily and into the Balkans.

Kesselring on paper may have appeared to have an impressive array of air power at his disposal. But as Commander in Chief, South, the about 3000 planes under his command were dispersed quite tenuously throughout the vast Mediterranean and the Balkans. And the new Fliegerführer Afrika, General der Luftwaffe Hoffmann von Waldau, could count on little more than 600 of those rather widely scattered forces. On the eve of Montgomery's offensive he had about 380 fighters, of which most were Italian and only 165 Me-109Fs; he had about 150 bombers, plus 75 Italian attack planes and a few seaplanes and reconnaissance aircraft. But of these only about half were operational, thanks in part to the disruption of Axis supply routes into north Africa by Allied air and sea effort.

Opposing Waldau was Air Marshal Sir Arthur Coningham, commander of the Western Desert Air Force, with some twelve hundred planes in Egypt and Palestine, predominantly fighters. Of these, more than eight hundred were ready to fly when Montgomery was ready to move. At the same time there was a small force of the USAAF on hand: forty B-24s, six B-17s, thirty-five B-25s, and forty-nine P-40s. Another thirty-five, a sampling of all types, were not operational at the time.

So it was that even before the battle opened the Luftwaffe and Rommel were at a numerical disadvantage. In fact, Montgomery's attack came at a time when Rommel was in Germany on sick leave. His deputy at the head of the Afrika Korps, General Georg von Stumme, died of a heart attack during the opening phase of the offensive and Rommel was rushed back to El Alamein. His appraisal and fear of the power of the RAF, which he had tried to explain to Hitler and a skeptical Göring, was revealed in the shambles of his army, the smashed panzers; El Alamein had been blasted into a graveyard of tanks. Luftwaffe airfields had been bombed and strafed so that Montgomery's troops could move forward unmolested by enemy aircraft. British and American bombers attacked shipping at Tobruk and later Benghazi and Tripoli.

Night-operating RAF Wellingtons bombed German gun positions and troop concentrations, and behind the front the Hurricanes of No. 73 Squadron swooped down upon the German and Italian troops out of the dusk to harry them and to shoot up their vehicles. Specially equipped (with a 40-mm. cannon under the wing) "tank busters," Hurricane IIDs of No. 6 Squadron and No. 7 Squadron (South African Air Force), scourged the Afrika Korps tanks.

The decisive ground fighting, under the air umbrella, was a triumph for Montgomery. Rommel fell back. "British air superiority," he stated, "threw to the winds all our operational and tactical rules. . . . The strength of the Anglo-American Air Force was, in all the battles to come, the deciding factor." But Hitler would not hear of this. "In the situation in which you now find yourself, there can be no other consideration than to hold fast, never retreat, hurl every gun and every man into the fray. . . . You can show your troops no other way than that which leads to victory or death."

With such chilling counsel from his Führer, Rommel, more battlewise, found his own solution to "the situation." He retreated. His forces began withdrawing on November 2 with Montgomery's troops in pursuit; by the fifth it was obvious that a new "desert fox" had come upon the scene. Strewn in the wake of the once invincible Afrika Korps were such expendables as burned-out tanks and other vehicles, victims of the flying tank busters and of British "Crusader" tanks. Left behind also were the Italian infantry (also regarded as expendable by the Germans) and German dead.

As Rommel recoiled toward Tunisia he received further disheartening news: Anglo-American landings had been made on November 8, 1942, in French Morocco and Algeria in northwest Africa. This was Operation Torch, led by Lieutenant General Dwight D. Eisenhower. Despite token resistance by the French the invasion forces were speedily landed and drove eastward for Tunisia.

With the advent of Torch came the introduction of New air units into the Mediterranean. "Borrowing" from the Eighth Air Force's not very considerable strength in England, the Twelfth Air Force was activated for the Torch landings and placed under command of Major General James H. Doolittle. From the Eighth Air Force (still mounting missions upon German-held France despite poor weather and small forces) Doolittle had been given two B-17 groups (the 97th and 301st Bombardment Groups); he also brought two P-38 units (1st and 14th Fighter Groups), the 33rd Fighter Group (P-40s), two groups of Spitfires with American pilots (31st and 52nd Fighter Groups), as well as the 15th Bombardment Squadron (L). The C-47s of Air Transport Command came to replenish the Allies with men, parts, and supplies.

Brereton, meanwhile, commanded the Ninth Air Force (successor to the U. S. Army Middle East Air Force), which moved in from the east with Montgomery while Doolittle's Twelfth came from the west with Eisenhower. Thus were the Afrika Korps and the hapless Luftwaffe strangled from both directions. Even so, the fight did not immedi-

*Flying over the pyramids of Egypt, this Air Transport Command C-47 represents one of the aspects of the United States into the war: supply and transportation. Rommel's lack of these decided the war in Africa.* (U. S. AIR FORCE)

*Mitchell medium bombers over the north African desert on the way to bomb German positions, supply routes, and harbors.* (U. S. AIR FORCE)

*Luftwaffe air base at El Aouina, Tunisia, under bombing attack by the Allies. German planes have been* *caught on the ground, some of them as they were taking off to defend the base, and burn uselessly.*
(U. S. AIR FORCE)

ately go out of either and until the Allies held air superiority over Tunisia (March 1943) the Messerschmitts and Stukas, and the panzers, took their toll. But it was a lost cause.

As the jaws of the Allied pincers closed on Tunisia, the Anglo-American air units again underwent transmutation with the formation of the Northwest African Air Forces under Major General Carl Spaatz. The NAAF merged both British and American units for a concentrated push on Rommel. Doolittle co-ordinated the heavy bombardment in the theater and Coningham the tactical operations. Tedder remained in over-all command in the Mediterranean. It was the beginning of the end for Rommel.

The Luftwaffe in Africa suffered too. Its bases were bombed and strafed. Its supply routes, whether by sea or air, were torn to bits by Allied

bombers and fighters. One attempt to fly aid to Rommel ended in disaster when on April 18, 1943, a large formation of German transports, about a hundred Ju-52s, escorted by Italian Macchi C-202s, Me-109s, and Me-110s, was intercepted off Cape Bon by Allied fighters. These were forty-six P-40s of the Ninth Air Force's 57th Fighter Group, a dozen P-40s of the 324th Group's 314th Squadron, and twelve Spitfires of the RAF's No. 92 Squadron. The latter were providing top cover for the American P-40s.

The Junkers were skimming the Mediterranean in three perfect V-formations about a hundred feet above the sea. Their mixed escort numbered about thirty fighters. One pilot upon sighting the trimotored transports thought it to be "the most beautiful formation I've ever seen. It seemed like a shame to

the German fighters fared poorly, flying around in "a confused and inferior fashion, possibly due to the low altitude. . . ." As the Warhawks destroyed the Junkers, the Spitfires and the remaining P-40s took on the Me-109s and Macchis.

When the battle was over, all but six of the P-40s and one Spitfire returned to their home bases. The German formations, however, were heavily decimated. Claims were necessarily high (partly because of the confusion of the fighting), ranging from seventy to fifty Ju-52s (the Germans admitted to the loss of fifty-one in addition to sixteen or more fighters of the escort. The massacre was but the climax to a deliberate campaign (Operation Flax) to sever Rommel's supply line into Tunis.

A prelude to that terrible Palm Sunday had occurred only a week before when B-25s, with P-38 escort, on a shipping sweep came upon some thirty-five Axis planes in an air convoy over the Sicilian strait. Both Mitchells and Lightnings bore in for the attack and accounted for twenty-five enemy aircraft, twenty-one of them Ju-52s carrying precious supplies for Rommel in Tunisia.

*Scourge of the Afrika Korps and the Luftwaffe: P-38s above the African desert. The heavy Lockheed fighter earned the name* der Gabelschwanz Teufel *("Forked-tail Devil") in north Africa. It was an especially devastating tank buster.* (ALLIE MOSZYK)

break it up. Reminded me of a beautiful propaganda film."

Captain James Curl, leading the low squadron of P-40s, however, was not moved by the beauty of the formations. Leaving the Spitfires, led by Squadron Leader Neville Duke, and a squadron of P-40s to handle the German fighters, Curl led three squadrons of P-40s in an attack upon the transports. With a wild whooping the Americans dived into the neat formations. The ensuing ten minutes have come to be known as "the Palm Sunday Massacre," as the Warhawks slashed the Ju-52s into flaming ribbons. The slow, clumsy Junkers crashed into the sea or smashed onto the beaches of Cape Bon. Even

*Several pilots who had participated in the "Palm Sunday Massacre," members of the 66th Squadron, 57th Fighter Group. Captain James M. Curl, who had led the low squadron in the attack upon the German transports, squats in center with a cigarette and drink in hand.* (U. S. AIR FORCE)

*Wrecking Rommel's supply line: B-25s, with P-38 escort, come upon Ju-52s in the Sicilian Straits on the* *way to Tunisia with supplies. In minutes twenty-five of the thirty-five German transports were destroyed.*
(U. S. AIR FORCE)

*By sea and by air the beleaguered Germans in north Africa were denied supplies by air power. A munitions ship blows up in the Mediterranean off Bizerte after being hit by Allied bombers (left). A giant Messer-* *schmitt 323, a six-engined transport with a wing span of 180 feet used for carrying supplies and troops, recoils under an air attack on an ill-fated run for Tunisia.*
(U. S. AIR FORCE)

Trapped in the massive pinch, his supplies cut off, his troops exhausted, Rommel was incapable of continuing the fight. It was on May 13, 1943, that Colonel General Dietloff Jurgen von Arnim surrendered the surviving Axis forces in Tunisia; it was an inglorious end for the once proud Afrika Korps. About 240,000 troops (of which 125,000 were German) had chosen not to fight to the death according to the Führer's wishes. Rommel, three days before the surrender, had escaped by air to Germany. At the time it was all that the Luftwaffe could do for him.

The Luftwaffe lost much in Africa, not the least of which was one of its brighter stars. He was twenty-two-year-old (in 1942) Hans-Joachim Marseille of Jagdgeschwader 27. His sunny disposition and prankish nature endeared Marseille to his squadron mates, if not always to his commanders. His skill as a pilot (first demonstrated during the Battle of Britain) and amazing marksmanship eventually earned Marseille the rank of *Oberleutnant* (first lieutenant). His Me-109, painted in desert colors with a large yellow 14 on its sides, was known throughout north Africa. If German records can be trusted Marseille destroyed no less than 158 Allied aircraft before he died.

Unlike most fighter pilots he had been a master of the deflection shot. Approaching from the side (most pilots preferred the classic tail attack), Marseille by a feat of mental computation was able to gauge the speed of the enemy plane relative to his own and knew the moment when he must fire his guns. The laws of physics did the rest.

Not even Marseille's youth, however, shielded him from the ravages of daily battle at high altitudes. When his score had reached 101 (he had exceeded the magical 100), Marseille landed and when his ground crew rushed to his plane to assist him out, he waved them away. His drawn face was a pasty white, and when he finally pulled himself from the cockpit, his hands shook and he moved like an old man. Marseille was finished for the time being as a fighter pilot.

After an enforced two-month leave Marseille returned to command his old 3 Staffel of JG 27 as a *Hauptmann* (captain) late in August 1942. It was about this time that Montgomery was preparing the Eighth for his push on Rommel. By September 1, obviously back in fighting trim, Marseille in the course of three sorties had shot down seventeen planes, most of them P-40s. There were plenty of enemy aircraft, for while Montgomery waited to strike at El Alamein, the RAF came over from Egypt.

On September 30 Marseille led his squadron to escort Stukas on a raid. Although no enemy planes were encountered, he ran into trouble. Smoke suddenly was seen belching from his cockpit and his engine burst into flame. Unable to see, Marseille nevertheless stayed with his plane, hoping, no doubt, that before he bailed out he could get as close to base as possible. He counted also on the plane not blowing up in mid-air.

With his wingman Rainer Pöttgen flying alongside radioing instructions, Marseille attempted to direct the 109 toward El Alamein. Before they reached the airfield, Marseille realized he would never make it and would have to get out of the stricken plane. He flipped it over on its back, released the canopy, then dropped out. As he left the cockpit, and as the plane dipped downward and fell away, the tail surfaces struck Marseille in the chest. His parachute never opened as the young ace fell onto the desert below.

## II

Hitler left Mussolini to flounder around in the Mediterranean for six months before he ordered the Wehrmacht and the Luftwaffe (specifically Lohr's Luftflotte 4 based in friendly Antonescu's Rumania) to strike. On April 6, 1941, with Rommel again on the offensive in north Africa, German troops invaded Yugoslavia and Greece. The curtain rose on a typical scene: Luftwaffe bombers destroyed the center of Belgrade, killing seventeen thousand people. This was in punishment for otherwise co-operative Yugoslavia's refusal to permit German supplies and troops bound for Turkey use of its railroads. Within two weeks Yugoslavia capitulated to the blitzkrieg.

A week later, on April 23, the Greek government surrendered also. The survivors of the small British force that had been attracted to Greece as Hitler had feared by Mussolini's invasion was withdrawn. The decision was made, however, to establish an

*Hans-Joachim Marseille, the "Star of Africa," whose final victory score before his death totaled 158.*

army on the island of Crete, southeast of Greece and almost directly north of the north African battlegrounds. Crete was a strategic island, indeed, and Churchill himself argued for its defense. Under Major General Bernard Freyberg a force of about forty-two thousand—British, Australian, New Zealand, and Greek troops—was established on Crete.

Hitler coveted the little island also and wished to make it "the crowning glory" of the Balkan campaign. He had said, in fact, when writing to Mussolini chiding him "with the warm heart of a friend" about the Grecian blunder, that he himself would not have taken that action "without a previous, lightning occupation of Crete, and to this end I wanted to bring you practical proposals—namely, to employ a German paratroop division, and an airborne division."

Having been denied the opportunity by his friend's precipitate invasion the previous October, Hitler ordered the aerial invasion of Crete in May. Curiously, Lohr himself had suggested such an investment of Crete once the Balkans were overrun. Göring, then based in Austria, rather liked the idea, for since the Battle of Britain, he was eager for a spectacular job for the Luftwaffe. Hitler, of course, approved, but

*German paratroops taking a British gun position, Crete, May 1941.* (H. J. NOWARRA)

*A stricken Ju-52, having dropped its cargo of German paratroopers into the inferno that is Heraklion aerodrome, falls burning to earth. This is the second wave of the assault on Crete, Hitler's "crowning glory" of the Balkan campaign, Operation Mercury. For the hapless German air-borne troops, Mercury was a winged messenger of death. After Crete—although it was taken by the Germans at great cost—German paratroops would never be capable of participating in any major future operations. Casualties were so high that these units were crippled for the rest of the war.*

(IMPERIAL WAR MUSEUM, LONDON)

not before remarking that *he* had thought of the idea several months before. He visualized Crete as a rampart to the Balkans as well as a base for aerial operations against Britain's African strongholds: Alexandria, Cairo, Suez, among other points in the eastern Mediterranean. Certain other voices, among them Keitel's, were raised suggesting that an air-borne invasion of the British colony of Malta, an island to the west in the central Mediterranean, might be more useful. But Hitler had his heart set on the "crowning glory."

It was code-named Operation Mercury and fell to

*Ceremonies celebrating the taking of Crete; survivors of the German 1st Parachute Regiment stand at attention to receive honors. The cost of taking Crete from the air all but ended German full-scale paratroop activity for the rest of the war.* (H. J. NOWARRA)

Kurt Student's newly formed Fliegerkorps XI, consisting of paratroops and air-borne troops. The first large-scale invasion of the war opened in the morning of May 20, 1941, when after an initial bombardment of the drop areas, nearly five hundred Ju-52s appeared over Crete dropping parachutists and pulling gliders. The plan also called for sea-borne convoys with reinforcements from the north, but which, as it eventuated, were driven off by the British Mediterranean Fleet. This was accomplished at great cost, however. The Mediterranean Fleet, operating to the north of Crete, was beyond the range of the RAF and within reach of Luftwaffe bombers and fighters of Richthofen's Fliegerkorps VIII based on the Greek mainland.

Thus did the entire investment of Crete devolve upon the air-borne troops. As with nearly all best-laid plans, a number of things went wrong with Mercury. Dust-laden airfields in Greece disrupted the takeoff of the Ju-52s; the first planes to leave stirred up clouds of dust that prevented subsequent takeoffs until the dust settled (a delay as long as twenty minutes). Another delay was caused by a shortage of fuel, during which the British, pre-warned by Intelligence, prepared for the invasion on Crete. Although the 28,000 troops on the island outnumbered the 15,000 air-borne troops committed to Mercury, the island garrison was exhausted after the Greek campaign itself and ill equipped. They could count upon only a dozen air-craft, Hurricanes and Gladiators mainly, while Richthofen commanded 650 aircraft, bombers and fighters, not counting transports and gliders.

The outcome was inevitable when the Ju-52s appeared over Maleme airfield, the major objective on Crete (this field lay at the western end of the island; other objectives, attacked by the second waves, were the airfields at Rethymnon and Heraklion, like Maleme on the north coast of Crete, but located near the center of the island).

After the initial bombardment by the bombers and strafing attacks by fighters, the Ju-52s released their gliders, which swooped down onto Maleme. Not all made good landings as they bounced into the unusually hilly terrain, splintering and tossing out their occupants. Some crashed into hillsides, injuring the troops they carried and killing some. Only the stunning effects of the preinvasion aerial attacks prevented the defenders from finishing the job of wiping out the glider troops. The Germans who had

landed safely began moving in on Maleme airfield.

The glider troops were followed by the parachutists, who jumped from low altitude to join in the fighting on the ground. The defenders fought back savagely and it appeared that taking Crete would be no simple matter. The decision was made to throw in more men. As the Junkers disgorged their cargoes, the island's defenders shot them to bits; one German battalion lost four hundred of its six hundred men. Casualties were inflicted either while the men dangled helplessly from their parachutes or when they were injured while landing in the unfamiliar rocky terrain. Some died as they vainly tried to extricate themselves from trees into which they had drifted; the rest fell in fighting with New Zealand troops.

And still they came on. A third wave of Ju-52s arrived in the afternoon of the second day, May 21, bringing the entire 100th Mountain Regiment. Maleme was by then precariously held by the Germans, but as the transports came in to land British artillery fire began to fall among them. Anti-aircraft shot the Junkers out of the sky and the artillery shattered them on the ground—and with them more German troops died.

The runway became a shambles of wrecked and burning aircraft; one divisional commander of the 100th Mountain Regiment said that "Maleme was like the gate of hell." A captured British tank was used to clear the wrecks off the runway to make way for those Junkers which had escaped the guns or were only damaged. By the end of the day there were no less than eighty wrecked Junkers along the edges of the runway.

To the weary defenders it appeared that Germany had an unlimited supply of manpower at Hitler's disposal, for despite the frightful slaughter, troops continued to pour in from the sky. Hitler's profligacy turned the tide; with Maleme taken, even more troops could be flown in. Exhausted, without air protection and supplies, it was obvious that the Crete garrison could not hold out. By May 24 General Freyberg realized the situation was hopeless. Three days later the ships of the Mediterranean Fleet appeared off the southern coast at Sphakia to evacuate the remaining defenders (more than fourteen thousand men, about half of the original number on Crete when the battle began) to Alexandria in Egypt.

Hitler had his "crowning glory." Crete had fallen

in ten days, but at what cost? More than 200 aircraft had been lost (119 of them Ju-52s), not counting the expendable gliders. More than 5000 German troops had died, of which 3600 were highly trained paratroopers. Crete had, in fact, eliminated the German parachute force from the rest of war. It had been a costly victory and an ironic one, especially after the center of the war in the Mediterranean shifted westward with the victories of Montgomery and the Torch landings of Eisenhower in north Africa the next year. Crete's strategic location was not what it once was; much more important was the island of Malta, still held by the British.

After the fall of Crete Hitler crowed, "There are no more unconquerable islands," conveniently and characteristically ignoring that island which lay across the English Channel. He had already become absorbed in his own massive blunder, Barbarossa, the invasion of Russia, which, thanks to Mussolini, had to be postponed while Hitler cleaned up in Greece and generally stabilized the Balkans. What was the Mediterranean to him when he planned to outgeneral Napoleon in a holy crusade against Communist Russia?

### III

Even as he denied the existence of "unconquerable islands," Hitler overlooked another: Malta, just to the south of Sicily in the central Mediterranean.

If Hitler chose to disregard Malta, astride the supply routes into north Africa, there were those more

*A Beaufighter such as was stationed on beleaguered Malta (an island Hitler chose to ignore) and had an important effect on the outcome of the war in the Mediterranean.* (IMPERIAL WAR MUSEUM, LONDON)

directly concerned who did not. Almost as soon as Italy declared war on Britain the Regia Aeronautica began its bombing runs from Sicily, less than sixty miles away, in June of 1940. By the end of the month the redoubtable *Faith, Hope,* and *Charity* were joined by a few Hurricanes, eventually more (some flown off British carriers), and Fleet Air Arm Swordfish, a Hudson, a Skua, as well as a handful of Wellingtons. It was possible then to peck away at Italian targets as the Italians rather half-heartedly bombed Malta.

It was when Hitler was convinced of Africa's importance—militarily nil, he believed, but if lost would have a "strong psychological effect on Italy" —that the strategic role of Malta was recognized. With the coming of the new year and the establishment of Fliegerkorps X in Sicily Malta was fated to suffer the harsher attentions of the Luftwaffe. The island's fortunes were to fluctuate with those of the newly arrived Rommel. By March the residents and troops on Malta could expect nearly daily visits from Luftwaffe bombers. The arrival of new Hurricane IIs in April turned the balance toward the defenders, whose Mark I Hurricanes had been no match for the Me-109Fs. The next month further relief came with the gradual withdrawal of Fliegerkorps X into the Balkans. In the comparative lull additional reinforcements arrived: a few Martin "Marylands" to be used as reconnaissance planes, some Blenheims to replace the Wellingtons, and a squadron of Beaufighters. Malta had not become suddenly a great impregnable armed camp, but it was a formidable hornet's nest of the Mediterranean. And besides the tiny air force, Malta harbored cruisers, destroyers, and submarines.

By November 1941 the effect of Malta was felt even in Berlin, and directly in Russia. Maltese-based ships, submarines, and bombers had ripped at Italian convoys bringing troops, supplies, and fuel to Rommel. Fuel especially was a precious commodity in the mobile desert war. Because of this deficiency Rommel's offensive into Egypt petered out and while he was forced to wait, the British prepared to push him back into Libya whence he had come. Even the exhaustion of his troops would not have deterred Rommel from trying to reach Cairo at the time, flushed with victory as he was. But Malta had.

Hitler turned briefly from his map of Russia and realized what was occurring elsewhere. It was then,

*Street scene, Malta 1942. The city of Valetta under Nazi aerial siege. Hitler did not regard tiny Malta with the same strategic romantic respect as he did Crete, consequently Malta was never invaded by the Nazis. It eventually became a most strategic island as the war in the Mediterranean unfolded: it would cost him Africa, Sicily and finally Italy.*

late in 1941, that he sent Kesselring and Lörzer to the Mediterranean. As Commander in Chief, South, Kesselring was ordered by Hitler primarily to "obtain air and sea supremacy in the area between southern Italy and north Africa in order to establish safe shipping routes to Libya"; to accomplish this it would be "particularly important to suppress Malta." He was also to co-operate with German and Italian forces in north Africa and put a stop to enemy shipping in the Mediterranean.

Beginning in December 1941 Malta became the chief target of the Luftwaffe in the Mediterranean. The attacks intensified through the first of the year and reached a crescendo in April 1942, when the Luftwaffe bombed the little island as often as two hundred (and on two occasions more than three hundred) times a day. By April 12 Kesselring informed Hitler that Malta's air and naval bases had been eliminated.

It was a premature appraisal, but even Tedder when he visited Malta a few days later was not heartened by what he saw. Only six serviceable Hurricanes remained and the airfields were pocked and torn; the docks were blown into the sea and the city of Valetta was filled with rubble. With invasion all but imminent the defenders and civilians alike faced starvation. With the Luftwaffe persistently overhead no convoys had been able to break through since February. On April 20 the American carrier *Wasp,* however, arrived to deliver forty-

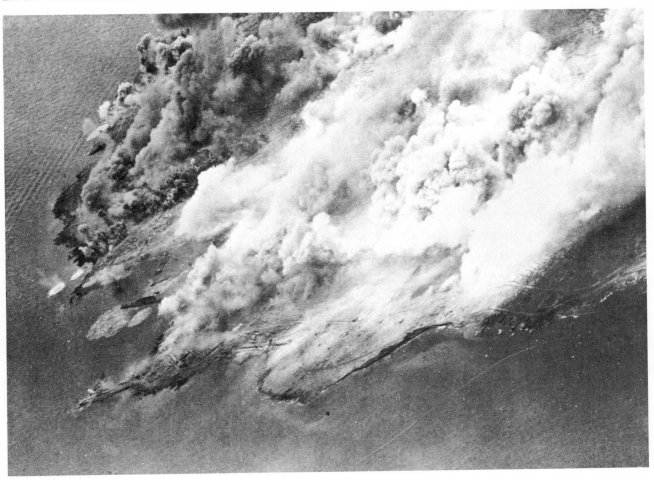

*Pantelleria, Italian island fortress between Tunis, north Africa, and Sicily, is taken out of the war by air power in Operation Corkscrew.* (U. S. AIR FORCE)

seven Spitfires. By the next day, after a night and day of bombing, only seventeen remained serviceable. The Spitfire, unlike the Hurricane, was superior to the Me-109F. When they arrived in sufficient numbers, it was hoped, the Luftwaffe's attacks would dwindle. On May 9 the *Wasp* in company with the British carrier *Eagle* dispatched sixty-four Spitfires (of which two were lost at sea en route) and within five minutes of arrival they were ready for action. The Spitfires did not solve Malta's problem, but a subtle change was imminent. "One lives here only to destroy the Hun and hold him at bay," one of the Spitfire pilots observed after a few days on Malta, "everything else, living conditions, sleep, food and all the ordinary standards of life have gone by the board. It all makes the Battle of

Britain and fighter-sweeps seem child's play in comparison. . . ."

Air Vice-Marshal Sir Hugh P. Lloyd, RAF commander on Malta, later wrote of that May 1942 that "Our diet was a slice and a half of very poor bread with jam for breakfast, bully beef for lunch with one slice of bread, and except for an additional slice of bread it was the same fare for dinner. . . . Officers and men slept in shelters, in caverns and dugouts, in quarries. . . ." The supply of ammunition and bombs was depleting. "Malta was faced," Lloyd concluded, "with the unpleasant fact of being starved and forced from lack of equipment into surrender. The middle of August was starvation date, and as we should all have been dead before relief arrived, the surrender date was much earlier. . . ."

On June 16, after a fierce air-sea battle, the first

*Pantelleria after Corkscrew. Italian and German air-craft destroyed in the bombardment of the island lie* *scattered in burned-out wreckage, never having got off the ground.* (U. S. AIR FORCE)

two merchantmen docked in Malta under a pro-tective cover of Spitfires. Despite the heavy losses, the proof was there that Malta would survive.

Developments in the camp of the enemy also as-sured the survival of the tiny island. Late in May Rommel, thanks to Kesselring's suppression of Malta, was on his way toward Cairo again. Plans for an invasion of Malta were postponed and units of the Luftwaffe were drawn away from Kesselring in expectation of the summer offensive in Russia.

The Italians, even Mussolini, continued to fret about Malta, but Hitler had lost interest again. He could point to the Afrika Korps and its victories, including the taking of Tobruk, which had held out for so long, and then the pressing on for Egypt. Even Rommel, who once offered to lead an assault upon Malta, was willing to dismiss the island from his mind. Egypt became the prize, but he was stopped at El Alamein, where he would meet with Mont-

gomery, who planned to "knock Rommel for a six" and "tidy up the battlefield."

When that occurred a recovered Malta contrib-uted to the defeat of the Afrika Korps in Tunisia in May 1943. Malta remained Britain's unsinkable aircraft carrier in the Mediterranean.

With north Africa in Allied hands, British and American strategists felt they could turn to Europe for the next assault. Although Stalin clamored for a Second Front, the Anglo-American leaders could not visualize a direct assault upon the coast of France at the time. Churchill believed that the Russians would benefit from, and that the Allies could undertake, a strike at what he called, in one of his less felicitous phrases, "the soft underbelly of Europe": Mussolini's Italy.

Unlike Hitler, the Allies chose not to overlook the islands of the central Mediterranean. To get at the underbelly two islands would have to be taken:

*The port of Messina, Sicily, a German stronghold, was heavily bombed by Northwest Africa Air Forces and the Ninth Air Force. Large-scale bombings were car-* *ried out before landings were attempted by ground troops. Sicily was the step before Italy itself; Messina was the heaviest hit of Sicilian targets.*

(U. S. AIR FORCE)

Pantelleria and Sicily. Tiny Pantelleria, about half-way between Tunisia and Sicily, the Italians referred to as their Gibraltar. While this was a rather grand conception of the island, it did lay in the path of any invader bound for Sicily. The very nature of Pantelleria—hilly, eroded, few beaches, a soil with a heavy volcanic ash content—made it a poor objective for amphibious troops. Its single airfield could put up aircraft that would spot any invasion forces far out at sea. Besides being heavily fortified, Pantelleria was garrisoned by ten thousand troops. While the Allies attempted to "neutralize" them, German and Italian forces in Italy could have time to prepare for their coming on the mainland.

After weighing the possibilities it was decided to bomb Pantelleria into submission from the air: Operation Corkscrew, beginning May 18, 1943.

Some fifty medium bombers and the same number of fighter-bombers opened the campaign by striking at the main harbor area and the airfield. By June 11, the date set for the invasion, British and American aircraft had dropped six thousand tons of bombs on Pantelleria. German and Italian fighters attempted to interfere with the assault, but with little success because of escorting Allied fighters.

In the evening before D-Day Mussolini had been informed by Vice-Admiral Gino Pavesi that "the Allied bombing could be endured no longer"; the Italian dictator himself authorized the surrender of Pantelleria.

When the assault troops began landing on the island the next morning a white flag appeared on a hill. The invasion proceeded with minimal resistance —the single Allied casualty being an infantryman who was bitten by a jackass.

For the first time in the history of warfare a sizable military objective had been taken by air power alone. True, it was a small objective (about forty-two square miles), but the significance of the fact was great and parlous.

In July Sicily, the next island steppingstone into Italy, became the setting for the first sizable Allied air-borne operation. The Luftwaffe, already bombed out of Sicily by Allied bombers based in Africa and Malta, did not interfere with this phase of the air and sea invasion. But everything else did: high wind, flak, smoke from preinvasion bombing, trigger-happy seamen, and fate. As the Germans learned at Crete, much could go wrong. In the night of July 9, 1943, gliders towed from Africa by C-47s were released over Sicily. In the near fiasco, because of an unfortunate high wind, only twelve gliders actually came to earth in the designated landing zone; about sixty-five swept into the sea and hundreds of the heavily laden troops of the 1st Airborne Division drowned. The remaining fifty-six gliders scattered widely over Sicily. Fortunately the defenders were more confused than the dispersed air-borne troops, mistaking the dispersal for a truly full-scale invasion. The Italian defenders, disheartened, could not bring themselves to fight with any resolution.

The glider drop, as at Crete, was followed by paratroopers. These, the American 82nd Airborne Division, were also scattered all over the place. Even as this ensued, a great convoy of ships carry-

*Sicily, August 1943. General Dwight D. Eisenhower and Air Force General Henry H. Arnold at Castelvetrano airfield after the fall of Sicily.*

(U. S. AIR FORCE)

ing the British Seventh Army and the American Eighth Army (under command of two new military stars, Bernard Montgomery and Major General George Patton) sailed forth from widespread ports, but mainly from north Africa, under an umbrella of Pantelleria-based P-40s of the 33rd Fighter Group and Malta Spitfires. The convoy reached Sicily untouched by Axis aircraft.

Co-operative efforts between the Luftwaffe and the Regia Aeronautica had deteriorated to nearly zero, so that no truly concerted attempt was made to interfere with the amphibious assault. The seaborne invasion proceeded more smoothly than had the one from the air, and within twenty-four hours all beachheads had been secured. In Berlin Goeb-

*Albert Kesselring (here a prisoner of war), former commander of Luftflotte 1 (Poland), Luftflotte 2 (Battle of Britain and Russia), and commander in chief of all German forces in Italy.* (U. S. ARMY)

mans fought tenaciously and brutally—Italian deserters were shot without mercy. But they were overwhelmed by sheer numbers and equipment and pushed into the northeast corner of Sicily around Messina. It was a battle, however ferociously fought, that could have but one outcome: the Germans were squeezed out of Sicily, which fell on August 17. It had not been a total victory, for the Germans had succeeded in evacuating much heavy equipment and troops. Even Hitler was disappointed, hoping as he did to make of Sicily "another Stalingrad."

It had not been that for the Germans, but for Mussolini it had been a Waterloo. He was deposed on July 25, even before Sicily officially fell, when

*Italy was "boned with the Apennines," which made fighting different on the ground as well as in the air. Twelfth Air Force Thunderbolts equipped with extra fuel tanks and bombs lift over the mountains to lend a hand to the American Fifth Army.*

(ARTHUR F. SCHRAMM/U. S. AIR FORCE)

bels cursed the day Germany had ever become allied with "the macaroni eaters."

By D plus (July 13, 1943) Spitfires from Malta were flown in to begin co-operative air-ground work with advancing Allied troops. Within a week American fighters of the 31st and 33rd Fighter Groups arrived to lend a hand. By the last week of July the hard-pressed Germans had begun to evacuate the island, although by no means without a fight. The tough 1st Parachute Division had been flown in from southern France via Rome to combine with the equally tough "Hermann Göring Division" to give battle where the Italians had all but capitulated. German supplies were flown into Italy and then transported across the narrow Strait of Messina, where Sicily and the Italian toe nearly touched. A heavy flak concentration made bombardment at this point costly to the Allies.

Taking advantage of the rough terrain, the Ger-

*Outstanding fighter-interceptor of the Regia Aeronautica was the Macchi-Castoldi 202 Folgore ("Lightning"). Developed from earlier radial engine designs, the Macchi C. 202 was the result of the combination of an Italian airframe, the work primarily of Macchi's chief designer Mario Castoldi, and a German in-line engine, the Daimler-Benz. The clean design resulted in a formidable aircraft, with a top speed of more than three hundred mph, plenty of armament, and, in the hands of a trained pilot, a dangerous adversary. Fortunately for the Allies, the number of Folgores produced was small because of supply problems. A small plane (the wingspan was just under thirty-five feet and length of fuselage a fraction over twenty-nine feet), the Macchi C. 202 might have even proved a match for the Mustang. (AERONAUTICA MACCHI)*

King Victor Emmanuel told him, "You are the most hated man in Italy."

## IV

Only five days after the first Allied troops (the British Eighth Army) landed on the Italian mainland at Reggio di Calabria, just across the Strait of Messina, Italy surrendered unconditionally, on September 8, 1943. But this surrender by the post-Mussolini regime under Marshal Pietro Badoglio, once celebrated conquerer of Ethiopia, did not end the war in Italy. It had been Mussolini himself who had once said, "If the Germans ever get here they will never go home." Badoglio had hoped to slip out of the war as gracefully as possible and merge with the winning side.

That was not quite how the Germans planned it, however, for Italy became a bitter battleground for the remainder of the war. Kesselring was to command the battle in Italy, with or without Italian co-operation. The "soft underbelly" had turned to stone; it proved, in the words of Samuel Eliot Morison, "to be boned with the Apennines, plated with the hard scales of Kesselring's armor, and shadowed by the wings of the Luftwaffe."

The day following Italy's surrender the U. S. Fifth Army landed on the beaches near Salerno, thirty miles south of Naples, on the west coast of Italy. To the east, at Taranto, the British 1st Airborne Division secured the finest port in southern Italy. Before the landings aircraft of the Northwest African Air Force, a remarkable amalgam of British and American units, cleared the air of the Luftwaffe or grounded it by bombing its bases. Offshore American-British naval gunfire contributed to the landings. When the troops went ashore at Salerno they were covered by Mustangs, Lightnings, Spitfires, and even Seafires of Fleet Air Arm. The wings of the Luftwaffe appeared to have been clipped.

However, on the same day that the British took over Taranto and began moving northward toward Foggia and its complex of airfields, the Italian fleet began putting to sea. According to the surrender terms they were to proceed to Malta. One group of Italian ships was attacked by Ju-88s with bombs and radio-controlled glider bombs. The flagship *Roma* was hit by a glider bomb, caught fire, and in minutes exploded and sank.

Allied ground forces meanwhile moved inexorably up the foot and ankle of Italy. If the Northwest African Air Force fighters and bombers helped to clear the way, there was still a good deal of stiff fighting on the ground. Fighters assisted in air-ground co-operation in missions ranging from strafing to directing artillery fire. The heavy bombers—B-17s and B-24s—of the Twelfth Air Force struck at airfields and rail yards, and the mediums—B-25s and B-26s of the Tactical Air Force—bombed lines of communication and enemy troop concentrations. Co-ordination between ground and air forces was accomplished through the so-called "Rover Joe" system, Rover Joes being controllers who traveled with advancing troops and who, as airmen on the ground, could understand the problem of the infantrymen and could also, by radio, communicate with the men in the air.

By October 1 the Fifth Army had fought its way into Naples from the Salerno beachhead and the Eighth Army, moving up from the south, had combined with the 1st Airborne Division which had occupied Foggia. The Allies by mid-October were solidly established in Italy with a front line running across the peninsula from Naples on the west and Foggia on the east. On October 13, 1943, Italy declared war upon Germany, and if the Army had lost its taste for battle and proved no match for the Wehrmacht, Italian partisans would strike at the Germans with decisive fury.

The road to Rome, low and high, was no easy road. The comparative ease with which the Allies had established the line Naples-Foggia across Italy was no intimation of things to come. If the Luftwaffe in Italy was forced to fight, in the phrase of Kesselring, "a poor man's war" because of the increasing Allied bomber offensive upon the fatherland and the turn of events in Russia, the German ground troops fought ferociously. The war in Italy became predominantly a footslogger's war, the fortunes of which frequently pivoted upon terrain and weather; the landscape was especially advantageous to defense. The venerable travel cliché "Sunny Italy" became a grim joke with the coming of winter. The war in Italy developed into a miserable GI war, but it was air power—Allied air supremacy—that tipped the scales.

The first winter halted the Allied advance at Kesselring's Gustav Line, cutting across Italy at the Volturno and Sangro rivers. It was a night-

*A British Beaufighter in American battle dress at Grottaglie, Italy (just north of the great naval base at Taranto). Beaufighters, both American and British, operated with Tactical Air Force in close-support work with the ground troops.* (U. S. AIR FORCE)

*Sunny Italy? Fifteenth Air Force Liberators at Foggia contend with the elements of an Italian winter: snow and rain, both of which brought an even more invidious*

*enemy, mud. Curtailment of air operations multiplied the miseries of the ground fighting.* (U. S. AIR FORCE)

mare of rock, mud, and cold. The race for Rome, for the time being, was stopped. Aerial operations too were crippled by one of the worst winters Italy had suffered in decades. For the Luftwaffe it was, in effect, a time of respite; not comfortable, but an opportunity to recuperate from Allied attacks. The once indomitable, numerous Luftflotte 2 (commanded by Richthofen) had dwindled to a remnant of around 350 aircraft.

Opposing the Luftwaffe was the newly constituted Mediterranean Allied Air Forces, which merged and shifted around the units that had comprised the Northwest African Air Forces and Mediterranean Air Command. General Eisenhower was ordered to England to prepare for the projected Allied landings in France; accompanying him were Tedder, Spaatz, and, eventually, Doolittle. The latter on January 6, 1944, assumed command of the Eighth Air Force. Lieutenant General Ira C. Eaker came from the Eighth Air Force to head the Mediterranean Allied Air Forces. The heavy units of Doolittle's previous command, the Twelfth Air Force, were used to form the nucleus of another strategic striking force, the Fifteenth Air Force, which would be capable of lashing at not only Germany itself, but also the Balkans, occupied Czechoslovakia, Poland, Hungary, and the Rumanian oil fields. Until he left for England, Doolittle commanded the Fifteenth, which then was taken over by Major General Nathan F. Twining, late of the Thirteenth Air Force and the fighting in the Solomons. The

Fifteenth Air Force was based in the airfields of Foggia and was, technically, formed to participate in the strategic bombardment of Germany and its satellites and not in the tactical fighting in Italy.

The Twelfth Air Force medium bombers and fighters remained in the Mediterranean. Brereton's Ninth Air Force, after returning some of its "borrowed" heavy groups to the Eighth Air Force, had its tactical units reassigned to the Twelfth and joined the Eighth in England. There it would be reorganized as a tactical air force for participation in the invasion of the Continent.

Thus was a great ring of steel being drawn around *Festung Europa.*

But while all these changes ensued, the Germans continued to hold the Allies in Italy on the Gustav Line with aid from snow-choked mountains, bitter cold, and muddy lowlands. The latter inspired the observation, credited to Private Elmer Ponks of Gladwin, Michigan, that "The trouble with this mud is that it's too thick to drink and to thin to plow."

The Allies' failure to pierce the Gustav Line gave birth to the idea of going around the right flank by sea and making an assault at Anzio and Nettuno behind the German lines on the west coast. While the expected surprise assault by the U. S. VI Corps was carried off on January 22, 1944, the effect was forfeited, as ten days were spent "consolidating the beachhead" before pushing inland. By then Kesselring had moved in tough panzer units, zeroed in the beachhead with artillery, and trapped the invaders in a small pocket for no less than four months. In Berlin the papers predicted "another Dunkirk." They were nearly right.

Meanwhile, attempts to breach the Gustav Line itself were unsuccessful; the road to Rome was blocked by strong German positions at the town of Cassino and in the heavily fortified mountains rising behind it. The inland road to Rome was dominated by the Benedictine monastery atop one of the peaks. The monastery, built by St. Benedict in the sixth century, was unquestionably one of the shrines of Catholicism, but it was also, as far as the Allied commanders who faced it believed, a German observation post, which surveyed the bogged-down misery of their troops for miles.

Shortly before he left for England, Eisenhower had issued a directive in which he had stated, "If we have to choose between destroying a famous building and killing our men, then our men's lives count infinitely more and the building must go. But the choice is not always so clear-cut as that. In many cases the monuments can be spared without any detriment to operational needs. Nothing can stand against the argument of military necessity. That is an accepted principle. But the phrase 'military necessity' is sometimes used where it would be truthful to speak of military convenience or even of personal convenience. I do not want it to cloak slackness or indifference."

There were divided views in the Allied camp. Eisenhower's successor, General Sir Henry H. Wilson, and his British commanders believed that the Germans were using the abbey as an observation post. American commanders disagreed, among them Fifth Army commander General Mark Clark, General Eaker, and his British deputy, Air Marshal Sir John Slessor. Wilson, however, heeded the demands of his commanders on the ground before the abbey. To assure himself, Eaker flew over the position in a Piper "Cub" and was certain he saw a radio antenna on the abbey itself and troops moving in and out. There were also, below and around the abbey, gun positions from which snipers harassed the Allied troops, artillery observation posts, gun emplacements, and ammunition dumps. Wilson, unaware of Kesselring's strict orders that the abbey was not to be entered by Germans (the German troops seen by Eaker may have been the guards posted at the gates), ordered the bombing of Monte Cassino. (According to Abbot Gregorio Diamare, the monastery was not occupied by German troops.) When leaflets were dropped upon the abbey warning of an impending heavy aerial and artillery assault, the German commander of the paratroopers in the vicinity of the abbey asserted that it was merely a ruse.

At eight-thirty in the morning of February 15, 1944, B-17s, Mitchells, and Marauders dropped five hundred tons of bombs on the historic shrine, reducing it to a pile of rubble. Although the tomb of St. Benedict escaped damage, the church and courtyard were destroyed and hundreds of Italian women and children who had taken refuge in the monastery died.

But the plan had failed. As soon as the bombing stopped, the Germans, who had promised to stay out of the abbey unless the Allies bombed it, moved into the ruins to set up gun emplacements. The position was now more impregnable than before. The Allies, therefore, continued to be stalemated on the Gustav Line and entrapped on the beach at Anzio.

A new plan called for a "mass air operation"

*Mitchells of the Twelfth Air Force pass a boiling Mount Vesuvius as they fly for Cassino to bomb a block in the road to Rome.* (U. S. AIR FORCE)

*The Abbey of Monte Cassino following the Allied bomb-*
*ings. The possible view—if Germans actually occupied*
*the abbey—may be noted in the background vista.*
(U. S. AIR FORCE)

upon the town of Cassino itself, which, theoretically, would blast a hole in the line through which the Allied troops would pour. Weather interfered until March 15, when, beginning with a B-25 assault at eight-thirty, more than a thousand tons of bombs were dropped by 275 B-17s and B-24s of the Fifteenth Air Force and 200 medium bombers (B-25s and B-26s) of the Twelfth. Like the abbey a month before, the town of Cassino was demolished. But as they had been warned by Eaker, who had not agreed with the plan, the troops entering the town were held up by rubble, craters, debris, and, after the shock had worn off, by the Germans who had sought refuge in shelters and tunnels under the

town. That was not all; some of the bombs from the heavies had fallen among Allied troops.

While the use of air power had accomplished at Cassino what was expected of it—it had, indeed, destroyed the abbey and the town—it had not enabled the ground troops to take Cassino. The ground forces, hindered by the rubble, had not been able to move in quickly enough, nor with sufficient number. It had been an error to employ aircraft as artillery.

While the battle at Anzio and Cassino continued, the medium bombers and fighter bombers initiated Operation Strangle, whose objective was "to reduce the enemy's flow of supplies to a level which will make it impracticable for him to maintain and operate his forces in Central Italy." Marshaling yards, railroads, bridges, roads—all systems of communication became the prime targets. When the Allied spring offensive along the Gustav Line opened on May 11, 1944, German troops, short of supplies, were forced back. Cassino fell on May 19 to Polish troops; French troops broke through the Gustav Line on the Garigliano River and the German retreat was on. On May 23 the Fifth Army broke out of the Anzio beachhead with the aid of heavy air support and took the city on the twenty-fifth. The

*Tactical Air Force Mitchells executing Operation Strangle at Terni, north of Rome, cutting the rail lines over which German troops in Rome might obtain supplies.* (U. S. AIR FORCE)

*The cost of Strangle: A Marauder is struck by an .88 flak shell during a mission over Italy.*

(U. S. AIR FORCE)

with the statement: "I, Mussolini, resume supreme direction of Fascism in Italy." This was not, as before, true. Supreme command of what remained of Fascist Italy north of Rome belonged to Kesselring.

The Germans were kept on the run by Allied ground troops supported by sorties by the Mediterranean Allied Air Forces. Bombers, fighter-bombers, and fighters harassed the retreating Germans, shattered columns of vehicles, and destroyed bridges in the path of retreat. The Luftwaffe in Italy, now commanded by General E. R. von Pohl, barely showed itself to contend these strikes. By early August the Allies had pushed up to Florence, after which several of their divisions and most of their air support were diverted to the invasion of southern France. This left only the veteran Desert Air Force for close support in Italy. In September the tactical units that had operated in France returned to Italy; but by this time Kesselring had dug in again on the Gothic Line, which ran from the Adriatic, just to the north of Ancona, to the Tyrrhenian at Leghorn, in time for another Italian winter. Although

entire Allied battlefront surged ahead. Kesselring hoped to establish new defensive lines in the path of the Allies but found his forces short of fuel and ammunition following the Strangle operations, and the retreat became a near rout. In the evening of June 4, 1944, troops of the Fifth Army were welcomed with flowers, shouting, tears, kisses, and wine in Rome.

Two days later Eisenhower's forces landed on the beaches of Normandy and for most, except those who were there, Italy became a secondary theater, a "forgotten front," as the combatants called it.

Although history's spotlight had shifted to the newly opened Western Front, and despite the fall of Rome to the Allies, the war continued in the Mediterranean for nearly another year. When Mussolini was, for the last time, delivered by Hitler from captivity, Il Duce from northern Italy postured

*Flying Fortresses pass over the ruins of an ancient Roman aqueduct near Rome—the ruins casting long shadows across a modern highway. Objectives of the Fifteenth Air Force bombers were transportation targets in northern Italy.* (U. S. AIR FORCE)

*Operation Dragoon, the invasion of southern France into which the bulk of Allied air forces formerly employed in the Italian campaign was drawn. Twelfth*

*Air Force C-47s deposit troops and supplies in an area between Nice and Marseilles, August 15, 1944.*

(U. S. AIR FORCE)

the Allies succeeded in breaking through the Gothic Line, the coming of the rains in late September brought a sequel to the previous winter on the Gustav Line.

It was the mixture as before, six months of cold, snow, and mud. While the ground forces were mired down or crouched in foxholes and the weather proved to be not too unreasonable, the air forces of the Mediterranean command, some 280 squadrons strong, pursued their mission: cutting off all Nazi supply routes into Italy and all withdrawal routes out. By this time, late 1944 and early 1945, it was unlikely that the Luftwaffe could have put up 280 aircraft to oppose the Allied assault.

Medium bombers and fighter-bombers ranged over the Apennines, over the plain of the Po River, and even across the Alps. The B-25s and B-26s of the Twelfth Air Force were specifically assigned targets in the Brenner Pass, an escape route directly

into Germany; the Desert Air Force pummeled Tarvisio to the east, the route into Austria. Bridges, railroads, and highways became unsafe for any kind of travel, from tank to bicycle. The strategic forces (Fifteenth Air Force and No. 205 Group, RAF) united with the tactical units in a ruthless interdiction of the battleground. By spring of 1945 only a trickle of supplies was reaching the beleaguered Germans.

If the Luftwaffe in Italy had been rendered all but impotent, the flak remained an ever present danger. A direct hit by the deadly "88" could cut a wing in half, detonate a bomb load, or sever an engine. The weather too was a danger, particularly over the mountains, where ten minutes of flying time might bring an abrupt change in the conditions. "The Apennines," observed Roderic Owen in his history of the Desert Air Force, "produced Jekyll and Hyde conditions. A blue sky to the west could

*Marauders cross the Alps in a bombing mission to Germany itself; once the Allies had moved into northern Italy it was possible even for medium bombers to strike at German objectives. Note the effect of the freezing air upon the "skin" of the B-26.*

(U. S. AIR FORCE)

*Hit by flak on a tactical support mission, this Liberator of the 779th Bombardment Squadron (464th Group, Fifteenth Air Force) falls over northern Italy.*

(U. S. AIR FORCE)

*With P-38 escort 97th Bomb Group (Fifteenth Air Force) Flying Fortresses from Foggia, Italy, set out to bomb the Linz marshaling yards in Austria. Heavy bombers could now close in upon Hitler from two directions, England and Italy.* (U. S. AIR FORCE)

mask scudding clouds to the east." Missions over the Alps were equally hazardous; aircraft which had not been damaged by the enemy simply disappeared in the overcast—frequently because of disorientation and a resultant flight into a mountain —and were never heard from again. The war may have bogged down, but death never took a holiday.

When not diverted to the tactical requirements of the ground war, such as bombing bridges and the Brenner Pass area, the B-17s, B-24s, Wellingtons, and Halifaxes of the Mediterranean Strategic Air Forces began reaching out for targets in occupied countries and even into Germany itself. By day Fifteenth Air Force bombers, escorted by P-38s and P-51s, struck at aircraft factories in Austria, railroad systems in Hungary, even the once dreaded objectives at Ploesti and Schweinfurt. As early as June 1944, using Foggia as a base, the Fifteenth completed the first shuttle mission to Russia, bombing rail targets in Hungary on the way out and a Rumanian airfield on the return trip.

No. 205 Group bombed many of the same targets at night without escort. Another specialty was mining the Danube River at night in low-flying (two hundred feet and lower) Liberators and Wellingtons. These "gardening" missions, as they were called, blocked the river traffic, denying Germany precious oil and coal. Beaufighters frequently accompanied the heavies to attack the vessels in the river and other nearby targets, such as railways.

In mid-April 1945 the Allies began their final drive into the Po Valley after an intensive air offensive by both tactical and strategic aircraft. The technique of "carpet bombing," the laying of a massive, concentrated bomb saturation upon enemy positions directly in front of Allied troops, was employed. First the heavies laid the carpet and were followed by the mediums and fighter-bombers to complete the devastation.

With Allied armor and air power in pursuit, the Germans fell back. By the end of April the polyglot Allied armies—British (including Canadians, English, and New Zealanders), French, Polish, Italian, and American—burst into the Po Valley and fanned westward toward Turin, north toward Milan, and eastward toward Venice. At the same time Italian partisans caught Mussolini trying to flee into Switzerland, shot him and his mistress, Clara Petacci, and brought their bodies to Milan, where they were displayed hanging by their heels like sides of beef.

The Germans were finished too and it devolved upon General Heinrich von Vietinghoff, Kesselring's successor (the latter had been transferred to the Western Front), to surrender the German forces in Italy. On May 2, 1945, the war in Italy ended unconditionally, with the German Army there a demoralized shambles and the Luftwaffe non-existent. It had been a hard war, no "soft underbelly" by any means, but it might have been harsher had not Allied air power paralyzed the ability of the German troops to move freely and had not the system of communications been consistently disrupted. Even the withdrawal, that final, bitter expedient, had been impossible. General Fridolin von Senger und Etterlin, who commanded the XIV Corps of the German Fourteenth Army, summarized the impact of Allied air forces in the final battle as well, in effect, as in the entire Italian air campaign. He said, "The effect of Allied air attacks on the frontier route of Italy made the fuel and ammunition situation very critical. It was the bombing of the Po crossings that finished us. We could have withdrawn successfully with normal rear guard action despite the heavy pressure, but owing to the destruction of the ferries and river crossings we lost all our equipment. North of the river we were no longer an Army."

# 2

# REAP THE WHIRLWIND

THE high road to Berlin left the German land-scape scorched with the ruins of its cities and the graves of hundreds of thousands of civilian dead. North Africa, the Mediterranean, Italy—all were merely collateral to Allied strategic air forces; the prime, the true target was Germany.

This, crudely put, "get Germany," was to be the mission of the strategic air forces—Bomber Command, RAF, the Eighth Air Force, and, once it was established at Foggia in Italy, the Fifteenth Air Force. The plan called for the Americans to bomb with reasonable accuracy by day upon con-

*Frustrating and dangerously protected targets were the German sub pens situated around the Bay of Biscay in France. Among the first attacked was Lorient in a long campaign of little result because of the practically bomb-proof installations, which the Germans boasted* *were impervious. By June of 1943, when this attack on Lorient occurred, individual bombing was abandoned in favor of entire groups dropping when the lead plane released its bombs. The result was a heavy target concentration—but even this did not knock out the sub pens.* (U. S. AIR FORCE)

*One of the major targets of the Allied Strategic Air Forces: the Luftwaffe, in the air in combat or on the ground in factories where it was replenished. This is an Me-109 assembly line at Wiener Neustadt, Austria.* (U. S. AIR FORCE)

the RAF and the Eighth Air Force commanders. There was general agreement upon the priorities, which gave first place to the German aircraft industry, second to the ball-bearings industry, third to oil, and so on. As revised slightly in Britain the list was headed by submarines (the industry, the pens from which they operated, and the vessels themselves) followed by, as in the original, aircraft, ball bearings, oil, synthetic rubber and tires, and military transport vehicles.

As finally emended by the end of April 1943, the list was preceded by what was termed as an "intermediate objective"—"German fighter strength" followed by the primary objectives once again with submarines first, "remainder of the German aircraft industry" second, ball bearings third, and oil fourth. This was not so much a revelation of dissension among the military planners as it was an admission

centrated targets while the British struck, generally at the same targets, by night. The American method was called "precision" bombardment (and there were times when it was, thanks to skillful crews and the Norden bombsight) and the British technique "area" bombing. The British method was less costly to aircrews and hard on German civilians who happened to live in the general area of a selected target. What it meant, in effect, was that German cities which housed German war industries were fair game for Bomber Command's Lancasters. This was not, even at the time, regarded as a "civilized method of waging war," as ironic a sophism as was ever coined by man.

It was reasoned in the higher reaches of the Allied High Command that in order to destroy Germany's war machine certain key industries must be bombed out of existence—just which was open to argument. A Committee of Operations Analysis was formed to study the problem of target selection and to provide priority lists. This American group submitted its recommendations in March 1943 to the British High Command (the Air Ministry and the Ministry of Economic Warfare) as well as to

*Bombs for Messerschmitt: Fifteenth Air Force Liberator in one of its first major missions attacks the Me-109 plant at Wiener Neustadt, Austria.* (U. S. AIR FORCE)

*A stick of bombs falls toward the Focke-Wulf factory in the suburbs of Bremen. Damage was extensive enough after this raid of April 17, 1943, to force the removal of the facilities deeper into Germany, to*

*Marienburg. Of the 107 bombers that attacked, 16 were lost to flak, bursting short in this photograph, and particularly aggressive fighter attacks.*

(U. S. AIR FORCE)

that before any serious consideration could be given to a heavy strategic bombardment of Germany the Luftwaffe would have to be eliminated. The German fighter was the single crucial obstacle to the Allied Combined Bomber Offensive.

The submarine was granted a high priority as a concession to the havoc it wreaked in the Atlantic at the time. It was a worthy though frustrating target, as the Eighth Air Force had learned in its early operations during the previous winter. Striking at the German submarine pens in France around the Bay of Biscay, the Eighth Air Force B-17s encountered heavy flak and aggressive fighters. The cost in crews and aircraft was high and the bombings

accomplished little or nothing, except to kill French civilians: and this was no accomplishment at all.

It was in the valley of the Ruhr that the greatest concentration of German industry lay, great sprawling factories in more than a dozen cities clustered on the banks of the Ruhr, the Rhine, and the Dortmund-Ems Canal. Bomber Command initiated the Battle of the Ruhr in May of 1940 with an inconclusive raid by a mere thirty-six bombers upon München Gladbach, directly southwest of the Ruhr proper. It was not until the spring of 1943 that Air Chief Marshal's Bomber Command was capable of mounting truly sizable attacks upon the Ruhr industries. In these attacks Bomber Command could expect little assistance from the depleted Eighth Air Force, whose heavy-bomber units were being shunted off to north Africa and the Mediterranean. Although the Eighth had flown its first mission in August of 1942, it had not actually dropped any bombs upon German soil until January 27, 1943, when it attacked the U-boat bases at Wilhelmshaven.

Carrying the battle into Germany and into the heart, Berlin, fell to Harris and Bomber Command. "At long last we were ready and equipped," Harris noted when the true Battle of the Ruhr opened on the night of March 5/6, 1943, with an attack upon Essen, home of the Krupps works. By "ready and equipped" Harris meant that he had the Lancasters and the electronic device—Oboe—to make the attack feasible. Oboe was so named because the sound its sending station directed over the target was continuous and low like that of the musical instrument. Because it required ground stations Oboe

had a limited range of about 350 miles (which covered only the central Ruhr area and was of no use for deeper missions into Germany). This limitation was circumvented when it was decided to install the Oboe set in a target-marking Mosquito instead of the bombers themselves. The Mosquitos could fly at an altitude at which the earth's curvature would not interfere with the signal (which was beamed at the aircraft and in turn beamed back to another station). If on proper course the pulse was the continuous note, if off course the signal broke up into dots and dashes. Course and distance were calibrated by Oboe with remarkable accuracy. The pathfinding Mosquitos then marked the target area with flares and the bombers followed to accomplish the mission.

It worked exceedingly well on the Essen raid, when 442 bombers dealt the first major blow to the Krupp factories. This was not the last as the

*A "Former Naval Person" (as he signed his messages to President Roosevelt) observes with evident satisfac-* *tion as a Lancaster takes off in England for a night mission to Germany.*

(IMPERIAL WAR MUSEUM, LONDON)

spring moved into summer. After one heavy raid Essen was left in a blazing ruin; in the center the Krupp plants were hardly more than a mass of smoldering wreckage. When Gustav Krupp von Bohlen viewed the result of Bomber Command's night visit the next morning he suffered a stroke from which he never recovered—and which saved him from prosecution as a war criminal after the war.

Other towns and cities in the Ruhr suffered under the growing power of Bomber Command: Duisburg, Bochum, Dortmund, Düsseldorf, and Wuppertal, among others. It was at Wuppertal on May 29/30, 1943, that the attack took an ominous turn for the Germans. That night more than seven hundred bombers succeeded in saturating Barmen-Wuppertal (scarcely touching the other section, Elberfeld-Wuppertal), causing monstrous fires and great loss of civilian life (2450). What Rotterdam and Coventry had been to the Allies, Wuppertal became to the Germans. Goebbels denounced the attack (which had knocked out five of the six major factories) as a "kind of aerial terrorism . . . the product of the sick minds of the plutocratic world-destroyers."

"A long chain of human suffering," he admonished "in all German cities blitzed by the Allies has borne witness against them and their cruel and cowardly leaders—from the murder of German children in Freiburg on May 10, 1940, right up to the present day." Freiburg, as Goebbels well knew by then, had been bombed by off-course Luftwaffe He-111s. But the death of fifty-seven civilians, among them women and thirteen children, had served him well in his denunciations of Allied bombing ethics.

The bombing of Wuppertal was one of the most effective area attacks up to that time and came near the close of the Battle of the Ruhr, which ended, as far as heavy concentration was concerned, by July 1943. Harris then turned his attention to Hamburg, next step on the road to Berlin.

II

The second largest city in the Reich, Hamburg was an important shipping and shipbuilding center; it housed other, lesser industries too, but the major concern was with the U-boat production factories. That was sufficient reason for a Bomber Command

*A Bomber Command Lancaster scatters incendiaries upon Duisburg in the Ruhr.*

(IMPERIAL WAR MUSEUM, LONDON)

attack on the city; another was, since it was beyond Oboe range, that it was susceptible to an H2S (also called "Home Sweet Home" for the two H's and the S). This radar device, carried in the pathfinder aircraft, operated much like a primitive television set— it scanned the ground below the attacking force, picking out certain features of the area. It was especially effective over cities situated near or on water. Hamburg was located some fifty miles inland from the North Sea on the Elbe River; its features were revealed remarkably even on the not yet completely perfected H2S.

During the Battle of Hamburg the radar-jamming device called "window" was also used. Tin-foil strips were released from aircraft and completely threw off radar-controlled flak guns as well as German night fighters. The battle was opened by Bomber Command the night of July 24/25, 1943, when nearly eight hundred Lancasters, Halifaxes, and Wellingtons planted the first seeds of a holocaust. Flying Fortresses of the Eighth Air Force followed up with smaller daylight raids on the twenty-fifth

*Aerial battleground at night. Starlike clusters are target indicators dropped by "pathfinder" aircraft.*
(IMPERIAL WAR MUSEUM, LONDON)

and twenty-sixth, concentrating on the city's dock areas. The climax came on the night of July 27/28, when 787 bombers were dispatched. Fires from the earlier attacks were still burning (fed by coke and coal stored in Hamburg for the coming winter); the succession of attacks had also disrupted attempts by firemen to extinguish the fires.

Hamburg, as a palpable target because of its major industry, had one of the most efficient Air Raid Precaution organizations in Germany; its shelter system was one of the finest. But for what occurred in the wake of the bombing in the early morning of July 28, 1943, stringent precautions and ingeniously constructed shelters meant nothing. The bomb loads combined high explosives with incendiaries, and when the newly made fires combined

with the fires of the preceding attacks the result was what one observer called a "lake of fire."

The first man-made fire storm was unleashed upon Hamburg in that lake. The heat generated a powerful suction that uprooted trees three feet thick and drew them into the fire. The same thing happened to human beings.

A secret German document prepared after the attack described the fire storm with undisguised awe—"beyond all human imagination"—and hopelessness:

Through the union of a number of fires, the air gets so hot that because of its decreasing specific weight, it receives terrific momentum, which in its turn causes the surrounding air to be sucked toward the center. By that suction, combined with the enormous difference in temperature (600–1000 degrees centigrade), tempests are caused which exceed their meteorological counterparts (20–30 centigrade). In a built-up area the suction could not follow its shortest course, but the overheated air stormed through the streets with immense force, taking along not only sparks but burning timber and roof beams, so spreading the fire more and more, developing in a short time into a fire typhoon as was never before witnessed, against which every human resistance was quite useless.

Searing winds of 150 miles an hour swept through Hamburg in a howling fury. Dwellings, trees, people—all incinerated in its path. Bomb shelters proved to be not havens, but deathtraps. The thousand-degree heat produced searing vacuums around them, asphyxiating and cremating the occupants. By August 3, when the Battle of Hamburg was over, half of the city was gone and perhaps 50,000 dead. (The number will never be known and ranges from 31,647 actually counted by December 1943 to the greater number, which is probably closer to the true figure. As a comparison, it might be noted that the most authoritative figure for the number of people killed during all of the bombings of Britain is 51,509.)

The survivors would ever refer to those few days and nights as *Die Katastrophe*. Goebbels reported that Hamburg *Gauleiter* Karl Kaufman called it "a catastrophe the extent of which staggers the imagination . . ." and that "the entire city must be evacuated except for small patches. He spoke of about 800,000 people who are wandering up and down the streets not knowing what to do." But

Goebbels found Kaufman "a bit too lyrical and romantic for so great a catastrophe. . . ."

Minister of Armaments Albert Speer, no romantic but a pragmatic realist, went so far as to inform Hitler himself that if such attacks were made on six other German cities devoted to German war production, it would bring "a rapid end to the war." The attack even galvanized the dilatory Göring, who attempted to rally the Luftwaffe into a real defensive force and to encourage the production of fighters for that force. But Hitler had the last word as usual. "Terror can only be broken by terror!" he ranted. "Everything else is nonsense. I can only win the war by dealing out more destruction to the enemy than he does to us. . . ." Whereupon he ordered Oberst Dietrich Peltz, the youthful *Angriffsführer England,* to plan a series of revenge attacks upon Britain. With the Luftwaffe then dispersed to the Eastern Front and the Allies overrunning Sicily, Peltz had little in the way of air power to attack England. When he did, beginning

around the first of the next year, it resulted in what the British called, somewhat disdainfully, the "baby blitz." The attacks were inconclusive and wasteful and demonstrated little more than the fact that the Luftwaffe was a victim of the inner decay of its own High Command.

### III

Hitler had no understanding of the meaning of air power, nor of the change that it had undergone since he had unleashed his Stukas on Poland. He remained ever the corporal with his feet in the mud and delusions of grandeur. Although he had ignited a world war, his vision remained limited by his own megalomania. He fixed his eyes to his battle map, a flat wall map, not a globe, and refused to look up. It simply did not dawn on him that since the Battle of Britain the only attacks upon the Reich itself had come from the air. Nor did he

*An Eighth Air Force Liberator is cut in half near Hamburg during a daylight attack upon the city's docks.*

*Flak stopped the B-24 before it reached the German city.* (U. S. AIR FORCE)

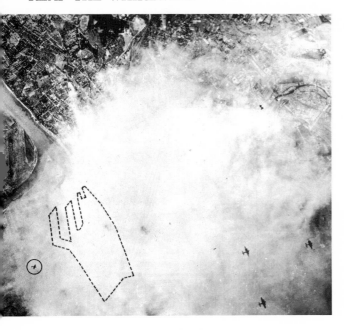

*A conception of the Hamburg catastrophe may be realized from the extent of the fires that obscured the city when Eighth Air Force bombers arrived the morning following the initial Bomber Command attacks. The Eighth Air Force target, the dock areas, is covered over with smoke (the target area is indicated by the dotted line). In the circle: a lone FW-190 pursues Fortresses of the 381st Bomb Group leaving the target.*

(U. S. AIR FORCE)

realize that in the inevitably impending Battle of Germany the Luftwaffe represented his first line of defense. Besides, defense was inconceivable to Hitler; he would listen only to plans for attack or the fight to the death.

When Hamburg was burned late in July 1943 Hitler and Göring were estranged to an embarrassing degree to the *Reichsmarschall*. The Luftwaffe had failed to bring off Sealion, it had permitted a thousand bombers to strike at Cologne and now Hamburg, not to mention the American Flying Fortresses, which flew over the Reich during the day. Insofar as Hitler was concerned, the Luftwaffe was "not doing its job."

Göring, cut to the quick not only by the Führer's tongue-lashings but by his refusal to shake hands, chose to withdraw from the scene of conflict. He would send deputies to Hitler's meetings and cultivate his own comfort and the vast art collection he had gathered in the wake of the German armies.

At the same time he simply shifted the guilt for his ineptitudes to the shoulders of others.

The first suggestion that all was not well in the Luftwaffe was revealed as early as November 1941. Ernst Udet, chief of the technical office of the Luftwaffe, had become Göring's chief scapegoat as well. Udet was blamed for the failure of the Battle of Britain, he was blamed for the decline in aircraft production that seemed to follow every successful campaign, and he was blamed for the fatal lack of a long-range heavy bomber. During the 1941 summer offensive in Russia a critical decline in aircraft production brought Udet under fire again. Göring placed Udet's functions in the hands of the superefficient Milch. Within five months Udet had become little more than a name in his own office.

In November Udet shot himself, first scrawling over his bed a final message: "Reichsmarschall, why have you deserted me?" The message was discreetly removed and Göring released the news that Udet had been killed "testing a new weapon." Although he seriously considered court-martialing Udet posthumously, Göring consented to an impressive state funeral attended by nearly all of the great German

*Victims of Göring: Udet and Jeschonnek both committed suicide because of Göring's practice of using them as scapegoats for his own failures.*

(H. J. NOWARRA)

airmen and with Göring himself leading the funeral procession.

The situation inside the German High Command was so bad that when Werner Mölders, an outspoken non-Nazi, was killed in a crash in attempting to fly to Udet's funeral, rumors hinted that he had been assassinated.

Having lost his chief scapegoat, Göring selected another, Jeschonnek, the young Luftwaffe chief of staff. Jeschonnek all but worshiped Hitler and Göring resented that also; but Hitler detested the Luftwaffe, so Jeschonnek's lot was not a happy one. It took a turn for the worse when Harris opened his offensive in the Ruhr, destroyed Hamburg, and appeared to be heading for Berlin itself. Then on the night of August 17/18, 1943, barely two weeks after the Hamburg mission, Bomber Command succeeded in making a surprise raid on Peenemünde, home of Hitler's "secret weapon," of which the world had been hearing so much.

This was the German rocket research center on the Baltic Sea, which was not as secret as Hitler had hoped. While a small force of Mosquitos dropped flares upon Berlin, creating the impression that the capital was to be the night's objective, close to six hundred bombers released their loads on Peenemünde. The mission was remarkably successful, although it did not wipe out the home of Hitler's "vengeance weapons." Two important scientists were killed, there was a delay in the development of the V-weapons, and certain phases of production and testing were moved from Peenemünde.

The shock of the attack and the confusion under which the Luftwaffe, led astray by the Mosquitos over Berlin, had responded to it created further tension in the higher reaches of the Luftwaffe. Unable to face what was inevitably in store for him the next morning, Jeschonnek shot himself. Like Udet he left a message: "I can no longer work with the Reichsmarschall. Long live the Führer." His death, attributed to a stomach hemorrhage, was not announced immediately, so that it might not be associated with the bombing of Peenemünde.

Jeschonnek's successor as Luftwaffe chief of staff was General Gunther Korten, another Hitler toady (and who later died in Hitler's bunker on July 20, 1944, when a bomb intended for his Führer exploded).

*If the Luftwaffe High Command degenerated under the pressure of total war, its pilots did not lack courage and determination. Here Major Heinz-Wolfgang Schnaufer, top-scoring (121—most of them four-engined bombers) night fighter ace, studies the tail of his Me-110. The British admired Schnaufer and called him "the Night Ghost of Saint-Trond" (for his base in Belgium).*

(H. J. NOWARRA)

Bomber Command lost heavily over Peenemünde to flak and to night fighters. Forty bombers did not return from that mission. Hitler thus could not say that the Luftwaffe was not doing its job. Nor could he have overlooked what the Luftwaffe had done during the same day over Regensburg and Schweinfurt when the Eighth Air Force lost so heavily to its fighters.

Despite Hitler's attitude, attempts were made sub rosa to prepare for the defense of Germany. To counter Harris's bombers a system called the "Kammhuber Line," the brain child of Josef Kammhuber, was devised. This employed an elaborate network of searchlight belts across the western approaches to the Reich and a lesser one to the west of Berlin. The night-flying Ju-88s, Me-110s, and Do-17s, carrying electronic devices, were controlled from the ground by the "Würzburgs," the German version of radar. These ground control stations were called *Himmelbetten,* and despite some disadvantages (for instance, when an enemy plane passed from the zone of control of one station into another, it could escape, for German night fighters were

A "Würzburg" radar installation, or Himmelbett. The giant radar antennas of the Würzburg proved to be remarkably effective, but were rendered all but useless when "window" was dropped during Allied bombing raids. (U. S. AIR FORCE)

A bombed-out railroad station that Hitler was unable to shun: the Potsdamer Station, Berlin. British and American heavy bombers had reached the heartland of Nazi Germany. (U. S. AIR FORCE)

strictly forbidden to operate except in their own zones), the system proved to be fairly effective.

However, when Kammhuber approached Hitler, hoping to expand the *Himmelbetten* through all of Germany, he ran into trouble. Basing his request upon the figures of American aircraft production which had been supplied him by German Intelligence, Kammhuber hoped Hitler would be impressed enough to give his blessing to the project. Instead Hitler refused to believe that the figure—five thousand military planes per month—was accurate (it was in fact quite accurate, if on the conservative side). Kammhuber was clearly exaggerating, Hitler insisted.

"Nonsense!" Hitler shouted. "I will not stand for such nonsense." Kammhuber left with his plan for the defense of the Reich a shambles. On September 15, 1943, he was notified that his Nachtjagdfliegerkorps XII would be disbanded and its units dispersed to various other *Luftflotten*. Kammhuber was demoted and the night-fighter system began to disintegrate. The nighttime protection of Germany continued, though with much less direction, with Kammhuber's twin-engined night fighters and the single-engined fighters of Jagdgeschwader 300, the contribution of Major Hajo Herrmann.

An ex-bomber pilot, Herrmann came forth with the suggestion that FW-190s, without radar, could be used at night to attack British bombers. With the Lancasters silhouetted by *Himmelbett* searchlights, or illuminated by flares, the FWs could readily find them and shoot them down. This simplistic approach appealed to Hitler—it would not require the construction of costly ground stations—and he smiled upon it. The one serious problem was flak. Herrmann, however, reached an agreement with flak commanders about timings and altitudes of the bursts, thus affording his fighters some immunity.

In time Herrmann commanded three *Geschwader,* the original JG 300 plus JG 301 and JG 302, which were nicknamed *Wilde Sau* ("Wild Boars") in honor of their tactic of diving heedlessly into enemy bomber formations at night. It had been the *Wilde Sau* which had accounted for most of the British bomber losses on the Peenemünde attack. The plan was courageous, and it cost Bomber Command dearly, but it was haphazard and unable to cope with the growing power of Bomber Command as well as the Eighth and Fifteenth Air Forces.

Discouraged, Kammhuber resigned in November of 1943; on November 18 Harris opened the first major phase in the Battle of Berlin. More than four hundred aircraft dropped their bombs upon the heart of the Reich. With the specter of Hamburg fresh in mind (and an even more recent burning of Kassel in October) the appearance of enemy bombers was a chilling experience to the inhabitants of Berlin. "Hell itself seems to have broken loose over us," Goebbels commented.

Hitler was not impressed by the portent. The hearts of several German cities lay in smoldering ruin but they served only as an excuse to berate the Luftwaffe or to chide Göring. Hitler could not, however, bear to look upon the devastation of his cities. When his train passed through bombed-out areas the window shades were discreetly drawn; what he did not wish to see he did not behold. But reality was catching up with him and there was an irony in his future: although he could not stomach the sight of ruined cities he would live out the final weeks of his life in the very center of one.

# 3

# KITES OVER BERLIN

Whatever the official conception of Berlin's strategic importance, to the eager pilot in the ETO (European Theater of Operations) it was the ultimate objective. It was, after all, the headquarters of the hated Hun. However little the absolute destruction of the Reich's capital might contribute to the ending of the war was, in truth, immaterial: the "Big B" remained an ever beckoning symbol. That it might contain millions of helpless (even innocent—but who considered that?) civilians was also immaterial, irrelevant, or incidental; this was Total War.

The professional German militarists, of whom Hitler was not one, conceded that Harris's Bomber Command devastated German cities, but that the effect upon German morale was minimal. It stiffened non-combatant attitudes in general (as it had those of the English) and aroused the German's sardonic sense of humor—frequently at the expense even of Hitler and Göring. But there was no great upsurge of civilian pleas for surrender.

But what the German professionals—Minister of Arms and War Production Albert Speer and Milch —feared most was American bombing by day, aimed at specific war industries. If the Americans were permitted to intensify and concentrate their attacks on any single target for any length of time the war would be lost.

By the turn of 1944 the Allied Air Forces approached that point, but it was a tragic paradox that in spite of it the war was not lost by Germany until another year and a half went by, months of great cost in lives and destruction. The paradox, simply stated, was this: although the Allied heavy-bomber strength by the middle of January 1944 made it possible to strike at Germany several times

*The major dread of German war production experts: American bombers attacking specific targets by day.*
(CECIL COHEN)

*Another source of discomfort to the German planners—American mass production. B-17s roll out of Boeing's plant at Seattle.* (THE BOEING COMPANY)

a week with immense bomber formations (ranging from four hundred to eight hundred bombers) and the advent of the P-51 Mustang made escorted missions deep inside Germany possible, German war industries did not crumble even under repeated blows, and Germany, therefore, did not crumble either.

Why?

There were several reasons, not the least of which was the ability of German industries to recover rapidly from the raids. The dispersal which followed the Schweinfurt-Regensburg mission also made it difficult to damage with any finality specific industries that might have clogged the German war machine. Weather was always a factor, of course, preventing or interfering with missions.

The year 1944, for example, opened with bad weather, forcing whatever missions that were mounted to depend upon "blind bombing" (radar) rather than visual tactics. Inexperienced operators of the H2X device (an American adaptation of the British H2S) scattered bombs across target areas and caused little real damage to specific targets. The much vaunted, very secret miracle devices were not miracle workers despite occasional success, such

as the bombing of docks, submarine construction yards, and the city of Kiel on December 13, 1943; and on this mission Oboe was used, not the more recent H2X. The former operated on a beam projected from sending stations in England, the latter was carried in the bombers themselves—the so-called "Pathfinders," and were not limited to the sending power of the stations in Britain.

The main target, in preparation for the forthcoming invasion of Normandy, was the Luftwaffe. Unless the factories could be seen it was not possible to concentrate the bombing pattern on the targets. The first opportunity to strike at the Luftwaffe in 1944 came on January 11, when the weather cleared over central Germany. An attack was mounted consisting of 663 Flying Fortresses and Liberators, with a fighter escort of Spitfires, P-47s, P-38s (allocated to the nearer outgoing and incoming legs of the mission), and P-51s (over the target areas). The targets were the FW-190 plant at Oschersleben, the Ju-88 plant at Halberstadt, and the Me-110 plants at Brunswick. These cities were grouped quite close together; they were also directly in line with Berlin, which lay about ninety miles beyond.

It was an impressive concept, but certain factors as usual intervened. If the weather over central Germany was fine, it was poor over England and complicated takeoffs and assembly over England. Along the way the weather worsened and the B-17s of the 3rd Bombardment Division and the B-24s of the 2nd Division were ordered back to England. Some of the B-17s of the 3rd Division, however, approaching the target, decided to continue on with the 1st Division, which was about fifty miles from Brunswick when the "recall" came. This decimated the force greatly, for only 238 bombers struck at their primary targets (the others bombed targets of opportunity).

Fearing that Berlin was the objective, the Luftwaffe reacted, after what had seemed a quiescent period, savagely. More than two hundred fighters, Me-109s, FW-190s, and Me-110s (armed with rockets) rose up to meet the bombers and their escort. The German pilots, their planes equipped with extra fuel tanks, could wait until the escorts were forced to turn back before dropping their tanks and lancing through the bomber formations. The two-engined fighters merely stayed out of gun range and lobbed rockets into the combat boxes.

## HOW THE TARGET IS LOCATED

H2X {AN/APS-15 / AN/APQ-13}  MICROWAVE ASV AND HIGH ALTITUDE BOMBING SET

FLIGHT SHOWN STARTING FROM ENGLAND TOWARD TARGET (BERLIN).
X SHOWS LOCATION OF FLIGHT OVER CHANNEL.

APPEARANCE OF PPI ON 50 MILE RANGE. BRIGHT LINE SHOWS HEADING OF 90°.

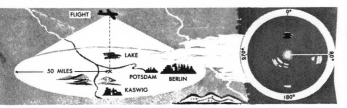

40 MILES FROM TARGET (BERLIN). NAVIGATOR MUST STUDY MAP TO LOCATE AREA BY TOPOGRAPHIC FEATURES.

PPI WITH 50 MILE RADIUS. BERLIN IS BRIGHT SPOT AT 40 MILES AND 100°. POTSDAM IS SMALL SPOT AT 30 MILES AND 100°. LAKE AT 25 MILES AND 0° SHOWS AS DARK SPOT.

25 MILES FROM TARGET. SECTOR SCAN IN OPERATION, AIRCRAFT HEADING IS NOW 100°.

10 MILE RANGE CIRCLES ON 50 MILE PPI SCALE SHOW BERLIN AT 25 MILES.

## OVERCAST BOMBING

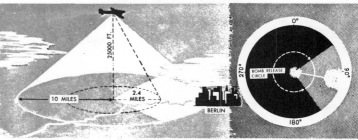

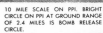

TARGET AT 10 MILES. SECTOR SCAN IN OPERATION.

10 MILE SCALE ON PPI. BRIGHT CIRCLE ON PPI AT GROUND RANGE OF 2.4 MILES IS BOMB RELEASE CIRCLE.

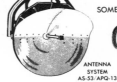

BOMBS AWAY. AT 25000 FEET AND 160 M.P.H. (INDICATED AIR SPEED) THE BOMB RELEASE POINT IS 2.4 MILES (GROUND RANGE) FROM THE TARGET.

ON 10 MILE PPI SCALE BOMB RELEASE CIRCLE AND HEADING LINE INTERSECT IN CENTER OF THE TARGET.

SOME OF THE COMPONENTS OF THE AN/APQ-13

ANTENNA SYSTEM AS-53/APQ-13    INDICATOR ID-XA-9 APQ-13(XA-1)    RADIO-FREQUENCY UNIT BC-1276A    CONTROL BOX C-71 APQ-13

*How H2X located targets and how overcast bombings were accomplished with the aid of newly developed navigational devices.* (ROBERT CHAPIN)

The P-51s, of the 354th Fighter Group (the first to be issued the Mustang), raced in to the defense of the bombers that attacked Oschersleben and Halberstadt, which seemed to be taking the brunt of the German attack. But there were only forty-nine Mustangs, which had to be shared between the two forces, and it was impossible to protect the Fortresses with any thoroughness. A further factor had interjected itself: the Mustangs had joined with the bombers earlier than scheduled so that fuel remaining for battling over the target was limited. Still, the pilots gave a good account of themselves. It was on this mission that Major James H. Howard, squadron commander of the 356th Fighter Squadron (of the 354th Fighter Group, Ninth Air Force) and a former Flying Tiger, won the Medal of Honor by taking on what one bomber commander believed was "the entire Luftwaffe."

Howard disclaimed that, saying that he had not even seen the thirty fighters "all at once the way the bomber people tell it." In an interview with *Stars and Stripes* writer Andrew A. Rooney, Howard told of his encounter. The bombers had passed over the target (Oschersleben) when the German fighters struck. The P-51s swept in to the defense of the bombers. In the initial fighting Howard became separated from the rest of his flight.

"The first plane I got was a two-engined German night fighter [Me-110]. I went down after him, gave him several squirts and watched him crash. He stood out very clearly, silhouetted against the snow that covered the ground. He went down in a cloud of black smoke and fire and hit the ground. Shortly after that an FW came cruising along underneath me. He pulled up into the sun when he saw me. I gave him a squirt and I almost ran into his

*B-17s of the 384th Bomb Group bombing through the overcast on instruments.* (U. S. AIR FORCE)

*The North American P-51 "Mustang," the plane that turned the tide in the daylight bombings of Germany. Capable of escorting the bombers all the way to and* *from the deep penetration targets, the Mustang was also an outstanding fighter plane.* (U. S. AIR FORCE)

canopy when he threw it off to get out. He bailed out.

"Then I circled trying to join up with the other P-51s. I saw an Me-109 just underneath and a few hundred yards ahead of me. He saw me at the same time and chopped his throttle, hoping my speed would carry me on ahead of him. It's an old trick. He started scissoring underneath me but I chopped my throttle and started scissoring at the same time and then we went into a circle dogfight and it was a matter of who could maneuver best and cut the shortest circle. I dumped twenty-degree flaps and began cutting inside him, so he quit and went into a dive, with me after him. I got on his tail and got in some long-distance squirts from three hundred or four hundred yards. I got some strikes on him, but I didn't see him hit the ground.

"I pulled up again and saw an Me-109 and a P-51 running along together. The 51 saw me coming in from behind and he peeled off while the Me started a slow circle. I don't remember whether I shot at him or not. Things happen so fast it's hard to remember things in sequence when you get back.

"Back up with the bombers again, I saw an Me-110. I shot at him and got strikes all over him. He flicked over on his back I could see gas and smoke coming out—white and black smoke. It could be that he had some sort of smoke equipment to make it appear that he was damaged worse than he was."

If he had doubts about his victory (he did not claim this plane in his report), Howard did not waste time in ascertaining it. He climbed back up to the level of the bombers.

"I saw an Me-109 tooling up for an attack on the bombers. They often slip in sideways, the way this one was doing. We were both pretty close to the bombers, and I was close to him. I gave him a squirt and he headed straight down with black smoke pouring out."

Although he had not come under fighter attack up to this point, for the Luftwaffe concentrated primarily on the bombers, Howard's luck was not all good. When he jumped the first plane all four of his guns were operating, but by his third attack only two functioned; finally only one. This was an early problem the Mustang pilots faced. Howard pulled away from the burning Me-109 and climbed again to bomber level, approaching from the left side of the formation.

"I saw an Me-109 over on the starboard side getting into position to attack the bombers," Howard related. "I dived on him from where I was and got strikes all over him with my one gun. He turned over on his back and skidded out. He thought he had lost me with the skid and he pulled out into a forty-five-degree dive. I followed him down and kept on shooting.

"I'd been with the bombers for more than an hour altogether by then and just before I left I saw a Dornier 217—I think it was—coming alongside the bombers, probably to throw rockets. I dived on him and he left, but I never did fire a shot at him." He was officially credited with shooting down four enemy planes, and given the Medal of Honor for singlehandedly standing off an entire *Gruppe* of enemy aircraft. Major Howard returned to his base, leaving when his fuel supply was dangerously low, to find that his Mustang had but a single bullet hole, through the left wing.

The fighting over Oschersleben had been ferocious; of the 174 Fortresses which bombed the A.G.O. Flugzeugwerke A.G. there, 34 were lost, most of them to enemy fighters. The day's total losses with 26 shot down over Halberstadt amounted to 60 bombers. Claims were made for 152 German fighters, although the actual loss was 39. But the bombing had been good, with a high percentage of effective hits within a thousand feet of the aiming point. There was heavy damage to the factory installations at Oschersleben and near Brunswick.

The heavy weather set in again the following day, thus precluding an immediate sequel and giving the Germans time to repair and disperse. And if the Luftwaffe again had proved itself formidable, the implications of the raid were not lost on Speer, who could see that the aircraft industry was under planned assault. Nor were they ignored by fighter general, General der Jagdflieger Adolf Galland, who recognized what the appearance of the Mustang so deep inside Germany meant. But while he called for more fighters, and Speer agreed with him, Hitler called for bombers with which he could avenge the attacks upon Germany by bombing England. The cross-purposes of the two points of view would in time have its effect.

But because the serious attacks upon the German aircraft industry had led to feverish productivity, the number of fighters being produced in the Reich

*Dornier 217, a later development of the Do-17, which was used to launch rockets into American bomber streams.* (H. J. NOWARRA)

rose instead of lessened. During the last half of 1943, for example, the average monthly fighter production had been about 850 aircraft (the Allies estimated it to be about 640); during the first half of 1944, under Speer's hand, it averaged 1581 (Allied estimate, based on the estimated damage to the industry, was 655). While the Allied air commanders did not underestimate the Luftwaffe, it was, as the year began, a greater threat than they had imagined.

As if to underscore this self-evident fact, a new directive issued by the Combined Chiefs of Staff dated February 13, 1944, called for the "progressive destruction and dislocation of the German military, industrial and economic systems, the disruption of vital elements of lines of communication and the material reduction of German air combat strength, by the successful prosecution of the combined bomber offensive from all convenient bases."

The next day Arthur Harris read the Air Ministry version of the directive. The over-all plan no longer contained any mention of "undermining the morale of the German people." Under Section 3, "Concept," Harris read:

Overall reduction of German air combat strength in its factories, on the ground and in the air through mutually supporting attacks by both strategic air forces pursued with relentless determination against

*James Howard, former Flying Tiger pilot, is being congratulated after receiving the Medal of Honor by Robert M. Lovett, U. S. Assistant Secretary of War for Air.* (U. S. AIR FORCE)

same target areas or systems so far as tactical conditions allow, in order to create the air situation most propitious for OVERLORD is immediate purpose of Bomber Offensive.

The primary objective was "the German Air Force"; "Other objectives" included "Crossbow" targets—the bombing of flying bomb launching sites, which had begun to burgeon across the English Channel—"Berlin and Other Industrial Areas," as well as targets in "South Eastern Europe," which came into the sphere of the Mediterranean Allied Air Forces and particularly the new Fifteenth Air

Force. The plan, appropriately, was given the code name "Argument." Harris was not convinced that striking such panacea targets would achieve the results hoped for. Among the assigned target cities was Schweinfurt, which was, Harris was hopefully informed, to be destroyed "at as early a date as possible."

This proposed directive, however, was not sent to Bomber Command for fear it could "lead to trouble with Harris." There was trouble anyway, for even a less strongly worded memo aroused Harris, who reiterated his objections to bombing such a distant, well-defended, and unprofitable target. It was not, Harris persisted, "a reasonable operation of war." But his chiefs, Portal and Sinclair, persisted also, and on January 27 Harris was officially ordered by letter from Deputy Chief of the Air Staff Air Marshal Sir Norman Bottomley to strike at Schweinfurt.

Bomber Command was to join the newly redesignated U. S. Strategic Air Forces (commanded by General Carl Spaatz), whose function was to co-ordinate the strategic operations of the Eighth and Fifteenth Air Forces. These operations, in turn, were co-ordinated with those of Bomber Command. This "Combined Bomber Offensive" was aimed at the

*B-17 of the U. S. Strategic Air Forces, whose primary objective was the Luftwaffe, as a prelude to a projected invasion of France.* (CECIL COHEN)

Luftwaffe, as per the directive of February 13, and would serve as an overture to Overlord.

Although Harris remained at his post, there were shake-ups in the American camp. Lieutenant General Ira C. Eaker was sent to Italy to take command of the complex Mediterranean Allied Air Forces. His old command, as head of the Eighth Air Force, was taken over by Major General James Doolittle. Major General Frederick L. Anderson, deputy for operations of the U. S. Strategic Air Forces, served as the direct co-ordinator of the bomber forces of the Eighth and the Fifteenth. The latter bomber command was under the direction of Major General Nathan F. Twining.

With this quite complex command structure it was hoped that an equally complex series of heavy attacks could be made upon Germany's airframe factories, aircraft assembly plants, and anti-friction-bearing plants and thus lay low the Luftwaffe.

II

By the night of February 19, 1944, the weather over Germany once again breaking, the time came for putting Argument into operation. Although England lay under a heavy coating of cloud, which would complicate getting away and possibly landing, and the Fifteenth Air Force was caught up in the frenzy of the Anzio beachhead, General Spaatz elected to "Let 'em go."

What was to come to be called the "Big Week" opened ominously with an attack the night of February, 19/20, 1944, by RAF's Bomber Command upon Leipzig. More than eight hundred bombers and fighters proceeded toward their objective upon what was hoped was a diversionary route; to German radar plotters it appeared that Berlin was the target. This brought out the night fighters slashing at the bomber stream. Even before the stream turned south, short of Berlin, for Leipzig, it had suffered heavy attack. Seventy-eight bombers, or nearly 10 per cent of the attacking force which succeeded in bombing Leipzig, never returned to England. It was not a propitious beginning for the intensified Combined Bomber Offensive.

Spaatz's "Let 'em go" still stood on February 20, and the largest force of aircraft up to that time lifted through four to five thousand feet of murk and set off for Germany. England literally shook under the roar of thousands of powerful engines. More than a thousand heavy bombers alone were dispatched. The escort consisted of no less than thirteen P-47 groups and two each of P-38s and P-51s from Eighth Air Force Fighter Command and from the Ninth Air Force. The RAF provided an additional sixteen squadrons of Spitfires and Mustangs.

The major targets lay in an area between Brunswick in the north and Leipzig in the south (with some other objectives to the north in Poland); all were associated with aircraft production. In this same area was Oschersleben, which had cost so dear on January 11. The men in the great air armada of close to two thousand warplanes flew toward their objectives with some trepidation. Again the route appeared to point toward Berlin.

The Luftwaffe came up to meet them and rammed into a wall of "little friends," or "peashooters," as the fighters were called by the bomber crews ("big friends"). Of the 941 Fortresses and Liberators that bombed Leipzig, Bernburg, and Brunswick (besides other targets of opportunity) a total of 21 was lost. Three fighters were listed as missing. A figure closer to 200 was actually expected.

The results of the bombing were good: production of the Ju-88 in Leipzig was knocked out for about a month. The Me-109 suffered too at the city's Erla plant, and so did the workers. About forty completed Messerschmitts were destroyed in the factory's wreckage, and over four hundred workers who had taken shelter in slit trenches and air raid shelters died in the attack.

The next blow fell upon Stuttgart that night when six hundred RAF bombers struck at aircraft factories in that area. The daylight attack was aimed at Brunswick, but cloud interfered with the mission by the Eighth Air Force and the Fifteenth could not participate at all. The next day—February 22, 1944 —proved to be better and the Fifteenth struck at Regensburg from the south while, as had been planned, the Eighth hit several target cities, among them Gotha, Oschersleben, Aschersleben, Bernburg, and Schweinfurt. The mission went awry because of poor weather over English bases, and several bombers of LeMay's 3rd Division collided in mid-air during the attempts to assemble above the clouds. LeMay ordered the mission scrubbed. The B-24s of the 2nd Division became so dispersed during their

assembly that they would have been unable to form into proper combat boxes in time for arrival over their targets; these aircraft were called back also.

This left only the B-17s of the 1st Division to continue with the attack from England, and the Fifteenth Air Force from Italy. Of the 466 bombers the Eighth Air Force dispatched only 255 dropped bombs (and of these only 99 actually hit their primary targets, because of cloud); of the 183 bombers sent by the Fifteenth Air Force 118 bombed the Messerschmitt plant at Regensburg.

The decreased forces ran into the Messerschmitts of Jagdgeschwader 1 and 11, which mauled the bombers even before they reached their targets. Forty-one bombers went down, although some degree of effective bombing was accomplished upon the Ju-88 night-fighter factories at Aschersleben (knocking it out for two months) and Bernburg. The Fifteenth Air Force did well at Regensburg, although at the cost of fourteen aircraft.

Fighter escort, which had proved so formidable on the Sunday opening day of the Big Week, was unable to contend with the Luftwaffe on Tuesday. This was partly because of the scattering of the bomber forces and partly because of the change in German tactics: attacking the bombers *before* they reached the target areas. The P-51s dispatched to furnish fighter cover over the targets found themselves in the wrong place or, because of the change in targets because of cloud, too distant from the bombers to provide effective help.

Wednesday offered only poor weather predictions, so after three successive days of operations, the Eighth Air Force "stood down," a welcome relief. But the Fifteenth Air Force continued from its end with a small force (102 bombers), which struck at the ball-bearing-producing plant at Steyr in Austria.

Thursday's weather brought a return of the massive co-ordinated attacks. The Fifteenth Air Force dispatched 104 bombers for a return visit to Steyr and a strike upon an aircraft component plant there. Eighty-seven actually bombed Steyr (the remaining 27 bombers, which had become separated from the main body, hit an oil refinery at Fiume); the Steyr bombers, despite heavy escort of Thunderbolts and Lightnings, lost 17 of their number.

From England the Eighth sent a force of B-17s to bomb Schweinfurt (the first attempt since the

*A 453rd Bomb Group Liberator homeward bound after bombing a Luftwaffe base during the "Big Week," February 21, 1944.* (U. S. AIR FORCE)

October 14 disaster), B-24s to hit Gotha's Me-110 works, and another force to the north to strike at targets in northeastern Germany and Poland (aimed at the FW-190 production). Schweinfurt, with its dreaded reputation, proved to be heavily defended, and the fighter escort was heavily engaged, losing 10 (and claiming 37 enemy aircraft). Bomber claims for German fighters were very high and, if not accurate, at least were an indication of the heavy fighting. Of the 234 Fortresses that dropped bombs on Schweinfurt's ball-bearing works, only 11 were lost.

Of the 239 B-24s dispatched to Gotha, 33 were lost, and bombing was very accurate. The Schweinfurt and Gotha attackers drew off the German fighters from the north, which left the force that was to bomb the FW-190 factory practically untouched.

With the coming of night Harris's Bomber Command contributed its share by sending a force of 734 four-engined bombers (most of them Lancasters) to a still burning Schweinfurt. Air Staff had finally had its way, although Harris, as usual, had the final word. The loss of 33 aircraft was not prohibitive (though serious enough), but as Harris had so long protested, Schweinfurt was too small a target to hit effectively at night (and too worthless by day). Of the first wave of bombers only 7 were plotted over the target—and of the second wave only 15. More than 300 bombers had placed their bombs within three miles of the ball-bearing works and 30 did not even come near it.

But a further truth was that, despite the day's accuracy and the night's additional damages, however inaccurate, it made little difference to Germany's supply of ball bearings, since nearly half of Schweinfurt's capacity for production had been dispersed since the October raid. But this kind of information was not being furnished to the planners of Argument by Speer and company.

Friday, February 25, 1944, dawned "bright and clear" over nearly every target in Germany. Those selected for attention were the Messerschmitt plants at Regensburg (scheduled for attack by both the Eighth and Fifteenth Air Forces), the Messerschmitt main plant at Augsburg, the ball-bearing works at

Stuttgart, and an Me-110 components factory at Fürth.

The Fifteenth Air Force, with the bulk of its bombers that day committed to targets in Italy, contributed 176 heavies to its portion of the Regensburg strike. It was upon this force that the Luftwaffe concentrated its attack. Previous experience had taught the Germans that fighter escort from the south was not as heavily "laid on" as from the west. The Fifteenth Air Force still lacked the long-legged (i.e., Mustang) fighters. So, with little or no cover during the phase of its deepest penetration and with small (comparatively) forces, added to the decision of the commander of the German Flieger-division 7 (a Generalmajor Huth) to concentrate on the southern force, the Fifteenth lost one fifth—a total of thirty-three bombers—of its attacking force. With its heavy escorts, including the Mustangs, which could furnish cover over targets even as distant as Regensburg, plus a total bomber strength of more than seven hundred, the Eighth Air Force lost 31 aircraft.

Those aircraft which fought through to their primary targets bombed them with what must have been disheartening effect to Speer. Regensburg and Augsburg, particularly, suffered under massive tonnages of bombs (five hundred tons on Augsburg alone). Regensburg had suffered so badly that for a time it was considered not worth salvaging. However, initial digging revealed that despite the rubble and heavy damage to buildings, the important machine tools had hardly been damaged at all.

To close the Big Week the RAF returned to Augsburg on the night of February 25/26, 1944, compounding the destruction to a despairing degree. The Big Week, which was of course named after the event, was terminated by the weather, not because the Allies believed that their work was done.

What "work," in fact, had been done? Had it actually been a "big week"? It was a popular, not official, designation (it was also called "Blitz Week" by airmen). The taciturn British called it nothing special—they were merely "getting on with the war." But for the Eighth and Fifteenth Air Forces, coming at last into their own, it had truly been a big week. More than 3300 Eighth and more than 500 Fifteenth Air Force bombers had attacked Luftwaffe targets and deposited close to ten thousand tons of bombs on them. In the six-day campaign

a total of 226 bombers were lost (damaged bombers that returned to their bases were also written off); 28 fighters were lost.

Strategic targets were hit as they had never been before; if the total objective had not been attained (for the aircraft industry was not wiped out), a great deal of serious damage was done. Production was crippled for several months (fewer, however, than was estimated by Allied intelligence) and measures were taken to counter this inside Germany. The result was that, because of the work of Speer's lieutenant in charge of the aircraft industry, Otto Saur, fighter production actually rose following the Big Week instead of falling.

This did not make the Big Week a failure, however. Besides the damage done to factories and the number of aircraft destroyed on the ground, the Luftwaffe suffered in the air. The experienced German fighter pilots lost in the encounters with the peashooters, particularly the Mustang, were irreplaceable.

The Luftwaffe night bombers were active too during the Big Week. While responsible air leaders called for more fighters to meet the aerial offensive, Hitler demanded retaliation upon English cities. A young though veteran officer, Dietrich Peltz, was selected to serve as *Angriffsführer England* and to direct the attack. Furnished with few aircraft and inexperienced crews, Peltz accomplished very little in his initial attempts during the spring and through 1943, when he could barely raise a force of 100 bombers for a mission. By the beginning of 1944 he had more than 500 bombers (Ju-88s, Dornier 217s, Heinkel 177s, Ju-188s, Me-410s, and a handful of FW-190 fighter bombers), of which about 460 were operational. With these, but still with green crews, Peltz carried out what was called "the Baby Blitz" (January–May 1944).

The weather showed no favoritism and the *Angriffsführer England* complained of its interference with the success of his missions. About the time that the Allies were sending nearly a thousand bombers per mission against Germany, Peltz averaged about two hundred, which concentrated upon London during the Big Week. The great number of incendiaries dropped indicated that the Germans hoped to raze the British capital; announcements which followed the raid—"several hundred aircraft" which dropped "hundreds of thousands" of incendiaries—were so exaggerated that the claims seemed ludicrous, perhaps more for the eager ears of the rancorous Führer than anyone else. The Baby Blitz did damage, killed people, destroyed property (a high percentage of which could hardly qualify as military objectives), but achieved little more than a smile from Hitler.

### III

After the Big Week came "Big B."
The advent of the peashooters made this possible;

*Fighter pilot Don Gentile with his commanding officer, Donald Blakeslee (right). Latter led the first formations of the 4th Fighter Group's Mustangs to Berlin, March 3, 1944.* (U. S. AIR FORCE)

the fighting during the Big Week proved that which everyone knew: there was no such thing as a "flying fortress." Without fighter escort to and from the target as well as target support, the bomber toll would be costly.

It was Göring, after it was all over, who said that the day he saw American fighters over Berlin he knew "the jig was up." It was a sign of military perspicacity which had, until that March 4, 1944, not been readily discernible . . . if then.

The fighters over Berlin were the Mustangs of the 4th Fighter Group (Eighth Air Force) and those of the Ninth Air Force's 354th and 363rd Groups. The 4th Group had evolved from the Eagle Squad-

rons, several of whose members continued to fly with the 4th. Early in January 1944 the 4th was commanded by the brilliant, young (about twenty-seven), pugnacious Colonel Donald Blakeslee. He had succeeded Colonel Chesley Peterson (who, at twenty-three, had been the youngest colonel in the U. S. Army), an Eagle veteran, detached for duty to the Ninth Air Force to assist in its planning for Overlord.

Blakeslee's Mustang may have been the first American Mustang over Berlin, but he did not fire a shot. In fact, the arrival of the Americans over the Reich capital, though epochal, was not as impressive as the newspapers would have had it. The International News Service, reporting from London under the March 4 [1944] dateline, reported the operation, "carried out in 56-below zero cold and covering 1,500 mile round trip distances," as if it had been a true success: "Escorted U.S. Flying Fortresses, plowing through clouds nearly six miles high, staged history's first American bombing attack on the Berlin metropolitan district today." The London *Evening Standard* editorialized to the effect that this daylight assault was "a sign of unshakeable comradeship" of the British and Americans (this was in answer to German broad hintings at disagreements between the Allies).

The first American attempt to reach Berlin actually occurred on March 3, but cloud, piled to nearly thirty thousand feet, caused the mission to be scrubbed except for a few bombings of opportunity targets short of Berlin. It was a bitter disappointment, for among the more "intrepid" pilots it had become a matter of pride and rivalry to be the first over Big B.

Blakeslee was without doubt one of the most intrepid and, since he led the fighters which spearheaded the first combat box of Fortresses in the run over Berlin, was probably the first of the fighters over the city. But thick, high clouds again interfered. Most of the Fortress forces returned to their bases, or bombed targets of opportunity, but the 95th and 100th Bombardment Groups stubbornly continued on to Berlin with Blakeslee's Mustangs countering the Luftwaffe.

Over Berlin, when the Eighth Air Force for the day dwindled down to a mere twenty-nine B-17s (eleven 100th Bomb Group, the rest from the 95th) and around twenty Mustangs (many had been forced to abort because of various mechanical troubles), the Luftwaffe struck. Even these forces were not impressive—the estimate was about thirty to thirty-five Me-109s and FW-109s. Green flares arched from the bombers, indicating enemy fighters were attacking.

Blakeslee led his fighters in on the German attackers. He himself jumped an Me-109 and fastened to its tail; when he pressed the gun nothing happened. His guns had jammed. Cursing, Blakeslee throttled the Mustang, overtook the German plane, and, as he flew alongside, waved to the pilot. The German waggled his wings in wondering gratitude and flipped away. Blakeslee climbed to a position over the clouded battle zone and directed the fighters to the spots of contention.

"The P-51s saved the day," one of the 100th's gunners said—the 100th lost one plane that day. The 95th lost four B-17s. The day's target had been the Bosch electrical plant in a suburb of Berlin, which actually showed through a break in the clouds for a moment or two. But then it covered again and most of the bombs were dropped with the help of radar; very little damage was done, in fact. But the German capital had finally been attacked by American bombers (German propaganda that night announced that the bombers had been turned back before they ever reached Berlin). Göring, apparently, had not communicated his perturbing divinations to Herr Goebbels.

Even so, it was the initial blow in a new phase in the Battle of Berlin—the final phase.

On March 6 the first full-scale attack took place, the targets being the Bosch works, the Erkner ball-bearing plant, and the Daimler-Benz factory, where aircraft engines were produced. These were not the only targets, for it was hoped that the Luftwaffe would come out to protect the *sancta civitas* of Germany. On this Monday, when even the weather momentarily seemed co-operative, the Luftwaffe co-operated also in its most deadly fashion. If German interception had not been very zealous since the Big Week, it was absolutely ardent on the first big mission to Berlin.

The Germans had devised a new tactic in an attempt to deal with the serious problem of the Mustangs over the target. Three *Gruppen* were dispatched as a unit, one to attack the bombers and the other two to engage the fighters. The newer, high-

flying Me-109 (equipped with the latest Daimler-Benz engine) bounced down upon the Mustangs and Thunderbolts, which on this day also made the trip to Berlin. Besides the Messerschmitts the Germans had mustered FW-190s, equipped with cannon and machine guns, as well as the twin-engined fighters (many drawn from the night fighter units) with their rockets fired out of bomber machine-gun range. About two hundred German aircraft met the oncoming American force.

The Fortresses and Liberators were covered in relays by Lightnings, Thunderbolts, and Mustangs across the North Sea and Holland and deep into Germany. The bomber formations stretched over a distance of fifteen miles from lead group to "tail-end Charley" of the last. The Lightnings and Thunderbolts weaved around the bombers to keep within striking distance of the slower-flying Fortresses and Liberators.

The bombers had flown only fifty miles into Germany when the German fighters struck. The high squadron of the 100th Bomb Group took the brunt of the first attack before the Thunderbolts could sweep in to their aid. Looking up from the lead bomber Major Albert M. Elton was shocked to see that of the nine ships in the high squadron, six trailed sheets of flame. More shock was in store, for another great formation—it seemed like fifty —of German fighters tore through the bombers again. The air filled with burning debris as the large planes were forced to leave the formation. Pilots attempted to keep the planes flying level so that the still living among the crews could jump. Bombs were jettisoned across the countryside on the way to Berlin.

Robert Koper of Beloit, Wisconsin, ordered the crew out of his burning B-17 and was the only man aboard when the ship blew up in the air. Jack Swartout, of San Francisco, piloting *Nelson King,* the lead aircraft of the 100th's 351st Squadron, watched an FW-190 come in head on as the guns rattled. He felt the ship shudder—and then a swift lurch. Swartout found the plane difficult to control even with the help of his copilot, F. G. Lauro. The Focke-Wulf had torn off the tip of the vertical fin. Another ship, flown by Richard Helmick, who saw the trouble Swartout and Lauro were in, pulled alongside to give some support to the stricken bomber—always a favored Luftwaffe

The first full-scale mission to Berlin: March 6, 1944, when Luftwaffe fighter pilots fought ferociously. A

Flying Fortress with an engine aflame falls toward Berlin. (U. S. AIR FORCE)

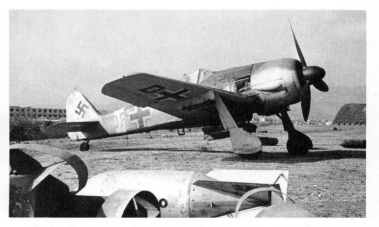

Chief challengers of American daylight bombers: the Me-109 and the FW-190, backbone of the Luftwaffe's fighter force. By 1944, when Allied bombers began attacking Berlin in great numbers, the Messer-

schmitt had just about reached the end of its line; the Focke-Wulf (designed by Dr. Kurt Tank) was a dangerous adversary. It operated also as a fighter-bomber (as did the 190 illustrated).

(IMPERIAL WAR MUSEUM, LONDON)

*Robert S. Johnson, one of the high-scoring fighter pilots of the 56th Fighter Group who fought over Berlin. Johnson's final score was twenty-eight (making him the fourth-ranking U.S. ace). He is seen here with his crew chief, Ernest D. Gould.* (U. S. AIR FORCE)

target. But Helmick had to abandon his position off Swartout's wing when another burning bomber began falling directly toward his plane, which he pulled out of the way.

Unable to join up with any other planes, Swartout turned *Nelson King* around for the long, lonely flight back to England. Before he left, however, the bomb load was dropped "somewhere in Germany."

For forty-five minutes the battle raged—from eleven fifty-nine when the first German fighters had hit until twelve forty-five—and Elton counted no less than seventeen bombers from the 13th Wing (95th, 100th, and 390th Groups) which went down aflame. And Berlin was still a half hour away. In vain, it seemed to the hard-hit groups of Elton's wing, did they look for their own fighters. One lone Thunderbolt flashed through the formation on the tail of an FW-190. The Thunderbolts that had been weaving above them when the Germans arrived were off fighting in another part of the sky.

It was over Berlin that the flak thickened as, for ten seconds, the bombers held a steady course on the bomb run. And on the edge of the flak zone the German fighters waited for the cripples. Mustangs and Thunderbolts tore into the German

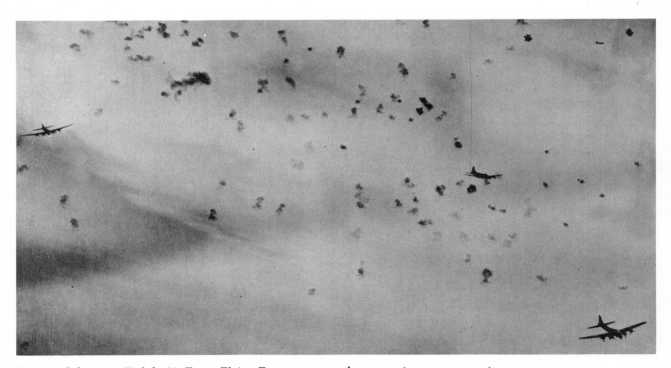

*German flak greets Eighth Air Force Flying Fortresses over the target.* (U. S. AIR FORCE)

fighters, but there seemed an overwhelming number of them and they fought recklessly, with determination and with seeming desperation. If the men in the bombers did not see the American fighters as often as they would have wished, the Luftwaffe saw them.

The 56th Fighter Group (commanded by Colonel Hubert Zempke made its first trip to Berlin that day in its Thunderbolts. Leading A Section himself, Zempke assigned B Section to a young Oklahoman, Robert S. Johnson. Each section consisted of thirty-five P-47s. Over Berlin they joined their archrivals, the 4th Fighter Group in their sleeker Mustangs—which the pilots referred to as "kites"—to take on the Luftwaffe.

If the October 14 mission to Schweinfurt could be called "Black Thursday," the March 6 Berlin attack was definitely "Blue Monday" for both sides. Sixty-nine heavy bombers of the 660 which bombed did not return to their bases in England and 11 fighters were lost in the melee. Bomber crews claimed they had shot down no less than 97 German fighters of all descriptions—the fighters claimed a more modest 82. As was inevitable in such a widespread battle, duplications of claims were made, especially by bomber gunners. But postwar evaluations of German records put the German losses for the day at 80, almost half of its attacking force. The loss in pilots was even more serious than the loss of aircraft.

When the bombers returned two days later, the effect of Monday's fighting was obvious. As 462 bombers dropped their loads on the Erkner bearing factory in a nearly clear sky few German fighters ascended to contest the privilege. Over 170 Mustangs, in turn, were on hand to protect the big friends. Consequently, most of the 37 bombers that fell that day had been flak-ed. But the Erkner friction-bearing factory was hit hard and with chilling precision. Berlin Radio was not advertising that, but it did announce that "a large number of enemy planes were destroyed" over Berlin and admitted that "Berlin has become the front line of the air war."

Hitler, however, was not listening.

The Big B had been attacked and rapidly lost its glamour; like Schweinfurt and Ploesti it stood for heavy losses even if from time to time it appeared that the Luftwaffe had gone under. Soon the more defiant bomber crews sang a bitter song:

*Don't take my boy to Berlin,*
*The dying mother said;*
*Don't take my boy to Berlin,*
*I'd rather see him dead.*

### IV

Captain Don S. Gentile, of Piqua, Ohio, one of Blakeslee's 4th Fighter Group hot-shots, was quoted in the *Stars and Stripes* after the March 6 Berlin mission as saying that "There were so many planes up there today that we were choosy about which ones we shot down."

This was considered a characteristic remark to attribute to a spoiling-for-a-fight fighter pilot, although difficult to assign with any certainty to Gentile. He was not given to such quotes. He was not clever and witty as were so many young pilots; Gentile's chief concern was to shoot down more enemy aircraft than any other pilot in the Air Force.

The 4th Group, with its comparatively long history, its Eagle Squadron traditions, and its youthful pride and combativeness, radiated a glow of cockiness, love of battle, competitiveness (among themselves and with the 56th Fighter Group, Zempke's "Wolfpack"). More typical of the general outlook of the 4th was a sentence penned by Captain Allen

*A 384th Bomb Group Fortress, its tail sheared by flak, follows the group's bombs into Berlin.*

(ROBERT CHAPIN)

*Milestone: a special photograph taken of the first airmen of the 384th Bomb Group who bombed Berlin —and returned.* (ROBERT CHAPIN)

Bunte, who after a battle had closed his official report with the words: "I claim one Me-109 destroyed and one hell of a lot of intrepidity."

Bunte, originally from Eustis, Florida, though never fated to become one of the aces, was one of the 4th's reliables. His intrepidity never deserted

him. Early in April 1944, while on a sweep deep inside Germany shooting up German airdromes, his Mustang struck a high-tension wire and burst into flame. Spotting a nearby lake, Bunte extinguished the fire by the simple expedient of splashing the Mustang into the water. His squadron (334th) mates assumed that was the end of Bunte. The plane nosed into the lake and sank. The impact knocked Bunte unconscious, but though under water he managed to come to in order to free himself of seat belt and chute harness. In time he surfaced, half inflated his dinghy, floated to a tree in the lake, and eventually staggered ashore.

There he was found by that rare human in those days, the "good" German, who wrapped him in a blanket, gave him a cigarette, and delivered him to the Luftwaffe and captivity.

In a galaxy of stars, it was Gentile who seemed to outshine the rest, even the redoubtable Blakeslee. Blakeslee, in fact, though a fine pilot, was not a marksman (he still managed to shoot fifteen enemy aircraft out of the air and to destroy two on the ground); his forte was that intangible, "aggressive leadership." Blakeslee spent more than three years leading his men into battle and, in his case at least, back. He carefully doctored his flight time,

*The Republic P-47 "Thunderbolt" (or "Jug" to fighter pilots), one of the toughest and most versatile aircraft of the Second World War. The early model D (left), the so-called "Razorback," arrived in England in the*

*spring of 1943; the later bubble canopy was introduced in the D models, as were other innovations to increase range and speed of climb. The P-47N (right) was the long-range model (actually designed for Pacific operations).* (B. B. GILKES; REPUBLIC AVIATION)

cutting a few hours here and there (or not at all when serving with a unit other than the 4th) so that he survived over a thousand hours of combat time. Blakeslee was a born warrior.

Gentile's chief rival in the 4th Group was the youthful Duane W. Beeson of Boise, Idaho. At nineteen Beeson enlisted in the Royal Canadian Air Force (1940), and later the 71st Eagle Squadron. He transferred into the 4th Fighter Group in September 1942, along with the other Eagle veterans, Gentile, Blakeslee, Howard Hively, Oscar Coen, et al. The 4th took over an RAF base at Debden, where they lived—because it was a permanent station—in comparative luxury.

The major discomfort seems to have been the change from the dainty Spitfire to the bulky Thunderbolt. Accustomed to the lighter British aircraft, the ex-Eagles found the heavy "Jug" not much to their liking. The P-47, like all untried planes, had its share of bugs and the "prima donnas" (as the 4th Group men were thought to be) found all of them. When he knocked down an FW-190 in a diving fight, Blakeslee was congratulated on the fact that he had proved the P-47 could outdive a Focke-Wulf. "It ought to dive," he is supposed to have said; "it certainly won't climb."

Blakeslee, using his persuasive powers, coaxed Major General William Kepner, head of the Eighth Air Force's Fighter Command, into acquiring some Mustangs for the 4th. At this time the P-51s were going to the Ninth Air Force fighter groups in expectation of tactical support for the coming invasion of *Festung Europa*. Blakeslee talked well for his group and acquired the P-51s in time for the initial assaults on Berlin by the Eighth Air Force. Since the Mustang more closely resembled the Spitfire than the P-47, the 4th Group pilots who had flown the English plane had little trouble in making the transition. Blakeslee promised Kepner that he would have his Mustang group in the air twenty-four hours after delivery of the new fighter. To his pilots he merely stated, "You can learn to fly them on the way to the target."

On the other hand, the 4th's friendly enemies, the 56th Group, equipped with the Thunderbolt, did very well with it. Zempke's Wolfpack led all the other fighter groups in Europe in the number of enemy aircraft destroyed. This did not sit well with the 4th Group pilots, who darkly hinted that

*North American P-51 "Mustang," the favored aircraft of the 4th Fighter Group.* (B. B. GILKES)

while they remained with the bombers as they were supposed to, the 56th went off hunting the "wily Hun" individually. Also, because the 56th was based closer to the English coast than the 4th, the Wolf-pack had more time (i.e., more fuel) to spend over the battle area. These were, of course, rationalizations, but they do reveal the curious philosophy which grew out of keeping "kill" scores. When Gentile spoke of being "choosy" about which planes were to be shot down, he may not have been merely tossing off a printable phrase. But woe to the man who had chosen the wrong plane. One fighter pilot, at least, was nearly court-martialed for shooting down his commanding officer's enemy plane. Since the CO was the number one and the fighter pilot was his wingman, or number two in pecking order, the plane they were attacking belonged, according to unwritten law, to number one.

The more zealous pilots were known to remove a fellow squadron member off the tail of an enemy by shouting the warning word "Break!", the signal that an enemy was getting onto your own tail. When you took evasive action, your savior moved in and shot down your victim. It was all in the game.

Beeson and Gentile never, as far as is known, stole from one another, but each followed the other's scores after missions—just as Bong and McGuire had in the Pacific. Beeson was the more volatile personality, more obviously aggressive, while Gentile revealed little emotion or anxiety. Both men raced neck and neck for several months, approaching the magical Rickenbacker number of twenty-six, until the Germans settled the question once and for all. Leading a low-level mission against a German airdrome in April 1944, Beeson was hit by flak, bailed out, and spent the next thirteen months in Stalag Luft I (with some time spent in solitary for having addressed one of his captors as a "Hun").

On the day that Beeson and the intrepid Bunte went down, Gentile had destroyed five German planes on the ground, which officially brought his score to thirty. (In the European theater enemy aircraft destroyed on the ground received official recognition; according to the American Fighter Aces Association, which recognizes only "aerial victories" against "piloted aircraft," Gentile's final score was 19.84—whatever that means.)

What it did mean was that the youthful (he was then twenty-four) pilot received newspaper space not only in his home town, but all across the United States—and even in England (where the official attitude toward aces continued to be aloof). Gentile was wooed by writers (Ira Wolfert literally moved into Gentile's room, there being a vacancy because his former roommate, Lieutenant Spiro Pissanos, had been forced down in France and taken prisoner). Other correspondents arrived to bring Gentile the attention and fame he had never conceived was possible. He found himself a celebrity with people bidding for his story, girls for his favors, and superior officers for his proximity. It was a heady life.

Gentile's combat record, he was the first to admit, was not entirely of his own making. If the PROs (public relations officers) tended to stress the individual achievements, for the simple reason that the public preferred its heroes singly, the pilots realized that, except for unusual incidents, practically every aerial victory was a two-man job. The wingman concept was an effective lifesaver and equally effective as an enemy destroyer.

Gentile had formed an interchangeable wingman team with a peer, John T. Godfrey. That grand phrasemaker, Winston Churchill, called Gentile and Godfrey "the Damon and Pythias of the twentieth century." But their friendship was purely military. It was so effective that legend has it that Göring said he would exchange two squadrons for the capture of Gentile and Godfrey.

While they were rivals, the two men in battle were all business and operated with a unique give-and-take which enabled them to survive for so long (Gentile was taken out of combat and Godfrey also, though the latter returned and was eventually shot down and taken prisoner; he finally escaped near the end of the war).

Working together the two pilots had developed a technique of interchanging the roles of number one and wingman as the situation demanded. During the March 8, 1944, mission to Berlin the two broke up a large attack upon a Flying Fortress combat box and accounted for six enemy aircraft between them. On the way home, all but out of ammunition, the two men attached themselves to a distressed Fortress, escorting it back to England until they broke off to land at Debden.

This was, of course, their primary function, and it was in this special category that these two young men proved formidable. Godfrey, particularly, had his personal reasons. His P-51, *Reggie's Reply,* was named for his brother, who was lost when his U. S. Navy ship had been sunk by a Nazi U-boat. Besides an exceptional personal motivation Godfrey had extraordinary eyesight—always a valuable asset to the fighter pilot. Quick reflexes and an aggressive spirit, supreme self-confidence, plus the will to excel and,

*Don Gentile and John T. Godfrey, Winston Churchill's "Damon and Pythias" fighter team of the 4th Fighter Group, after an escort mission to Berlin.*

(U. S. AIR FORCE)

*Bombs falling Berlin-ward toward Hitler's Chancellery and Goebbels' Ministry of Propaganda buildings, east of Potsdamer railroad station.* (U. S. AIR FORCE)

most of all, to survive combined to produce the kind of pilot both Gentile and Godfrey were.

Youth was an essential because of the physical, mental, and emotional drain of air fighting, not the least of which was sucking on an oxygen mask. The tension immediately preceding a mission as well as the letdown after were debilitating. The blackout which came under the pressures of a fast dive, the recovery (if you recovered), and a sharp skidding turn were never pleasant. The world grew dim around the edges or completely black for a fraction of a moment as the pull of gravity pulled blood away from the brain. Tremendous cold too was a hazard. So was gnawing fear, however much self-confidence the pilot had built up; perhaps he was better than any enemy flier, but there was always the chance that flak would get him. And even the non-superstitious succumbed to the apprehension that at some unknown point luck would run out.

Fighter pilots like Gentile and Godfrey had courage, but they also knew fear—and admitted it. There came the point in their flying careers when even the competition of the "sport" would not sustain them,

*Gentile's* Shangri-La *sweeping past the photographers —and about to be "pranged," that is, cracked up for no reason at all.* (U. S. AIR FORCE)

when it seemed (especially after a very close call) that surviving one more mission was impossible. Instinct and training and the exhilaration of battle brought the pilot through, but many a very brave man landed at his base and found himself shaking so uncontrollably that he was unable to get out of his plane. There were very few "iron men" like Blakeslee, who seemed impervious to the wear and tear of operations and who fought being taken off combat duty "to fly a desk."

As in the Pacific, star performers in Europe were taken off operations when they acquired a certain notoriety and shipped back to the States for the full treatment—adulation and interviews. Blakeslee had little respect for the celebrity treatment, especially after Gentile, on returning from his last mission, and responding to an audience and a full battery of newsreel cameras, decided to "beat up the field." Near the ground he elected to "fly right into the lens" and succeeded only in "pranging his kite," to Blakeslee the supreme delinquency. After so many missions in his P-51 Gentile managed finally to bounce it into the ground for the benefit of the press. Although he was not seriously injured—still the base doctor saw to it that he was kept out of the reach of Blakeslee for several days—the kite was pranged

indeed, its propeller bent in two directions and its back broken about halfway between cockpit and tail. *Shangri-La* would never fly again.

Blakeslee, who always threatened to throw any man out of the squadron who pranged a kite in a pointless buzz job, was livid. He raged at the newsmen, "You people have just ruined one good man!" Thus ended Don Gentile's last combat mission; since he was scheduled to be taken off operations, it made little difference to his career as a hot-shot combat pilot, although it was an ignominious way to end it. He and Godfrey returned to the United States (just in time to miss out on the "fun" of D-Day). Both were given appropriate greetings by their home towns—Piqua, Ohio (Gentile), and Woonsocket, Rhode Island (Godfrey)—and, to dramatize the efficacy of teamwork in aerial combat, appeared together—both sporting rather dashing mustaches—at War Bond rallies. Gentile was a lion, a role Godfrey did not deny him, but Godfrey soon grew restless and wished to get back to the 4th Fighter Group.

Gentile was denied any chance of returning to

*Godfrey and Gentile, back home, doing their War Bond rally circuit. Gentile never returned to combat, but Godfrey was quickly shipped back to Europe after he publicly stated his views about "brass hats."*

(U. S. AIR FORCE)

combat; he married and became an Army Air Forces test pilot (like Bong, his Pacific competitor, he was killed while flying a jet). Godfrey may have gotten himself shipped back to Europe because of certain statements he made about the Air Force training system "spoon-feeding" its future combat pilots. The "kid-glove policy by 'brass hats' in this country is endangering the lives of all youngsters now in training camps," he intimated.

"They won't let the kids fly when it's cloudy. They won't let them do this or that—until it makes you ill. They wouldn't let me fly the Ohio River with a two-thousand-foot ceiling. I can remember taking off in England when you jumped straight into overcast and stayed that way up to thirty thousand feet or more. . . ."

This did not sit well with the "brass hats," although taking any truly drastic measures against one of the country's best-known heroes would have been extremely indelicate and risky. So, as phrased by Grover C. Hall, Jr., ". . . his status as outstanding AAF warrior evoked the quality of mercy and it fell as a gentle rain. . . ." Godfrey was told to keep his mouth shut and was permitted to return to combat.

But when he did, early in August of 1944, the Luftwaffe was no longer so much in evidence, and like so many fighter pilots of the Eighth and Ninth Air Force, he took to shooting up trains in lieu of aircraft. Strafing missions were considered more dangerous than escort missions because of the hazards of ground fire and the proximity of the ground itself—not to mention high-tension wires, trees, and other obstacles. While churning up Herzberg airfield in Germany, Godfrey was struck by flak and plowed into the ground. Though he attempted to hide out for a couple of days, he was captured by the Germans. He succeeded in escaping from his Stalag Luft (on his third attempt) and made it back to the Allied lines on April 17, 1945, at Nuremberg. By then the air war was all but over in Europe.

While Gentile and Godfrey were the most celebrated of the 4th Fighter Group's high-spirited crew, there were many others of note also: Duane Beeson, already mentioned; Ralph K. "Kid" Hofer, who liked to hunt on his own and disappeared one day in July 1944 over Hungary; James Goodson, who was known as "the King of the Strafers"; and Howard Hively, Fred W. Glover, Willard Mil-

*Gun-camera views of a fighter strafing a German train in the final months of the war, when Luftwaffe planes became scarce.* (U. S. AIR FORCE)

"Beware of thin cirrus clouds . . ." *haven of German fighters which pounced upon fighters and bombers. In* *the foreground an H2X ("Mickey")-equipped B-17 accompanies other Fortresses over Germany.*

(CECIL COHEN)

likan, Nicholas Megura, James A. Clark, Kendell E. Carlson, and Pierce W. McKennon, to name but a few more of the dozens of colorful characters of a colorful group.

When the war ended the group was commanded by Colonel Everett W. Stewart. Blakeslee had returned to the States, to other duties and to marriage. When he left the 4th Group, it was with a minimum of emotional display, as befitted the man. But, as a curious sequel to the Gentile incident, the always alert Blakeslee unwittingly revealed his inner feelings during a simple flight after he had been relieved of his command and forbidden to fly in combat. While coming in for a landing, bemused and out of

sorts, he put down but without remembering to lower his landing gear. Blakeslee, the imperturbable, had pranged his own kite.

It was time to go home; and he did.

When the war ended there were fifteen fighter groups in the Eighth Air Force (and eighteen in the Ninth); the entire war effort, obviously, had not fallen on the 4th Fighter Group. It was that this unit closed the war as the highest-scoring group in the ETO (1016 enemy aircraft). Second was its archcompetitor, the 56th Fighter Group, Zempke's famed Wolfpack, with 1006. 5 enemy aircraft destroyed (both in the air and on the ground).

"A fighter pilot must possess an inner urge to do

combat," Zempke once told his men. "The will at all times to be offensive will develop into his own tactics. If your enemy is above, never let your speed drop and don't climb, because you'll lose too much speed. If you're attacked on the same level, just remember you can outclimb him. Beware of thin cirrus clouds—the enemy can look down through them but you can't look up through them. Don't go weaving through valleys of cumulus clouds, either with a squadron or by yourself. The enemy can be on your tail before you know it.

"When popping down out of a cloud, or up, always do a quick turn and look back. You may have jumped out directly in front of a gun barrel. When attacked by large numbers of enemy aircraft, meet them head on. In most cases half of them will break and go down. Handle all those remaining in an all-out fight until you're down to one—then take him on.

"If there are twenty aircraft down below, go screaming down with full force to pick out the most logical target at the point of firing. Then pull up to a good altitude and develop an attack on one of those remaining enemy pilots who had been shaken out of his helmet by your sudden onslaught.

"I stay with the enemy until he is destroyed, I'm out of ammunition, he evades into the clouds, or I'm too low on gas and ammo to continue. When you have your squadron with you and the enemy has so much altitude you never would get up to him, stay below and to the rear of him—he'll be down.

"Learn to break at the proper time to make a head-on attack—the enemy doesn't like it. Don't run. That's just what he wants you to do. When caught by the enemy in large force, the best policy is to fight like hell until you can decide what to do."

Zempke, a forestry major from the University of Montana and a prewar Army Air Corps pilot, happened to be in Russia demonstrating the P-40 to Soviet Air Force pilots when the Japanese attacked Pearl Harbor. During December 1942–January 1943, as commanding officer he brought over the 56th Fighter Group and its massive new Thunderbolt fighter (the P-47B). Zempke's group joined the 78th—which had lost most of its P-38s and pilots to the north African invasion. It too was issued the heavy, ungainly, but powerful P-47.

The Wolfpack went into combat in April of 1943

and by November of that year had exceeded its own goal of a hundred enemy aircraft destroyed by Christmas. It was the first American fighter group in Europe to achieve this score—which was more than mere scorekeeping, for it represented, in the words of fighter commander Major General William Kepner, "an untold number of our bombers . . . saved."

The 56th Fighter Group had its full share of aces, among them Zempke himself. Others included Gerald W. Johnson, Walker Mahurin, David Schilling, Robert S. Johnson, and Francis Gabreski. Zempke, Schilling, and Gabreski were called by the Germans "the Terrible Three," in recognition of their deadliness as fighter pilots.

Gabreski was enrolled as a pre-med student at

*Hubert A. Zempke, commanding officer of the 56th Fighter Group—the "Wolfpack." His Thunderbolt is fitted with the new "paddle blade" propeller, which increased the P-47's rate of climb.* (JOSEPH ORAVEC)

Notre Dame when he enlisted as an aviation cadet in July 1940; he was commissioned the following March. On December 7, 1941, Second Lieutenant Gabreski was serving with the 45th Fighter Squadron of the 15th Fighter Group and stationed at Wheeler Field, Hawaii. The Japanese bombing and strafing of the field, Gabreski recalls, was "effective." But so was U.S. antiaircraft gunnery later. When he was able to take off some two hours after the attack had begun (and, in fact, was over), Gabreski and the other eleven pilots in their P-40s had their formation broken up over Pearl Harbor by American antiaircraft fire. Gabreski remained with the 15th Group for almost a year (a year of near inactivity) and then was transferred to 8th Fighter Command in England because of "linguistic qualifications." He was able to speak Polish as well as a little Czech.

So for a while Gabreski continued with near inactivity, serving with Intelligence as interpreter. But "I wanted to fly airplanes." That became a clear, rather loud statement after a month, and the Air Force, wishing to keep Captain (as he was by then) Gabreski happy, shipped him to Ferry Command at Prestwick, Scotland, where he flew airplanes, all types, from the B-24 to the P-38.

"It was pretty dull after two months and I started saying 'get me out of Ferry Command!'" Which was easier said than done; Gabreski languished for another month until in November 1942, after a chance meeting with Polish fighter pilots serving with the RAF in London, he got himself transferred to No. 315 Squadron ("Deblin"). Technically Gabreski was assigned as a liaison officer to the Polish Air Force on TDY (temporary duty). Flying the Spitfire, Gabreski participated in twenty combat missions, acquiring good training in aerial combat.

So it was that when the 56th Fighter Group was forming up, Gabreski was ready when asked by Colonel Robert Landry, then lining up "talent" for the group. Gabreski joined the group as the operations officer of the 61st Squadron; in time he commanded this squadron as "Keyworth Blue Leader."

Making the transition from the Spitfire to the Thunderbolt posed no serious problem for Gabreski; he soon learned to love the plane's ruggedness. During an escort mission to Oldenburg, Germany (November 26, 1943), Gabreski was leading a section of the 61st Squadron when he caught sight of a large

formation of Me-110s. These were the rocket-firing fighters which tore up the bomber formations so badly. In turn, the 110s were themselves escorted by single-engined fighters above.

Keyworth Blue Leader immediately swept in to break up the attack. With the squadron behind him, fanning out and selecting their targets, Gabreski made a pass on the Messerschmitts. The Big Thunderbolt tore through the formation and Gabreski kicked it into a turn and looked back to see what the result had been. He spotted a lone Me-110

"Keyworth Blue Leader" Francis Gabreski in his 56th Fighter Group Jug. Gabreski was the third-scoring fighter ace of the war and the number one living ace when the war ended. (U. S. AIR FORCE)

which had broken away from the others and seemed headed for home. Undoubtedly he had made a hit, for the plane had begun a descending spiral.

Gabreski closed in "rapidly, firing on the way. At first I was really wasting ammunition. Then I got a real good burst into the cockpit and the engines. All my guns were bearing on the airplane when—about a hundred yards away—it exploded and instantly decelerated.

"It appeared to me as if I would ram right into him; quickly I pushed forward on the stick. Burned parts of the plane came through the vent system into my cockpit, fragments of the Messerschmitt hit the Thunderbolt, but I managed not to run into an engine."

In seconds Gabreski had swept through the debris and, finding himself still air-borne and his P-47 apparently operational, scanned the battle area. He saw another Me-110 maneuvering into position out of the bomber's gun range in order to begin lobbing rockets. Gabreski throttled the Thunderbolt into position and with a few short bursts sent the second Messerschmitt burning in a steep dive.

Though outnumbered, Gabreski's section had suc-

*Gabreski and Steven Garick discussing fighter tactics in England after a fighter sweep over France.*

(U. S. AIR FORCE)

ceeded in breaking up the attack by the rocket launchers (for which he was awarded with the Distinguished Service Cross).

It was only after he had returned to his home base at Halesworth that he actually realized what the exploding Messerschmitt had done to his P-47. The wing's leading edges were crushed and the left wing was badly torn. The engine cowling was dented and gouged and the plane was scorched. A 20-mm. shell was lodged in the engine. One cylinder was cracked but not seriously enough to have impaired the engine's efficiency.

Having studied his aircraft, Gabreski walked into

the debriefing session and claimed "two Messerschmitt-110s destroyed and one P-47 half destroyed."

By the summer of 1944 Gabreski had thirty-one aerial victories to his credit—the highest score in the European theater. (His ground-destroyed score was 2.5 officially.) He had accumulated hundreds of hours of combat time and at least a dozen decorations, including those from the Polish, British, and French governments. The air war had changed a great deal in the twenty-one months he had been flying in fighter planes. The war was not over, but it was more difficult to find the Luftwaffe air-borne. Consequently, the fighters went down to the deck to shoot up the Luftwaffe in its own nests, on the ground.

On July 20, 1944, after escorting bombers on a mission, Gabreski led the fighters in an airdrome strafing. This had become customary at this phase of the war. Having spotted the airfield, near Coblenz, Gabreski decided to finish off its parked planes.

If no planes rose to challenge the Thunderbolts, there was plenty of flak. Gabreski dived the big aircraft down to treetop level and began working the field over, leaving a trail of pockmarked concrete in his wake along with burning planes. Racing over the field close to the ground Gabreski found himself "overshooting a plane on the ground. I stuck the nose down a little to get on the target and the propeller hit the ground. Oil sprayed all over my windshield and canopy. . . .

"The engine was obviously failing and this meant I must either belly-land or bail out. But bailing out meant climbing up into the flak. So I found a nearby wheat field and despite excess speed—about one hundred and seventy, two hundred miles an hour—I set the plane on the ground with the wheels up. Just before I struck, I kicked to the side so that the wing crumpled and took much of the shock of the impact.

"Crumpling and crackling, the plane plowed across the field and then stopped. The aircraft was still in one piece—but smoking. That scared me. I tried to open the canopy but couldn't open it more than four or five inches. I removed the parachute but I still couldn't push through the narrow opening. The smoke got thicker and thicker. I was really frightened by that time; my adrenalin was flowing

*German fighters burning on their base after American fighter planes strafed the field. (This photo came from the gun-camera of Colonel Ben Rimerman, who destroyed six planes.)* (U. S. AIR FORCE)

*Thunderbolts "on the deck" (in this photo caught during takeoff). It was at about this height that strafing missions were carried out and during which Gabreski's propeller struck the ground and he ended up in a German POW camp.* (U. S. AIR FORCE)

heavily and I managed to pull the canopy open enough so I could jump out and began running from the burning plane. There was a crackle and whistle which I realized was bullets from some troops approaching the plane.

"I outran the troops and moved into a nearby woods, where I found a shelter inside which there was a religious shrine. I hid under the shrine and when the soldiers searched the shelter I was hidden within a foot of the search party.

"After that, for four days, moving only at night, I walked for what I thought was Luxembourg. On the fourth day I became more ambitious and even walked in the daytime. I walked right by a farmer and a little boy with a few cows."

The two immediately set up a hue and cry and within minutes Gabreski was in the hands of the Wehrmacht and on his way to Stalag Luft I at Barth on the Baltic Sea in northern Germany. There he would join the Air Force elite, among them Gerald Johnson of his own 56th Fighter Group, Duane Beeson of the 4th—and, eventually, even Zempke.

Gabreski was turned over to the Luftwaffe and sent to the interrogation center at Dulag Luft. As one of the Terrible Three, his fame had obviously preceded him. He opened the door and walked in to confront the interrogator—"we called him 'Stone Face' Scharrf." The stone face cracked into a smile.

"Well, Colonel, we've been expecting you for a long time."

# 4

# DER GROSSE SCHLAG

When Colonel Hubert Zempke was knocked down at the end of October 1944 he, like Gabreski, was greeted by a Luftwaffe officer with a sense of humor.

"Now," he said beaming, "when we get old Blakeslee, the war will be over."

He was close to the truth; only his reasoning was wrong. The war was over, or should have been, but Hitler refused to concede to the facts. The Germans faithfully fought on, trusting in the intuition of a madman; the slaughter and destruction continued despite the inevitable outcome.

The beginning of the end had finally come with the invasion of Normandy on June 6, 1944—D-Day. Hitler's vaunted Atlantic Wall, despite its various fiendish killing devices, the brain children of that military darling, Rommel, had a hole in it. It was an opening which literally ascended to the skies. On the eve of D-Day the Supreme Commander Dwight D. Eisenhower could say with near certainty to troops about to embark upon what he called a "great crusade," "You needn't worry about the air. If you see a plane it will be ours."

Assaulting the beaches at Normandy, though successful, was no simple walk-in; and had Eisenhower been overly optimistic in his appraisal of the air situation, and had the Luftwaffe been able to lash out in force, the story of the bloody beaches of Normandy would have been tragically bloodier.

Where was the Luftwaffe?

The American GI was pragmatic; he wanted to believe his Supreme Commander, but he would also wait to see how it all turned out. But it was true, except for a few ineffectual fighter sweeps over the landing beaches, there were no German aircraft.

The most persistent inquirer as to the absence of the Luftwaffe was the German soldier, while the beaches churned and seethed under the pounding of Allied naval guns, heavy bombing, medium bombers, and fighter bombers. Sperrle's Luftflotte 3, with headquarters in Paris, could only count on about 320 operational aircraft—and of these only 125 were fighters—to meet the overwhelming sea and air invasion, plus the literally thousands of Allied planes (the American Eighth and Ninth Air Forces alone dispatched 8772 aircraft; to these were added some 5656 by the RAF's Second Tactical Air Force, Air Defence of Great Britain—formerly Fighter Command—Coastal Command, and Bomber Command). Considering the number of aircraft in the air that day, Allied losses were reasonably low—and most could be attributed to flak—reaching a total of 113 (71 American). Only 33 German aircraft were claimed to have been destroyed—an index to the minimal countermeasures attempted by the Luftwaffe.

This was yet another consequence of the Combined Bomber Offensive of the previous winter.

*The Normandy beach one month before D-Day. P-38 pilot Albert Lanker of the 10th Photo Reconnaissance Group obtained this "dicing" shot showing the various types of obstacles Rommel had distributed along the coast of France. (*U. S. AIR FORCE*)*

*German soldiers scatter as Lanker comes in closer to "dice" the timber ramps, which were mined or armed with saw-toothed blades for dealing with landing craft.* (U. S. AIR FORCE)

*Lanker photographs gun positions dug into the side of a cliff at Normandy; a pillbox is situated at the bottom of the cliff.* (U. S. AIR FORCE)

*Before the Normandy landings heavy bombers joined the mediums, and the fighters, in cutting off all arteries —roads and railroads—into the invasion area. A Flying Fortress bombs a rail junction at Versailles two days before D-Day.* (U. S. AIR FORCE)

Anxious Luftwaffe chiefs had begun bringing the fighters closer to home to fight off the bombers over Germany. The invasion, which everyone expected any minute, began to take on secondary importance to the protection of the Reich.

On the morning of D-Day Geschwaderkommodore Oberst Josef Priller of Jagdgeschwader 26 commanded three *Gruppen* which had been dispersed all over France. One, I/JG 26, was based at Rheims in northern France; another, III/JG 26, had been flown to Metz, also in northern France, closer to the German border. The third, II/JG 26, had been sent all the way to Gascony in southern France and based near the city of Mont-de-Marsan.

Priller, whose victory score had reached a total of more than ninety "kills," was as outspoken as he was headlong in his fighter tactics. He raged over the dispersal of his units from his base at Lille. With invasion obviously in the air, he bluntly told an officer at Fliegerkorps II that he thought

they were all insane; the squadrons they had so stupidly scattered all over France would be needed along the coast. Priller, with a reputation for a hot temper, was permitted to abuse even a general, but was then told that the weather had turned bad on June 5 (the original date set by Eisenhower) and the good days of May had gone by, so there would be no invasion.

At the Lille airdrome Priller, who had remained to oversee the movement of his *Geschwader*'s supplies, records, and ground crews, commanded two aircraft—FW-190As—on the morning of June 6. One of the planes was his; the other belonged to his *Rottenflieger* (wingman), Feldwebel (Flight Sergeant) Heinz Wodarczyk. Angry, disgusted, and certain that something real was brewing, Priller suggested to Wodarczyk that for the moment there was nothing further for them to do except get drunk. Which they did.

He was awakened in the early morning by a

nervous caller from Fliegerkorps II. There was a good deal of air activity and something seemed to be going on in the Channel; perhaps—as a precaution —he should place his *Geschwader* on the alert. Hung over, sleepy, and still disgusted, Priller, once more or less awake, erupted in fine style. Verbally he strafed the Fliegerkorps, then the Luftflotte High Command, on up to Göring himself. Had the fools forgotten that they had ordered all his planes away? His whole damn *Geschwader* at Lille was already on the alert with its total air force of two planes.

"Who the hell am I supposed to alert?" he shouted. "I'm alert. Wodarczyk is alert!" He hung up.

But the phone rang a few moments later. Flieger-korps again, informing him that all was well, there was no alert, and there would be no invasion. Well, they were wrong again.

The phone rang for the third time just before eight o'clock later that morning. The invasion *was* on. An attempt would be made to get his *Gruppen* back. Meanwhile, could he do something? The two FWs were ready to go, of course—but that readi-ness was for the trip to join his *Geschwader*. He and Wodarczyk could get down to the invasion area and strafe the beaches. Invading troops would be like sitting ducks to aerial attack. But how many other Luftwaffe planes would be in on the show?

The two men ran to their "Butcher Birds" and before they took off Priller ordered Wodarczyk to stick to him as he had never stuck before. They

might very well be the only German planes over the invasion area—and he did not really expect that they would make it.

The two planes raced southward from Lille and crossed the Somme (near Abbeville they saw great loose formations of Allied fighter planes, but suc-ceeded in skirting them). Near Le Havre, approach-ing the Normandy beaches, Priller led Wodarczyk into the clouds. Through breaks in the cloud they saw a sight that shook the imagination: thousands of ships dotted the Channel, ships of every descrip-tion from small, skittering landing craft to great bat-tleships which pounded the beaches with their big guns. The beaches were black with troops, supplies, vehicles, and the debris of battle.

The air was black too: fighters, bombers, supply planes, antiaircraft bursts. But except for their two Focke-Wulfs, there were no German planes. With amazing objectivity, Priller looked upon the impres-sive sight of Allied endeavor and said, "What a show!"

Their contribution, he knew, would be very small. What with the planes, the ships with their flak, and the barrage balloons, they just might make one pass before they fell.

Coming from the east, the first beaches they came to were those of the British—"Sword," "Juno," and "Gold," a stretch of about fifteen miles.

"We're going in, Wodarczyk," Priller said. "Good luck." He pushed the throttle all the way, eased the control column forward, and hurtled down on Sword beach. Barely a hundred feet over the sand, and racing at more than 350 miles an hour, Priller and Wodarczyk opened up with their machine guns

*British-built "Horsa" gliders on June 6, 1944—D-Day —awaiting American air-borne troops to board for France.* (NATIONAL ARCHIVES)

*Gliders carrying air-borne infantry were towed by C-47s; so-called "snap" takeoff is demonstrated here as the C-47 catches the glider towrope. Glider was then released over the landing areas in France.*

(U. S. AIR FORCE)

radar installations by the RAF had its effect. Then on D-Day itself the heavy onslaught hammered at airfields, destroyed planes on the ground, and furnished close support to the troops on the beachheads. It was not till around eight in the evening —thanks to a breakdown in communications—that the first German reinforcements left Cologne for France. All of twenty-two fighters took off in the twilight with Villacoublay (near Paris) as their destination. The hastily trained pilots got lost in the darkness, ran into Allied fighters, encountered bad weather, and suffered accordingly. Only two of these planes actually arrived at Villacoublay. The rest were shot down, crashed upon landing at advanced bases under Allied attack, or suffered accidents because of pilot error. By the next day—D plus 1—

and cannon. Their unexpected and sudden attack sent men scurrying for cover, but despite the confusion and terror, some fire came back at them. The two planes whipped over the British beaches, the target of countless antiaircraft guns from the ships, and came to the eastern edge of the Americans' "Omaha" beach, where at an altitude of less than fifty feet over the carnage they dodged balloons. Their ammunition spent, Priller and Wodarczyk climbed for the clouds to the south and inland, away from the beaches of Normandy. They had made their pass and were miraculously unscathed. As the two lone aircraft zoomed away from the flak and ground fire, there were men in the British ships who were happy to see them make it after their incredible show of courage.

Priller and Wodarczyk, however, were the only representatives of the once irrepressible Luftwaffe to appear over Normandy on D-Day (a handful of Ju-88s bombed the beachheads during the night). All the "conquests, glories, triumphs, spoils" had "shrunk to this little measure."

There had been plans and promises: when the invasion came the *Oberkommando der Luftwaffe* would dispatch reinforcements to Sperrle for meeting it on the beaches. But preinvasion strafing and bombing of airfields and particularly of German

*A Marauder of the Ninth Air Force passes over Allied landing craft headed for the beaches of Normandy. The B-26 is painted in special invasion stripes, making it easier to identify by ship crews and ground troops.*

(U. S. AIR FORCE)

only one of the original twenty-two aircraft was still operational.

Aerial activity on D-Day, and for days following, was one-sided; the Allies had complete air superiority. A German soldier could write home that "the American fliers are chasing us like rabbits." So were British Mustangs and Typhoons pursuing troops as well as paralyzing troop movements by rail and road. Bridges too were destroyed if no vehicles were found. (For weeks in advance of the invasion railroads and bridges over which reinforcements might have come into Normandy were also destroyed. So, of course, were other such targets in other areas, so as not to give away the location of the landing areas. However, on the night before the invasion, leaflets were dropped from Allied planes

*Flying arsenal: a Marauder of the 386th Bomb Group moves in on an objective literally bristling with guns. Note the cut-out gun position below the tail; also the forward firing guns just below the wing—and a bomb about to fall from the bomb bay.* (U. S. AIR FORCE)

*The business end of a Hawker "Typhoon"; a fighter-bomber of considerable impact, particularly in low-altitude operations against trains and troops.*
(IMPERIAL WAR MUSEUM, LONDON)

advising the French inhabitants to get out of the general zones of invasion.)

Field Marshal Rommel had hoped to catch the invaders on the beaches and, with sufficient reinforcements, stop them at the water's edge. But when he called for additional Panzer forces, these were denied him. Hitler had ordered that no panzers could be used without his permission. Thus as the Allied bridgehead widened and deepened and the German commanders phoned frantically, Hitler slept. He did not awaken until three in the afternoon, when he did grant permission to Rommel to add the 12th SS Panzer and the Panzer Lehr divisions to his already available 21st Panzer Division, which had begun moving into Normandy from the vicinity of Caen.

But it was too late; reinforcements were harried by Allied aircraft and did not arrive in force until June 9; by this time, in the words of Rommel's chief of staff, Hans Speidel, "the initiative lay with the Allies." And they had come, despite Hitler's wishful thinking, to stay. Within three weeks of landings thirty-one Allied squadrons were operating from airfields in and around the beachheads. Traveling over the roads of France was a hazard. By the end of July seventeen of the Ninth Air Force's eighteen fighter-bomber groups were operating from

Normandy airstrips—gashed through the hedgerows —to join the various tactical aircraft—fighters and medium bombers—of the RAF and the U. S. Air Force.

No one was safe, not even generals. In the afternoon of July 17, 1944, as he raced in an open staff car on a return trip to his headquarters after visiting various trouble spots, Rommel was attacked by Spitfires of No. 602 Squadron. The planes dived on the car, driving it off the road, where it overturned. Rommel, flung from the car, suffered a fractured skull. Although he survived the serious injuries, Rommel later committed suicide as an alternative to standing trial for high treason for his complicity in a plot on Hitler's life which occurred three days later.

On July 10—the day Gabreski went down—an attempt was made to kill Hitler with a bomb. It failed in its primary purpose, although several high officials then in Hitler's bunker were killed, among them Jeschonnek's successor, Luftwaffe General Gunther Korten. He, in turn, was to have been succeeded by Werner Kreipe. The latter, however, because of certain mannerisms was known around Führer headquarters as "Fraulein" Kreipe. Hitler would not hear of his appointment (although Kreipe had proved himself a competent staff officer), dismissing the idea with the remark that he would not "have any woman around the place."

The job fell to General Karl Koller, once a staff officer of Luftflotte 3 (during the Battle of Britain) and then serving as Chief of Operations of the Luftwaffe. Koller was experienced, capable, and all but totally fed up with the Reichsmarschall. He was summoned to Karinhall, Göring's country estate not far from Berlin. The setting was mythical, a sprawling hunting lodge gone baroque beyond the wildest dreams of an extravagant prince. Göring named it for his first wife, a Nordic (Swedish) beauty who had been a particular favorite of Hitler and who, if possible, exceeded him in virulent anti-Semitism. Karinhall thus became a shrine to her (for a time the first lady of the Reich) and a symbol of Göring's position in the government. In time he had Karin's body removed from its grave in Sweden and placed in a magnificent vault at Karinhall. Her macabre proximity seemed not to upset Göring's second wife, a former actress, Emmy Sonnemann.

As the war turned more sour, Göring could be found more frequently in the comfortingly medieval setting, away from the realities of the twentieth century.

The great main hall of Karinhall was dominated by a massive stone fireplace; the log walls prickled with antlers of such stags as were unlucky enough to have run into the Great Hunter (one of Göring's official titles was that of Reich Master of the Hunt). The skins of bear decorated the floor.

Koller, embittered and driven by the realities, found such trophies uninteresting. When Göring told him that he wished to appoint Koller chief of staff of the Luftwaffe, he assumed that Koller's reluctance to accept was attributable to the fact that he had not been asked before. Koller than asked if he could speak frankly. Göring granted permission.

Although he did not use the colorful language Priller employed, Koller was as blunt as Galland in his criticism of his chief. Göring had not shown his face in the Luftwaffe operations headquarters in a year. He kept in touch only by phone, and at that, it was all too frequently through an adjutant and not directly. Also, Koller had a large file of unanswered telegrams sent to Göring, requesting decisions on important matters. As a precaution, these were filed in the official War Diary—a complete record in an official state paper of Göring's abandonment of his authority and duty.

Göring's heavy head was by then buried in his hands. Whimpering and moaning, he finally pleaded, "Koller, you must help me. You must accept. I'll be good, I promise."

Koller accepted, later admitting that when Göring was contrite he was "irresistible." The Luftwaffe had a new, hardheaded chief of staff, but did the *Chef des Generalstabs der Luftwaffe* have an air force? When Koller assumed his duties, he too might very well have asked the one great question of D-Day: "Where is the Luftwaffe?"

II

The Luftwaffe had been frittered away in the Battle of Britain, had been squandered in the Russian offensive, and was being consumed by the Allied air offensive. And when Hitler elected to activate Barbarossa, the Russian sneak attack, he

Wo ist der Luftwaffe? *Lightnings, in invasion stripes, on the prowl. This kind of formation would have been* *near suicide had there been a Luftwaffe to worry about.* (U. S. AIR FORCE)

*Henschel 123s in Russia; during the early months of Barbarossa even such obsolete aircraft as these were more than a match for the inferior Russian Air Force. These aircraft, also of the Stuka class, were used for dive-bombing.* (H. J. NOWARRA)

Hans von Seeckt at the Kazan tank schools and at Lipesk's aviation center. The wheels of a blind but inexorable justice turned greedily, for if Hitler bestowed, Russia absorbed: men, tanks, and aircraft.

Barbarossa, which erupted on June 22, 1941, marked the final resurgence of the Stuka, that unlovely harbinger of blitzkrieg. By this late date it would have seemed improbable that yet another classic blitzkrieg could be executed successfully. But it was, despite the warnings through British sources in Moscow and the near-pathological suspicion with which Stalin regarded an ally; he trusted his friend Hitler until the Heinkel 111s bombed Russian airfields and three great German army groups moved along a front stretching two thousand miles. With first light the Stukas came to bomb the airfields and to assist the panzers. In the first day an estimated two thousand Russian aircraft were destroyed, most of them on the ground. It was like a repeat of the Polish campaign.

*Heinkel 111 bombing up for a mission in Russia.*
(H. J. NOWARRA)

*Heinkel bomber on the way to its target in Russia.*
(H. J. NOWARRA)

placed the German war machine in a precarious position: war on no less than three fronts. The major front, of course, lay in the east, where the objective was "to vanquish Soviet Russia in a swift campaign."

No less than four *Luftflotten,* comprising nearly two thousand operational warplanes—two thirds of Germany's aerial strength at the time—were unleashed by Barbarossa. It was overwhelming, swift, surprising, and ironic. For Hitler now returned, with interest, to the Russians the Stukas and panzers which had been fostered there in the heyday of

*The Polikarpov I-16, which first saw combat in the Spanish Civil War, later in the little-known war between Japan and Russia (May 1939–June 1940), and later on the Eastern Front after the launching of Barbarossa. Called* Mosca *("Fly") by friend and* Rata *("Rat") by foe, the I-16 was one of the world's first modern fighters. Conceived in 1932 and first flown late in 1933, the I-16 could boast several advanced design ideas for the time, including a retractable landing gear. Though a tough plane to take off with and land, it was good in flight. By 1941, however, it was obsolescent.* (NAVY DEPT., NATIONAL ARCHIVES)

The Russians fought courageously, but poorly led and ill equipped, they fell back under the onslaught. Russian aircraft, most of them obsolete, were no match for the Me-109, particularly the new "F" model. Even the Stuka was capable of dealing with such aircraft as the Polikarpov I-15, a biplane with a fixed landing gear (the I-153 was a variant of the same plane with a retractable undercarriage). The "Rata" (Polikarpov I-16) was a more formidable, though also outdated, fighter plane, and while it could deal with the Stuka, it was no match for the Messerschmitt.

It would have appeared then that the Great Military Thinker had done it again. The German war machine rolled practically unchecked into Russia, averaging as much as ten miles a day. By September the German armies had pushed hundreds of miles into Russia all along its broad front. The Russians had fallen back, were taken prisoner or killed;

Russian casualties totaled into the millions. By late September, although German forces were practically at the gates of Moscow, the Russians gained an inestimable ally, "General Winter." By December it was obvious to all but Hitler that the new blitzkrieg had failed. As if to assure the ultimate failure, he appointed himself the Supreme Commander of the German forces on December 16; by this time, thanks to Japan, Russia had yet another ally of which it could be suspicious: the United States.

Both the Luftwaffe and the Russian Air Force were tied down to their armies; but Russia enjoyed one advantage. Its British and American allies, however suspect, employed strategic air forces. Germany had no such advantage. Even though the Russian air forces were virtually destroyed in the first phase of the blitzkrieg, the Germans were not capable of destroying the Urals factories deep inside Russia. The "Urals Bomber" (the four-engined Ju-89 or the

*The Russian Yak-9, one of the newly developed Soviet fighters that proved capable of taking on the Luftwaffe.* (U. S. AIR FORCE)

Do-19) which Wever had projected simply did not exist when it was needed. Despite Barbarossa Russian aircraft production rose sharply. It took time, but the Russians, particularly with the aid of General Winter, rammed the German war machine right back to Berlin.

Barbarossa was not proving to be the "swift" war Hitler had foreseen. During the spring and summer the Germans would revive the offensive, only to have winter set in again. Operations of aircraft became nearly impossible because of the ferocious cold. Vehicles froze to the ground, engines not kept running did not run again, some burst when the water-cooling system solidified. Planes skidded on icy landing strips, many crashed in the fog, others simply disappeared and were never heard from again. While the Wehrmacht and the Luftwaffe remained frigidly immobile, the factories of the Urals turned out new tanks—the powerful T-34—and new aircraft—the Lavochkin 5, the Yakovlev 9, and the Ilyushin 2 ("Sturmovik")—to which were added Hurricanes, Tomahawks, and Airacobras.

The Luftwaffe suffered further loss of numbers

—again to Hitler's ambitions—when Kesselring was withdrawn from the Russian front and sent to the Mediterranean as Commander in Chief, South and other units were withdrawn to reinforce the defenses of the Reich, under attack by both the RAF and the U. S. Air Force.

When winter came in 1942 it was obvious to all but its author that Barbarossa was a serial, not a short story, and that the ending would be sad. The summer offensive had brought the Sixth Army of General Friedrich Paulus up to the Volga, just north of Stalingrad. But once there, with troops exhausted, supply lines long, and forces thin, Paulus ran out of steam. The Luftwaffe, lacking numbers, was reduced to purely support actions in conjunction with the infantry or artillery. Bombers were employed as transports, carrying supplies to troops. When Paulus suggested that the Stalingrad front be withdrawn so that his flanks would not be exposed, Hitler replied, "I will not leave the Volga!"

He was not, of course, actually there. Paulus was, and with his armies composed of reluctant Rumanian, Italian, and Hungarian troops, besides Germans, he feared the consequence of the Russian winter offensive. In brief, the consequence was that twenty-two German divisions were encircled in and around the rubble of what had been Stalingrad. Hitler, in spirit, stood fast on the Volga.

His pleas for permission to withdraw having been denied, Paulus next had the problem of supplying 250,000 men. This would require some seven hundred tons of material each day: How was he to keep Hitler on the Volga if his troops were starving, freezing, and out of ammunition and fuel?

Hitler solved that too. He cornered Göring at a situation conference at the Führer headquarters and told the Luftwaffe chief that unless the Sixth Army could be supplied by airlift at Stalingrad the army was lost.

Göring, anxious to get back into Hitler's good graces after so many Luftwaffe "failures," answered, "We will do the job!" Göring, so out of touch with any practical operation of the war, had no idea of what he promised. At the time, no air force in the world was capable of airlifting such tonnages every day, even in the best of climates. Over the protests of several men wiser than he, among them Jeschonnek and Von Richthofen (who termed the whole idea as "stark, staring madness"),

Göring ordered the Stalingrad airlift to begin. It was hoped that at least three hundred tons could be taken into the surrounded area every day, but even that, despite heroic efforts on the part of the Luftwaffe, was never realized.

Aircraft fell to the weather, to the resurgent Russian Air Force, especially to such aces as Alexander Pokryshin and Ivan Kojedub, accident—and "madness," for Hitler ordered Paulus to hold Stalingrad to the end. Paulus, who *was* on the Volga, surrendered on February 2, 1943. Hitler never forgave him for not committing suicide. Of his army only ninety thousand men remained—the entire army was lost and with it went enough aircraft for an entire *Fliegerkorps,* close to five hundred—most of them Ju-52s and He-111s. And with these aircraft went more than two thousand men.

After the calamity of Stalingrad the Germans were able to attempt only one more summer offensive (July 1943), with the Luftwaffe replenished—at the cost of the reserve strength in Germany. But by this time the Soviet Army had been welded into a huge, powerful, relentless weapon. By winter a

*A German air base in Russia following a bombing attack by the Soviet Air Force, which destroyed Ju-52* *transports sorely needed to airlift supplies to the tottering Wehrmacht.* (H. J. NOWARRA)

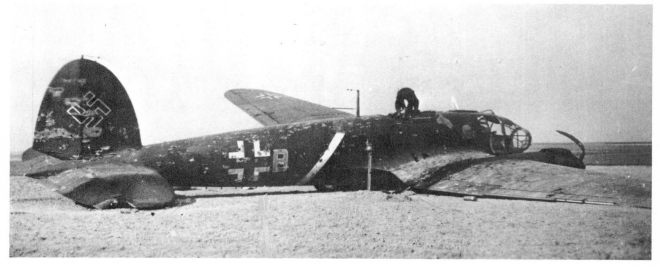

*The zeal of Russian fighter pilots is evident in this badly shot-up He-111.* (H. J. NOWARRA)

broad wedge had been driven into the German positions across the Dnieper River. The Russian offensive refused to be halted and by the summer of 1944 the Crimea and Leningrad were free of German troops and Soviet forces entered Rumania. The Germans and, more ominously, the Russians pursuing them were on the way to Berlin. By July 12, 1944, the Berlin Radio could warn its people, "The enemy is at the gates of the Reich!"

The Luftwaffe had failed the Führer again, despite the sacrifices of the summer before, when no less than seventeen hundred planes had been scraped away from the defense of the homeland and the broiling Mediterranean. That had been done at a time when the fighters especially might have been put to good use in Sicily or over Hamburg of *Die Katastrophe*. Hitler could not grasp the reasons behind the failure of the Luftwaffe, whose strength he had dissipated over the entire, all but interminable Russian front, where it was at the mercy of German ground commanders from one end of the line to the other, demanding the services of tired aircrews and tired aircraft.

It was also at the mercy of growing numbers of Russian and other Allied fighters. Where, indeed, was the Luftwaffe now that the barbarians menaced the very gates of the fatherland?

It was, by the summer of 1944, outnumbered, outgunned, outmanned, and outdated. The fate of the

Stuka, obsolete since the Battle of Britain, was representative of the entire German Air Force.

The Stukas, like most German aircraft (and Russian, for that matter), were confined to ground-support roles. Despite the improvement in Russian aircraft, the Stuka still operated as an effective tank buster. In the summer of 1944 the Stuka had returned to Poland—and so had the Russians. The indestructible Hans-Ulrich Rudel, veteran of literally thousands of operational flights, was stationed with his Stuka Geschwader 2 near the Polish town of Mielec, about sixty miles east, and slightly north, of Krakow.

Not only did Rudel's Stukas have to contend with Russian tanks and aircraft, they had also begun to run into American Mustangs. This too symbolized the approaching end. On July 25, 1944, Rudel encountered a formation of P-51s and for the first time in his career ordered his Stukas to jettison their bombs, abandon their mission, and return to Mielec.

Rudel's own account of this encounter (in *Stuka Pilot*) is curious. According to his count there were "nearly three hundred of them." He succeeded in bringing his fifteen Stukas back to his base but heard that "a neighboring unit suffered heavy losses from this huge formation of Mustangs."

At this time there was a total of fifty-eight Mustangs operating in Russia, the fighter cover for seventy-six P-38 fighter-bombers that had come from Italy on a shuttle bombing mission. While the heavy bombers bombed Ploesti, the P-38s with their P-51 cover attacked other Rumanian oil fields, after which they continued on to Russian airfields.

Flying top cover for the P-38s delighted the P-51 pilots, who harbored little love for the twin-boom plane. Ernest Shipman, a very young Mustang pilot with the 31st Fighter Group (307th Squadron), was already an ace when he took part in the battle Rudel had witnessed. Like his squadron mates Shipman resented the "condescending attitude" of Lightning pilots. The fact that some P-38 pilots had already shot down Mustangs (apparently mistaking them for Me-109s) added to the natural animosity.

How it felt to be very young and a fighter pilot flying the "fastest in-line fighter in the world" was preserved in a contemporary diary kept by Shipman. He was a typical young American air enthusiast who had avidly read the adventures of *G-8 and His Battle Aces;* at the same time he was a thorough student of tactics.

*Hans-Ulrich Rudel, whose specialty was destroying Russian tanks in a Stuka; he is also credited with the destruction of eleven Russian aircraft.* (H. J. NOWARRA)

"On this particular day [July 25, 1944]," he wrote, "we [flew] top cover for one of the two P-38 groups while it strafed a German airfield in Poland [this was Mielec]. We stayed around until the 38's left the field after starting a number of fires and then left for home ourselves.

"We were quite close to the front on the German side and the German army was in full retreat. There wasn't a cowpath that wasn't clogged with men and vehicles. Our guns were full of ammunition and the enemy was literally crawling over the ground below us, but we did not attack. This was because of the orders that had come down to us from the top. As you can guess our mission to Russia was to impress the Russians with the power and glory of the American air forces rather than to impress the Germans. We were to go to Russia in one piece, fly pretty formations and come home in one piece."

The mission had not been mounted as a troop-strafing one. The squadron leader, therefore, did little more than acknowledge the comments of his pilots who noted the presence of enemy troops below. He did not order an attack. But, as Shipman phrased it, "popular opinion swung it and we went down after them. After three passes we pulled up and headed for home.

"We were on course for about half an hour when somebody called in Enemy Aircraft. Col. [Yancey] Tarrant, the group C.O., immediately got nasty on the radio and said we were over the Russian lines, the planes we saw were probably Russian, and to stop clowning around. He was apparently more worried about our looking intact for the Russians than putting some of the enemy out of commission. How he knew whether the planes that had been spotted were friendly or not I shall never know for he was leading another squadron that was completely out of sight of us."

The moment Tarrant's voice went off the air, another cut in.

"Russian, hell—those planes are Stukas!"

At the same instant Shipman saw them, "black angular ships swooping low over what appeared to be a mill by the side of a stream. One look convinced me that our squadron, which numbered twelve ships that day, was heavily outnumbered. But on the other hand the enemy ships were Stukas, a flock of sitting ducks.

"The enemy planes were dive bombing in threes,

a stunt I had never seen before. The building they were attacking shuddered with the impact of their bombs as each wave pulled up from its bomb run. We were at 2000 feet and approaching at what was about 10 o'clock to them. Brown [the squadron leader] pulled down in a diving turn to the left and the rest of us followed. What happened in the next five minutes will always be a little confused in my mind."

*The Ju-87 Stuka, which enjoyed a temporary resurgence as a battle plane in Russia, but then once again was fated for slaughter by the newer Russian fighters and the American Mustang.* (U. S. AIR FORCE)

The Mustangs bounced the Stukas, Shipman estimated, about three or four waves behind the lead bombers hurtling three abreast upon the Russian building (probably a small factory). The American planes had by then been seen by the Germans, for they immediately began jettisoning their bombs. Even with the diminished weight, the Stuka was a poor contender, lacking speed although capable of making abrupt turns. Shipman had dived into the formation and found himself on the tail of a Stuka.

"My first burst went wild but a little correction put my guns on the target. In spite of the hits I was getting on the fuselage, the ship ahead of me showed no ill effects. I fired again. Before I had a chance to see what happened, I saw tracer going by my

canopy and I broke around to the left all in one motion. The ship whose tracer I had seen was a P-51; he was shooting at the same Stuka as I and I had been clumsy enough to get between him and his target. I never found out who that eager beaver was.

"There were plenty of other ships in the neighborhood and I chose the nearest one. He began to smoke almost immediately. It looked as though I almost had one in the bag when tracer began to come over my canopy again. After what had just happened I decided to ignore it. I had found this Stuka and if whoever it was behind me wanted one he could look for his own—the sky was full of them. I took another squirt at the plane ahead of me and then noticed something about the tracer arching over my head. Instead of the usual two lines of tracer that we fired for aiming purposes, there were four or more coming from behind me. I looked over my shoulder into the airscoop of a Stuka. The model we were attacking carried two twenty-millimeter cannons, one under each wing, and this one was no exception. These were blazing away, accompanied by machine guns in the wing roots, down the leading edges of the pants on the non-retractable landing gear and, I think, in the nose. [Besides being used as a dive-bomber the Stuka was also used for strafing and strafing necessitates considerable armament.] I got the hell out of there fast. The only reason I didn't get it on the spot was, I suppose, that the pilot had little experience with aerial gunnery, being in a ship and at a job that called for ground gunnery exclusively.

"Somewhere about here I got into a pass to the right on three of them. I started to fire at ninety degrees and got the lead ship in the engine and the front cockpit (I'm sure of this because the films showed it). Flames started coming out from under his belly and he went out of my sight. Now I'm not sure if it was on a continuation of this pass or on another one to the right that one of them tried to ram me.

"I was after the second ship of a group of three and we were all turning as tight as possible. The Stuka can make a mighty tight turn and I was really wasting ammunition because I didn't have the proper lead. I closed down as close as I could and then began to break away. The third Stuka was in a vertical bank to the left. As I pulled up I looked over at him. Looking down into the canopy I could see the pilot and the rear gunner, both looking up at me. Then the German wrenched his ship into a bank that could only crash his ship into mine. I pulled back on my stick as I had a few times before. The Stuka rolled up at me and disappeared under my plane. The last I saw of it was its left wing, black with a white cross on it, as it arched toward my plane. Fascinated is a poor word, but that's what I was as I stared at my right wing, expecting to see it dissolve as that Stuka went through it. In a second the danger was past, for my wing remained as big and beautiful as ever. . . .

"This episode rattled me but not to the point where a passing Stuka had no appeal. I started after him and then noticed that he was smoking and wobbling badly. I assumed that he was on his way in, which he was. Another was not far from this one and taking off for the big timber. I came down on him from above, not realizing that in doing so I was giving his rear gunner a beautiful shot. I was getting fine hits up and down his fuselage when something hit my ship with a concussive thump—more of a shock wave than a sound. I stopped firing and thought to myself, *I'm hit.*

"However, my controls responded and my engine sounded okay, so I decided that the damage couldn't be too serious. The Stuka was still in front of me and I went back to work on it. The smoke began seeping into my cockpit. I was on fire! I forgot about the Stuka and everything else. The only thing I thought of was getting clear before the tanks went. I pulled up, for at all times during this fight I had not been 2000 feet above the ground and the hills in the neighborhood went up to 800 or so feet. I wanted out, but paused in my stampede not knowing whether to roll over first and then drop out, pulling the canopy, or pull the canopy and then roll over. It may sound silly but that minor point kept me in the plane while the fire burned itself out. I realized suddenly that I wouldn't have to bail out after all for the smoke was subsiding.

"When I realized this I banked over to take a look at the Stuka I had been after. As I watched, it crashed in flames against a hill. Simultaneously the smoking Stuka I had passed up crashed and exploded not fifty yards away. I checked my tail and, seeing that was clear, took a look around. The Stukas had disappeared and so had the squadron."

The valley over which the battle had occurred was, to Shipman, an amazing sight. Besides the two Stukas which he had just seen crash, there were perhaps ten others strewn through it. Great black curls of smoke rose up from the crashes. The Stukas had virtually been slaughtered. (Shipman, however, as he gazed down had no idea that all crashes represented German planes, but the sight of a dozen destroyed aircraft in so small a space was one he had never seen before.)

Shipman then heard the voice of Tarrant on the radio ordering all Mustangs to return to their base. "With my ship in the shape it was in, I decided that he had a point.

"Turning back to the course we had been flying, I began checking ahead for the squadron. I saw several P-51s ahead and headed for them. As I approached a flight of Russian-flown P-39s came over the 51s ahead of me and started into a dive after them. They were making a pass from the rear and this brought them close to me. When I was sure that they could see me I wiggled my wings like hell. The lead 39 wiggled acknowledgment and the Russians swung off to our right and, presently, out of sight.

"I was closing the gap between me and the ships ahead when another 51 came up from the left. By odd coincidence it was my wingman. I was surprised and relieved to see him. We closed up with the other ships and headed for home.

"Then I began checking on my battle damage. My hydraulic pressure was at zero, there were several holes in my wings, and the cracks around the ammunition box cover on my right wing were smoke stained. There was a hole in this cover and from the signs I concluded (wrongly) that a stray slug had set off some rounds in the ammunition boxes, causing the smoke that had given me such a scare."

Although the length of the mission, the impromptu strafing of German troops, and the Stuka slaughter had consumed much fuel, none of the Mustangs were forced to make emergency landings because of a lack of fuel. However, like Shipman's, some planes were shot up.

"With my hydraulic pressure at zero I knew that my gear would not lower in the usual way and that I would have to rock it down. This involves putting the gear handle in the down position and letting gravity pull the gear into place. When the pilot feels the gear hit bottom, he rocks his ship wildly to throw the weight of the oleo struts into a fully down position. This causes the spring loading locking pins to snap into place, locking the gear in the down position. I did not call in for an emergency landing because others were calling in emergencies and with my wingman checking on my wheels from his vantage point, there wasn't much more to be done.

"I told my wingman to keep an eye on my wheels when I put them down. We went into our landing peel-off and went through the procedure described above to lower my gear. I called my wingman and asked him what he thought. He was flying behind and below me, where he could see my wheels, and he called back that they looked down and locked. But as I glided down toward the landing strip a red flare arched up in front of me. I poured on the coal and went around wondering if my wheels *were* down as I rocked the ship all over the sky. On my next try I got another red flare. My gas was getting dangerously low and so when I got a flare again on my next pass, I called the tower asking if my wheels looked down and locked to them. They called back assuring me that they were. I then asked, 'Why all the red flares?' The tower came back with the bland answer that my flaps weren't down.

"The flaps are hydraulically operated as well as the wheels and zero hydraulic pressure means no flaps. I got on the radio and told the tower that my goddam flaps wouldn't come down because my goddam hydraulic system was shot out. (If I recall correctly, this is a watered-down version.)

"On my next pass I landed without any greater mishap than several good bounces. This business about the flaps is an example of how far the asinine regulations of the swivel-chair air force back in the States could go.

"As I sat filling out my Form 1 the crew chief, who had been inspecting my plane, climbed up on the wing root, next to my cockpit, with an excited expression on his face. He wanted me to take a look at the battle damage my ship had received. I complied and was not long in finding out what had excited him so. The smoke that I had mistaken for a hit in my ammunition box had actually come from a burning gas line in my right wing. An incendiary bullet of what would be the equivalent of our .30 caliber had neatly clipped the gas lead from my right wing drop tank installation. The gas in the line had been set on fire and would certainly have

fired the whole ship if the drop tank had been attached. As it was, a fire must have been gayly burning for thirty seconds or so in the wheel well, not more than a few inches from the rubber tire.

"My gun camera films were fairly clear. They revealed the strafing of the enemy vehicles and, along with the films of the others in the squadron, dozens of enemy planes. One of my films came close to giving me heart failure a week or so after we were safely back at our base in Italy [San Severo]. My camera showed a Stuka at fairly close range with one or two others further ahead of it and off to the sides. Toward the end of that particular film, the scene shifted downwards disclosing another Stuka which appeared huge on the screen. That one had been out of sight under my nose, and probably with his rear guns working away like fury, all the while I was firing on the one ahead of it. I had no idea how close he was, nor even that he had been there, until we ran off the films."

Five days later the 31st Fighter Group participated in a more conventional action: escorting Fifteenth Air Force Liberators to targets at Budapest. The strategic forces were concentrating on oil targets (the most important, most effective of all, it was learned after the war). Shipman's squadron that day was led by a man the others called, with minimal affection, "Wild Willie S——, the Village Idiot." But he developed radio trouble and before he peeled off for a return to San Severo, turned the squadron over to Shipman. Flying blightly as a flight leader, Shipman was reasonably happy with his lot—this was to be his final mission for a while and he expected to take some time off for a visit to Cairo. Now, "the Village Idiot" had handed him the responsibility of the entire squadron, despite the fact that the deputy squadron commander was himself on the mission, flying at the head of "Blue Section."

This arrangement did not seem right to Shipman, who discussed it with Blue Section leader (himself not eager to lead the entire squadron). Finally, however, Shipman took over Blue Section and the deputy squadron commander assumed responsibility for the squadron—reluctantly. Their two Mustangs shifted across the sky as the formations joined up with the heavy bombers. "There was usually a certain amount of confusion during the time when contact was made, by radio, between the bombers and

*Mustangs of the 31st Fighter Group (Fifteenth Air Force), carrying wing tanks which will be dropped in an instant, peeling off for an attack.* (U. S. AIR FORCE)

the fighters," Shipman noted. "This was because of the number of planes involved and the necessity for one small part of these to be distinguished from the others and located in the vastness of the sky.

"Contact was invariably made but rarely without some difficulty. On this particular, and for me unfortunate, mission things surprisingly went like clockwork. While we were making contact with the wing of bombers we were responsible for, we heard other bombers calling in enemy aircraft that were attacking them from above at six o'clock."

Minutes later Shipman saw a P-38 some distance away on the tail of an Me-109. The German plane trailed a long plume of white, glycol from the engine's cooling system, apparently hit by the P-38.

But the Messerschmitt raced away from the battle area as the great armada continued on its way. The battle gave Shipman "some useful information. This was that P-38s, the pilots of which were considered trigger-happy by our pilots, were in the neighborhood. This always meant that we had to be on our guard against the enemy forces as well as our own."

Shipman positioned his section above the Liberators, where the P-51s weaved back and forth to keep as close as possible to the slower bombers. Just as he had led his planes on the outward leg of the course, Shipman looked back at the bombers and saw two or three Me-109s and an FW-190 "diving in a long diagonal slant through the bombers." Ordered to deal with the enemy fighters, Shipman (as did the other pilots in his section) had to prepare for combat. This was not as simple a procedure as the layman believes.

"The sudden turn in events meant that I must drop my [auxiliary fuel] tanks, make a sharp diving turn to the left, keep an eye on the enemy planes and make the usual hasty preparations for a fight: . . . tightening the straps on the oxygen mask, turning on the gun switches, the gun sight, checking the gasoline situation, checking the maneuverability of the flaps and pushing the three components of the throttle quadrant—the prop pitch, mixture, and throttle controls—into full forward position. There is also the necessity, when leading a section . . . of a hasty check on the disposition of the planes moving into battle."

Shipman's luck began to fail when he jettisoned his drop tanks; one tank did not fall. Already in a sharp turn, which even under perfect trim conditions would have brought the Mustang into a stall, Shipman fought to keep the plane from going out of control. The drag of the unjettisoned tank finished the job. "My ship shuddered and mushed down through the air on its left wing. I fought to regain full control before my plane fell into a spin. In this I was successful but I had lost sight of the German planes." The enemy fighters had swept through the formation and disappeared into thick clouds below.

What followed contributed to Shipman's total disenchantment with the P-38 and its "trigger-happy" pilots. One of the twin-boomed fighters, apparently mistaking the P-51 for an Me-109, dropped down on him and shot Shipman out of the sky. His plane was in such condition that he could do nothing but bail out, cursing the P-38 all the way down to enemy territory. Ernest Shipman, ace with seven victories to his credit, became an enforced guest of the Third Reich for the rest of the war.

### III

The Normandy invasion preparations had resulted in placing all air forces, tactical and strategic, in England under the direct command of General Eisenhower. The strategic bombardment program was thus temporarily set aside as heavy bombers were employed in more or less direct support of ground troops.

Even after the Allies were firmly established in France heavy bombers were used tactically—bomb-

ing enemy airfields or enemy troop concentrations in proximity to Allied troops. This was not how the strategic planners would have wished it. As early as March 1944 General Spaatz in his paper "Plan for the Completion of the Combined Bomber Offensive" outlined the particular American point of view and suggested that oil targets be struck instead of transportation, as was being then put forth as supreme. Advocating transportation targets were Harris (who continued to view the oil industry as a panacea target), Tedder (who was Eisenhower's air operations

*Ernest Shipman, 31st Fighter Group, ace with six victories to his credit before being downed by an overzealous P-38 pilot.* (ERNEST SHIPMAN)

*Eighth Air Force Liberator bombing German positions at Saint-Malo, Brittany (southwest of the Normandy beachheads), as heavy bombers were employed in tactical missions shortly after D-Day.* (U. S. AIR FORCE)

supervisor for the invasion), and Brereton, the commander of the Ninth Air Force.

By late March Eisenhower, after listening to the arguments pro and con, himself voted in favor of transportation—railroads, bridges—but reaffirmed his confidence in Spaatz (with whom he had had such fine relations in the African invasion) by leaving the way open for a resumption of the strategic program with a concentration on oil as soon as possible after Normandy fell to the Allies. In making this choice Eisenhower noted that he was certain "there is no other way in which this tremendous air force can help us during the preparatory period, to get ashore and stay there."

Though Spaatz was certain the Luftwaffe would vigorously defend oil targets—and thus be forced into attritional air battles—he doubted that it would be concerned much with rail centers. These were remarkably (and relatively) easy to restore what with the highly efficient German employment of slave labor. Then too, in France there was the certainty of civilian casualties.

However, once Eisenhower had made his decision, Spaatz, while doubting its ultimate effect, believed it was justified. The fact that German units were denied access to the invasion area meant that enemy troops on the beaches would be forced to fight without reinforcements for hours and even days because

*Interdiction: isolating the Normandy battlefields in preparation for D-Day. This railroad bridge, which crossed the Seine just south of Rouen, was taken out by British Second Tactical Air Force and U. S. Ninth Air Force medium bombers. By June 12 all seven rail bridges that linked Brittany with Normandy on the Seine were knocked out; so were thirteen road bridges.* (U. S. AIR FORCE)

delicate yet, as it turned out, powerful arrangement and it worked—not without slight international friction: but it worked.

One of the concerns of the British, concurrently, had come about in May of 1943 when a beautiful young WAAF, Constance Babington-Smith, scrutinizing a reconnaissance photo, spotted a curious pilotless aircraft on a launching site on the island of Usedom in the Baltic Sea. The place was Peenemünde, Germany's experimental station for rocketry. Later similar sites were picked up on other aerial photographs in France north of the Seine. Coupled with Hitler's ominous references to secret weapons that would decide the outcome of the war, the discovery of these sites was chilling. The launching sites apparently pointed in the general direction of England. Understandably, to the British the destruction of these sites took precedence over synthetic petroleum plants.

Flight Officer Babington-Smith had spotted the first of the German *Versuchsmuster* weapons—a long-range missile. This was the V-1 (originally designating an experimental type), a flying bomb. By the time the V-2, a rocket, appeared Hitler had a weapon which indeed (had he realized it) might have decided the war. It was no longer "experi-

the area had been cut off. Bridges were down, railroads were disrupted, and roads were a perilous shambles.

The command structure which accomplished this was anything but simple. Both the RAF and the U. S. Air Force were loath to be commanded by a fellow ally. Careful balances of command, therefore, had to be devised which could accomplish the job without injuring national pride. Where an Englishman was commander, it was likely that an American would be his deputy; and vice versa. It was a

*A Douglas A-20 "Havoc" on a hunt over France; a former German airfield is scarred with the bombs of earlier missions.* (U. S. AIR FORCE)

*A Fortress of the 401st Bomb Group bombing the German rocket weapon development center at Peenemünde. It was here that fuel for the V-1 bombs was produced. The campaign against V-weapon sites and centers was code-named "Crossbow."* (U. S. AIR FORCE)

mental," but a *Vergeltungswaffe* ("vengeance weapon"). The V-1s and V-2s, however, were not launched until after D-Day, when they did blindly cause death and destruction of little military import beyond contributing to the joy of Hitler. It was an example of science corrupted by the license of war.

The more conventional air weapons were used to assure the success of Overlord. Much of the load of the preparatory missions fell to the U. S. Ninth Air Force, by D-Day the largest tactical air force in the world, composed of medium bomber units (Douglas A-20s, Douglas A-26s, and Martin B-26s), fighters (predominantly P-47s, plus P-38s and a single P-51 group), and troop carriers (Douglas C-47s). The Ninth operated in conjunction with the British Second Tactical Air Force with its assorted aircraft:

Spitfires, Mosquitos, Mustangs, and Typhoons. These forces, along with the so-called Air Defence of Great Britain (formerly Fighter Command), came under the direction of Air Commander in Chief of Allied Expeditionary Air Force, Air Chief Marshal Sir Trafford L. Leigh-Mallory. Harris continued to control Bomber Command and Spaatz controlled the American Stragetic Air Forces.

Harris undoubtedly spoke for both men when he pointed out that the "only efficient support which Bomber Command can give to Overlord is the intensification of attacks on suitable industrial centers in Germany as and when opportunity offers. If we attempt to substitute for this process attacks on gun emplacements, beach defenses, communications, or dumps in occupied territory, we shall commit the irremediable error of diverting our best weapon from the military function for which it has been equipped and trained to tasks which it cannot effectively carry out. Though this might give a specious appearance of supporting the army, in reality it would be the greatest disservice we could do to them. It would lead directly to disaster."

After Eisenhower's decision such theory could be violated in practice if the need arose—and it did. Until the heavy—that is, strategic—forces could be drawn away from their primary function, it devolved upon Leigh-Mallory to employ his tactical air forces in preparing the Overlord assault areas for the invasion. The attack began on French rail centers and switched to bridges (which proved most attractive as targets), so that by D-Day every bridge across the Seine below Paris had been destroyed. As for the railroads, suffice it to say that the only German troops which reached Normandy after D-Day walked there. Airfields within 130 miles of Normandy were rendered unusable. Radar stations, ranging from Ostend (Belgium) to the Channel Islands, were knocked out. At the same time tons of bombs were dropped upon the burgeoning V-weapons sites. For every attack upon the actual assault area, two others were made elsewhere, so that the Germans would have no idea of where the invasion would come. By a curious quirk, only Hitler of all the German military "minds" had guessed that the attack would open at Normandy. By the time he had offered this observation his stock as a great military philosopher had fallen among the professional military men in Germany. His errors, in fact,

*Dance of death: Coastal Command Beaufighters attacking a German minesweeper in the North Sea.*
(IMPERIAL WAR MUSEUM, LONDON)

had given the High Command so bad a name among the professionals (rather than for his crimes against humanity) that a number of them had attempted to assassinate him. In this too they failed.

As Harris had indicated, bombing the coastal defenses was not effective, although the medium bombers and the fighter bombers (the Thunderbolts) performed this function with great dispatch and, frequently, at great cost. Flak was thick and deadly and the medium bombers and fighter-bombers of necessity operated at a vulnerable altitude.

The British Second Tactical Air Force participated in unusual low-level missions in the preinvasion period in Mosquitos. Group Captain P. C. Pickard led nineteen Mosquitos of Nos. 487, 464, and 21 Squadrons on a jailbreak. A large number of French

Resistance leaders were imprisoned at Amiens and it seemed a worthy project to release them. On February 18, 1944, in near-scrubbing weather, Pickard led his planes in the attack. Although the raid was successful—more than 250 prisoners escaped through the bomb-breached walls—Pickard's Mosquito was shot down by two FW-190s and he and his navigator, Flight Lieutenant J. A. Broadley, were killed. So were 102 prisoners, unfortunately. But the main prisoner, a Monseiur Vivant, an important leader in the Resistance movement, went free.

Another Mosquito mission of unique distinction was accomplished by six aircraft of No. 613 Squadron led by Wing Commander R. N. Bateson. The target was a single building, the Kleizkamp Art Galleries, in The Hague. The Gestapo had taken over the building and used it for storage of records and a file on the Dutch. Bateson led his Mosquitos to the town, circled it, and then at a height of fifty feet above the street, flew toward the art gallery. The German guard standing in front of the building looked up and saw six aircraft racing directly for him; he threw down his gun and ran. Seconds later two bombs skipped through the gallery doorway; another two went through windows on either side of the door. The bombs that spilled over detonated in a German barracks, burning it to the ground.

Although Dutch officials were killed by the bombs that struck the art gallery, the official files of the Gestapo were blown to the winds, burned, and otherwise destroyed. The surviving Dutch keepers of the files returned to work, replacing the destroyed cards with fake information, thus thoroughly disrupting the Gestapo's efficient system. All Mosquitos returned safely to England.

Such missions, while not strategic by any definition, were typical of the imaginative daring of the RAF crews. This same daring and imagination, coupled with that of the Ninth Air Force's crews, opened great holes in the German defenses at Normandy and across France into Germany. Typical of the kind of mission that fell to the medium bombers is one gleaned from the history of the 387th Bombardment Group (M). The language is typical in its laconic recital of the salient facts.

"On June 7 it was learned that the 17th German Panzer Division was moving north to the invasion beachhead. The report called for a mission to deny this route to the Germans. Because of bad weather the formation attempting to bomb the rail junction at Rennes was not successful, but it did get good results on a railroad west of Vire and on a choke point of vehicles near Saint-Lô. The next morning a highly successful mission was flown against the railroad junction at Pontabault. The best strike was made by Lieutenant Rudolf Tell, bombardier in Captain Robert E. Will's flight, whose bombs hit the target perfectly.

"The afternoon mission [June 8, 1944; D plus 2] proved to be one of the most remarkable ever flown by the Group. Capt. Rollin D. Childress was to lead eighteen aircraft [Marauders] to a fuel dump in the Forêt Grimbosq, south of Caen. At the take-off at 1958 hours, the ceiling was 900 feet. The formation assembled without difficulty; but on going up through the solid overcast it became widely dispersed. Eleven of the planes returned to the base.

One crash-landed at Gravesend. One, piloted by First Lieutenant Raymond V. Morin, crashed while attempting to land at Friston in ceiling zero weather.

"Captain Childress rallied three aircraft with his own and continued on, sometimes at deck level in quarter of a mile visibility. He managed to find the target, and his bombardier, First Lieut. Wilson J. Cushing, bombed it with great accuracy from 6000 feet. As the formation of four turned off target, moderate extremely accurate flak shot down the fourth airplane, piloted by Capt. Charles W. Schober. The airplane exploded in mid-air and no parachutes were observed. Included in Capt. Schober's crew was Capt. John D. Root, group weather officer.

"The remaining three aircraft, proceeding homeward, braved terrible weather conditions over England and landed at the base at 2230 hours. Captain Childress was congratulated on his tenacity and perseverance by Col. Millard Lewis, commander of the 98th Combat Wing, and by the group commander, Lieut. Col. Thomas H. Seymour.

"The effectiveness of the bombing was attested to by a congratulatory telegram from the ground forces which stated that the important fuel dump, the immediate supply for an entire Panzer division, was destroyed."

Once the beachhead was secure, there remained the problem of moving inland. This "breakout," it was concluded, could be implemented by concentrated air power, employing not only the fighter-bombers and mediums of the Ninth, but also the Fortresses and Liberators of the Eighth Air Force. Where the Germans had managed to stiffen their positions in the face of the advancing Allies the plan was to slash a hole through the German lines with a heavy concentration of aerial bombardment. The official code name for this operation was "Cobra."

Weather, the usual menace, helped to get Cobra off to a poor start. On July 24, 1944, the Ninth Air Force's fighter-bombers took off, but three of its six groups returned to base upon being recalled because of the bad weather. Leigh-Mallory, who was in France and saw the impossibility of effective bombing, postponed the attacks, and later in the day canceled them.

Unfortunately, when this word came down to the Eighth Air Force it's more than fifteen hundred heavy bombers were already on the bombing runs;

only a few of the planes in the last formations received word in time to turn away from the target area. Visibility was so bad over the target that the lead formations did not attempt to drop on the primary targets: German positions directly in front of the Allied troops. Some bombers did drop, but made several runs before identifying the correct drop zone. About three hundred bombers succeeded in dropping on what was hoped to have been the proper targets. But these hopes were not fulfilled.

Accident and error unleashed an envenomed Cobra which did not discriminate between friend and foe. On one bomb run a lead bombardier found his bomb release stiff and in attempting to loosen it dropped some of his bomb load. The other ships in the formation, fifteen in all, seeing the bombs released from their lead ship, dropped their bombs also. The bombs fell two thousand yards inside Allied positions, killing sixteen troops of the Ameri-

A direct flak hit has sheared off this Marauder's engine. This occurred over Toulon Harbor, in southern France, where another invasion was under way. The B-26 was one of the Twelfth Air Force mediums borrowed for the second invasion of the Continent.

(U. S. AIR FORCE)

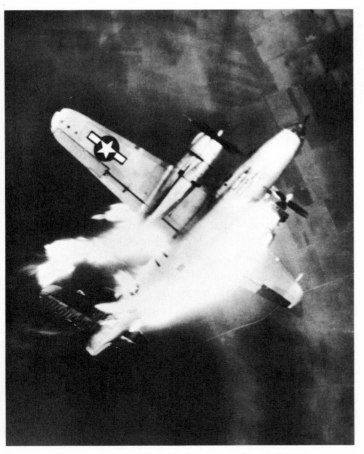

A Marauder, hit by flak, is enveloped by flame as it falls into France. Despite Allied aerial supremacy flak, as always, took its toll. (U. S. AIR FORCE)

can 30th Infantry Division and wounding about sixty. A single B-24 flew over a Ninth Air Force field in France, at Chippelle, at which instance something struck the B-24's nose turret. The bombardier recoiled from the sudden impact and inadvertently struck a toggle switch. Seconds later two Ninth Air Force medium bombers ready to take off on a mission blew up with their crews and full bomb loads after being struck by the toggled bombs. Other planes were damaged also.

At another point a Thunderbolt swept down, turned, and ran in on an ammunition dump, which blew up with pleasing violence. Except that the pilot had made a wrong turn and had attacked an Allied dump. To complete the day's toll, three heavy bombers were knocked down by flak, presumably German.

Despite the day's misadventures, the second application of Cobra followed the next day, when weather conditions promised better possibilities of success. There were other forces at work also. The previous day's activities revealed to the Germans the point at which the Allied breakout was most likely to occur. Consequently, while the U. S. Army soldiers moved out of the bombing zone, so did those of the Wehrmacht. In some areas this meant retaking ground once held by the Allies because of the evacuations away from the bomb lines. Those Germans who suffered the saturation bombings, however, were in no condition to hold or take any ground for some time after. Although casualties were not excessive, for the Germans had dug in intelligently, the effect upon communications and especially upon morale was "shattering," to employ the word most often used by the Germans.

The very sight of literally thousands of enemy aircraft (1507 Flying Fortresses and Liberators, 380 Marauders and Invaders, and 559 Thunderbolts) was dispiriting, and the cry again was heard, "Where is the Luftwaffe?"

To Generalleutnant Fritz Bayerlein, commander of the Panzer Lehr division, the battlefield looked like the dead and pocked *Mondlandschaft* (moon landscape). His unit was heavily hit, with a good number of his troops "either dead, wounded, crazed, or dazed." The command post of his 902nd Regiment had been in the center of the bomb carpet and that was entirely gone; thirty or more of his tanks lay toppled on their backs or upended in bomb craters. Bayerlein's divisional flak guns were all but useless because of the great number of enemy aircraft; half the guns were knocked out in the opening minutes of the attack.

But, as on the day before, "gross errors" took their toll. In general, the bombing was more accurate than the first Cobra, but human error as ever resulted in bombs falling short and consequently within American lines. The 30th Infantry suffered again as heavy bombers released some of their bombs, killing 120 and injuring 380. Among the dead was Lieutenant General Lesley J. McNair.

In short, the effort did not equal the effect. Even if it were possible to accept Allied casualties as one of the "fortunes of war," the actual accomplishment was less than expected. Allied troops did not "pour through the great gaps" in the enemy lines, although the way was broken for the infantry of the First U. S. Army, followed later by the rampaging tanks of Patton's Third Army in August.

While the Cobra carpet bombings had been effective on a limited scale, they only served to underscore Harris's view on the "irremediable error of diverting our best weapon from the military function for which it had been equipped and trained to tasks which it cannot effectively carry out." The use of heavy bombers in close support of troops was, in effect, a military perversion, although at the time an expedient one. Nor was it abandoned merely because it did not function to perfection. As a substitute for artillery, capable of delivering greater firepower in a given time, the heavy bombers were incomparable, although in theory it was a step backward.

If the ground-support role of the high-altitude heavy bomber proved to be less than successful, the co-ordination between ground troops and the fighter-bombers, particularly the Thunderbolt, was excellent. Thunderbolts frequently teamed up with Allied tanks, with which they communicated with two-way radios as had the "Rover Joes" in Italy.

*Liberators assembling over England for a mission to bomb in front of Allied troops in France.*

(CECIL COHEN)

*Liberators in a "carpet" bombing mission over Tours, France, during the "Cobra" operation to force a break in the German lines for Allied troops. Smoke markers indicate drop point—the entire formation releases the bombs when the lead bomber drops. Such bombings so close to friendly troops were not truly effective and were often fatal to foe and friend alike.*

(U. S. AIR FORCE)

Jug pilots could spot enemy gun positions, antitank traps, and German tanks, warn their own forces, and attack the enemy. The fighter-bombers strafed and bombed German troop concentrations and artillery installations, engaged an intermittently emergent Luftwaffe, and played an important part in the interdiction campaign, the isolation of the Germans in the battlefield by cutting off their lines of communications: bridges, railroads, and highways.

After the breakthrough at Saint-Lô the Allies swept across Normandy; another invasion, in southern France, was also successfully launched and the German blitzkrieg machine was squeezed even as it was rammed back toward the Rhine. As winter approached the possibilities for fighter-bomber cooperation with ground troops diminished—and Spaatz could again consider the release of his heavy

bombers for the continuation of the attack upon Germany behind the Rhine. He hoped to strike particularly at oil targets and the Luftwaffe. Berlin too became an important target city by the end of June. With the coming of winter Spaatz could take up the Battle of Berlin again.

Robert Chapin, lead navigator of the 384th Bombardment Group, upon reflection did not regard Berlin as tough a target as the cities related to the oil targets (Brüx, Blechhammer, Merseburg, Ruhland, and, among others, Ploesti). But Berlin, he knew, "was tougher psychologically." The "most frustrating missions," however, were those to the V-weapons sites, for the slightest mist would obscure the heavily camouflaged installations. These sites, too, were not very vulnerable to bombing and never did get knocked out of operation until ground troops overran them. But not before Hitler's indiscriminate "vengeance weapons" (flying bombs and V-2 rockets) took 8938 civilian lives and left nearly 25,000 seriously injured in their blind wake. From the first flying bomb, the "doodle bug," which fell on England on June 12, 1944, until the final V-2, which fell on March 27, 1945, a corner of England with London at its center was even more of a "Hell's Corner" than Kent had been during the Battle of Britain.

The V-weapons, though terroristic, were militarily pointless, however much they supposedly advanced "civilization" toward the Space Age.

The weapon which Chapin recalls that really "shook up the troops" was the jet fighter. As he sat in the nose of a B-17 one day, Chapin heard the pilot announce the approach of a jet fighter. Chapin, as usual busy with his navigational computations, and bombardier Richard Crown, likewise preoccupied with his own work, rarely actually saw enemy fighters even in the height of combat. The dawn of the Jet Age, however, was too important to miss. The two men peered out of the plexiglass nose.

"Where?" Chapin asked.

The pilot called out the "clock" position directly out in front of their plane (as lead team Chapin and Crown flew in the lead aircraft along with the command pilot, at this time Colonel Theodore Ross Milton). At a point that appeared to be miles distant, Chapin saw a tiny dot which suddenly expanded into a strange-looking aircraft that "zoomed out of nowhere" and through the bomber formation.

Although it did no damage, the very appearance and incredible speed of the plane had a disquieting effect upon the men in the bombers. Not even the Mustang could overtake the Messerschmitt 262.

Several factors, luckily for the Allies, inhibited the full employment of the Me-262, an aircraft which could very readily have had a decisive effect upon the air war over Germany. When he saw the Messerschmitt demonstrated for the first time, Hitler, gorged with the virulence of vengeance, glanced at the fighter and snapped, "Can that thing carry bombs?"

Neither Göring nor Messerschmitt wished to say nay to their Great Captain, so they answered with a qualified yes. The qualification lay in the fact that the Me-262 was designed as a fighter-interceptor, to meet the greatest need in Germany at the moment: to stop the Allied heavy bombardment from obliterating German cities and, worse, from destroying the German synthetic oil industry. The jet plane could carry a light bomb load, but that would seriously impair its performance; so would operating at a low level as a fighter-bomber. In short, all the advantages of the fact that it was a jet aircraft would be sacrificed. Hitler's so-called "Blitz Bomber" would not be superior to Allied fighters.

Hitler's meddling from the moment of the Messerschmitt's inception, therefore, canceled it out as any kind of potent weapon. Not until after D-Day did Hitler relent to the degree that he would permit the Me-262 and the word "fighter" be mentioned in the same sentence. He conceded that it just might serve the function for which it was conceived—but not if it interfered with bomber production. Bomber production was in itself an interference, for to meet Hitler's demands the fighter would have to be converted into a bomber—it would need bomb clips installed, it would require a bombsight, all of which took time.

Adolf Galland, then general of the fighters, was

*Thunderbolt of 365th Fighter Group seeks out enemy positions for American tanks. In communication with tank commanders by two-way radio, pilot of P-47 would spot targets such as German tanks and anti-* *tank gun positions, or warn of tank traps. American artillery frequently dealt with these targets in co-operation with tactical pilots or American tanks.*

(U. S. AIR FORCE)

*A Spitfire pursues a V-1 flying bomb ("doodle bug" to the English) over the English countryside. The Spitfire, the P-47, and the P-51 were capable of overtaking the bomb, and either shot it down or tipped it out of its trajectory by flipping it with the wing of the pursuing plane.* (U. S. AIR FORCE)

*The V-1, the first of Hitler's "vengeance weapons," known as "doodle bugs" to the English. Pilotless, these were brought down by balloon barrage, antiaircraft fire, and fighters capable of speeds in excess of four hundred miles an hour. These included the Spitfire XIV, the Thunderbolt, the Mustang, and the first of the war's operational jets: the Gloster "Meteor."*

(U. S. AIR FORCE)

*Antiaircraft fire tracks a doodle bug over London at night. Many were knocked down in this way.*

(IMPERIAL WAR MUSEUM, LONDON)

so outspokenly opposed to the perversion of the Me-262 that he argued himself out of his post. Dismissed, Galland was given the opportunity to form a jet fighter unit, Jagdverband 44 (ironically, he ended the war as he began it, as a squadron commander). This, the second jet fighter unit (the earlier one was Jagdgeschwader 7, *Gruppen* of which had gone into combat in October of 1944), like its predecessor had come too late. Even so, the two Me-262 units took a high toll of American bombers while they operated.

Like any new aircraft, the Me-262 had its share of bugs, and with Hitler assuming the role of aircraft expert, it had even more than its fair share. Accidents occurred during testing and training; despite this the first operational unit was hurried into service. One of the first operational jet units was the so-called "Kommando Nowotny," named in honor of its leader, Major Walter Nowotny, a fighter ace with a score of more than two hundred "kills" to his credit. It was Nowotny's jets that first "shook up the troops" of the Eighth Air Force. Prior to that, most of the jet type of fighters encountered were the odd but quite ineffectual Me-163 (*Komet*).

Nowotny died as result of an engine failure after

*A V-2 missile on its blind way to England.*
(NATIONAL ARCHIVES)

he had taken off to knock down his 258th enemy aircraft. As he came in to land he reported his left jet engine had gone out. Thus crippled, he became an easy target for a swarm of Mustangs which pounced on his tail. When he came within sight of his own home base at Achmer, either Nowotny's Me-262 was hit by the American fighters on his tail or he crashed into the ground. The former is more likely, for via radio Nowotny's voice was heard: ". . . attacked again . . . hit . . ." His fighter then disintegrated in a sudden flash of flame.

As for Galland, he was shot out of the sky while attacking a formation of Marauders of the 17th Bombardment Group over Neuburg on the Danube. Neuburg was a major aviation center, complete with airfield and plant. According to Galland's own account, he was shot down by a Mustang, whose pilot had surprised him while he was attacking the Marauders. According to Air Force files, no claim by a fighter pilot of an Me-262 was made that day (April 26, 1945), although two claims were made by Marauder gunners of the 34th Bombardment Squadron. Since the jet did not go down immediately, perhaps the Mustang pilot did not think he had succeeded in his attack.

But he had. Galland himself was injured and his instrument panel was a shambles. His engine pods

*One of Hitler's secret "vengeance weapons" (a V-1)*        *begins to fall into Piccadilly, London.* (U. S. AIR FORCE)

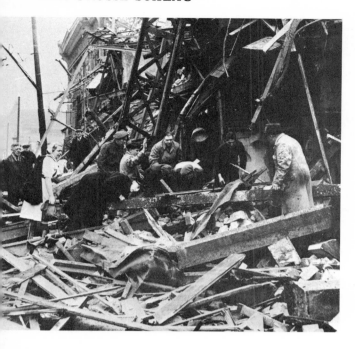

*A V-2 hits the target: Smithfield Market, London. More than 100 people died, 123 were seriously injured, and Hitler was not one day closer to victory.* (NATIONAL ARCHIVES)

*Lead navigator Robert Chapin, lead bombardier Richard Crown, and Group Commander Theodore R. Milton of the 384th Bomb Group. Chapin recalls that of all of Hitler's surprises, the introduction of the Messerschmitt 262 jet fighter "shook up the troops" most.* (384TH BOMB GROUP)

were tattered and running ragged. Afraid that if he were to bail out he would be shot up in his chute, Galland returned to his base at Riem. Despite his poorly operating engines, Galland brought the plane in for a landing. Unable to control the fuel feed, he could only cut off the engines completely once he was over the field and ready to land. Trailing twin plumes of black smoke, he approached the landing strip—only to find that the field was under attack by Thunderbolts. Because his radio had also been destroyed Galland had not received the warnings of this. With the engines flared out Galland could do nothing else but land.

The Messerschmitt wobbled down to earth and then Galland found he had other problems. His nosewheel had been shot flat, and at a speed of 150 miles an hour his landing was extremely noisy and rough. The Thunderbolts ignored the crippled jet in favor of smashing up the field. When he could, Galland jumped from the plane and into the nearest bomb crater, where he cringed under the bombardment. Finally a mechanic ran to an armored tractor, which he drove through the rubble and the shellbursts to Galland. Hobbling onto the vehicle, Galland said nothing, but in heartfelt gratitude slapped the courageous mechanic on the shoulder. Galland ended up in the hospital at Munich, where it was found he had two shell splinters in his knee. That mission was his last of the war.

Despite the jets, the great formations of bombers continued to bomb Germany. Once the initial shock of their presence was over it was possible—and necessary—to deal with them.

## IV

To Hitler, it must have seemed those pagan gods to whom he prayed were not listening. His Atlantic Wall and his most brilliant general had not kept the Allies out of Normandy; his vengeance weapons had failed to bring Churchill to his knees and his Blitz Bomber neither blitzed nor bombed.

Further: the Allied strategic bombardment effort, for all the internal argument, was having its effect. The oil strikes had begun seriously to curtail the training program for new Luftwaffe pilots. Due to the fuel shortage, training flights were carefully rationed. Many young pilots were sent to certain de-

# WARM YOUR GUNS FOR JERRY'S FINAL BRAINSTORM

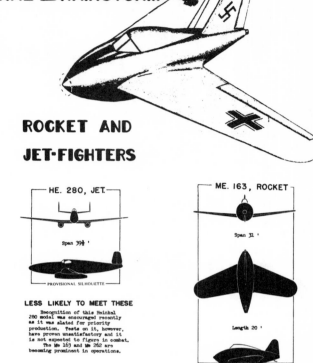

**You'll likely be meeting these soon and**

**our tip is you'd better sight 'em first!**

ME. 262, JET.

Span 40'

Length 35¼'

PROVISIONAL SILHOUETTE

They're still trying to pump "soup" into the superman. Becoming more frequent are the appearances of these hopped-up go-buggies, and they're one of the last-ditch hopes of the Nazi overlords.

Suffice it to say if they become prominent, we'll have adequate counter-measures for them. Tests already show they'll walk away from conventional aircraft. Which from the bomber's viewpoint means one thing: You have less time to sight him, less time to hit him, and he has less time to shoot at you.

Because of advantages in overtaking speed, he's most apt to attack from the tail, or dive and pull up from below. The rocket-driven Me 163 may use power in "bursts", gliding alternately. Defensive fighter support remains your prime protection, but if he gets through to the formation, you've got to be proportionately faster in everything you do -- recognizing, sighting, firing.

Apparently least armored on these customers are the fuselage and personnel area. Confirmed victories for our fighters are already reported, and it is expected that our bombing attacks on production centers and equipped airbases will prevent these ships from becoming much of a factor in this war.

Fuel capacity is a vital problem with them -- all types consume it voraciously. Also the production-geared Me 163 requires special airbase structures in which to refuel. This makes them especially vulnerable to attacks on their sources of supply. Determined bombing may keep them out of your sights -- but if they get there, know your sighting and use it fast!

## POSITION FIRING

| Angle Off ° | Rule For Present Fighters | Rule For ME163 and 262 | Change |
|---|---|---|---|
| 90° | 3 rads | 2 1/2 rads | Reduce 1/2 rad |
| 45° | 2 rads | 1 1/2 rads | Reduce 1/2 rad |
| 22-1/2° | 1 rad | 1 rad | None |
| 11-1/4° | 1/2 rad | 1/2 rad | None |
| 0° | Point Blank | Point Blank | None |

**AIMING CHANGES LITTLE**

The normal type of attack is still to be expected, but is at higher speeds. Hence the direction of the necessary deflection is unchanged.

Within 45° of the nose or tail, no change need be made in aiming rules. On attacks nearer the beam, present aiming rules must be reduced by 1/2 rad.

However, proficiency must be practiced to a maximum to assure speed in tracking.

## ROCKET AND JET-FIGHTERS

HE. 280, JET.

Span 39¼'

PROVISIONAL SILHOUETTE

**LESS LIKELY TO MEET THESE**

Recognition of this Heinkel 280 model was encouraged recently as it was slated for priority production. Tests on it, however, have proven unsatisfactory and it is not expected to figure in combat. The Me 163 and Me 262 are becoming prominent in operations.

ME. 163, ROCKET

Span 31'

Length 20'

*The Air Force alerts its combat crews to "Jerry's Final Brainstorm," the Messerschmitt rocket and jet fighters and the Heinkel 280.* (RAYMOND C. WIER)

struction, even in the superior jet fighters, because they were ill trained and lacked experience. And those veterans who might have compensated for some of that inexperience were already dead or being worn out in interminable operations.

The squeeze on oil even cut into operations. While Speer had succeeded in increasing the production of aircraft, the denial of fuel chained them to the ground. Because of this Luftwaffe interception would be sporadic and only very important targets would be defended. Fuel and oil would be hoarded until Berlin, or Vienna or some similar critical target area, was attacked and the Luftwaffe, assumed dead, would rise out of the ashes.

Hitler hated being on the defensive; his was a philosophy of attack. The thought of surrender was inconceivable—even after France had been won back and Allied troops had crossed into Germany.

(This occurred five years and eleven days after Hitler had launched *Fall Weiss* upon Poland.) "As far as I was concerned," Field Marshal Gerd von Rundstedt, Commander in Chief, West, later said, "the war ended in September [1944]." For Rundstedt, perhaps, but not for the German people, not for troops on both sides, and not—especially—for Hitler.

"I think it is pretty obvious," the Führer said in conference one day with some of his staff, "that this war is no pleasure for me." It is unlikely that any more fatuous statement has ever been made. "For five years," he continued in a characteristic outburst of self-pity, "I have been separated from the world. I haven't been to the theater, I haven't heard a concert, and I haven't seen a film. I live only for the purpose of leading this fight, because I know if there is not an iron will behind it this battle cannot be won.

"I accuse the General Staff of weakening combat officers who join its ranks, instead of exuding this

*The Messerschmitt Me-262 of Jagdstaffel 77. Had Hitler not interfered with the production and design of this aircraft the last months of the war might have proved gloomier and bloodier than they were. This was not, however, the first operational jet; the British Gloster Meteor was used against doodle bugs as early as July 1944—the Me-262s of KG 51 went into action a month later.* (U. S. AIR FORCE)

*A hidden Me-262 plant at Obertraubling, Germany. Final assembly was completed here before the jets were delivered to jet units.* (U. S. AIR FORCE)

iron will, and of spreading pessimism when General Staff officers go to the front. . . ." This was the old refrain, for in the twilight of the Third Reich the former corporal harked back to the good old days of the First World War, when the military situation, for him at least, was much simpler than it was in 1944.

"If necessary," he conceded, "we will fight on the Rhine. . . . We'll fight until we get a peace which secures the life of the German nation for the next fifty or hundred years and which, above all, does not besmirch our honor a second time, as happened in 1918. . . ."

By September, when Rundstedt believed the war was over, the Allied advance lost its impetus. The rapid advance across France had stretched the supply lines. Patton's Third Army, for example, came to a halt for five days because of a lack of fuel. All fuel, all ammunition, all essential supplies had to be brought in by truck from the Normandy beaches or the port of Cherbourg to the front lines —distances ranging from four to five hundred miles. Also, along the German West Wall (called the Siegfried Line by the Allies) were fortifications which ran from the Netherlands southward to Switzerland. Despite his defeatism, Rundstedt held the West Wall firmly.

*Lancasters bombing through the overcast by day; the target is a vengeance weapon base in France.*
(IMPERIAL WAR MUSEUM, LONDON)

It had been Eisenhower's plan to invade Germany along a broad front through the West Wall, but the critical problem of supply intervened. Two of his commanders urged Eisenhower to give one of them his own head for the plunge into Germany: Montgomery in the north was certain he could penetrate into the Ruhr (provided he was given priority on supplies and reserve troops intended for other units), and Patton promised with equal certainty that he could reach the Rhine. Eisenhower rejected both ideas and continued to favor his "broad front" concept.

He did, however, approve of an attempt, suggested by Montgomery, to drop troops by air into the Netherlands to assist the British Second Army across river obstacles. Although the drop, the largest air-borne operation of the war and code-named "Market," was executed successfully, it fell short of its intended objective because of unexpected, stiff German resistance. Montgomery had hoped that "Market," plus its ground phase, "Garden," would open up a corridor through the Netherlands which would lead directly into the heart of Germany. To Eisenhower "Market-Garden" had furnished "ample evidence that much bitter campaigning was to come." And when it came, the whim of Hitler's vaunted "iron will," it was with dismaying surprise.

Hitler called the operation ultimately (for the code name changed biweekly in the interest of supersecrecy) *Die Wacht am Rhein.* Whether this was a bitter allusion to Allied occupation of Germany after the First World War or a flicker of rare sardonic humor it would be impossible to ascertain. But Hitler's plan when he told his military leaders was regarded as a form of madness. Late in November the Allies had taken Antwerp, which served as an important port. Hitler's grand plan had come to life one day when he heard the word "Ardennes" mentioned.

"Stop!" he shouted and raised his hand for silence. "I have made a momentous decision. I am taking the offensive." He then dropped the personal pronouns and brought his hand down upon a map.

"Here," he said with eyes afire and his racked body electric for the first time in years, "out of the Ardennes. Across the Meuse and on to Antwerp!"

This was a stunning decision, and Hitler's military advisers saw little chance of success. It was a plan that might have worked in 1940, when Britain

*The curse is off Ploesti, although the flak is as thick as ever. Fifteenth Air Force B-24s deal a hard blow to Hitler's major oil source. Without oil neither the Wehrmacht nor the Luftwaffe could operate effectively.*
(U. S. AIR FORCE)

and France were on the run and German troops invincible—and there was still a Luftwaffe. (Rundstedt's comment was typical of the general outlook: "If we reached the Meuse we should have got down on our knees and thanked God—let alone try to reach Antwerp.") By driving a wedge between Eisenhower's armies (thus, Hitler predicted, trapping the British on the sea as at Dunkirk) Hitler would prove that, despite Allied victories, Germany was not finished and would not capitulate—"Never! Never!"

To make this impression, Hitler scraped together all possible troops, with the main blow falling to two panzer armies, Josef Dietrich's Sixth SS Panzer Army and Hasso von Manteuffel's Fifth. All possible armor was thrown into the gamble, about eight hundred tanks. Göring promised no less than three thousand fighters for the Luftwaffe's part of "the Watch on the Rhine"—code-named *Der Grosse Schlag* ("the Great Blow").

After waiting for a weather prediction which promised several days of poor flying weather, grounding Allied aircraft, Hitler suddenly unleashed his Ardennes counteroffensive on December 16, 1944. This came as a shock to the Allies, confident that the German capability for another offensive was a thing of the past. The Fifth Panzer Army smashed through the American lines, as consternation in the various Allied capitals evidenced a fear of success and a second Dunkirk. The Germans knew that the American defenses in the Ardennes sector were thinly held, and it was there that the deepest thrust was made; this became popularly known as "the Battle of the Bulge." It was a stunning surprise, and during the period from the sixteenth through the twenty-sixth of December the Americans suffered terrible losses; but the Watch on the Rhine failed and, in fact, never even reached the Meuse. When the weather cleared, Allied aircraft ripped up the panzers and cut off supply lines. The German thrust literally ran out of gas.

Though the gamble was lost, Hitler continued stubbornly to insist that his generals continue with the attack even though it was obvious by the end of December that it had failed. But having sacrificed men and tanks (the totals of casualties exceeded 120,000 troops and about 600 tanks), there still remained the Luftwaffe and *Der Grosse Schlag.*

The Great Blow would answer once and for all

*Winter 1944–45: weather such as this on the base of the 92nd Bomb Group in England and over the Continent furnished Hitler with the setting for a surprise blow in the Ardennes.* (U. S. AIR FORCE)

that haunting question, "Where is the Luftwaffe?" Göring had promised three thousand fighters. These had been husbanded for what Galland had assumed would be a true great blow, upon the Strategic Air Forces' heavy bombers; instead Hitler diverted them to the land battle in the Ardennes.

When Hitler heard of Göring's promise, he smiled sardonically and told Manteuffel, "Göring has reported that he has three thousand planes available for the operation. You know Göring's reports. Discount one thousand, and that still leaves a thousand for you and a thousand for Sepp Dietrich." The number that actually participated in *Der Grosse Schlag*—which Luftwaffe pilots called Operation Hermann—was closer to 900 (numbers vary from 790 to 1100; after the war Göring claimed 2300). Planes and pilots were even drawn from JG 104, a training unit.

Like the Ardennes offensive itself, Operation Hermann was prepared with the utmost secrecy and unleashed with devastating surprise. In the early morning of New Year's Day 1945 hundreds of Me-109s and FW-190s warmed up on various German airfields behind the lines. Both experienced and inexperienced pilots were to take part in the surprise attack upon Allied airfields in the Netherlands and Belgium and a single base in France, a total of seventeen. Because the formations were a mixed bag, the

*"Bulge" weather on the Continent, which grounded the Allied planes while Hitler's panzers smashed through the American lines.* (U. S. AIR FORCE)

fighters were guided toward their targets by Junkers 88s. At a point near the target areas, the inexperienced pilots would have to rely upon special maps to find their targets; the Ju-88s turned back at the Rhine. The approach was made at very low level to avoid enemy radar; strict radio silence was observed.

Pilots, aircraft, and fuel had been hoarded for this great blow. For the second time within two weeks the Allies were dealt a shock by the Germans. The most successful attack was made upon the British Second Tactical Air Force base at Eindhoven. About forty German fighters swept in low over the field at the moment Mitchell bombers were lining up to take off. Hawker Typhoons of No. 438 and No. 439 Squadrons, Royal Canadian Air Force, were also caught on the ground; those pilots who attempted to take off were shot down only a few feet off the ground, encumbered as they were by bomb loads and unretracted landing gears. Some pilots abandoned their planes and ran for cover. Soon Eindhoven was strewn with burning wrecks. A single Spitfire took off in the maelstrom of smoke and fire, shot down one of the attackers, and then crashed into the ground itself.

Other Spitfires, of the No. 131 Wing (Nos. 302, 308, and 317, Polish squadrons), returning from a fighter sweep, however, were air-borne and upon

returning to their base found it under attack by about fifty German fighters. Within minutes eighteen of the attackers had been shot out of the air at the cost of a single Spitfire.

The American base at Asche, near Chièvres, Belgium, was jumped at around ten o'clock in the morning. A dozen Mustangs, led by Lieutenant Colonel John C. Meyer, deputy commander of the 487th Squadron (352nd Fighter Group, Eighth AF), were preparing to take off on a morning patrol. Early morning fog had kept the planes grounded, but by eight it had begun to burn off, clearing slowly from east to west. The twelve Mustangs, motors warming on the frozen airstrip, awaited word from Meyer to take off. All were unaware of the approaching Messerschmitts and Focke-Wulfs hugging the floor of the valleys of the mountainous Eifel district, leading to Asche. They swooped in behind the veil of fog. It was approaching ten before Meyer could gun his engine and begin the takeoff. As he thundered down the runway he was surprised to see antiaircraft puffs bursting at the far end of the field. He called the control tower, asking if its radar had picked up "bogies" on its screen.

*During a break in the weather C-47s of the 9th Troop Carrier Command come over to drop supplies to Americans encircled in Bastogne, Belgium.* (U. S. AIR FORCE)

*John C. Meyer, who was caught up in "the Great Blow," the Luftwaffe's last wasteful gasp during the Battle of the Bulge.* (U. S. AIR FORCE)

"Negative."

*Petie,* Meyer's Mustang, picked up speed and raced toward the eastern end of the field and the ever thickening bursts. As the Mustang's wheels left the strip Meyer saw, as if out of nowhere, an FW-190 coming his way. With wheels still lowered, his engine striving for altitude, Meyer knew he was a sitting duck. But the German pilot, briefed to strafe the field, turned aside and fired on a C-47 (Dakota) on the edge of the runway. Shaken but apparently reprieved, Meyer hauled up his undercarriage, quickly went through all the "drill" for battle, and fired at the German fighter, still intent upon destroying the transport on the ground. The FW, hit by six .50-calibers, slammed to the ground beside the Dakota.

Another pilot, William T. Whisher, following Meyer, began firing at another Focke-Wulf thirty seconds after he had left the ground. He was two hundred feet above the earth, an unlikely height for a dogfight, and within a hundred yards of the German aircraft. The "Butcher Bird" winged over, smashed into the ground, and burned. In the ensuing half hour, most of it over the base, Whisher knocked down another FW-190 and two Messerschmitts.

"There were plenty of Jerries left to shoot at," Whisher commented. Meyer meanwhile managed to gain a little altitude and found this to be only too true. What with trying to ascertain the identity of the aircraft—for now Thunderbolts too had joined the battle—sorting out the Me-109s from the Mustangs and the FW-190s from the Thunderbolts, plus twisting his neck to clear his tail, Meyer was busy indeed. There was still another hitch: the antiaircraft gunners were firing up at him as well as the enemy, and his P-51 was taking hits. A large chunk flew off his wing.

In spite of this distraction, Meyer got onto the tail of another FW-190. American ground gunners (still shooting at him) proved to be less effective than the American airman: pieces of the cowling flew away from the German fighter, the propeller slowed up and windmilled, and the pilot pointed the nose down. As Meyer watched, the FW, with wheels up, skidded into a field. The plane struck on its belly, bounced, thumped again, and then tossed over onto its back, over and over, flared, and broke up in a great flash of fire.

Turning back to the congested sky, Meyer found he had flown away from the base. Low on fuel and practically out of ammunition, he realized he had to land. A call to base informed him that the field was still under attack; it would be pointless to attempt to land there. Meyer then found what appeared to be an airfield and just as he was about to put down, three Me-109s bounced upon the Mustang's tail.

The four aircraft darted and maneuvered in an aerial ballet; Meyer got one of the Messerschmitts in a good spot, there was only a short burst from his guns, and he realized he was now really out of the battle. Suddenly, as it so often was in air combat, a swarm of planes filled the air around him: Mustangs. Drifting through the sky, looking for landmarks and checking for "bandits," Meyer worked his way back to Asche, which by eleven o'clock was clear.

Nearly half of the enemy attackers, twenty-three in all, had fallen to the guns of the 352nd Group —with no losses to the group itself. A few planes had been lost, but no pilots. Except for a few

*A Luftwaffe pilot leaves his stricken plane over the Bulge after being shot up by James Dalglish, 354th Fighter Group, Ninth Air Force, flying a Thunderbolt.* (U. S. AIR FORCE)

immolation (and perhaps sensing it), had sacrificed the German Air Force to his own peculiar gods, just as he had the Wehrmacht and the German people. "If the war is to be lost," he believed, "the nation also will perish. This fate is inevitable. There is no need to consider the basis even of a most primitive existence any longer. On the contrary," he told Speer, "it is better to destroy even that, and to destroy it ourselves. The nation has proved itself weak, and the future belongs solely to the stronger eastern nation. Besides, those who remain after the battle are of little value; for the good have fallen."

He had seen to that personally. He established himself in the Reich Chancellery in Berlin, by early 1945 a city of rubble, which he declared he would "defend to the last" despite the fact, as he believed, that the German people were "unworthy of my genius." While his armies desperately fought the Russians in the east and the British and Americans in the west, Hitler awaited the inevitable. But when

holes in *Petie* (many of which could be credited to friendly antiaircraft fire), Meyer was untouched (but it had been his last fight—in which he scored his twenty-fourth aerial victory—for before he took to the air again he was injured in an automobile accident, hospitalized for three months, and then returned to the United States).

When Operation Hermann ended the question arose again, "Where is the Luftwaffe?" The Great Blow had been, as all had wished in Hitler's headquarters, a surprising one. But it was the last. The Allies had lost 156 aircraft (120 British and 36 U.S.); the Germans lost over 200; only sixty Luftwaffe pilots were taken prisoner. Over fifty irreplaceable air leaders were thrown away in *Der Grosse Schlag;* even the reserves were sacrificed. Many of the losses could be attributed to inexperienced German pilots who inadvertently collided over their targets or were readily shot down by Allied pilots or antiaircraft.

The Luftwaffe? Hitler, approaching his Wagnerian

*Jug pilots of the 354th Fighter Group discuss a strafing of German supply columns and communications targets. Left to right: Omer W. Culberson (Minneapolis), Orrin D. Rawlings (Depue, Illinois), Glenn T. Eagleston (Alhambra, California), James B. Dalglish (Rome, New York), and Lloyd J. Overfield (Leavenworth, Kansas.)* (U. S. AIR FORCE)

*And what they did: when the weather cleared over Belgium Ninth Air Force fighter-bombers tore Hitler's Ardennes offensive to bits. Here is what remained of* *a German convoy after the P-47s caught it on a highway in Belgium.* (U. S. AIR FORCE)

he went, he wished the whole world to go with him.

"He had a special picture of the world," observed General Heinz Guderian, "and every fact had to be fitted into that fancied picture. As he believed, so the world must be, but, in fact, it was a picture of another world." How true: much of Germany and its cities bore the aspect of *Mondlandschaft*.

v

Although Hitler's mad counteroffensive had failed, no one in the Allied camp was aware of the extent of that failure: its losses in men, machines, muni-tions, and expenditure of a continually diminishing supply of fuel. The Ardennes battle had in fact upset the Allied ground battle timetable and inter-fered with the strategic aerial plan. Heavy bombers diverted to ground co-operation led to some re-covery of the German synthetic oil industry, for example.

There was little optimism in the Allied camp in early 1945. There seemed little hope for an early end to the war in Europe. A realist, Spaatz visualized the possibility of the war's continuing on into autumn. If, as revealed by *Der Grosse Schlag,* the Germans could muster counteroffensives in the future, it would be a very hard summer.

*Winter 1944. Flying Fortresses heading for Germany to bomb railroad targets that did not yield to the heavy bomber. Easily repaired by slave labor gangs, these targets did not loom very large in the opinion of General Spaatz of the Strategic Air Forces.*

(U. S. AIR FORCE)

ously Bomber Command attacked important rail centers and the Ruhr waterways, and contributed to the vexing Battle of the Atlantic by placing "Tallboys" (a twelve-thousand-pound, extremely destructive bomb devised by B. N. Wallis, inventor of the "Dam Buster" bombs) into the battleship *Tirpitz,* which turned over and blew up.

Harris deployed his heavies mainly in the Ruhr; the Mosquitos harassed Berlin as did the Eighth Air Force's Fortresses and Liberators. Flak was more of a menace than the Luftwaffe, and great forces of bombers crossed German skies, night and day, with little opposition.

As the ground forces closed in upon Hitler in his bunker in Berlin, British and American air power was employed in assisting the Russian advance from the east. This was mainly in the form of heavy bombardments of major transportation centers: Chemnitz, Leipzig, Cottbus, Berlin, and Dresden. In conjunction with a new Russian offensive, which opened the second week of January, various strikes by British and American bombers were made. In some quarters it was believed that such co-ordination of plans should prove disheartening to the Germans. Chief of Air Staff Sir Charles Portal, while voting for oil targets as top priority, believed also that the Allies "should use available effort in one big attack on Berlin and attacks on Dresden, Leipzig, Chemnitz, or any other cities where a severe blitz will not only cause confusion in the evacuation from the east but will also hamper the movement of troops from the west."

The Germans, on the other hand, were in worse condition than the Allies realized. Despite the use of the strategic bombers in the European land battle, the Lancasters, Fortresses, Liberators, and Mosquitos continued to appear over Germany with devastating effect. The Fifteenth Air Force, for example, was not tied down to the Battle of the Bulge, and its heavy bombers contributed its share to the bombing of the oil centers during that critical time. To Spaatz, oil and jets were the major anxieties and as soon as possible he hoped to aim his strategic forces at these targets. Even Harris's Bomber Command began attacking the despised panacea targets, namely the oil plants. By November 1944 Bomber Command was carrying heavy loads of explosives to various oil targets both night and day. Simultane-

*A twelve-thousand-pound "Tallboy" devised by Barnes Wallis of the Dam Buster bombs and which proved terribly destructive to German cities.* (U. S. AIR FORCE)

What emerged from this hopeful attempt to co-operate with an ally—a touchy and not always co-operative ally—was a classic example of the terrifying impact of total air war. This was the devastation of the city of Dresden by RAF Bomber Command and the Eighth Air Force beginning on the night of February 13, 1945, and continuing into the next day. Eight hundred Bomber Command heavies initiated the attack in a night raid and 311 Eighth Air Force B-17s completed it the following day. And the day after an additional 200 American bombers returned to churn up what was already a catastrophe.

The horror and terror on the ground was incredible, destruction was extensive, and the loss of life was frightful. The beautiful little city, its population swollen by an influx of refugees from the east fleeing before the Russians bent upon revenge, pillage, and rape, and its predominantly wooden buildings, ideal for incendiaries, all but vanished in a howling whirlwind of incineration. Although it is unlikely that the true toll will ever be known, the number of people probably killed at Dresden was about 135,000 (as compared with the atomic bombing of Hiroshima, which killed 71,379). Harris had been correct, they had reaped the whirlwind.

By April of 1945 the great European air war was virtually over. The most important targets remained those associated with the oil industry. Berlin, the objective of the Russians (although Stalin assured Eisenhower, rather significantly on April Fools' Day, that the German capital was of no military importance), continued to take a tremendous pounding from the air. On March 18 the Eighth Air Force mounted its largest daylight raid on Berlin—1250 Fortresses and Liberators escorted by 14 groups of Mustangs. Bombing through the overcast by instrument (H2X), they did great damage to transportation and industrial targets in the city. But on this day the German jets came out in numbers for the first time—three dozen intercepted the heavy bombers in spite of the poor weather and claimed 15 "kills" (two probable) of the day's total American loss of 24 bombers and 5 fighters. Only two Me-262s were shot down in the encounter. German flak, too, was particularly telling, and at least 600 bombers were damaged, 16 so badly that they were forced to crash-land behind the Russian lines beyond Berlin.

The success of the jet fighters that day was a foreboding development, an indication of what might materialize if the Luftwaffe could muster pilots, aircraft, and fuel. On April 10 no less than 50 jets intercepted a large (1232) raid on the Berlin area. The objectives were airfields, marshaling yards, jet assembly plants around the capital at Oranienburg, Rechlin-Larz, Brandenburg-Briest, Burg, and Parchim.

Mustangs of the Eighth Air Force attacked the "blow jobs" and shot down twenty in the vicinity of Oranienburg and other targets near Berlin. Another ten jets were claimed by bomber gunners, particularly those of the 13th Combat Wing (95th, 100th, and 390th Bomb Groups) over Berlin. A loss of at least thirty jets was the most severe of the war, to which could be added hundreds destroyed on the ground. The Eighth lost ten bombers in the widespread fighting, but the jets were as good as finished. That the slower P-51s had been able to deal so devastatingly with the Me-262s was undoubtedly because of the inexperience of most of the German pilots.

What occurred over and within Germany could no longer be called "battles." Deep underground, in his ill-ventilated, artificially lighted bunker Hitler marshaled forces he no longer had for battles that could not be fought. He believed, almost to the end, that some miracle—if not a miracle weapon—would save him from the Russians slashing at the gates of Berlin. For a brief time his "miracle" was Generaloberst Gotthard Heinrici, who with minimal forces somehow managed to hold the Russians in check temporarily in the face of military madness and hopelessness. By mid-April the Russians opened their final drive into the heart of Berlin. Within days the lone remaining outpost in all of Germany was the bunker under the Reich Chancellery. The glorious battle had degenerated into street fighting like that out of which the Third Reich had sprung; there were no more strategic targets, only fear-driven, depleted scarecrows. Chaos had indeed come to those who had lit the torch of war.

On April 16, 1945, General Carl Spaatz dispatched a message to Major General James Doolittle (Eighth Air Force) and Lieutenant General Nathan Twining (Fifteenth Air Force): "The advances of our ground forces have brought to a close the strategic air war waged by the United

*The 384th over Dresden (after the terrible February 13–14, 1945, attacks that burned the city). The target is the rail yards, over which escaping Germans were expected to travel.* (U. S. AIR FORCE)

States Strategic Air Forces and the Royal Air Force Bomber Command. . . .

"From now onward our Strategic Air Forces must operate with our Tactical Air Forces in close co-operation with our Armies.

"All units of the U. S. Strategic Air Forces are commended for their part in winning the Strategic Air War and are enjoined to continue with un-diminished effort and precision the final tactical phase of air action to secure the ultimate objective—complete defeat of Germany."

Four days later Hitler celebrated his last, that is, fifty-sixth, birthday in the grim, unreal setting of his bunker. When Hitler emerged around noon to receive the tributes of his few remaining faithful (among them Goebbels, Martin Bormann, Speer, Von Ribbentrop, Himmler, Jodl, and Keitel), plus some SS troops and a contingent of Hitler Youth (children would have been a more appropriate des-ignation). Hitler had aged, and those who had not seen him for a while were shocked at his ap-pearance. He was bent, he dragged one foot, his hands trembled, and his color was ghastly.

Göring arrived later in the day to pay his re-spects; his plans were made. He evacuated Karin-hall, had the Luftwaffe pack his treasure into a great convoy of trucks, and after dynamiting Karin-hall, paid his visit to Hitler and fled to the south. Luftwaffe chief of staff Koller bitterly noted that Göring, as usual, had left him to deal with Hitler's fury. Göring's plan also included bargaining with the Allies, assuming that he would be able to do better than Hitler; after all, wasn't Göring a figure of fun to the Allies? They hated Hitler but they laughed at the Fat One. When he offered his services as peacemaker, the Führer (who had suffered a physical collapse) revived long enough to accuse the Reichsmarschall of "high treason" and ordered his arrest. He refused, however, under the urging of Goebbels and Bormann, to have Göring executed.

Göring was stripped of his offices, and appointed in his place as *Oberbefehlshaber der Luftwaffe* (of a non-existent Luftwaffe) was the faithful Robert Ritter von Greim, formerly chief of Luftflotte 6. In addition to this empty command, Hitler also presented Greim with a potassium cyanide capsule. Hitler had already begun to discuss his own impending end and Greim begged to be permitted to remain in Berlin to die with his Führer. So did Hanna Reitsch, famed prewar woman glider pilot and a dedicated Nazi test pilot.

On the night of April 28 Hanna Reitsch, with Greim as a passenger, flew a small Arado trainer off the streets of Berlin. Hitler had ordered them out of the bunker so that Greim could order Luftwaffe support for the decimated army of General Walther Wenck, attempting to break through the Russian armies encircling Berlin. It was, of course, another pointless gesture, and the little Arado managed to get off the rubble-strewn street and into the air despite the Russian small arms and anti-aircraft fire. Flying over the ruins of Berlin, aflame it seemed from end to end, Hanna Reitsch headed north. She survived the war, but Greim could not face the future he saw for Germany. Nor could Hitler, betrayed on all sides, who committed suicide in his bunker and then was burned along with his bride of a few hours, Eva Braun.

*With the Luftwaffe burning on the ground, Allied fighters, in air-ground co-operation, made a shambles* *of any German convoy that attempted to move.*
(U. S. ARMY)

cerebral hemorrhage) to inform him of the "plight of the civil population in Occupied Holland," which the Prime Minister believed to be "desperate." Perhaps three million people faced starvation in an area still held by the German Twenty-fifth Army, isolated but still holding out in "Fortress Holland."

"We believe," Churchill told Roosevelt, "that large numbers are dying daily, and the situation must deteriorate rapidly now that communications between Germany and Holland are virtually cut. I fear we may soon be in presence of a tragedy."

General Eisenhower too was aware of this dire possibility. "I still refused to consider a major offensive into the country," he wrote in his *Crusade in Europe*. To stop the Allied advance the Germans had opened the dikes, which flooded the Dutch countryside with sea water. To forestall further such desolation, Eisenhower held his forces in check, knowing that the German Army in Holland was virtually helpless insofar as it mattered in the Battle of Germany. If he pressed his advantage Eisen-

*Last-ditch weapon: pick-a-back bomber. The lower plane, the Ju-88, was loaded with explosives, and the upper FW-190, with pilot, was supposed to fly the Ju-88 to its selected target, release it, and guide it the rest of the way by radio.* (U. S. AIR FORCE)

Greim, captured by the victorious Allies, said upon swallowing the capsule the Führer had so thoughtfully given him, "I am head of the Luftwaffe but I have no Luftwaffe."

There was no Luftwaffe, just as there were no remaining strategic targets. Even the fighters were forbidden to strafe because of the general shambles and the possibility of hitting released prisoners or Allied troops.

However, among the final "targets" of the Eighth Air Force's B-17s were a racetrack and a golf course. These unusual objectives were to be hit from an altitude of about four hundred feet. The mission was not carried out with any levity, for behind it lay a great national crisis. On April 10 Churchill had communicated with Roosevelt (only two days before the American President died of a

*Caught in the guns of Mustang pilot Bernard H. Howes, this pick-a-back is abandoned by the pilot (just below the tail of the Ju-88).* (U. S. AIR FORCE)

*Göring at journey's end; dismissed by Hitler, pursued by the Gestapo, but undismayed, Göring hoped to negotiate a peace with Eisenhower.* (U. S. ARMY)

*Hanna Reitsch, Germany's leading woman aviator, glider pilot, and jet test pilot. She flew Greim into and out of Berlin while the Russians encircled it and Allied bombers bombed it into rubble.* (U. S. AIR FORCE)

*Robert von Greim, last chief of the Luftwaffe.*
(H. J. NOWARRA)

hower realized that "Not only would great additional destruction and suffering have resulted but the enemy's opening of dikes would further have flooded the country and destroyed much of its fertility for years to come."

The early flooding contributed to the starvation then afflicting the Dutch. But there was even more. A general railway strike in September of 1944 called by the government in exile from London inspired a German retaliation. All food supplies to western Holland were cut off for two months, thus hindering the stock-piling of food supplies. Further, all

". . . but I have no Luftwaffe. . . ." *Robert Ritter von Greim,* Oberbefehlshaber der Luftwaffe, *Berlin, April 1945.* (U. S. AIR FORCE)

means of Dutch transport were seized by the Germans to doubly ensure the edict. By November the first deaths by starvation occurred; by the spring the estimate was that a thousand Dutch died every day.

To alleviate the situation the Allies proposed a plan to the *Reichskommissar* in the Netherlands, Dr. Artur von Seyss-Inquart. The Allies would halt their westward advance into Holland if the Germans ceased their ruin of the Dutch earth and permitted wholesale drops of food and other supplies to the Dutch by air. Attempts were made, meanwhile, to provide relief by limited means but to no great effect, and the Luftwaffe's flak continued to be as deadly as ever.

To work out a solution Eisenhower sent his chief of staff, Brigadier General Walter Bedell Smith, into Holland to discuss it with Seyss-Inquart. Although Generaloberst Johannes Blaskowitz refused to surrender his troops, it was agreed that the Allies could fly large formations of bombers over certain areas of Holland at very low level and drop the supplies. Aircraft were to be de-gunned, no ammunition could be carried, and no photographs could be taken.

The two drop points were the racetrack at The Hague (one of the Nazi's major rocket-launching

centers) and a golf course at Rotterdam. Eisenhower accepted the proposals although he honestly believed that the "continued occupation of Holland was senseless" and warned Blaskowitz and Seyss-Inquart that he would "tolerate no interference with the relief program and that if the Germans were guilty of any breach of faith I would later refuse to treat them as prisoners of war."

The mercy mission, as the Air Force called it, was prepared with great enthusiasm by the men in the bombers. RAF's Bomber Command flew one of its most gratifying daylight missions (Operation Manna) on April 29, 1945, when the Lancasters and Mosquitos of Nos. 1, 3, and 8 Groups initiated the operation with more than 250 aircraft participating. No. 8 Group was comprised of nineteen—mostly Mosquito, with the rest Lancaster—squadrons of the legendary Pathfinder Force, which had so skillfully marked the targets in the wasted Ruhr. For Manna it marked the several drop zones assigned to Bomber Command: the Valkenburg airfield at Leiden, the racetrack and Ypenburg airfield at The Hague, the Waalhaven airfield and Kralingsche-Plas in Rotterdam and Gouda.

On May 1, after three days of cancellations because of the weather, the Eighth Air Force dispatched three wings, the 13th, 45th, and 93rd, of the 3rd Air Division. Its Flying Fortresses were loaded with nearly eight tons of food. At the premission briefing Sergeant Cecil Cohen, who among other duties functioned as the photographer in his 34th Bomb Group, recalled that he was told to take along a small reflex camera and "to get everything you can, but under no circumstances show the camera from a window." Cohen decided that he would take shots through the open bomb bay before and after the drop. Although the day's mission had not been scrubbed as the previous three, it was not an ideal day for flying, especially at low level.

As recalled by First Lieutenant Jerome Kagel, "The weather was bad—rain and gusty winds threw our ships about like model airplanes in a wind tunnel."

Cecil Cohen prepared his camera for his part in the mission. He placed filters over the lens to cut some of the haze. But the plane apparently had strayed from the designated corridor as they approached the Dutch coast—"one of the meanest in the world for flak." As they came in lower, it

*Cecil Cohen in the waist of a Flying Fortress en route to Holland.* (34TH BOMB GROUP)

dren danced around when they saw our planes. I even spotted a few enemy soldiers intermingled with the civilians.

"The people seemed to get all out of bounds as our supplies rained down. They ran toward the tumbling boxes of rations apparently heedless of the danger of being hit by bundles which fell with terrific impetus. I wouldn't be surprised if in their eagerness and their anguish for food some of them were hurt by the boxes or from being jostled in that tremendous throng. The whole thing made an exciting, heart-wrenching picture that will remain with me for a long time.

"I was soon absorbed in the amazing spectacle below, as I saw—actually saw—thousands of people mobbing the streets, gazing skyward and waving frantically at us. Boulevards, street corners, everywhere, civilians clustered, looking up at these former dealers of destruction that were now playing the lead roles as angels of mercy."

Cohen, meanwhile, was recording the mercy mission (military installations were of no real interest). To get another angle he stood on several boxes

was possible for Cohen to pick out German gun emplacements; there were even German troops moving around beneath their Fortress with seeming unconcern. But not a wary flak unit, which began firing at the straying plane. The pilot all but stood the big Fortress on one wing—Cohen and the other aircrew in the plane's waist were piled in a heap against the side—and returned to the correct flight path. Inside Holland they came down very low and the air was bumpy. On his stomach in the bomb bay, Cohen for the first time in his Air Force career became airsick. The strange position, the rough air had done it—and the result was the spoilage of the filter on Cohen's camera. It would be impossible to clean, so he merely threw it overboard and took several photographs with a filterless lens.

"When we came over the racetrack," Kagel saw "a surging crowd of excited people, hundreds of them, of every age. They filled the grandstands and seemed to be everywhere—on the paddock, along the track, hugging the guard rail. Women and chil-

*Passing over a windmill, the crew of a Flying Fortress is greeted by arm-waving Dutch.* (U. S. AIR FORCE)

*Operation Manna: supplies rain down upon a drop site in Holland as this 390th Group Fortress opens its bomb bay.* (U. S. AIR FORCE)

*No other words required.* (U. S. AIR FORCE)

that he had stacked in the nose of the plane. With a couple of crewmen grasping his legs, about half of his body projected from the upper nose of the B-17 as he snapped pictures blowing in the wind. If any German saw him, there were no official complaints registered. Aircraft did return to England with flak holes in their wings, but no serious incident marred the mission. For ten days these missions continued, missions the crews found more gratifying than their missions to Berlin—or Dresden.

Flight Lieutenant R. E. Wannop, RAF, summed up the emotions of all men when he described one of the final missions. "We crossed the Dutch coast at two thousand feet and began to come down to five hundred. Below lay the once fertile land now covered by many feet of sea water. Houses that had been the proud possessions of a happy, carefree people now stood forlorn surrounded by the whirling, surging flood, some with only a roof visible.

A double line of poplar trees would show where once there had been a busy highway.

"Children ran out of school waving excitedly. One old man stopped at a cross-roads and shook his umbrella. The roads were crowded with hundreds of people waving. . . .

"Nobody spoke in the aircraft. . . .

"My vision was a little misty. . . .

"Perhaps it was the rain on the perspex. . . ."

The last Manna mission was flown on May 8, 1945; the Third Reich on that day lay in ruins and Hitler's wretched heirs surrendered to the Allies. Signing for Germany, Generaloberst Alfred Jodl, German Chief of Staff, said, "With this signature, the German people and Armed Forces are—for better or worse—delivered into the victor's hands."

Hitler's war was over; the most powerful air forces the world had ever known could turn to the shriveled Greater East Asia Co-Prosperity Sphere.

*Greim's Luftwaffe: May 8, 1945.* (U. S. AIR FORCE)

# BOOK II
# The Divine Wind

*The purity of youth will usher in the Divine Wind.*

—VICE-ADMIRAL TAKIJIRO OHNISHI

# 5

# "TYGER! TYGER! BURNING BRIGHT"

THE Boeing B-29 ("Superfortress") was not—as the legend goes—designed specifically to bomb Tokyo, but it did to a devastating degree. Its inception, the idea of General Henry Arnold, dates from November 1939—more than two years before the Pearl Harbor attack. This conception was inspired by the Nazi blitzkrieg in Europe and the high probability of a German victory and the possibility of a Nazi foothold "somewhere in the Americas" from which aerial attacks could easily be mounted against the United States.

The B-29 was designed to fly over longer distances, at higher altitudes, and at greater speeds and to carry heavier bomb loads than the B-17 and the B-24. The advent of war put the project on an emergency basis and orders were placed for the B-29 off the drawing board, even before the aircraft had been tested. Consequently, the development of the B-29, called "the three-billion-dollar gamble," was fraught with hazard and potential tragedy. An innovational concept—a new engine, pressurized crew stations, and remote-control gun turrets, to name a few—the B-29 also carried a full load of bugs. One of the most critical was a tendency for engines to catch fire. The second test model, flown by the chief test pilot on the project,

Edmund T. Allen, caught fire on February 18, 1943, during a test flight from Boeing Field, Seattle, and crashed, killing Allen and ten experienced B-29 specialists aboard. In addition, the plane, which Allen was attempting to land even while a sheet of flame trailed from his right wing, rammed into the Frye Packing Plant, killing several workers inside.

Despite such tragedies—for even after the B-29 went into combat in-flight engine fires plagued it—the gamble proved worthwhile. The B-29 emerged as the most formidable air weapon of the war. Although originally intended for use against Germany, by the summer of 1943 Air Force planning proceeded along a course aimed at Japan. Early in November, General Oliver P. Echols, Assistant Chief of Air Staff for Matériel, Maintenance, and Distribution, could state with more authority than historical truth that "the B-29 airplane was thought out and planned as a high-altitude, long-range bomber to attack Japan, her cities and industrial keypoints." The employment of the aircraft made the general's slight exaggeration a portentous historical truth.

With practically all of the bugs ironed out of the B-29 there still remained the problem of its deployment and command. The Pacific remained a

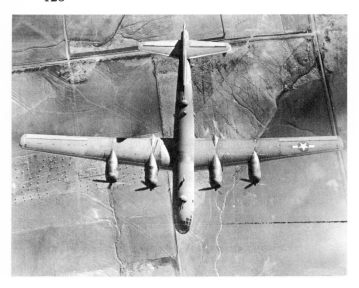

The Boeing B-29 "Superfortress," an aircraft designed for a very special mission. (U. S. AIR FORCE)

pail of worms, with its arguments over definition of command boundaries, supply distribution, and personality clashes. Once the Marianas were taken and bases established it was possible to attack Japan more efficiently than was possible from Indian and Chinese bases. But this would mean that the B-29s would "violate" the air over MacArthur's territory as well as the air over Nimitz's territory. The solution devised by the Joint Chiefs of Staff was the establishment of the Twentieth Air Force, under its direct control and with General Arnold as executive agent for the Joint Chiefs. This solved the problem of the B-29 units but, in effect, compounded those of logistics and administration, which devolved upon the theater commanders. The strained interservice relations (Navy vs. Air Force) were stretched nearly to the limit by the advent of the B-29 in the Pacific.

Since it became reasonably evident by the "Trident" conference in Washington (May 12–27, 1943)

The advent of the B-29 initiated an internal tug of war. Chennault—and especially Chiang Kai-shek—hoped to have them for the Fourteenth Air Force. Here Chennault conducts members of the Chinese Aero-

nautical Affairs Commission around a Fourteenth Air Force base. At this time not only did Chennault command the Fourteenth, he was also chief of staff to Chiang Kai-shek of the Chinese Air Force.

(U. S. AIR FORCE)

that Germany was checked and that, given time
and some luck, the Allies might open a second front
in Europe by May 1944, it was decided that the
B-29 would not be employed in Europe. To assuage
the feelings of Chiang Kai-shek, who believed he
was being given short shrift by the Allies, the B-29s
were earmarked for China. On their part, the Allied
planners did not believe that the war in the East
could be decided in China, preferring to move
toward Japan from the east and south. But with
Chiang Kai-shek's seemingly unlimited manpower,
it did seem feasible to furnish supplies to the
Chinese—provided the Generalissimo could get
them to fight the Japanese and not each other.

The thought of pouring U.S. divisions into China
did not sit well with the U. S. Chiefs of Staff; nor
did another suggestion that Chennault's Fourteenth
Air Force be equipped with B-29s, plus additional
fighter groups to escort them, for the bombing of the
Japanese homeland. The latter idea, however, had
its points, the most important of which was that a
bomber offensive out of Chinese bases, or at least
so the Air Force hoped, might "tremendously stim-
ulate Chinese morale and unify the Chinese people
under the leadership of Chiang Kai-shek."

At the same time Kenney in the southwest Pacific
wrote Arnold that he assumed "that I am still to
get the first B-29 unit. . . . If you want the B-29
used efficiently and effectively where it will do the

*Building a B-29 air base in China with manpower.
Rocks are brought to field site from the nearby hills
in horse-drawn carts.* (U. S. AIR FORCE)

most good in the shortest time, the southwest Pacific
area is the place and the Fifth Air Force can do
the job." The generally deteriorating military situation in the China-Burma area, however, favored the
CBI (China-Burma-India) as the recipient of the
first B-29s.

Arnold's solution was to establish the Twentieth
Air Force directly under the control of the Joint
Chiefs of Staff; this very effectively denied the B-29

*An American construction engineer called this a "ten-
ton, five-hundred-coolie-powered, rice-burning roller."*

*Stones, mud, and gravel were ground into the strip
by manpower also.* (U. S. AIR FORCE)

to the various warring factions. He kept the super-bomber out of the hands of Stilwell, MacArthur, and Nimitz, none of whom were particularly impressed with the strategic potential of what was then being called the VLR (very long-range) aircraft for employment by VHB (very heavy bomber) groups.

These groups (the 40th, 444th, 462nd, 468th) had been in existence since November 1943 and were assigned to the Twentieth Air Force in June of 1944 as the 58th Bombardment Wing (VH) of the 20th Bomber Command. The first B-29 landed at Kharagpur, about seventy miles west of Calcutta, India, on April 2, 1944. Before this was possible two months of very hard labor had been put in by the 853rd Engineer Aviation Battalion and the 382nd Engineer Construction Battalion (which had been borrowed from Stilwell's Ledo Road project). The labor force eventually numbered six thousand U.S. troops and twenty-seven thousand Indians. The preparation of the Indian bases was an epic in itself, for the B-29 required longer runways, which, in addition, had to be thicker than normal to withstand the weight of the great plane.

At the same time, since the B-29s would be based in India, out of the reach of the Japanese, staging areas in the neighborhood of Chengtu, China, were also constructed. Again conditions were at once contemporary and primitive, with American engineers directing Chinese laborers, doing most of the work literally by hand, numbering into the thousands. By May 10 the Chengtu bases were also ready for the B-29. These bases were within range of the Japanese homeland.

But there remained, as always, the problem of logistics. Before a mission could be mounted from Chengtu, supplies—fuel, ammunition, bombs, parts: everything—had to be moved from the Calcutta area, across the Hump, to China. Roughly it required six B-29 flights over the Hump and back to make possible one B-29 bombing mission upon Japan.

This in itself was a formidable undertaking. The Himalayas were the highest, most treacherous mountains in the world and the B-29 was not yet the world's most efficient aircraft. Even on the flight from the United States to India several of the planes were left behind with engine problems along the way and two were completely destroyed at Karachi.

*A B-29 resting on a handmade strip in China.*
(U. S. AIR FORCE)

The capricious engines continued to plague crews—and the heat of India contributed to the problem of overheating. Merely starting an engine could cause a cylinder to blow and the aircraft to catch fire. Crews looked at the crossing of the Himalayas in their unproved "superbomber" with skepticism. That they should be put to such inglorious work as hauling supplies instead of bomb loads was expressed in their own description of themselves as "a goddamed trucking outfit."

Two days after the India-to-China supply run had been initiated, a B-29 was attacked for the first time by enemy aircraft. The encounter occurred on April 26, 1944, late in the afternoon, when a B-29 (piloted by Major Charles H. Hansen) carrying a cargo of fuel had reached the Indo-Burmese frontier. The B-29 was cruising at sixteen thousand feet when Major Hansen saw, two thousand feet below and about five miles distant to the starboard, a formation of twelve Nakajima Ki. 43 "Oscars" (the Ki. was an abbreviation for *Hikoki,* meaning "aircraft").

Alerting his crew to battle stations, Hansen observed the Oscars as six of them began spiraling up toward their lone plane and the remaining six continued on in formation toward the Hump. The six Oscars that approached the B-29 then broke up into two formations of three on each side of the big bomber. They remained out of range, obviously studying the B-29, a plane none had probably ever seen before. This went on for nearly fifteen minutes as the nervous gunners on the bomber tracked the

Oscars. Suddenly the lead Oscar whipped out of formation and twisted in toward the B-29 almost directly from the starboard side. The wings winked with fire as the Oscar closed and a burst of fire cut across the B-29's midsection. A scream on the intercom meant that someone had been hit (Sergeant Walter W. Gilonske, a waist gunner, was wounded in this attack). The remaining Oscars followed in upon the bomber, now crippled—the top gun turrets were out, the 20-mm. tail cannon failed, and the twin .50s jammed. The latter were quickly cleared, however.

One of the Oscars came within a hundred yards of Sergeant Harold Lanhan's tail guns and left the battle smoking. The remaining Oscars continued attacking, but without conviction, for about twenty-five minutes and then left the battle. The American bomber had taken eight hits and, once Sergeant Gilonske was attended to, continued on to Chengtu unchallenged by other enemy aircraft.

Meanwhile, the B-29 crews operated primarily as

*Kenneth B. Wolfe, first commander of 20th Bomber Command—which was specially set up to keep the B-29s under control of the Air Force.* (U. S. AIR FORCE)

"truck drivers," which did not contribute to their efficiency in high-altitude formation flying, bombing, gunnery—the essentials to their primary mission. It was two months (less two days) before the first shakedown mission was scheduled for the 58th Bombardment Wing. Brigadier General Kenneth B. Wolfe, commanding 20th Bomber Command, hoped to compensate for the training deficiencies by bombing the target at night, each plane going in individually rather than in formation. Arnold, in Washington, rejected this and insisted upon a "daylight precision" attack because "the entire bomber program is predicated upon the B-29's employment as a visual precision weapon."

Wolfe rescheduled his shakedown operation, crammed some training time into the already strained program (B-29s flew in bomber formation over the Hump even while on trucking missions), and believed the wing ready for a strike upon the Makasan railway shops in Bangkok, Siam (Thailand). This would not yet be a strike against the Japanese homeland, but might very well interfere with Japanese operations in northern Burma.

The mission was set for June 5, 1944—the first B-29 mission of the war. One hundred of the big bombers were in readiness in the Kharagpur base area; the takeoff was to begin at 5:45 A.M., before the heat of the morning could overheat the engines and to afford as much daylight as possible for the long flight of about a thousand miles to—and, most importantly, a thousand miles from—Bangkok.

One plane of the 462nd Group developed mechanical problems and simply never left the ground. The 40th Group also left one plane behind. During takeoff at Chakulia Major John B. Keller's aircraft began behaving peculiarly about halfway down the runway: the nose of the plane lifted off the runway and for thousands of feet the B-29 maintained this curious attitude—its nosewheel in the air and the tail skid bumping against the ground. Then it left the ground and appeared to be taking off normally. The left wing suddenly dropped and Keller brought it up with a quick turn of the control column. But the wing dropped again and the plane, seemingly out of control, plowed into the ground, exploded, and left a flaming trail across the earth. Bombs exploded inside the fuselage, tearing it to bits and immediately killing all inside the plane except the copilot, Lieutenant B. A. Elsner, who could be heard whispering something about an engine failure before he died.

The remaining ninety-eight B-29s, led by Colonel Leonard F. Harman (commanding officer of the 40th Group), proceeded with the mission. If the takeoff had been complicated by ground mist, formation was rendered all but impossible by cloud and haze. Confused, apprehensive, the pilots joined up with the wrong elements, and as weather thickened, even the rudimentary formations disintegrated. It seemed better to risk what little Japanese opposition was expected singly than to chance a collision in mid-air. As was also expected, one by one planes developed some mechanical trouble or other and began turning back—a total of fourteen before the target was reached. Of the remaining eighty-four aircraft, seventy-seven actually dropped their bombs in the target area (and of these, forty-eight were forced to depend upon radar because of the overcast; the radar teams were not well trained, it might be noted).

After about six hours of touchy flying, with no improvement in the weather, the planes began arriving over Bangkok at 10:52 A.M.—and continued to arrive in a long stream (instead of the intended diamond formations) for over an hour. Japanese antiaircraft began bursting around the big bombers, and what might be called the Battle of Bangkok began. No flaming bomber went down before these guns—nor to any of the nine fighters that rose gingerly to make a few passes (a dozen in all) without effect.

But neither was the scattered, rather haphazard bombing very effective. The mission was regarded as an "operational success"—for a first mission. Bombs had fallen into the target area, some directly upon assembly and boiler shops, although it was admitted that the damage could not be expected to bring about a noticeable "decrease in the flow of troops and military supplies into Burma."

No aircraft was lost through enemy action, although the return trip to Bengal was more perilous than the long bomb runs over the target had been. With the monsoon season fast approaching, the weather, as a result rough and threatening, took its toll; as did the still emerging bugs. Fuel ran low because of faulty systems, engines froze up, propellers were feathered, and pilots fought to keep on course in the high winds, black clouds, and rain.

*New weapon of war with teething troubles; the B-29 with engines warming up. Ground crew under wing is ready with fire extinguishers.* (U. S. AIR FORCE)

After ten to twelve hours in the air, the B-29s began coming to earth wherever possible in friendly territory. Some landed in the home base area but others were scattered, after emergency landings, in a dozen British bases. Two of the big bombers were lost when the pilots were forced to ditch in the Bay of Bengal; another—with two engines malfunctioning—was abandoned over Yu-Chi (about sixty miles from Kunming), and a fourth crash-landed at the British base at Dumdum without injury to crew, although the B-29 was a total wreck.

Thus the shakedown mission to Bangkok had cost five B-29s (counting the one which exploded on takeoff) and fifteen lives. There were those who question the "operational success" of that mission. Still, a mission had taken place, seventy-three B-29s had made the round trip, bombs had fallen upon enemy installations, and crews had proved themselves and so, with some reservations, had the aircraft. It had been demonstrated that heavy loads could be carried over great distances and that was what the B-29 had been designed to do.

The question of what was to come next was answered with sudden unexpectedness. Even before all the strays had been reassembled from the initial mission Wolfe received urgent word from Arnold. A B-29 attack upon the Japanese homeland (which

*Warming up; the giant waiting for the word to take off on a mission.* (U. S. AIR FORCE)

had not been bombed since the Doolittle raid of 1942 except for small strikes in 1943 by the Eleventh Air Force, based in the Aleutians, on Paramushiro in the Kurile Islands) must be carried out by mid-June—a "maximum effort" which Arnold explained would help to divert the Japanese from their east China offensive then threatening Chennault's forward fields and also would tie in with an "important operation" in the western Pacific.

Wolfe hoped for a force of fifty B-29s for June 15 and an additional five if the mission could be postponed five days. Even such not very impressive numbers would put a strain upon the stockpile of supplies in China. Arnold was not pleased and called for an effort of no less than seventy bombers for June 15; if the Hump flights must be increased to accomplish this, then that too must be done. Wolfe proceeded as ordered, pressuring his crews over the Hump and cutting down on fuel for the fighters. But he knew that as The Day came, no matter how impressive the number, the inevitable arithmetic would set in and the maximum effort would be less than that.

The flight from the Chinese bases around Chengtu to the selected primary target—the Imperial iron- and steelworks at Yawata—was about sixteen hundred miles, making the round trip thirty-two hun-

dred miles. Wolfe had had bomb bay fuel tanks, necessary for so long a mission, for eighty-six B-29s. This was a little better than Arnold's minimum of seventy. With a good deal of hard work in blistering heat, no less than ninety-two "Dreamboats" (one of the code words for the B-29) began moving into China on June 13. Of the ninety-two, seventy-nine arrived in China; of the thirteen that had not, for various mechanical reasons, one B-29 and its crew was lost.

Four bombers already at Chengtu were added to the arrivals, so that eighty-three stood ready for the mission. More mathematics ensued what with mechanical failures and by the afternoon of June 15 a total of sixty-eight B-29s would be air-borne for Japan. The force was led by Brigadier General La-Verne G. Saunders, commanding officer of the 58th Wing, in a plane from the 468th Group and piloted by Group Commander Colonel Howard Engler. Fifteen B-29s followed their aircraft, *The Lady Hamilton,* but the sixteenth faltered, smashed back to earth, and burned—without a single injury to any of the crew.

Takeoff had been set for shortly after four o'clock in the afternoon, which would bring the B-29s over Yawata before midnight. It would be no daylight precision attack. Soon after the mission was airborne more of the not yet debugged bombers were forced back by mechanical failures. Four canceled out early in the flight. The first of forty-seven B-29s which dropped bombs on Yawata flashed the signal "Betty" to 20th Bomber Command headquarters at 11:38 P.M. For the first time since 1942 bombs rained down upon Japan. "Betty, Betty" tapped the radio operator—an echo of the *Tora, Tora* ("Tiger, Tiger") of the Pearl Harbor attack.

The sky was lashed with searchlights and a few fighters came up, as did the antiaircraft fire, but as at Bangok, no damage resulted from enemy action. A half-dozen planes jettisoned their bombs because of mechanical problems, two bombed the secondary target (Laoyao Harbor), and five others bombed various targets of opportunity.

Despite the lack of enemy opposition, there were losses nonetheless. Besides the aircraft which crashed and burned during takeoff, five others were lost during the mission and another—making the total loss of seven B-29s—on a postmission reconnaissance flight. One of the bombers that was lost

*Help from a very small friend: the jeep guides the B-29 to its hardstand. Note copilot leaning out of his cockpit window.* (U. S. AIR FORCE)

was destroyed by Japanese aircraft. Captain Robert Root's plane had developed engine trouble, so he set it down at the Chinese base at Neihsiang, near the Chinese-Japanese lines. As he settled into the airfield he radioed for American fighter protection while he and the crew worked on the B-29.

No American fighters arrived, but within a few minutes after the plane had landed two Japanese fighters swept down from across a low mountain range. Harry Zinder, *Time* correspondent, watched the approach of the fighters, shouted to the men inside the plane, and took refuge in a ditch about fifty yards from the bomber.

"The fighters roared across," Zinder reported later, "pulled up and then turned down on our ship. They spattered bullets across the fuselage and wings, then started a little fire on the left side. We hugged the ground closer as bullets kicked up dust and grass alongside the ditch. They made many passes. When the fire was fully blazing they left."

During the lull, Root and the others who had been

inside the plane jumped out (two of the crew were injured) and ran for the ditch to join Zinder and the others. They had barely settled into it when they heard the sound of engines again.

"There were fifteen this time—six bombers and nine fighters. The fighters peeled off first and did a strafing job, and then the bombers went to work and finished the job. We were in the ditch again, renewing our prayers. We felt sure they must have seen us because we could see their bomb bay doors open, see their bombs fall on the ship and around it. We decided to spend the rest of the morning in the ditch."

The B-29 was nothing but a wreck, and while the Americans lay in the ditch, covered with tree branches and grass, Japanese planes continued to come over intermittently to bomb and strafe the already long-destroyed bomber. Their vengeance fulfilled, the Japanese finally stopped coming. Their long, unreasoning attack was an indication of the fury the renewed attack upon the homeland had engendered. The men who had been aboard the B-29 were flown out of Neihsiang in a B-25 dispatched from the nearby base at Hsinching.

Although headlines in the United States proclaimed the news of the Yawata attack and such phrases as "glowing mass of ruins" and "reduced to huge rubbish heap" were used with poetic abandon, the report by Colonel Alan D. Clark, who flew the mission as an observer, contained the sentence "The results of the mission were poor." He noted that only a few bombs actually fell into the target area and that some bombs fell as far as twenty miles away. This he attributed to inefficient "blind bombing" (i.e., radar) because radar operators were yet inexperienced and untrained. Where the bombs had scattered through industrial and business districts, the Japanese declared that the buildings destroyed were "hospitals and schools."

Japanese propaganda also claimed the destruction of one B-29 and the capture of a crew, no member of which was less than a major in rank. Most of the men claimed by the Japanese, important squadron leaders most of them, had not even been on the mission. Japanese radio also claimed the destruction of B-24s that, like the high brass, had not participated in the mission. The general outcry revealed that, even if the official American evaluation of the mission was "poor," it had incensed the Japanese. It was time to apologize to the Emperor again.

Even more important to the future and its portents was the "important operation" with which the Yawata mission was co-ordinated. On the same day the Marianas campaign opened with the assault upon Saipan. With that island secured, on October 12, 1944, Brigadier General Haywood S. Hansell brought the first B-29, *Joltin' Josie,* into Saipan's Isley Field. Brilliant, young (forty-one), Hansell had recommended the taking of the Marianas as a base for the giant bombers. On the day that *Joltin' Josie* set down on Saipan the strategic air war took an ominous turn for Japan.

II

While the Twentieth Air Force underwent its growing pains, some of which proved tragically fatal, the two major Pacific forces were converging on the road back to the Philippines.

MacArthur's southwest Pacific forces leapfrogged out of New Guinea and onto Morotai Island (in the Halmahera group south of the Philippines) as Nimitz's Pacific Ocean areas forces struck in the Palaus, taking Peleliu and Angaur islands, east of the Philippines. With American forces in the Palaus (in the western Carolines), such strong Japanese bases in the central and eastern Carolines as Truk were neutralized; so were once and for all the bases in the Bismarck Archipelago, Kavieng and Rabaul. From bases on Angaur the 494th Bombardment Group of the Seventh Air Force was within bombing range of Japanese airfields in the Philippines, among them Clark Field, which had not been much in the news since the gloomy December days of 1941. The 494th, nicknamed "Kelly's Cobras" for the group commander Colonel Laurence B. Kelly and equipped with B-24s, arrived in the Palaus in October (1944) after a remarkable mass flight from Hawaii. Within twenty-four hours the group was off to bomb Yap and Koror, the latter

20th Bomber Command B-29, an aircraft of the 468th Bomb Group, returns from bombing Anshan, Manchuria. The city was an important steel-producing center; later it would house a school for training kamikaze pilots. (U. S. AIR FORCE)

*A Navy Vought OS2U "Kingfisher" dips over Angaur Island in the Palau group of the Carolines as invasion forces head for the beaches. The central Pacific forces were on the move closer to Japan.*

(NAVY DEPT., NATIONAL ARCHIVES)

of the Philippines—at Leyte—was advanced two months. The Joint Chiefs of Staff, then meeting with their British counterparts in Quebec, approved the idea, as did also Roosevelt and Churchill. Only MacArthur remained, and he was incommunicado on the Morotai invasion. However, Sutherland, certain of his chief's views, agreed to the advanced

*Japanese ships burning in a Palau island harbor; a Yorktown Hellcat noses into the picture at left.*

(NAVY DEPT., NATIONAL ARCHIVES)

a neighboring island of the Palaus, and returned without a loss. The group would soon be employed in the preparation for MacArthur's promised return to the Philippines. The Morotai operation placed units of Kenney's Far East Air Forces (which in June, had joined the Fifth and Thirteenth Air Forces under his command) within bombing range of Japanese targets in Java, the Celebes, and Borneo, as well as the Philippines. Setting up bases on Morotai, the Thirteenth Air Force (under the command of Major General St. Clair Streett), with its B-24s, began bombing Balikpapan, Borneo's Ploesti. Like the Seventh, the Fifth and Thirteenth Air Forces soon turned to softening up Leyte in the Philippines.

Meanwhile Halsey's carriers had also been striking at the Philippines during the Palau and Morotai operations. Halsey described Japanese aerial resistance as "amazing and fantastic" in its apparent impotence. He heard also from a Navy pilot shot down over Leyte and later rescued that guerrillas he had met told him that there were no Japanese on Leyte. Halsey immediately recommended a startling change in the Pacific timetable. Why not bypass the Palaus completely, he suggested to Nimitz, and strike at the middle of the Philippines instead of Mindanao (the southernmost island)? Nimitz, to a great extent, agreed. Although Peleliu and Angaur were taken (the former at great cost), the invasion of Yap was canceled and the invasion

*Closing in: a Liberator examining destruction to bridges over a river in Burma.* (U. S. AIR FORCE)

RR SIDING

WATER BUFFALO
(FEMALE)

SECTION HOUSE

BOX CARS

*Reconnaissance photograph of a railroad in north Borneo, Netherlands East Indies. Patient study of the* *photo reveals the careful attention to detail by Air Force intelligence men.* (U. S. AIR FORCE)

date and to Leyte over Mindanao (despite the fact that Leyte was out of the range of Allied fighter cover). Sutherland, however, could not quite agree with Halsey's view that the Japanese air force in the Philippines was "a hollow shell operating on a shoestring."

There was some truth in this view, but that was not quite the way it really was. True, the Marianas "Turkey Shoot" had taken an irreplaceable toll in men, aircraft, and ships from which the Imperial Fleet would never recover—and certainly not in the less than six months which had passed. But, as usual, the Japanese had formulated a desperate plan, which they, with even more optimism than Halsey, called the *Sho* Operation; *sho* is the Japanese word for "victory." Conceived after the Marianas debacle, Operation *Sho* was expected to bring about the "decisive battle" for which the Japanese Navy had yearned since Midway. *Sho* was actually four plans in one, depending upon where the enemy's next major invasion would come. If, as was expected, it came in the Philippines, *Sho*-1 would be placed in operation; if the blow came in Formosa, Nansei Shoto, or Kyushu (the southern-

most of the home islands), it would initiate *Sho*-2; *Sho*-3 was to activate if Kyushu, Shikoku, and Honshu were the obvious objectives; *Sho*-4 was the plan should Hokkaido be the enemy's target. Whichever plan was to be the final one, all were basically

*A Corsair lands on Peleliu Island airstrip in the Carolines just two weeks after the island's invasion.*
(NAVY DEPT., NATIONAL ARCHIVES)

the same: all possible forces would be rushed into action to defeat the enemy, and wherever that was, it was to be a "theater of decisive action."

It might have come at any of the expected points, but the most likely was in the Philippines (although for a time the Chiefs of Staff considered bypassing the Philippines and striking Formosa instead). MacArthur would want to keep his word about returning to the Philippines. Also, the Allies' ostensible ally, the Soviet Union, let a little hint slip through its foreign office in Moscow, which informed the Japanese Ambassador that the China-based Fourteenth and Twentieth Air Forces had been ordered to plan missions which would isolate the Philippines.

It would then be *Sho*-1; the Philippines would be the scene of the all-out decisive battle. Moscow had not informed Tokyo just where it would come— which of the several islands that comprised the Philippines—but the plan called for the last-ditch battle to be fought on the main island of Luzon. By late September reinforcements, ground and air, were sent to the Philippines. More ominously, on October 6 General Tomoyuki Yamashita, who had achieved notoriety (not necessarily deserved) as the "Tiger of Malaya" and the conqueror of impregnable Singapore, arrived to take command of the Fourteenth Army. He replaced Lieutenant General Shigenori Kuroda, who had, during the two-year occupation of the Philippines, grown soft. The "Tiger" would—and did—put some stiffening into the neglected defenses of the Philippines. The ground fighting would not prove to be a "hollow shell operating on a shoestring."

As Yamashita dug in, the Imperial Navy formulated its *Sho*-1 plans, although the date of activation remained unknown. Admiral Soemu Toyoda, Commander in Chief, Combined Fleet, would gamble the entire fleet in the operation. Like all Navy men, he distrusted the Japanese Army and expected little assistance from that quarter; the outcome of the battle, he believed, would depend upon his fleet. The idea was to destroy the "barbarians" before they could establish themselves back in the Philippines.

Toyoda's plan was as complex as it was grandly impressive—and therein lay its ultimate flaw. But he knew that if the Philippines fell, the shipping lanes to the south would be cut. This would deny fuel to the Imperial Fleet if it was to operate in

home waters; if it escaped to southern waters, then it would be cut off from ammunition and guns from the homeland. "There was no sense in saving the fleet," Toyoda admitted with resignation, "at the expense of the loss of the Philippines." The Japanese philosophy in the face of reality was turning suicidal. The old, almost arrogant confidence in victory was gone, despite the name of the operation; but the stubborn determination remained.

That something was in the wind became clear about the second week of October. Kenney's forces continued to harass the Japanese as before, with some attention in mid-September given to Philippine airfields by Liberators. Then Halsey unleashed the Third Fleet, particularly Mitscher's carriers, whose planes began raking over Marcus Island (east of Iwo Jima) and then, almost at Japan's doorstep, Okinawa in the Ryukyus. The next day, October 11, 1944, Mitscher's Task Force 38 Hellcats swept down upon an undeveloped air facility at Aparri on Luzon in the northern Philippines. The attacks were surprising and destructive, but on the twelfth, when the Navy aircraft turned to Formosa, the jittery Japanese activated both *Sho*-1 and -2.

Reinforcements from the Second Air Fleet of Vice-Admiral Jisaburo Ozawa's carrier forces rushed to Formosa. This all but stripped Ozawa of his planes and pilots—replacements for the Marianas losses. Vice-Admiral Shigeru Fukudome, once Yamamoto's chief of staff, commanding the Sixth Base Air Force, observed the early clash of the American and Japanese planes from his command post in Formosa. As he watched, the sky blossomed with flame and smoke; explosives flashed for a moment and then a trail of smoke marked the death fall of a plane.

"Well done! Well done!" Fukudome declared, certain that the falling aircraft were American; but they were not, as he later learned to his "sudden disappointment." Most of the burning aircraft were Japanese, which cleared the way for American dive bombers and strafing of Formosa's ground installations and parked planes by fighters. U. S. Navy pilots claimed 193 planes shot down and 123 destroyed on the ground the first day of the three days of the Formosa attacks. On the second day, the thirteenth, Japanese planes did break through the all but overwhelming numbers of Hellcats to place torpedoes into two cruisers, the *Canberra* and the *Houston,* both of which had to be towed out of the battle area.

Besides these damages Task Force 38 had lost seventy-nine planes and sixty-four men in the air battles, as well as a number of seamen aboard those ships which had suffered attack. But the cost to the Japanese was great: between five hundred and six hundred aircraft. The result was the near decimation of Ozawa's carrier strength, although a number of land-based aircraft remained in the Philippines. The aerial aspect of the *Sho* plan was truly a "hollow shell."

With perverse alacrity the Japanese High Command, only too eager to believe the exaggerated claims of the few pilots who had returned from the attack on the American fleet, turned the great defeat into an overwhelming victory. Somehow the two hits on American cruisers multiplied into sinking aircraft carriers, battleships, and, in fact, just about all of Halsey's Task Force 38. The Third Fleet, Tokyo announced, had "ceased to be an organized striking force." There was literally dancing in the streets in a three-day celebration in Japan.

Americans on recently taken Peleliu were showered with leaflets heralding the destruction of Task Force 38 (which the leaflet writer called the "58th Fleet") at Taiwan (Formosa):

### For Reckless Yankee Doodle

Do you know about the naval battle done by the American 58th Fleet at the sea near Taiwan and Philippine? Japanese powerful air force had sunk their 19 aeroplane carriers, 4 battleships, 10 several cruisers and destroyers along with sending 1,261 ship aeroplanes into the sea. . . .

When he heard the claims emanating from Japan, Halsey wired Nimitz "the comforting assurance that he [Halsey] is now retiring toward the enemy following the salvage of all the Third Fleet ships recently reported sunk by Radio Tokyo."

This message was made public on October 19. Two days before, with initial landings made upon islands in the entrance to Leyte Gulf, Toyoda ordered *Sho*-1 under way. This, he was finally certain, was the big American invasion—which explained the heavy aerial assaults upon Formosa and other possible staging areas into the Philippines.

With the activation of *Sho*-1, the Combined Fleet began its complex movements toward the Philippines. While it was still en route, MacArthur three

days later splashed through fifty yards of water, stepped ashore, and announced: "People of the Philippines: I have returned." Within two days more than 130,000 American troops and 200,000 tons of supplies had been placed ashore at Leyte by "MacArthur's navy," the Seventh Fleet (Vice-Admiral Thomas C. Kinkaid). And still the Combined Fleet pressed toward the Philippines determined to interfere with the amphibious operations, which were all but over.

Toyoda's plan, roughly, was this: Vice-Admiral Jisaburo Ozawa, commanding what was called the main body, consisting of all of the then operational carriers (one large, three light, and two converted battleship-carriers) plus three cruisers and ten destroyers, would leave the Inland Sea of Japan and head for the Philippines. He would expose his carriers to the Americans in the Philippine Sea, east of the northern coast of Luzon. The objective was to lure the American carrier forces away from the beaches of Leyte.

While the American carrier planes were thus diverted from the landing beaches, three other forces would converge upon the unprotected Americans and destroy them. Two of the forces came from the south, starting out from Lingga Anchorage (at Singapore), and after a refueling stop at Brunei Bay (Borneo) split up for a co-ordinated attack upon Leyte. The largest of these forces, under Vice-Admiral Takeo Kurita, consisted of no less than five battleships (two of them being the superships *Musashi* and *Yamato*), ten heavy cruisers, two light cruisers, and fifteen destroyers. Kurita's mission was to slip up the South China Sea, veer southeastward around the island of Mindoro, and thread his way through the Sibuyan Sea, traversing across the north-south axis of the Philippines and through the San Bernardino Strait into the Philippine Sea, all of this hopefully with the American carriers lured away to the north. Once in the Philippine Sea, Kurita would lead his forces (what was left of them: and he was prepared to lose at least half) around the island of Samar to a position off Leyte, where he would raise havoc with the American landing operations.

Another force, under Vice-Admiral Shoji Nishimura, which had split with Kurita's at Brunei Bay and which consisted of two battleships, one heavy cruiser, and four destroyers, was to bear east just north of Borneo. It would then negotiate the Sulu

Sea, pass north of the island of Mindanao, and come through the Surigao Strait (south of Leyte), where, in conjunction with Kurita's forces, the Nishimura force would pound the Leyte American positions and ships to bits.

But this was not all. Another force, under Vice-Admiral Kiyohide Shima (two heavy cruisers, one light cruiser, and seven destroyers), which had sortied from the Inland Sea and refueled at Bako (in the Pescadores off the coast of Formosa), was to combine with Nishimura's force for the attack upon Leyte, which came from the south.

It was a grand plan, dear to the heart of any Navy man worth his salt: great armadas of magnificent ships cutting through the seas on a split-second timetable converging upon the hated foe for a battle to the death. There were, however, a number of factors that, in fact, stripped the grand plan of its grandeur.

The split-second timing, for one. With ships converging from both north and south, communications became critical and communications between the different forces were not good. And those which might have been good could be (and in some instances were) knocked out by American attackers. Another flaw was that Toyoda had, in fact, set Sho-1 into motion too late to interfere with the landings on Leyte, which began on October 20. By the time the Kurita and the Nishimura-Shima forces were due off Leyte (October 25) the most vulnerable phase of the amphibious landings would be over. Not that the Japanese armada could not have done serious damage to the American positions, but the main chance had already evaporated when Sho-1 began.

There was one other, more serious imperfection in the Grand Thinking, as if the High Command had refused to learn anything from such battles as those at Midway and the Marianas. The Combined Fleet, virtually all of it, was venturing forth with practically no air cover.

Ozawa's carriers were just what they were intended to be, a ruse. The total aircraft borne by his four carriers were 108 (a single American fleet carrier carried 80 or more). The Marianas losses, and the more recent Formosa strikes, had seriously depleted the number of aircraft and pilots. Two carriers, for example, the Junyo and Ryuho, re-

mained behind in the Inland Sea because there were no planes for them.

Since Ozawa held no illusions, the only hope for any substantial air cover must come from land-based planes. Most of it would come from Vice-Admiral Shigeru Fukudome's Second Air Fleet—the survivors of Halsey's carrier attacks—moved from Formosan bases into the Philippines; Fukudome could muster about 300–350 planes. The First Air Fleet, already in the Philippines, demoralized and depleted, was placed under the command of Vice-Admiral Takijiro Ohnishi, one of the original architects of the Pearl Harbor attack. When he assumed command of the First Air Fleet on October 17, 1944—the day that Sho-1 went into motion—Ohnishi had few aircraft with which to provide air cover for Kurita's advance toward the American landing beaches. He had about sixty—at most a hundred—operational aircraft and eager, young, and inexperienced pilots. Ohnishi also had a scheme—in the words of Rear Admiral Toshiyuki Yokoi "conceived in futility and prepared for in despair"—that, Ohnishi hoped would put these few earnest young men and their obsolescent planes to very effective use. He called his conception kamikaze.

Also based in the Philippines was the Fourth Air Army, commanded by Lieutenant General Kyoji Tominaga, which had aircraft spread throughout the Philippines. But the Imperial Navy planners had few illusions of aid from that quarter. Japanese Army pilots were not noted for their intrepidity; still, Tominaga had about 150 aircraft of all types, which could be hurled against the invaders. However, mere numbers—Fukudome's 350, Ohnishi's 100, Tominaga's 150, and Ozawa's carrier planes amounting to 108: a total, roughly, of about seven hundred—were not so impressive when it is remembered that the pilots generally were very young and the aircraft old.

Two American fleets poised to challenge Toyoda's elaborate Sho-1 plan. Assigned to carry out and cover the actual landings was Kinkaid's Seventh Fleet with its six battleships, four heavy and four light cruisers, thirty destroyers, a dozen destroyer escorts, thirty-nine PT boats, as well as numerous landing craft, transports, and troop ships (more than seven hundred ships). Kinkaid's forces included also eighteen "baby flattops," the CVE (small escort carriers), which carried about five hundred assorted aircraft.

The Third Fleet (Halsey), with six battleships, six heavy and nine light cruisers, and fifty-eight destroyers, was also a formidable force. Its main punch lay in Mitscher's Fast Carrier Force, eight fleet (heavy) carriers and eight escort carriers with over a thousand aircraft aboard—Hellcats, Helldivers, and Avengers.

*Closing in: a Navy task group steams for the Philippines.*
(U. S. NAVY)

The command arrangement, although not as complex as that of the Japanese, was a bit intricate. Kinkaid was under MacArthur's command, but Halsey was not. He was directly under the command of Nimitz. Both Kinkaid and MacArthur seemed to understand that the function of Halsey's forces was to cover the beachhead at Leyte. Kinkaid's ships were excellent for amphibious operations but could not be expected to deal with an all-out surface attack by the Japanese fleet. Halsey, a crusty independent thinker, understood the need for protecting the landing areas, but as an airman, he also had a bloodthirsty gleam in his eye for the Japanese carriers. His understanding was that his primary task

was the destruction of the Japanese fleet (with special emphasis on the carriers) and that "strategic support" of the Leyte landings was of secondary importance.

Since Halsey was his own boss in the operation, the confusion, plus a near success by the Japanese, brought about the most trying moments of the Leyte Gulf battles and a naval controversy which has never been resolved.

Troops of Lieutenant General Walter Krueger's Sixth Army had been ashore for three days before the first guns in the Battle for Leyte Gulf were fired. As Kurita led his massive armada through the Palawan Passage (west of the Philippines), he was picked up on the radar of the submarine *Darter* (Commander David McClintock), which had surfaced near the *Dace* (Commander Bladen D. Claggett) to enable the two sub commanders to discuss plans via megaphone. As soon as contact had been made the two U.S. submarines submerged and headed for Kurita's ships. When he was within range McClintock opened the attack with torpedoes, which pierced the side of the *Atago*, a cruiser that also happened to be Kurita's flagship. It sank in less than twenty minutes, taking more than three hundred men with it; the indomitable Kurita transferred to the destroyer *Kishinami*—and later to the battleship *Yamato*. The *Darter* had opened the battle in fine style; besides sinking the *Atago* the submarine had also crippled the *Takao*. The *Dace* too drew blood by sinking the heavy cruiser *Maya*, which was forced to limp back to Brunei Bay accompanied by two destroyers. The initial action thus subtracted five ships from Kurita's force. This skirmish did not bode well for *Sho*-1.

Halsey, alerted by Commander McClintock's contact report, ordered the Fast Carrier Force to prepare for action. It consisted of three carrier groups—all veterans of several weeks of action and in need of rest. A fourth group, under Vice-Admiral John S. McCain, had been ordered to Ulithi, in the Carolines, for rest and reprovisioning. This deprived Task Force 38 of three large and two escort carriers. When word came in that Kurita's ships were steaming along Palawan, Halsey did not feel it necessary for McCain to hasten back to the Philippines—there were still plenty of aircraft in the remaining three groups.

Halsey positioned them east of the Philippines

*Heavy seas: Hellcats with wings folded and lashed to the flight deck in the Pacific.*
(NAVY DEPT., NATIONAL ARCHIVES)

running from central Luzon (Rear Admiral Frederick C. Sherman's Task Group 38.3), north of the island of Samar (Rear Admiral Gerald F. Bogan's TG 38.2), and off the southern point of Samar (Rear Admiral Ralph E. Davison's TG 38.4). Just south of this lay the Leyte Gulf area, which was guarded also by the Seventh Fleet. Since a large Japanese ship concentration had been sighted to the west, Halsey's search planes, launched in the morning of October 24, did not venture to the north-northeast of Luzon, where they might have sighted Ozawa's carriers approaching from the north.

Kurita's ships, since their harassment by the *Darter* and *Dace,* had pushed onward and easterly, rounded the island of Mindoro (where they were sighted by a submarine), and continued—obviously for the San Bernardino Strait—through the Sibuyan Sea. It was about at this point that Kurita's ships were sighted by Helldiver pilot Lieutenant Max Adams of the *Intrepid.* Halsey ordered his forces to prepare for strikes upon the oncoming enemy force; he also ordered McCain's Task Group 38.1 to refuel and to return to Philippine waters instead of proceeding to the Carolines. They might be required after all.

Before the American planes found the Japanese ships, Japanese land-based aircraft had spotted Sherman's task group and nearly all of Fukudome's

available aircraft were dispatched to strike at the group. There were about sixty bomber and torpedo planes accompanied by more than a hundred Zeros and Zekes. Radar picked them up, coming in three nearly equal waves of about sixty mixed aircraft each.

Most of Sherman's planes (from the *Lexington, Essex, Princeton,* and *Langley,* the latter two escort carriers) had already been launched for the search to the west for Kurita's ships. On deck were the bombers and torpedo planes, plus some escort Hellcats, awaiting contact so that the strike could be launched immediately. A few fighters circled over the ships of Sherman's group on combat air patrol: a dozen Hellcats, plus four others assigned to submarine patrol with four bombers.

Two large raids of more than a hundred aircraft were discovered approaching from the west before Sherman could launch his strike. A third group of enemy planes were quickly spotted at a distance of sixty miles. Both the *Princeton* and the *Langley* scrambled twelve fighters; the *Essex* contributed seven (these were led by Commander David McCampbell), and the *Lexington* launched its

*A Curtiss SOC-4 is catapulted from a cruiser on a search mission. The slow biplane was considered a sitting duck and replaced by the Kingfisher. But it served also as fire-direction craft for naval gunfire on invasion beaches—with proper escort by fighters.*
(U. S. NAVY)

*Navy Hellcat having its wings folded for storage.*
(NAVY DEPT., NATIONAL ARCHIVES)

eleven remaining *Hellcats.* The strike on Kurita was canceled for the time being as far as Sherman was concerned. Defense, not offense, was the issue.

McCampbell, commander of Fighting 15 aboard the *Essex,* had been scheduled to accompany the strike on Kurita. His other aircraft, twenty-nine Hellcats, had already taken off to strafe airfields in the Manila area. His Hellcat was ready for takeoff on Number one catapult, but he had orders not to participate in defensive scrambles. As the situation became more acute, as it became obvious that the Japanese strike was a massive one, McCampbell felt justified in taking off when Admiral Sherman himself ordered "all available fighter pilots to man their planes immediately."

Despite the fact that the fueling of his Hellcat had not been completed and because of the general hubbub, such as the bellowing through bull horns: "If the Air Group Commander's plane is not ready to go, send it below!"—because of this urgency, McCampbell signaled for his launch with only a full belly tank but with each of his two main tanks half full. This was something to consider as, with head tight against his headrest, he felt his Hellcat hurled into the air. The six other Hellcats followed. McCampbell was joined by his wingman, Lieutenant Roy W. Rushing. With the five other Hellcats trail-

ing, the two others headed for the oncoming enemy aircraft.

After several minutes of climbing McCampbell looked around for a sign of enemy planes. He saw a large formation—about sixty aircraft—too distant to identify. The formation was so beautifully composed that he was all but certain it was American.

"Are there any friendlies in this area?" he radioed Combat Information Center on the *Essex.*

"Negative, negative."

"In that case, I have the enemy in sight."

About two thousand feet above him and Rushing were twenty bombers, Vals and Bettys. Three thousand feet higher flew perhaps forty fighters, Zekes, Oscars, and Tonys. A total of sixty against his seven. Upon radioing the *Essex* again—"Please send help" —he was informed that none was available.

As he and Rushing climbed to get above the fighters, the five other Hellcats dived on the bombers. The Japanese bombers dived away through the clouds and lost contact with their escort—which soon became busy with its own problems. Before, however, the Japanese fighters became aware of the presence of McCampbell and Rushing, several of

*David McCampbell, Hellcat pilot, U.S.S.* Essex.
(NAVY DEPT., NATIONAL ARCHIVES)

their number fell to the guns of the Hellcats. The two Americans began picking away at the large enemy gaggle by coming up behind a straggler and blasting him out of the sky, and then finding another.

The first Japanese to fall under McCampbell's six .50-calibers was a Zeke. Under the impact of the heavy slugging, the Zeke began breaking up and then, after flaring from a wing root, disintegrated in the air. Certain of this victory, McCampbell ticked off a little pencil mark on his instrument panel: one.

After his second flamer, the enemy fighters became aware of their attackers and formed into a defensive circle, the so-called Lufbery Circle, nose to tail for mutual support. It was then all but impossible to hook onto a Zeke's tail without being fired upon by one of the Japanese fighters in the circle.

McCampbell led Rushing up to twenty-three

thousand feet to keep an eye on the circling Japanese aircraft and to try to decide what to do next. Another call to the *Essex* did not result in any reinforcement, although one of the five Hellcats which had gone after the bombers responded and joined the two Hellcats above the circle.

Then to their surprise, the circle opened up and the Japanese fighters strung along, apparently hoping to return to their bases in Luzon. The problem of fuel supply had begun to take effect. The Japanese planes then formed into wide, straggling Vs for the journey home. The three Hellcats dived on the disorganized Japanese fighters. Within seconds McCampbell had added a third tick on his instrument panel. For some reason the Japanese did not attempt to fight back as the American Hellcats decimated the formation.

The American planes dived, fired; a Japanese

*The* Princeton *after being struck by a bomb during the Battle of Leyte Gulf. The elevator has fallen below decks; explosions of gassed-up aircraft in the hangar* deck caused serious damage and casualties. The carrier was finally sunk by American guns.

(NAVY DEPT., NATIONAL ARCHIVES)

plane fell burning into the sea or the jungle below as the victorious Hellcat climbed for altitude and another dive. After an hour and thirty-five minutes of combat—after which his short fuel supply was dangerously low—McCampbell had nine ticks on the instrument panel. Rushing, who had depleted his ammunition, had accounted for six. The other five Hellcats had destroyed nine aircraft, most of them bombers. The seven *Essex* Hellcats, without losses, had shot down at least twenty-four Japanese aircraft. Other, and larger, forces had fared as effectively: planes from the *Princeton* claimed thirty-four, *Lexington* Hellcats splashed thirteen, and four Hellcats from the *Langley* claimed five Japanese aircraft destroyed. The big Japanese raid was thoroughly dispersed and Fukudome's Luzon-based air strength was all but finished as far as the Leyte Gulf battle was concerned.

However, one lone Judy appeared as if out of nowhere, ran the gauntlet of antiaircraft fire from various ships, and planted a 550-pound bomb on the *Princeton*'s flight deck before being shot down. Although not ordinarily a death blow, the bomb ignited the fuel in six Avengers in the hangar below decks; the planes were armed with torpedoes and the fire that resulted led to a series of explosions during the salvage and rescue attempts. One of the explosions tore off the *Princeton*'s stern, great chunks of which ripped over the decks of the cruiser *Birmingham,* which stood alongside assisting in the fire fighting. The stunning blast of metal and fire transformed the *Birmingham,* in the words of its captain, Thomas B. Inglis, into "a veritable charnel house of dead, dying, and wounded." Blood ran literally like water and made the decks unsafe and slippery for rescuers and medical men. The dead numbered 229 (more than had died on the bomb-struck *Princeton*) and 420 were wounded, more than half seriously.

Despite this single strike upon the *Princeton* (which was later ordered sunk by Halsey when the battle took a new turn) and the subsequent tragedy of the *Birmingham,* the Japanese air forces had not fared too well that day.

General Tominaga also hoped to contribute to *Sho*-1 and ordered his planes to attack the Seventh Fleet's shipping in Leyte Gulf. About 150 Japanese Army planes took off in the early morning attack and ran into the aircraft from Rear Admiral C. A. F.

Sprague's baby flattops. Those Japanese planes which succeeded in fighting through the Hellcat screen came under heavy fire from the hundreds of ships in and around the gulf. Although some hits were scored upon the shipping, no serious damage was done, and when the day's fighting ended Tominaga was minus at least half of his total air force.

Kurita, meanwhile, gingerly though courageously negotiating the Sibuyan Sea, had requested air cover from Fukudome. None was forthcoming, for Fukudome's planes had been expended in what had been a fruitless search for the American carriers. As for Tominaga's planes, "No request was made of the army; I [did] not know whether there were any Army planes there or not." Although his ships bristled with great numbers of antiaircraft guns—even the big guns on some ships could be raised to fire into the air—Kurita kept a wary eye on the sky.

Some three hundred miles to the south Nishimura's force, with its seven warships entering the eastern Sulu Sea, was having its sky problems also. Spotted early in the morning, Nishimura's ships came under attack from *Enterprise* and *Franklin* (of Davison's Task Group 38.4) planes. Although the aircraft were forced to break off their attack prematurely because of dwindling fuel, some damage had been done to the battleship *Fuso* and the destroyer *Shigure.* Further: the Americans were now alerted to two forces, Kurita's in the Sibuyan Sea and Nishimura's in the Sulu Sea, both obviously headed for Leyte Gulf. As Nishimura pressed on after the American planes had left him, he saw no Japanese air cover for his ships, nor did he see the ships of Shima, which were to join his for the attack upon the landing beaches. Nishimura proceeded unperturbed; he had a rendezvous. His son, Teiji, had died in the Philippines and, with his meager forces, Nishimura was resigned to joining him. Not that the Japanese seaman was suicide-bent—he took precautions with his lone reconnaissance plane, which showed him to be more cautious than some of the others thrusting toward Leyte. But he proceeded, promising to "storm the center of the eastern shore of Leyte Gulf at 0400 on the 25th" with a premonition of disastrous outcome. When the American planes were forced to break off their attack, Nishimura was granted a few hours' reprieve.

Kurita's main force, however, was not so—temporarily—fortunate. It was a formidable array of ships plying eastward in the Sibuyan Sea. Kurita, in his flagship *Yamato,* led the first of the two formations; the second was formed around the *Kongo.* Each of these formations consisted of more than a dozen ships, ranging from giant battleship to destroyer (but, of course, no carriers). One of the units in Kurita's formation was the battleship

aircraft fire—the *Yamato* alone carried 150 anti-aircraft machine guns and even each cruiser had a hundred of them mounted and pointing skyward. The planes swept in to the attack and despite the concentrated barrage ejected their torpedoes and dropped their bombs. A Hellcat which had taken a direct hit by the AA flared and blew up. Two Avengers went down, but they made ditchings in the

*A Wildcat goes into action aboard an escort carr*

*Musashi,* which was one of the two largest battle-ships on earth—the other being the *Yamato.*

Early in the morning the *Yamato's* radar picked up signs of enemy aircraft approaching from the east: these were twenty-five bombers—Avengers and Helldivers—escorted by nineteen Hellcats from the *Intrepid* and *Cabot,* two of Bogan's escort car-riers standing off San Bernardino Strait. Led by Air Group Commander William E. Ellis, the Amer-ican planes flew westward in near-perfect weather. There was no opposition to their flight—a surprising absence of Japanese aircraft was especially puzzling —until they approached the Japanese fleet. There they were were met by an intense barrage of anti-

water and the crews paddled to safety in their dinghys.

Although the heavy antiaircraft fire made obser-vation difficult, returning pilots were certain they had placed two "fish" into the side of a "*Yamato*-class battleship" and one into a heavy cruiser. Bomb-ers too claimed hits with their thousand-pound bombs.

This opening round of the battle was scarcely over when another *Intrepid* strike appeared over Kurita's ships. This force, with near-miraculous de-termination, was with one exception thirty miles closer to the San Bernardino Strait than when the first American strike had come. The exception was the cruiser *Myoko,* which because of a serious torpedo hit could not keep pace with the other ships and was ordered to return, as best it could alone, to Singapore. The *"Yamato*-class battleship" which had been hit was the *Musashi,* but the huge battleship seemed scarcely touched as it continued on its way into the Sibuyan Sea.

By now Kurita realized he had prowed into a

mained to go to his aid. Supposedly some land-based aircraft did take off to help him, but these were either lost or shot down by the Hellcats or heavy Japanese antiaircraft fire.

If the attacks were "almost enough to discourage" the Japanese, they were most encouraging to the American airmen, to the point of exaggeration. A normal reaction this, but it would lead to nearly

*baby flattop" of Leyte Gulf.* (U. S. NAVY)

hornet's nest. There seemed to be no end to the American bombers and fighters determined to destroy his fleet. His chief of staff, Rear Admiral Tomiji Koyanagi, said, "We had expected air attacks, but this day's were almost enough to discourage us."

Avengers, Helldivers, and Hellcats from six carriers, the *Intrepid, Cabot, Lexington, Essex, Enterprise,* and *Franklin,* converged on the Japanese First Diversion Attack Force. The great battleships were like magnets as bombs and torpedoes rained down upon the dodging ships. Kurita's call for help from Philippine-based planes went unheeded, and by the afternoon, even if heeded, no planes re-

fatal consequences. As these battles developed and Mitscher's pilots hammered at Kurita's ships, Halsey pondered an obsessively haunting question: Where were the Japanese carriers? Now that he knew where Kurita and Nishimura's ships were, he knew the Japanese had planned a big operation. It was unlikely that the carriers would be omitted from such an undertaking. This was troubling, especially when it was noted that carrier planes had taken part in the early attacks upon Sherman's northern carrier force.

Ozawa had, in fact, launched his hundred-odd planes in the hope of luring the Third Fleet to the north. Because his pilots were anything but expert

*Curtiss SB2C "Helldiver," the standard Navy dive bomber during the last two years of the war, circles an escort carrier. The baby flattop and the Helldiver* *were introduced in the Gilbert Islands campaign late in 1943.* (NAVY DEPT., NATIONAL ARCHIVES)

in carrier landings he had given permission to the pilots who survived the attack on the Americans to land on Japanese bases on Luzon. Most of these planes were lost in the aerial fighting over Sherman's group; a total of twenty-nine returned to Ozawa's carriers, which were now all but empty. This was unknown to Halsey, who fretted over empty shells.

A merciful night fell upon the Sibuyan Sea, after Kurita's force had suffered well over 250 American attacks. Five hours of desperate fighting had cost the Americans a mere eighteen aircraft, but it had cost the Japanese their superbattleship *Musashi*. The indestructible had been destroyed and the unsinkable had sunk to the bottom of the Sibuyan Sea—about half of the ship's twenty-two-thousand-man crew went with it. Captain Toshihira Inoguchi prepared his final report, conveyed his apologies to the Emperor, and went down with his ship. Other ships, the *Yamato* (sister to the *Musashi*) and the *Nagato* among them, had also suffered hits but were able to go on.

One of the last glimpses that the last of the

returning American pilots had of Kurita's fleet was that it appeared to be a smoking shambles; also, Kurita had ordered the ships to turn around, which made it appear that he had decided to give up the thrust for Leyte. For an hour and a half he led his ships—four surviving battleships, six heavy cruisers, two light cruisers, and eleven destroyers: still an imposing array—westward. At nightfall he turned eastward again. He would make the San Bernardino Strait at all costs.

However, the entire timetable was upset; he would never be able to rendezvous with Nishimura's and Shima's forces coming from the south for the assault upon Leyte.

Nishimura had escaped the full fury of the carrier plane attacks and true to his mission continued on toward Leyte. By the morning of October 25 he would emerge from the Mindanao Sea through the Surigao Strait for the early morning rendezvous with Kurita (which meeting was by this time academic). Nishimura had no real idea where Shima, who was in full charge of his own small armada, was; nor did he know of Ozawa's carrier disposition. He did know, however, where the American ships were and that they were numerous. This report, radioed by a scout plane dispatched by Nishimura, was the single bit of intelligence which Kurita received during the entire Battle of Leyte Gulf.

Nishimura's fate was not sealed by aircraft, although it was one of the several (at times simultaneous) actions of the sea-air battles over Leyte Gulf— none of which, incidentally, actually took place in the gulf.

During the night of the twenty-fourth Nishimura, as he quite literally steamed "Into the jaws of Death, Into the mouth of Hell," was harassed by PT boats in the Mindanao Sea. The little boats did not stop the seven Japanese ships, but they tracked them through the night. Around three in the morning Nishimura ran into the great forces of the Seventh Fleet, which had been prepared by Rear Admiral Jesse B. Oldendorf. On the battle line were six old battleships, five of them resurrected from the mud of Pearl Harbor. Nishimura ran the gauntlet of guns to the right and to the left of him. As his ships stopped dead in the water, burning, he merely pressed on toward Leyte. "Their strategy and intelligence," a U. S. Navy officer commented, "seemed to be inversely proportional to their courage." One by one the ships were blasted from the water, and at around 4:19 A.M. Nishimura, in his flagship *Yamashiro,* joined his son in death. His tactics had provided Oldendorf with a sea warrior's dream: "capping the T." With his battle line representing the horizontal line of the "T" Oldendorf could train full broadsides upon the approaching Japanese ships, coming in a straight line up the vertical line of the "T." Thus only Nishimura's forward batteries were able to fire at the battle line, which rained massive fire down upon the Japanese ships. By the time the *Yamashiro* capsized and sank only two of the original seven ships remained afloat, the *Shigure,* which miraculously escaped serious damage, and the *Mogami,* which, burning, scuttered away from the terrible scene.

About this time Shima, with his seven ships (none heavier than a cruiser), rounded the point of Panaon Island and entered the strait. All apparently was not well, for he had barely begun to steam for Leyte when one of his cruisers was struck by a

torpedo from PT-137. It gave him pause to see the burning hulks of those ships that had preceded him, but he continued onward. A couple of his ships released torpedoes at radar blips but hit nothing. Then he came upon the retreating *Shigure* and the blistering *Mogami.* The radar screen picked up many enemy ships awaiting him. Within a few minutes daylight would be upon him. Shima, who took orders only from Toyoda in Tokyo, and who operated independently of Nishimura, Kurita, and Ozawa, with unique discretion in a desperate situation, decided to get out.

He did not do this without some confusion: his flagship, in making the turn, collided with the already crippled Nishimura survivor, the *Mogami.* The decision to run did not end the battle for Shima, for as he fled the scene he was pursued and harassed, bombarded by ship and bombed from the air. With the coming of day the carrier planes from Sprague's baby flattops chivvied the fleeing Japanese. Just before 9 A.M. Avengers swept in with torpedoes to finish off the burning *Mogami,* which had managed to make seventeen knots through the night, although to one observer it appeared like an entire city block on fire. The agony was ended by the Avengers off the southern tip of Panaon Island. Only the *Shigure* of Nishimura's entire force returned to a friendly port.

Shima lost only one ship in this phase of the battle: the crippled *Abukuma.* On the twenty-sixth it was found by B-24s of the Fifth and Thirteenth Air Forces operating out of Noemfoor, Biak, and Owi. Shima and his suriving though bloodied ships faded into the Pacific.

"Someone had blundered," Tennyson had written nearly a century before. Nishimura had literally marched "Into the jaws of Death" in a neat but suicidal single file. Neither he nor Shima had coordinated their movements. Shima had managed to plow into the *Mogami* and had not succeeded in making himself felt (except in this one ironic incident) in Surigao Strait. The southern approach to Leyte Gulf as far as *Sho-*1 was concerned was an utter debacle.

Another blunder was yet to follow. Late in the afternoon of October 24 and during the time that Nishimura was being destroyed on the following day Halsey set off in pursuit of Ozawa's carriers. As soon as a search plane had located the Japanese carriers, Halsey had no doubts about what he would do: get the carriers and destroy the Japanese fleet. He felt justified in turning away from Kurita's force (seemingly in retreat in the Sibuyan Sea), believing that the enemy was in a "fatally weakened condition" and that even if Kurita did turn about and emerge from the San Bernardino Strait he could be thoroughly dealt with by the Seventh Fleet's baby flattops. The reports of excited pilots had, of course, exaggerated the damage to Kurita's still powerful fleet.

With the discovery of Ozawa's carriers, Halsey set off in pursuit to the north. In doing this he removed all of his ships from the vicinity of San Bernardino Strait. Upon leaving he informed Kinkaid of the Seventh Fleet that he was off on the chase taking "three groups to attack enemy carrier force at dawn." This was literally true, for the fourth group (which Kinkaid imagined was guarding San Bernardino), McCain's Task Group 38.1, was still on its way back to Philippine waters. There was an additional element: Halsey had also promised to form what he called "Task Force 34" "if the enemy sorties," presumably through the San Bernardino Strait into the Philippine Sea. At least this is what Kinkaid assumed. But when Halsey took Ozawa's bait, he did not form TF 34. Instead he made full speed northward taking all of his ships, carriers (under Mitscher's command), battleships, cruisers, and destroyers—the entire Third Fleet, excepting McCain's group—with him. Halsey fully expected to meet Ozawa in a full-scale engagement and, of course, had no inkling that the six Japanese carriers were capable of putting up a mere twenty-nine aircraft. Besides the carriers, Ozawa's so-called "main force" (generally called the Northern Force by American historians) was screened by three cruisers and ten destroyers. It was little else but a lure, but its composition was impressive.

So was Kurita's an impressive force. To the con-

*Thomas C. Kinkaid, who believed that some of Halsey's ships guarded San Bernardino Strait and the vulnerable baby flattops.*

(NAVY DEPT., NATIONAL ARCHIVES)

*William Frederick Halsey (whom no one—except newspaper writers—addressed as "Bull"); Japanese carriers were his special obsession at Leyte.*

(NAVY DEPT., NATIONAL ARCHIVES)

sternation of all, a Seventh Fleet Antisubmarine search plane from the escort carrier *Kadashan Bay* reported sighting a large Japanese fleet emerging from San Bernardino Strait and off the northern coast of the island of Samar. It was 6:47 A.M., October 25, 1944. Just ten minutes before, a radioman on the *Fanshaw Bay* (another escort carrier) had intercepted Japanese talk that was assumed to be a jamming attempt. But then, just a few minutes later, antiaircraft bursts appeared in the northwest; the American search plane had come under fire from Kurita's ships.

There was no doubt about it, a tremendous force of Japanese ships were intent upon rounding Samar just twenty miles away. Nothing stood between Kurita and the landing beaches at Leyte but the three escort carrier groups of the Seventh Fleet, the thin-skinned CVEs. A new man reporting aboard one of the new carrier escorts was generally informed that the initials stood for "Combustible, Vulnerable, Expendable." Carrying a few planes (from eighteen to thirty-six), the "jeep carriers" or "wind wagons" were not intended for intense surface battles; they were designed for the close support of amphibious operations, providing for combat air patrol and for antisubmarine patrols.

The CVEs were accompanied by destroyers and destroyer escorts, but neither were these any match for Kurita's force, the largest Japanese force since Midway. The big guns (18.1 caliber) of the *Yamato* opened up on the northern group ("Taffy 3" under Rear Admiral Clifton A. F. Sprague) of escort carriers. Even as the first shellbursts started splashing around them, the CVEs launched their fighters and bombers. The great Japanese fleet bore down upon the "wind wagons." The situation appeared hopeless—the Japanese not only outnumbered the American ships, but had the advantage of greater speed (thirty knots against the CVE's seventeen) and greater firepower.

"The enemy was closing with disconcerting rapidity and the volume and accuracy of fire was increasing," Clifton Sprague later remembered. "At this point it did not appear that any of our ships could survive another five minutes of the heavy-caliber fire being received. . . ."

Sprague, immediately sizing up the desperation of his plight, broadcast an appeal for help in the clear. This was picked up by Kinkaid aboard his flagship *Wasatch* in Leyte Gulf. It was Kinkaid's first inkling of the proximity of the Japanese force approaching Leyte and, according to plots, only three hours distant. Kinkaid was in a serious quandary. He knew that the CVEs were incapable of standing off the heavy ships of Kurita; he had the Leyte Gulf beachhead, transports to consider—and, because of the night battle in Surigao Strait and the mopping up in the strait in progress, he had ships short of fuel and ammunition. He nevertheless ordered Oldendorf to form a striking force of three old battleships, four American and an Australian cruiser, and two squadrons of destroyers and make for the battle area. All possible aircraft were converged off Samar.

Kinkaid then learned that Halsey had *not* left any forces behind to guard San Bernardino Strait. The air was charged with messages requesting help.

Kurita's ships closed upon the carriers and screening ships of Taffy 3. A vicious, if uneven, surface battle ensued in which the American destroyers *Johnston* and *Hoel* and the destroyer escort *Samuel B. Roberts* were torn to pieces by the heavy Japanese guns and sank into the Philippine Sea. Great volleys of gunfire bracketed the CVE *Gambier Bay* —merciless fire from Kurita's heavy cruisers, of which the *Chikuma* was most persistent. Even as the *Gambier Bay* capsized and sank the *Chikuma* continued to pour shells into the little carrier from short range.

With the Japanese cruisers in the van, Kurita's force bore down upon Taffy 3. It seemed only a matter of time before the entire group would be wiped out and the Japanese ships would then descend upon the middle group ("Taffy 2," commanded by Rear Admiral Felix B. Stump). The small guns of all the Taffy ships would just not do.

It was some time, too, before air attacks from the baby flattops could contribute to the battle, because of the confusion caused by the sudden appearance of Kurita. The bulk of the aircraft had already been launched to provide ground support on Leyte. This meant that most aircraft were not armed for bombing battleships. Despite heavy Japanese gunfire Taffy 3 put up forty-four Avengers and sixty-five Wildcats and Hellcats. Not that every plane was prepared for battle, however. Many Avengers were armed with mere hundred-pound bombs, which could not penetrate heavy decks; the *Gambier Bay*'s nine Avengers, for example, were more formidable

*"Taffy 3" under attack by Kurita's force, which had come through the San Bernardino Strait. The escort carrier* Gambier Bay *is bracketed by Japanese shell-* *fire during the Battle of Leyte Gulf (which some critics of Halsey called "The Battle of Bull's Run"), October 25, 1944.* (NAVY DEPT., NATIONAL ARCHIVES)

on paper than in the air: two of them were armed with depth bombs with wrong fuse settings, two carried no bombs at all, and two which carried torpedoes took off with practically no fuel at all. Within minutes after leaving the deck of the *Gambier Bay* these two Avengers were forced to ditch in the water.

These mishaps did not occur because of any lack of efficiency but because of the general desperation. Men of deck crews—handling the planes as well as rearming and reloading them—worked with remarkable dispatch, often under heavy fire. Aircrews took

off, bombed and strafed, landed again to take on more ammunition. Landings were made under impossible conditions, despite strong cross winds if the fleeing CVEs happened not to be facing into the wind.

The stricken *Gambier Bay* was avenged by torpedo bombers of sister ship *Kitkun Bay*. Led by Commander Richard L. Fowler, six Avengers loaded with five-hundred-pound bombs found a large cruiser, the second in line of the ships bearing down upon Taffy 3. By the time Fowler had found the Japanese ships, the weather being intermittently squally and rainy, plus their having run into heavy Japanese antiaircraft fire, he had lost two Avengers and had no fighter cover.

Waiting for a good moment, when the sun suddenly broke through the cloudy skies, Fowler led his four Avengers in a diving attack out of the sun upon the cruiser (the *Chokai,* which had assisted in the sinking of the *Gambier Bay*). Inexplicably, no antiaircraft fire interfered with the Avengers, and within seconds eleven five-hundred-pound bombs were hurtled at the *Chokai.* Five struck amidships around the stack, one hit the stern as two others splashed into the water, and three others smashed into the bow. The *Chokai* took a sudden turn to port, careened for some hundreds of yards as it shook with three tremendous explosions. Steam and black smoke shot hundreds of feet into the air, taking the aggressive *Chokai* out of the battle. (The cruiser, unsalvageable, was later sunk by Japanese destroyers.)

Almost simultaneously Wildcats and Avengers from Taffy 2, whose carrier escorts lay about thirty miles south of those of Taffy 3, came upon the scene. These were actually two strikes with an aggregate of twenty-eight fighters and thirty-one Avengers, the latter armed with torpedoes. These planes added to the confusion of the Japanese ships and added another victim to the credit of the carrier planes: the *Chikuma.*

Air attacks stopped another cruiser, the *Suzuya,* but, as Kinkaid well knew, could not stop Kurita's fatal rush upon Taffy 3's hard-pressed forces. But once again "Someone blundered." For no reason that the beleaguered Americans could understand, the advance ships in Kurita's force stopped firing, turned about, and retired to the north. The more powerful, faster—and actually more victorious— Japanese fleet had broken off the action on the threshold of victory.

There were, for Kurita, several good reasons to call off the chase. One was, he wished to assemble his dispersed forces for the run in on Leyte. Another was, he lived in fear of heavy aerial attacks; it seemed that the attacks by carrier planes had been increasing; they had stopped three of his cruisers (his only serious losses in the entire engagement). Sprague's Taffy 3 had lost one small carrier—and would lose another before the day was over—besides two destroyers and a destroyer escort.

Further food for blunder: Kurita's staff had

*A Navy Wildcat takes off the airstrip at Tacloban, Leyte. This was a substitute "carrier deck" after the escort carriers were sunk or damaged off Leyte Gulf. The truck hauls away the wreckage of another plane.*
(U. S. AIR FORCE)

magnified, somehow, Taffy 3's potential. The escort carriers were mistaken for full-sized fleet carriers, and all the other ships were amplified one size larger. Kurita, then, was worried about the carriers. For all he knew, the planes had come from the Halsey-Mitscher force. Nor had Ozawa, with characteristic lack of communication, informed Kurita that he had succeeded in his role of decoy. But Kurita did know that Nishimura had been wiped out, which meant that only his force was left for shooting up the beachhead. Of his original force of five battleships, he still had four; of the ten heavy cruisers, five had been sunk (or were sinking) and three had left for safer seas in damaged state; and there were still ten destroyers. He still had a little more than half of his original force left and he was about two hours' running away from his primary objective, Leyte Gulf.

The more he reflected upon that objective the less he thought of it. The planes worried him. He had intercepted radio instructions for American pilots to land on airstrips at Tacloban and Dulag. These instructions, unknown to Kurita, were emergency measures for aircraft whose carriers had been sunk. To Kurita, however, it appeared that land-based American aircraft would soon pound down upon him as he approached the objective. What would be the point of wasting his survivors upon empty landing craft? Certainly by now all the transports would have scurried to safety.

After much soul-searching, decisions and counterdecisions, Kurita steamed back for the San Bernardino Strait (still minus any sign of Task Force 34) and for Brunei. Even this passage was made under harrowing conditions. McCain's carrier group had come upon the scene to speed him on his way. The Thirteenth Air Force provided B-24s for additional harassment and, insult to tragic injury, Kurita's retiring ships were bombed by two Japanese bombers.

Kurita's retirement did not end the battle around Leyte. His will to survive was not common to all Japanese, for early in the morning a Zeke dived out of the sun at the *Santee*, an escort carrier in Rear Admiral Thomas Sprague's Taffy 1 (Thomas Sprague was not related to Taffy 3's Clifton Sprague). The Zeke came in strafing the deck of the *Santee* but instead of pulling away crashed into the flight deck on the port side. The plane crashed

through the deck and exploded on the hangar deck, killing sixteen men and wounding scores of others. Soon after, another Zeke plunged into the *Suwanee*.

It appeared to the American crews that these planes had deliberately crashed onto the carriers. The first kamikazes had struck.

To the north, Taffy 3 was hit after it had appeared that Kurita had spared it. Dedicated young Lieutenant Yukio Seki led a formation of five Zero fighters, each carrying a bomb, toward the American carriers (like Kurita, Seki was sure the CVEs were fleet carriers). Of the northern group, the *Kalinin Bay, Kitkin Bay,* and *White Plains* were damaged by the diving Zeros. Seki may have been the pilot of the plane that smashed into the *Saint Lo,* which was so badly hit that the escort carrier sank, the first loss to a kamikaze.

These were planes from Ohnishi's land-based force, not from Ozawa's alluring carriers. The absence of the Third Fleet from the scene of action had generated many a sulphurous query. Kinkaid's unheeded requests for help off Samar produced a message to Halsey from Nimitz himself which was touched with Tennysonian mischief.

Halsey had snatched at Ozawa's bait, honestly believing that he was in fact accepting a challenge. With his 64 ships, the carriers of which mounted more than 780 aircraft (401 fighters, 214 dive bombers, and 171 torpedo bombers), Halsey went off in pursuit of Ozawa's 17 ships and a total of 29 planes). It was to deal with these that Halsey ultimately formed Task Force 34 (under the command of Vice-Admiral Willis A. Lee). This powerful force was detached from the Third Fleet's battleships, cruisers, and destroyers and was to proceed ten miles in advance of the three carrier groups. At the same time Halsey turned over command of the carriers to Mitscher and ordered the arming of the aircraft for an early morning strike on the Japanese ships. After the carrier planes had finished with Ozawa's ships and planes, Lee's battle line—TF 34—would move in for the mopping up. It was not, as Kinkaid assumed, off the San Bernardino Strait; and, as events unfolded, TF 34 turned out to be neither here nor there.

During the night search planes, suffering mechanical difficulties, lost track of the Japanese ships. At daybreak, however, the carrier decks boomed with the engines of aircraft being readied for the first strike. Combat air patrol was stationed over the American ships and search planes fanned out to relocate the Japanese. At the same time the first strike group—about 180 planes, bombers, torpedo bombers, and fighter escort—was launched and dispatched in the general direction of the Japanese fleet. They would, on first sighting, be ready for the attack. These planes had been air-borne for about an hour and a half before a fighter plane spotted Ozawa's full force, the large carrier *Zuikaku,* three light carriers (the *Chitose, Chiyoda,* and *Zuiho*), two battleships that had been converted to carriers (the *Ise* and *Hyuga*), three light cruisers, and eight destroyers. Halsey's meat.

Target co-ordinator of the first strike was Commander David McCampbell of the *Essex.* What was surprising was the lack of enemy planes, which lack was attributed to "tactical surprise." A few, between fifteen and twenty, planes took off the four true carriers (the *Ise* and *Hyuga* carried no planes) to intercept the American planes. One Avenger fell into the sea, but most of the Zekes were either shot down or driven off by the swarms of Hellcats and for the rest of the battle were seen no more. As usual with the Japanese ships, intense antiaircraft fire—varicolored to identify the bursts of the several batteries—swept up to meet the American attackers.

The philosophy of battle was in keeping with Hal-

*Halsey's bait: a Japanese carrier—the* Zuiho, *its aft flight deck buckled, bomb-pocked, and burning from strikes by Navy dive bombers, attempts vainly to dodge further blows. This oiler converted into a carrier is disguised as a cruiser; note fake guns painted forward of the buckled deck. Moments after this photo was taken the* Zuiho *sank.*

(NAVY DEPT., NATIONAL ARCHIVES)

sey's battle plan: Get the Carriers. McCampbell, flying above the battle area, assigned the *Essex* planes to a light carrier (the *Chitose*), which took eight bombs and was clearly seriously damaged. Avengers also ran in with torpedoes and more bombers, from the *Lexington,* before they could be diverted to a more profitable target, dropped more bombs on the burning, exploding *Chitose.* Other aircraft, however, attacked the *Zuikaku,* claiming hits although McCampbell saw little to back the claims. Another carrier, the *Chiyoda,* was struck and lay dead in the water. A destroyer, hit in the side by an Avenger's torpedo, blew up and sank. So did the *Chitose* as McCampbell watched.

The *Zuikaku* had been hit and its communications so badly shot up that Ozawa was forced to leave it, the flagship, to direct his end of the strange battle from the light cruiser *Oyodo.* There was jubilation on Halsey's flag bridge aboard the *New Jersey,* when first word was flashed to him at 8:50 A.M. (more than two hours after the first planes had left his carriers). At the close of round one the American planes had sunk a carrier and a cruiser and had damaged other ships, two of which may have been carriers—and this was only the beginning. It was a great day for the carriers: Halsey's.

But it was not destined to be Halsey's day.

As strike after strike went out to mangle the Japanese ships and excited word came back to the *New Jersey*—co-ordinator of the third strike Commander Theodore Hugh Winters of the *Lexington* watched the *Zuikaku* slip under the water flying "a battle flag of tremendous size, perhaps fifty feet square"—as these reports of the destruction to Ozawa's fleet came in from the north, Halsey also received disturbing word from the south. These were the dispatches from Kinkaid appealing for aid to deal with Kurita steaming out of San Bernardino Strait.

*Question* [a part of the first message read] IS TF 34 GUARDING SAN BERNARDINO STRAIT

*Negative* [a somewhat bewildered Halsey replied, for Kinkaid should not have known of TF 34, which was to be formed only when Halsey ordered it and that when the Japanese fleet, i.e., the carriers, had been located] IT IS WITH OUR CARRIERS NOW ENGAGING ENEMY CARRIERS

And then came word from his carrier pilots. The *Zuiho,* the last of Ozawa's carriers, was stopped during the third strike by a small force of planes, led by Commander Malcolm T. Wordell, which with bombs and torpedoes put it under the sea also. What a day for sea dog Halsey! When the great *Zuikaku* went down all the carriers that had attacked Pearl Harbor nearly three years before had been destroyed, most of them by aircraft. As for the *Zuiho,* its sinking was vengeance for the sinking of the old *Hornet* in which the Japanese carrier had participated.

But the pleas kept coming from Kinkaid, whose Taffy 3 was under attack by Kurita's great force. Messages, at least nine, came in so rapidly that some canceled the others out. Communications were not good and messages were delayed or overlapped, so that Halsey found it difficult to assess the true situation: 0802, ENEMY VESSELS RETIRING SURIGAO STRAIT. Halsey breathed a sigh. Then at 0822, ENEMY BBS [battleships] AND CRUISER REPORTED FIRING ON TU 77.4.3 (Taffy 3). Then at nine o'clock: OUR CVES BEING ATTACKED BY 4 BBS 8 CRUISERS PLUS OTHERS REQUEST LEE COVER LEYTE AT TOP SPEED.

Halsey had already ordered McCain to stop refueling and to speed westward at once. He wanted Lee's ships to finish off Ozawa.

0922: CTU 77.4.3. UNDER ATTACK BY CRUISERS AND BBS . . . REQUEST IMMEDIATE AIR STRIKE . . . ALSO REQUEST SUPPORT BY HEAVY SHIPS . . . MY OBBS [old battleships] LOW IN AMMUNITION . . .

Then at ten—WHERE IS LEE . . . SEND LEE (this message had been sent in the clear with no attempt to hide from the Japanese the desperation of the plight of Sprague's Taffy 3 baby flattops). Halsey could not believe that the situation was really that critical. Surely the Seventh Fleet could stand off the Japanese, even if only with their aircraft, at least until McCain arrived with his large force.

And then the Tennysonian clincher, a message from Nimitz himself. (It should be mentioned at this point that messages sent in code were sent with padding of nonsense phrases—set off by repeated letters—to confuse Japanese cryptographers. Before the dispatch was handed to the recipient, the pad-

*Superbattleship* Yamato *is hit forward of the No. 1 gun turret by a Helldiver piloted by Arthur L. Downing* *as it fled the Philippines. Photograph was taken by Downing's radio operator, John L. Carver.*

ding was torn off and discarded. But it was not to be on this October 25, 1944. As for Tennyson, one of the lines he had used to rhyme with "Someone had blundered" was "All the world wondered," a line that evidently had stuck in the memory, even if not precisely, of a naval yeoman.).

The message was dispatched, in code, from Pearl Harbor thus:

TURKEY TROTS TO WATER GG FROM CINCPAC ACTION COM THIRD FLEET INFO CTF 77 X WHERE IS RPT WHERE IS TASK FORCE THIRTY-FOUR RR THE WORLD WONDERS

The padding preceding the double "G" was dropped, but that following the double "R" was not. The standing rule was that no padding used was to make any possible kind of sense. Despite the "RR," what followed *did* seem to make sense. In

that form, then, it was handed to Halsey—and also to Kinkaid (CTF 77), which made it appear like a public rebuke.

"I was stunned as if I had been struck in the face," Halsey later remembered. "The paper rattled in my hands. I snatched off my cap, threw it on the deck, and shouted something that I am ashamed to remember. Mick [Rear Admiral Robert B.] Carney rushed over and grabbed my arm: 'Stop it! What the hell's the matter with you? Pull yourself together!' . . . I gave him the dispatch and turned my back. I was so mad I couldn't talk."

For an hour Halsey brooded before he ordered the bulk of Task Force 34 about, in company with Rear Admiral Gerald F. Bogan's Task Group 38.2, to head for Leyte. The remaining carriers, under Mitscher, continued to harass Ozawa's diminishing forces until darkness intervened. When it turned

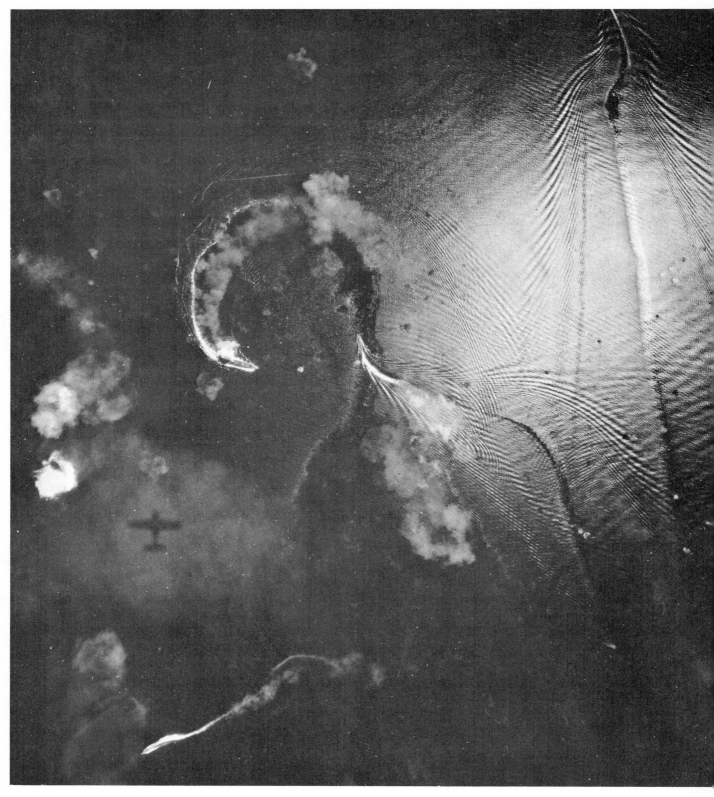

*Finale: Battle of Leyte Gulf. Halsey's carrier planes catch the survivors of Kurita's fleet in Tablas Strait (southeast of Mindoro Island). The Japanese did not* *echo the query "Where is Task Force 34?" The wake of a dodging Japanese ship forms its own question mark: Had Sho-1 truly succeeded?*

about, Task Force 34 was about forty miles from Ozawa's fleeing remnants. "I turned my back," Halsey bitterly commented, "on the opportunity I had dreamed of since my days as a cadet. For me, one of the biggest battles of the war was off." This turnabout, Halsey maintained, was his only blunder during the battle. He was off on another fruitless dash, this time to the south to intercept Kurita. By morning Kurita had slipped back into the San Bernardino Strait. Halsey missed that battle opportunity also.

But by October 26 the Battle of Leyte Gulf—and Sho-1—were finished. Of all the Japanese involved, only Ozawa had "succeeded" in his mission: he lost four carriers, a light cruiser, two destroyers, and all of his aircraft. He limped into port with many severely damaged ships. It was an expensive "success," for it virtually ended Japan's carrier force for the rest of the war.

Sho-1 had failed utterly. The Philippines would in time, and at great cost in lives, fall to the Americans because they had not been blasted out of Leyte Gulf. And the Pacific, in the phrase of the time, became "an American lake." Ozawa himself, after the war, summarized the ultimate result of the confusing, action-packed days of Leyte Gulf: "After this battle the surface forces became strictly auxiliary, so that we relied on land forces, special attack (kamikaze), and air power. There was no further use assigned to surface vessels, with exception of some special ships."

Sho-1 had cost the Japanese no less than twenty-six ships as against six lost by the Americans. The once great Imperial Japanese Navy was simply no longer of any consequence. There was much bitter land fighting and it was not until March of 1945 that Manila, on Luzon, was taken by MacArthur's forces. By this time the outcome of the war was imminent. Less than a week after Manila had fallen Tokyo had been set aflame by B-29s of the 21st Bomber Command operating out of Saipan. The great fires had finally come to Japan and the air war had assumed its ultimate twentieth-century form, a searing, fearful symmetry.

# 6
# WHISTLING DEATH

O N THE same day (October 20, 1944) that Mac-Arthur stood upon the beach at Leyte and dramatically announced his return to the Philippines the first flight echelons of the 73rd Bombardment Wing arrived in Saipan. It was fervently hoped that from the Marianas the B-29s would prove more effective than they had in their initial operations from the bases in India and China.

The problems confronting Brigadier General Kenneth B. Wolfe in these far-flung parts were rather difficult to understand in Washington. The mechanical quirks, particularly of the engines, the transporting of supplies over the Hump, the weather—all of which conspired to put the big superbomber out of commission and inoperational when Washington ordered missions—were not easily solved under the primitive conditions at Chengtu and Kharagpur. But in Washington it seemed that if a hundred-plane mission was ordered, Wolf could at least manage to have half that number ready when the mission was run. There were many aborts and accidents—all, of course, the unfortunate growing pains of a new air force and a still not fully tested plane.

Wolfe returned to the United States and a promotion in "an important command assignment"—which could also be read "kicked upstairs"—at Wright Field as head of Matériel Command. Placed in temporary command of the 20th was Brigadier General LaVerne Saunders. Barely a month later

Major General Curtis E. LeMay arrived to assume command of the B-29s. "With all due respect to Wolfe," Arnold confided to General Spaatz later, "he did his best, and he did a grand job, but Le-May's operations make Wolfe's very amateurish."

LaVerne G. Saunders, who led some of the first B-29 raids against Japan and who replaced Wolfe as head of 20th Bomber Command. Saunders was injured in a B-25 crash after LeMay had come to succeed him as commander of the B-29s in the Pacific.

(U. S. AIR FORCE)

Wolfe, it might be pointed out, was an engineer, not a combat airman. The experience gleaned during the early B-29 missions was invaluable to Wolfe, who supervised the plane's future development and production.

LeMay was that rare man at the right time: a thoroughly contemporary warrior, hard-bitten, practical, an experienced tactician, and, so far as his men knew him, lacking in sentiment and emotion—they referred to him, among other epithets, as "Ironass." He was that; cool, determined, and in his way perhaps ruthless, but he, at the cost of endearment, saved their lives. He was the complete professional.

Before he accepted command of the 20th, LeMay insisted upon learning to fly the B-29 and learned to his dismay that the "engines overheated, cylinder heads often blew out the moment an engine started turning over, ignition was faulty, oil leaked excessively, fuel transfer systems gave endless trouble. There were scores of other defects readily apparent or—worse—appearing insidiously when an aircraft was at work and at altitude."

After he arrived in India, late in August 1944, LeMay began shaking up the command: he stepped up crew training (as he had in Europe); he realized that something must be done to improve the maintenance of the tricky aircraft, and he did not at all like the diamond formation flown by the big bombers; he believed in the concentrated combat box he had originated in Europe. There were performance improvements, but there was no getting around the problem of logistics.

By October, while the Philippines battle raged, it was decided to switch the concentration of attack from the steel industry (specifically the coke ovens, the heart of the industry) after nine B-29 missions to Japan's aircraft industry. Shipping too was regarded as an important target, since it was so essential to Japan's war industry, and the B-29s were employed in dropping mines into important harbor areas, such as Shanghai and Singapore, as well as areas in Indo-China and Sumatra. But what with the efforts of Kenney's ship busters and the Navy's submarines and carrier planes, shipping emerged as a lesser target.

Another idea was put forth also: the saturation bombing of a half-dozen urban industrial areas. The susceptibility of Japanese cities to fire was no legend.

But when LeMay took over the 20th Bomber

*Preparation: construction crews digging coral for use in construction of B-29 runways on Saipan, Mariana Islands.* (U. S. AIR FORCE)

Command the scattered operations were dispersed in three ways: support of operations in the China-Burma-India theater, support of the Pacific war, and —the 20th's major mission—operations as a separate strategic "global air force." The capability of the B-29 was demonstrated on November 5, 1944, with an attack upon Singapore, an important Japanese naval base. The round trip of nearly four thousand miles was in itself an obstacle, but of the seventy-six B-29s dispatched more than fifty bombed the primary target, the King George VI Graving Docks. Bombing was amazingly accurate and the docks were knocked out of commission for about three months. The cost of the mission was two B-29s and twelve men, including the leader of the 468th Group, Colonel Ted S. Faulkner. The losses were attributed to the hazards of the extremely long flight, not to the Japanese, whose opposition proved quite feeble.

And so it went on, missions of questionable consequence; and then with unexpected suddenness LeMay was transferred out of 20th Bomber Command. His job was taken over by Brigadier General Roger M. Ramey—one of Kenney's former "operators" and ex-chief of staff of 21st Bomber Command. Although he continued to mount missions,

*Preparation: even as bulldozers made room for others, the first B-29s began arriving on Saipan for the opening of an aerial assault upon Japan.*

(U. S. AIR FORCE)

Ramey was afforded no opportunity to operate in the classic Kenney style. His major concern was to get the 20th out of the CBI theater and into the Pacific proper. The forty-ninth and final mission of 20th Bomber Command (a night attack upon a tank farm on Bukum Island near Singapore) was flown on the night of March 29/30, 1945, after which the four combat groups (the 58th Bombardment Wing) left India for Tinian and Guam in the Marianas.

Twentieth Bomber Command in its roughly ten months of combat operations had fallen short of the goals projected for it in Washington. As James Lea Cate observes in *The Army Air Forces in World War II,* ". . . the strategic results of VHB operations from Chengtu were not a decisive factor in the Japanese surrender." The bold plan, code-named

*Prepared: Isley Field, Saipan, two weeks before the first B-29 took off for Japan. Seventh Air Force*

*Liberators are parked on hardstands.*

(U. S. AIR FORCE)

"Matterhorn" and entitled *Early Sustained Bombing of Japan,* Cate notes, rather sardonically, "was neither early nor sustained. It achieved no significant results of a tangible sort and the intangible effects were obtained at a dear price."

This is a rather stern appraisal and like all such can only be reached long after the fact. Not that the men of 20th Bomber Command were not aware of its deficiencies—they themselves were not deficient. It was only that they had so much to learn and learning invariably implies error. While there was a goodly amount of human error, the bulk could be laid to the machine and to nature. It would be, in a sense, an error to call the 20th a failure simply because it did not fulfill its officially defined mission: the failure may very well lay in the military pretentiousness, and prematurity, of that definition.

But what of the intangibles? If the 20th had not destroyed Japanese industry it had these intangibles to its credit, as enumerated by Cate: "To bolster Chinese morale; to take the war home to the Japanese people, badly misinformed by their officials, in raids which might tie down in the main islands fighter planes needed elsewhere; and to combat-test a new plane and a new type of bombardment organization." These were no small achievements, however intangible, though the price was dear.

II

LeMay arrived on January 19, 1945 at Guam to succeed Brigadier General Haywood S. Hansell as head of the 21st Bomber Command. It then consisted of three wings, the initial 73rd and the 313th and 314th. These were to be joined later by the 20th's 58th Bombardment Wing (March), the 315th (April), and the unique 509th Composite Group (May). Besides these "very heavy bomber" units, fighter groups were also stationed in the Marianas, notably those of the 7th Fighter Command and, later, the 301st Fighter Wing. And then there was the U. S. Navy, which LeMay often found to be his major opposition.

Twenty-first Bomber Command had begun operations about five months before LeMay's arrival. The first mission (October 28, 1944), actually a training mission to much bombed, bypassed Truk, was not very impressive. Because the schedule of arrivals was somewhat off, Hansell could raise only about twenty B-29s for the strike (on the submarine pens at Truk), and after a delay owing to the possibility that the B-29s might be called upon to assist the Navy in the Battle of Leyte Gulf, eighteen planes finally took off. Four B-29s, including the lead plane carrying Hansell, were forced to return to Saipan. The remaining fourteen succeeded in dropping their bombs in and around the Dublon sub pens on Truk. To the men of the 497th and 498th Groups the sight of their bombs falling reasonably close to the target was a pleasing one (though as bombing goes, it was only partially effective). Japanese anti-aircraft fire proved even more ineffective at the high bombing altitude (twenty-five thousand feet), and one lone Zeke managed to get off the ground but chose to stay out of gun range.

Six shakedown missions were carried out between the first and last to Truk (on November 11). The former Japanese naval bastion (which served until war's end as an American practice bombing range) was hit four times, and Iwo Jima, about 730 miles

*Curtis E. LeMay, commander of the 21st Bomber Command, Saipan, 1945.* (U. S. AIR FORCE)

*Isley Field, Saipan, after a Japanese strafing. More than a dozen Zekes swooped down and destroyed three B-29s and damaged others. The Japanese lost thirteen* *planes in the attack and three others were listed as "possibles."* (U. S. AIR FORCE)

north of Saipan between the Marianas and the home islands, twice. Isley Field on Saipan had suffered strafing and bombing raids on November 2 (as the B-29s were bombing Truk for the third time) and November 27. The planes were believed to have come from Iwo Jima, a staging area for Japanese fighters. Bombing results of the initial missions were not very effective.

Even so, it was Japan itself that 21st Bomber Command aimed for, specifically the aircraft industries. So it was that on the first of November *Tokyo Rose* (an F-13, the reconnaissance version of the B-29), with Captain Ralph D. Steakley piloting, appeared over Tokyo. It was the first American aircraft to fly over the Japanese capital since April 1942. The day was bright and clear as the bomber lazily passed back and forth over the city taking photographs for thirty-five minutes. It was a shocking experience for the Japanese (to the degree that *two* B-29s were reported). With a minimum of fuel but a maximum of photographs, Steakley brought *Tokyo Rose* home. (The plane was named in honor of the English-speaking lady propagandist who

broadcast the latest American popular music and military "secrets.") Among the prints were shots of the Musashino plant located in a suburb of Tokyo about ten miles from the Emperor's palace. In this plant Nakajima manufactured nearly 30 per cent of Japan's combat aircraft engines.

Twenty-four days later, after additional photo missions and weather delays, *Dauntless Dotty* took off from Saipan runway, skimmed the water, pulled up, and headed for Japan. At the controls of the B-29 was 73rd Wing commander Brigadier General Emmett O'Donnell; copilot was Major Robert K. Morgan, whose B-17, *Memphis Belle,* had been one of the most famed of the early Flying Fortresses. Behind *Dauntless Dotty* followed 110 Superfortresses loaded with bombs and fuel—and ammunition (for no less than 500 to 600 Japanese fighters were expected to meet them; actually there were only 375 in the entire home islands). But there were more formidable obstacles in the way; seventeen B-29s turned back en route with various mechanical troubles (six, which made it all the way, could not bomb because of similar failures).

Bugs, therefore, eliminated twenty-three bombers from the mission. Of the remaining eighty-eight a mere twenty-four bombed the primary objective, the Musashino engine plant; the rest (sixty-four) bombed various sections of Tokyo and the dock areas.

The anticipated heavy fighter counteraction did not materialize, although more than a hundred, a miscellany of Zekes, Tonys, Nicks, and Irvings, as well as others—no doubt scrapings of the defense barrel—came up to intercept the B-29s. American gunners claimed seven of the defenders destroyed, with another eighteen as probables and nine others damaged. The Japanese pilots varied as much as their aircraft, some being apparently timid (and likely half-trained), while others were highly com-

petent pilots and aggressive. Of the eleven damaged B-29s that returned to Saipan, eight had been hit by Japanese gunners (the other three bore the marks of hits from their own sister ships).

Of the ninety-four planes that made the full trip, two were lost, one in combat. A pilot of one of the defending Tonys, with either himself or his aircraft hit, deliberately dived into one of the Superfortresses. The impact slashed off part of the bomber's tail and the plane fell into the sea about twenty miles off the coast of the main island, Honshu. The other loss, a B-29 which had run out of fuel, ditched into the Pacific, but the crew was saved by the quite extensive, precautionary Air-Sea Rescue system that had been arranged in advance. Bombing Japan from the Marianas did not entail the risk of

*Reconnaissance photo taken from* Tokyo Rose, *the first American plane to fly over Japan since the Doo-* *little raid of 1942. This is the Musashino aircraft factory, near Tokyo, November 1, 1944.*

(U. S. AIR FORCE)

*B-29s lining up for the first bombing mission to Tokyo.*
(U. S. AIR FORCE)

amount of damage (besides killing fifty-seven and injuring seventy-five). High winds of near-gale velocity, plus obscuring cloud, which would be characteristic of practically every mission to Japan, made accuracy extremely difficult.

If anything, it was the high wind that swept through the bomber formations, generally above the thirty-thousand-foot level at which the B-29 was designed to operate, that might have been called "divine" by the Japanese. For nearly six months it would hamper the operations of the giant bombers, more certainly than the kamikazes.

The mission then was not militarily very significant, but it was the opening blow of the Battle of Tokyo. Once again American bombers had dared to appear over the Emperor's palace, despite the vows of the Imperial High Command and in the

*Takeoff for Tokyo; the first mission, November 24, 1944.* (U. S. AIR FORCE)

crossing the Hump (as had the China missions), but it did encompass a great deal of over-water flying.

Two losses—and only one in combat—was not too bad a toll. Nor, in fact, had the bombing been too bad—although strike photos picked up a mere sixteen hits in the target area. Actually three times that number fell into the factory and did a small

face of antiaircraft and fighter attack. And it would not be years before the silver giants would appear again. The renewal of the attack on Tokyo may not have opened very impressively, but it was the merest intimation of the devastation, the terror, and the horror to come within the next few months.

The missions during those months were generally executed according to the standard doctrine of day-

*The major adversaries of the B-29 over Japan in the final months of the war: the Kawasaki Ki. 61* Hien *("Tony"), left, and the Mitsubishi J2M* Raiden *("Jack"), interceptor fighters. The Tony was generally used by the Army and the Jack by the Navy. The*

*Jack replaced the Zeke, once its several bugs had been ironed out, as the Navy's chief fighter.*
(U. S. AIR FORCE; NATIONAL AIR AND SPACE MUSEUM, SMITHSONIAN INSTITUTION)

light precision high-altitude bombings which had proved effective, if not decisive, in Europe. Hansell, one of the proponents of that doctrine, adhered to it in spite of Arnold's growing interest in the possibilities of area incendiary attacks. Hansell's term as head of 21st Bomber Command was characterized by what he himself termed a "deplorable" bombing record for accuracy; there was a high percentage of aborts; there were ditchings—and losses because of these ditchings—because of inferior maintenance. These were valid problems which Hansell sought to overcome, but there was little he could do about the weather, whose 180-mile-an-hour winds blew even the big B-29 across the skies of Japan, canceling out almost all the validity of Hansell's adherence to high-altitude precision bombardment.

The advent of LeMay, who took over, ironically, the day after Hansell's final and most effective mission, did not change all that immediately. That last mission, against the Kawasaki Aircraft Industries at Akashi on the Inland Sea about twelve miles from Kobe, just about blew the factory out of operation. Sixty-two of the seventy-seven B-29s dropped their bombs on target and succeeded in cutting aircraft engine and airframe production by 90 per cent. And all the B-29s returned safely. Not until after the war was it learned that Hansell had planned and executed so successful a mission. For some weeks

after, LeMay would continue to send out the B-29s with inconclusive results as before: no targets were wiped out.

As was customary, as soon as he arrived LeMay got a tough training program under way. It was obvious that the crews had much to learn about formation flying, among other essential operational tech-

*The Musashino aircraft plant, which, before the B-29s began striking it, produced nearly three thousand aircraft engines a month for Japanese warplanes.*

(U. S. AIR FORCE)

niques. Since he often confined his comments to monosyllables, or managed a sentence now and then in rebuke, LeMay soon did not qualify for any kind of popularity poll. But his crews were learning how to make it to the target and back and how to hit that target.

The U. S. Navy, which after all "owned" the Marianas, was a special problem. LeMay took the Navy on too. He managed somehow to get hold of a construction priority list and had to scan five pages before he found the Air Force mentioned. "They had built tennis courts for the Island Commander; they had built fleet recreation centers, Marine rehabilitation centers, dockage facilities for inter-island surface craft, and every damn thing in the world except subscribing to the original purpose in the occupation of those islands. The islands were attacked and taken and held because we needed them for air bases to strike against Japan."

LeMay sent the list to Arnold and started shaking and moving. In time the facilities were improved. However, when Brigadier General Thomas S. Powers, commander of the 314th Wing, arrived (also in January) at Guam with the first B-29s of his wing, the "only thing they'd built for him was a coral airstrip down through the jungle. He and his airmen slept on that, the first night they arrived. Next morning they had to tackle the jungle with pocketknives: no other equipment. This was the only manner in which they could clear away the brush and make space to set up their tents."

LeMay noted that Nimitz had "built himself a splendid house, way up on the very highest peak of the island. That was Living." After a round of socializing with the Navy, LeMay felt obligated to reciprocate. He invited the "Neptune" types to dine in his tent on flight rations out of cans. A far cry from Nimitz's "soup, fish course, then the roast and vegetables and salad, and a perfectly swell dessert, and demitasses, and brandy and cigars. . . ."

LeMay's table was not quite so grand. "I'll give the web-footed guests credit, and report they stood up like real men throughout it all. Didn't complain, told stories, were right good company. They ate the canned goods because they were pretty hungry, and had been working hard. I don't remember exactly what was being built that week. Maybe a roller-skating rink."

This near-tragic, not quite comic situation existed because of the command arrangement in the Pacific: Nimitz vs. MacArthur and now vs. LeMay (and eventually vs. the Japanese). The Navy, committed to the sea-air war, understandably looked after its own; it always had, it was tradition. If ships had refrigerator facilities it only followed that they must contain special goodies for the theater commander. Not that the web-footed types deliberately scuttled LeMay, he simply loomed less in their thinking. For all the success of the carriers, the Navy persisted in thinking in terms of ships at sea. Clearly, however, it was obvious that the Pacific war was primarily an air war.

But for some time even LeMay might have doubted that. He sent the B-29s out some sixteen times after he had taken over from Hansell and the results were hardly improved. It was something to think about and LeMay, in his way, did. He thought about those jet streams encountered at bombing altitude and how engines burned out so fast. He thought about bombing accuracy and how it rarely occurred. He thought about the subject, bandied about for so many months, of area bombing at night with incendiaries instead of (or coupled with) high explosives. He thought about clouds.

And he thought, especially, what it might cost in lives.

It was after a mission to Tokyo (February 25, 1945), in which General Power's 314th Wing (with only twenty-two planes at that date) made its first mission, that a new idea came to LeMay. Washington had ordered a "maximum effort" and, with the 314th's Superfortresses, LeMay was able to dispatch 231 of the big bombers. Each of these planes carried a single five-hundred-pound general-purpose bomb, the rest of the load consisting of E46 incendiaries.

Weather, as usual, interfered with the mission, but 172 Boeings dropped more than 450 tons of bombs on Tokyo depending on radar. The results were no better than before because of the scattered effect. But a reconnaissance photo taken after the raid showed an ominous black patch in one corner of Tokyo. A square mile of the city had been obliterated (27,970 buildings had been destroyed—although this was not known until after the war). Where the fire bombs had been concentrated, results had been impressive.

It had not been an unqualified success, but it had provided LeMay with concrete evidence to back

*B-29s after a bombing mission to Japan; the Japanese coastline is at left.* (U. S. AIR FORCE)

up a decision. When his plan was announced to the men who were to fly the mission, the revelation was a shock. The B-29s, designed to bomb from an average altitude of thirty thousand feet, would come in at low level (*Ploesti!*) at between five thousand to seven thousand feet. The mission would be made at night—the B-29 was designed for daytime operation; the previous nighttime missions even with radar had not accomplished much. They would not fly in LeMay's combat boxes, but singly—to avoid collision in the dark. They would carry only incendiary bombs. And finally, no guns and no ammunition.

Consider the final point. If gunners, guns, and ammunition remained behind, more bomb load could be carried. That made some sense, but what about Japanese night fighters? As far as was known, Japanese night fighters were all but non-existent and, according to Intelligence, Japanese radar was inferior to any other radar then in use. Of course, carrying no guns meant that the B-29s would not shoot at one another.

The low-level aspect was not too attractive either.

Way up at thirty thousand you felt quite secure from Japanese antiaircraft fire. What would happen at five thousand feet? Again, the Japanese had no radar to compare with that used with German flak guns, so that should not entail too great a risk. The Japanese would have to depend upon searchlights to find the B-29s, and that was hardly ideal—especially for a fast-flying aircraft.

The fire bombs—M47 (napalm) and M69s (oil)—would set difficult-to-contain fires which in turn would destroy the supposedly very combustible Japanese cities. A large proportion of Japanese military and industrial targets were concentrated in a few major metropolitan areas (unlike Germany), and these targets were surrounded by the flimsy dwellings of the workers. Also, hidden among the dwellings were small "shadow" factories devoted to turning out war materials. Work of this nature was done also in private homes. Defining the boundary between purely industrial and residential Japanese targets was all but impossible.

That was LeMay's decision: a medium-level,

nighttime maximum effort with incendiary bombs and without guns. After months of frustrating, inconclusive strikes, maybe this kind of tactic was the solution. Perhaps; if not, LeMay would have to be the goat. It was, ultimately, his idea, his responsibility, and—for all he knew—his funeral. And if it went wrong, if he was wrong, it would be the funeral flight of a lot of young airmen. If it went right, it also meant the funeral of a great number of Japanese—soldiers, civilians, women, and children. It was not an easy decision to make.

In the early morning of March 10, 1945, as he waited for the report of Bombs Away from Power, leading the mission, LeMay revealed, in what must have seemed an unusually long utterance for him, the real meaning of his decision. "If this raid works the way I think it will," he said, "we can shorten this war."

At 5:35 P.M., March 9, 1945, two groups of Power's 314th Wing—the 29th and the 19th—began lifting their seventy-ton, bomb-laden B-29s off the eighty-five-hundred-foot strip of North Field, Guam. A total of fifty-four took off after the green flare arched through the air, signaling that the mission to Tokyo was on. If tradition meant anything, the men of the 19th Group took off with resolution. Their predecessors had been bombed out of Clark Field in the Philippines the first day of the war; they had been pushed out of Java by the forces of the East Asia Co-Prosperity Sphere; they had participated in the Battle of the Coral Sea and as Kenney's war-weary kids had bombed Rabaul. That was as close as they had come to the Empire before the wrack of war had consumed their battered B-17s and dispirited them.

The Guam aircraft took off first because of their longer flight to Tokyo. The B-29s of O'Donnell's 73rd Wing followed from Isley Field (Saipan), and those of Brigadier General John H. Davies' 313th Wing (North Field, Tinian) left soon after. It took about two and three-quarter hours for the entire force, 334 Superfortresses carrying close to two thousand tons of fire bombs, to take off. There were a few aborts, but a total of 325 aircraft reached the target.

Shortly after midnight (it was now March 10) the pathfinders had arrived over Tokyo. Although turbulence and heavy cloud had been encountered on the flight, over Tokyo and particularly at the low altitude, visibility was very good. The pathfinders had no trouble finding the target area, a section of Tokyo about three by four miles, a densely populated, congested part of the city crowded with home industries and shadow factories. The dwellings were predominantly of wood, plaster, and bamboo construction.

It was simple to find the target because of the Sumida River, which ran through it, and the city's location to the north of Tokyo Bay. The pathfinders released their napalm bombs (M47s), timed to drop at intervals of a hundred feet. When the pathfinders had completed their work, a rough, blazing "X" lay in the heart of Tokyo. The fires ignited by the M47s would preoccupy Tokyo's courageous but not very efficient fire fighters. The remaining B-29s then followed—for about three hours—flinging their heavy loads of M69 clusters at the burning "X." These were timed to fall into the area at fifty-foot intervals; there were over eight thousand of these, which would place a density of about twenty-five tons per square mile. The fiendish aspect of the M69 was that it was devised as a cluster of bombs which would burst at two thousand feet altitude and spread the smaller blazing parts around the area into which it fell.

The bombers came in from altitudes varying from forty-nine hundred feet to ninety-two hundred feet and began dropping their bombs. To LeMay, anxiously waiting at Guam, the word came in: "Bombing the target visually. Large fires observed. Flak moderate. Fighter opposition nil."

That much of his plan had worked. Antiaircraft had been confused by the change in tactic as well as the large number of aircraft. As the fire spread, antiaircraft gunfire lessened, the gun positions being overrun by flame. Searchlights, too, poked up into the sky, but when the fire caught the searchlights were not needed: the sky was bright with flame. A number of Japanese fighters did come up and about forty closed in for attacks while a searchlight beam held one of the bombers. But no serious damage was attributed to Japanese fighters. Forty-two B-29s sustained damage from the antiaircraft fire and it was this which may have accounted for the fourteen B-29s that fell on the mission. Nine of the crews were lost; many may have fallen into their own fire in Tokyo, others may have crashed into the sea; however, five of the crews were saved by

*Tokyo still smoldering after LeMay's first fire bombing, March 10, 1945.* (U. S. AIR FORCE)

Air-Sea Rescue. Some may even have gone down, victims of the tremendous heat turbulence over which they flew. Returning crews reported being tossed thousands of feet upward as they came in to bomb. At least one B-29 was flipped over onto its back, out of control from an updraft of heated air, fell thousands of feet before the combined efforts of pilot and copilot brought it back under control, and headed back for the Marianas on strained, slightly bent wings.

Within thirty minutes of the first Bombs Away, the fire in Tokyo was completely out of hand. The fire department found it impossible to cope with the wide-ranging, rapidly spreading holocaust. Fire-fighting equipment, like the buildings in the target zone, went up in flames. Hoses shriveled up and burst into flame from the heat or flying debris, fire engines simply melted away (nearly a hundred were burned), and 125 firemen died in the fruitless attempts to contain the vicious conflagration. The mixture of the napalm and oil bombs was unquenchable, particularly when combined with the Japanese build-

ing construction and, nature's tragic contribution, a fairly strong wind.

Tokyo did not suffer a firestorm in the manner of Hamburg or Dresden; not the whirling, sucking inferno of those German cities, but a massive plunging fire—comparable to a moving prairie fire—sweeping all before it. The heat rose to more than 1800 degrees (F.) If this heat could fling about a 74,500-pound (empty) aircraft as if it were a leaf in the wind, only the imagination can conceive of what it did to the Japanese trapped in the immolation. No city on earth—not Warsaw, or Rotterdam or London, or Hamburg, or Berlin, not even Dresden (or to come: Hiroshima and Nagasaki)—suffered so great a disaster, so much agony, so much human despair and loss of life.

Radio Tokyo announced that about 130 Super-fortresses had "carried out indiscriminate bombings of the city area" but that the various fires had been put under control by eight o'clock in the morning. The fire, in fact, had burned itself out—there was little more destruction for it to do. The final statement was the nearest to the truth: "War results thus far verified include fifteen planes shot down [there were fourteen] and fifty others damaged." But the frightful truths soon spread throughout Tokyo and the official broadcasts became more shrill and more honest: ". . . the sea of flames which enclosed the residential and commercial sections of Tokyo was reminiscent of the holocaust of Rome, caused by the Emperor Nero." LeMay was quickly painted as a contemporary mad Nero and the mission was called by Radio Tokyo a "slaughter bombing." There are no other kinds of bombings, realist LeMay might have pointed out.

Nearly sixteen square miles of the main section of Tokyo had been wiped out, and along with it twenty-two industrial targets which had been marked for pin-point destruction by the Twentieth Air Force. One fourth of all the buildings in Tokyo had been destroyed; those few which remained standing—those made of concrete and brick—were nothing but burnt-out shells which had served as ovens for those hapless thousands who sought shelter in them. Sheer fright had led to panic, which contributed to the heavy toll in lives. An official of the Japanese Home Affairs Ministry summed up, succinctly, what had occurred: "People were unable to escape. They were found later piled upon the bridges, roads, and

*Burned-out Tokyo; the result of the B-29 fire bombings.* (U. S. AIR FORCE)

in the canals, eighty thousand dead and twice that many injured. We were instructed to report on actual conditions. Most of us were unable to do this because of the horrifying conditions beyond imagination."

The dead had succumbed first of all to the heat—some seemed to burst into flame as if by spontaneous combustion, some suffocated; others who sought refuge in the waters of the river drowned in the panic of the mobs rushing for the water. Those who hoped to save themselves in the smaller canals were broiled alive. Shelters were little more than death traps where the victims either burned, suffocated, or were literally torn limb from limb by one another.

Official figures listed 83,793 dead and 40,918 injured. It is likely that the death toll was much higher—and it is equally likely that its true figure will never be known. More than a million people were rendered homeless in the single bombing, placing a serious burden on Home Defense organizations in Japan. And there could be no questioning the terrible effect upon morale. The real war had come in full fury to Japan; the small flame ignited at Pearl Harbor had burgeoned into a pillar of fire.

LeMay's plan had worked and subsequent fire bombings, to a greater or lesser extent, proved that it had not been a fluke. When the results of the Tokyo bombing, and those which followed upon Nagoya, Osaka, and Kobe, were analyzed, the Joint Target Group in Washington voiced its full approval for the change in bombing techniques and compiled a target list designating thirty-three urban areas of Japan where its industries would suffer most from incendiary attacks. The assumption was that these attacks would pave the way for the projected Allied invasion of the home islands of Japan.

LeMay had another conception in the back of his mind; he believed that with proper support—supplies, crews, and B-29s—air power alone could force a Japanese surrender. In both, tactics and strategy, he was right. Japan was finished as a warmaking power, despite its still intact 2,500,000-man army awaiting the American invasion in the home islands (the Imperial Navy too could still muster 1.5 million men). The slaughter which might have ensued had the invasions, Operations Olympic and Coronet, planned, respectively, for the fall of 1945 and early spring of 1946, occurred would have made the fire bombings of LeMay's B-29s seem like little pin pricks in casualties.

Despite the fact that militarily Japan was practically finished and to continue the war only meant growing casualty lists, the Japanese war lords insisted upon fighting on, however hopeless the war had become. They would not sacrifice "face" even at the cost of hundreds of thousands of lives. To have continued on in the face of certain defeat was no longer as much an aspect of Japanese military thinking as it was of Japanese culture and psychology.

### III

A wide cultural gap separated the American and Japanese soldier. They killed each other but they did not understand one another; they shared neither the orthodox conventions of war nor certain values, emotions, and ways of thinking. The concept of surrender was alien to the Japanese; he fought until he died or, if he was not killed, charged screaming at his enemy in a suicidal, pointless evasion of surrender. When captured Allied soldiers asked that their families be notified of their imprisonment—and comparative safety—the Japanese were appalled. Why did these soldiers wish their families to know about their disgrace?

The Japanese did not surrender (especially in the early months of the war), because it was shameful and he could no longer, because of his shame, regard himself as Japanese. He also believed that the American enemy tortured and killed his prisoners—a powerful rumor was that at Guadalcanal all prisoners were disposed of by driving tanks over them. This explains why so few Japanese were taken prisoner (another was that they frequently made themselves walking booby traps and killed themselves and their captors) and why they treated prisoners so badly. Once "face" was lost, the prisoner was not fit for human treatment.

The Japanese were inculcated from birth with a number of basic beliefs: that things of the spirit were superior to material things, "to match our training against their numbers and our flesh against their steel." That Japan did not have the material resources of the United States meant nothing; Japanese spirit and discipline would win in the end.

Their training manuals invariably opened with the formula: "Read this and the war is won."

Another important concept was that of "place." At the top was the Emperor (just as Japan was at the top of the hierarchy of nations), who was above all material things. At the bottom was the lowly soldier, whose pleasure—whose duty—was to die for the Emperor. And war directives were issued by the High Command in the name of the Emperor whether he knew it or not. As the spiritual leader of Japan, the Emperor was above all that was mundane; if he was not a political nincompoop and a moral idiot he might just as well have been. His position was rarefied, detached from the life of Japan—although he symbolized Japan in the minds of his people, like the flag or an icon.

Dutiful Japanese believed what they were told. Radio Tokyo when it finally was permitted to announce certain defeats—the loss of Saipan, the fall of the Philippines—assured the Japanese that all was well because this had been predicted by the military leaders and therefore was perfectly all right.

When the B-29s began appearing over the home islands in greater profusion an official of the Aviation Manufacturers' Association spoke over Radio Tokyo saying, "Enemy planes finally have come over our very heads. However, we who are engaged in the aircraft production industry and who had always expected this to happen have made complete preparations to cope with this. Therefore, there is nothing to worry about."

The Japanese war hero was generally anonymous; it was taken for granted that he would conduct himself properly on the battlefield. If he died in combat for the Emperor he was sublimely fortunate and had gained spiritual immortality. Who needed medals and newspaper announcements to hail the common deeds of a true warrior?

Ruth Benedict in *The Chrysanthemum and the Sword* reproduced one of the broadcasts of Radio Tokyo, of which the moral is obvious. The hero is still anonymous, but he is an officer; individual accomplishments of mere enlisted men hardly ever attracted any attention. The broadcast told this story:

After the air battles were over, the Japanese planes returned to their base in small formations of three or four. A Captain was in one of the first planes to return. After alighting from his plane, he stood on the ground and gazed into the sky through his binoculars. As his men returned, he counted. He looked rather pale, but he was quite steady. After the last plane returned he made out a report and proceeded to Headquarters. At Headquarters he made his report to the Commanding Officer. As soon as he had finished his report, however, he suddenly dropped to the ground. The officers on the spot rushed to give assistance but alas! he was dead. On examining his body it was found that it was already cold, and he had a bullet wound in his chest, which had proved fatal. It is impossible for the body of a newly-dead person to be cold. Nevertheless the body of the dead Captain was as cold as ice. The Captain must have been dead long before, and it was his spirit that made the report. Such a miraculous fact must have been achieved by the strict sense of responsibility that the dead Captain possessed.

The Japanese listener was expected to believe this story—and probably did. There was a power much stronger than life itself. It was this belief in that power, plus a number of other beliefs, which made the Japanese soldier different from his occidental enemy. To the Japanese adding futility to futility was, within the patterns of his culture, not unnatural. Futility was, after all, a Western concept.

Those values which made up the Japanese national character and the Japanese warrior produced the war's most bizarre weapon, the kamikaze. The word, meaning "the divine wind," evoked the miraculous delivery of the Japanese from a Mongol invasion in the thirteenth century, when Kublai Khan's invasion fleet was dispersed and some of its ships capsized by a sudden typhoon. Obviously by the autumn of 1944 only a divine miracle could spare the Japanese another invasion.

Initially the Special Attack Corps, as the suicide units were called, were established on a limited basis: to participate in the *Sho*-1 defense of the Philippines. Time was running out on Japan and only unorthodox methods might save the Empire. The only offensive weapon remaining was the land-based aircraft of the Navy and Army. Ground troops must wait until the enemy attacked before they could participate; most of the carrier force—and the most experienced pilots—had been wiped out in the Marianas; the Navy's ships were depleted or crippled. Ordinary bombing rarely stopped the American ships because of antiaircraft fire and protective fighters which interfered with the bomb run. The invaders, and especially their carriers, must be stopped by deliberate crashing of a bombed-up aircraft onto a ship. And the only way of assuring that the aircraft would continue on its fatal trajectory was by having its pilot remain in the plane.

The idea was not new. A fatally stricken pilot or plane had crashed into ships, gun positions, or other planes before. But this resulted only after all other means had failed. And some crashes, however heroic they appeared to be, were not deliberate. The concept of a one-way mission had been introduced as early as Pearl Harbor with the midget submarines, which hardly had a chance, but the chance, however slim, was present. There was none of this in the kamikaze. The sacrifice of one's life for the Emperor was not therefore a new idea, but it had generally occurred in the heat of combat. But to devote a period of training to nothing else but sacrifice—this was regarded even by some Japanese commanders as a farfetched tactic.

One of the earliest suggestions for implementing this idea was submitted shortly after the Marianas Turkey Shoot by Captain Eiichiro Jyo, commander of the light carrier *Chiyoda,* who read the handwriting on the wall and himself wrote: "No longer can we hope to sink the numerically superior enemy aircraft carriers through ordinary attack methods. I urge the immediate organization of special attack units to carry out crash-dive tactics, and I ask to be placed in command of them."

Coincidentally, Jyo died on the same day that the first kamikaze Zero sank its first American ship. The *Chiyoda,* one of the units of Ozawa's decoys-for-Halsey force, was sunk by American carrier planes during the Battle of Leyte Gulf. Jyo went down with his ship.

Meanwhile, Vice-Admiral Takijiro Ohnishi, after serving in various high-level capacities, including the position of Chief of General Affairs, Bureau of the Aviation Department, in the Ministry of Munitions and as chief of staff of Navy land-based aviation during the early—victorious—battles in the Philippines and Malaya, arrived back in the Philippines to assume command of the First Air Fleet. The condition of the air fleet, depleted, its planes tattered and worn, its men dispirited, must have assured Ohnishi that the desperate plan he brought with him was the right one.

Before he had fully taken over his command Ohnishi personally traveled the fifty-odd miles from his post in Manila to Mabalacat Field (a part of Clark Field), where he placed his idea before Commander Asaichi Tamai, executive officer of the 201st Air Group (Sentai). American forces had already landed on Suluan Island at the entrance to Leyte Gulf; the *Sho*-1 operation would be put into force. The mission of the First Air Fleet—with its barely one hundred aircraft—was to provide cover for Kurita's advance into Leyte Gulf. To accomplish this, Ohnishi explained, the American carriers must be stopped—"we must hit the enemy's carriers and keep them neutralized for at least one week."

Ohnishi, his face impassive but obviously strained, went on, according to one of his officers, Captain Rikihei Inoguchi. "In my opinion," Ohnishi said, "there is only one way of assuring that our meager strength will be effective to a maximum degree. That is to organize suicide attack units composed of Zero fighters armed with two-hundred-and-fifty-kilogram [about five hundred pounds] bombs, with each plane to crash-dive into an enemy carrier. . . ."

When, after some discussion, the idea was placed before the twenty-three non-commissioned pilots of the 201st Air Group, Inoguchi described the reaction: "In a frenzy of emotion and joy, the arms of every pilot in the assembly went up in a gesture of complete accord." These volunteers were then placed under the command of Lieutenant Yukio Seki. Ohnishi had his first *Kamikaze Tokubetsu Kogekitai* (Divine Wind Special Attack Squad), twenty-four pilots and twenty-six Zeros. The unit, named *Shimpu* (another interpretation of the Japanese character for *kamikaze*), was divided into four sections, all poetically named: *Shikishima* (a poetic name for Japan), *Yamato* (an ancient name of Japan), *Asahi* (morning sun), and *Yamazakura* (mountain cherry blossoms).

It was not planned to send the full contingent upon suicide missions. Some pilots would escort the kamikaze planes, to protect them from enemy interference and also, if possible, to return and report on the success or failure of the mission. When the kamikaze idea was initiated and the secret became known among the young airmen of the First Air Fleet, it was seized upon as the one means of salvation for Japan. Emotions ran high and strong men literally sobbed when they were either accepted or denied membership in the unique unit. The two dozen men in Seki's *Shimpu* squadron were envied, for theirs would be an honor not all pilots would be privileged to share. That, at least, was the original intent: the kamikaze unit would help to turn the tide in the *Sho*-1 operation and Japan would win the war.

According to Inoguchi, when Ohnishi addressed Seki's men for the first time, the scene was charged with emotion.

"You are already gods," he told them, "without earthly desires. But one thing you want to know is that your crash-dive is not in vain. Regrettably, we will not be able to tell you the results. But I shall watch your efforts to the end and report your deeds to the Throne. You may all rest assured on this point. . . ." It would be the fulfillment of their lives, to be remembered to the Emperor. Their gratitude could barely be contained.

While Seki prepared his few men and planes for their first sortie, one of the units, the *Yamato*, was detached and flown four hundred miles to the south to Cebu, an island almost directly to the west of Leyte. Here Commander Tadashi Nakajima, flight operations officer of the 201st Air Group, organized yet another kamikaze unit. Volunteers leaped at the opportunity and Nakajima soon had an additional twenty pilots for the special attacks being planned for the American fleet. The only two pilots who did not volunteer had been hospitalized. Nakajima had led a flight of eight Zeros; besides his own aircraft and the four kamikaze planes, there had been escort planes. One of the pilots of the escorts (none of whom knew of the kamikaze plan), Lieutenant Yoshiyasu Kuno, when he learned of the plan, appeared before Nakajima in an excited but subdued state. He all but accused the commander of denying him the opportunity of participating in the special attacks, as if it were a kind of discrimination.

Nakajima assured him. "One of the Zeros we brought here from Mabalacat is reserved for *your* special attack mission." The Zero Nakajima had piloted was equipped to carry the five-hundred-pound bomb. Kuno left in a state of elation.

As the Battle of Leyte Gulf developed, the two kamikaze squadrons waited impatiently for an opportunity to strike at the hated enemy. This was an important factor too in their attitude. The Japanese had been indoctrinated since they were young that the United States had insulted the Empire, in its commercial dealings, in military demands—espe-

cially in the hated naval treaties and in diplomatic moves. Not until October 21 was the first sortie attempted. Lieutenant Seki, suffering from a debilitating attack of diarrhea, was to lead the *Shikishima* unit in the first attack. The takeoff was preceded by ceremony during which water was drunk from a container, a gift of Ohnishi, by the mission pilots. They then climbed into their Zeros to the sound of those pilots remaining behind singing an old song which closed with the words *Ogimi no he ni koso shiname/Nodo niwa shinaji* ("Thus for the Emperor I will not die peacefully at home").

Before he took off, the haggard Seki gave Commander Tamai an envelope containing a cutting of his hair. This was to be sent home to Seki's family, a recent wife and a widowed mother, as a memorial in traditional samurai manner. The four suicide planes took off accompanied by escort Zeros—and then all returned. They had not been able to find the American fleet. With tears in his eyes, Seki apologized for the failure of the mission.

The failure of the Cebu kamikazes was even more embarrassing. As three special attack planes and two escorts warmed up on the airstrip, American carrier planes swarmed down and shot them up, puncturing tanks, riddling the Zeros—all of which exploded and burned. This mission had not even gotten off the ground. After the carrier planes left, Nakajima prepared another three Zeros for a mission which would be led by Lieutenant Kuno—who had so feared he would be left out of the great events. The Zero pilots, hoping to find the source of their earlier ignominy, took off late in the afternoon. Poor weather intervened and two returned. They had not found the American ships. Kuno did not come back—nor was any American ship struck by a Japanese plane that day.

Weather and poor reconnaissance continued to add to the frustrations of the kamikaze pilots. Seki, for example, ventured out four times, four days running, only to return each time after a fruitless search for the enemy. The fifth time, leading his *Shikishima* unit (five kamikaze Zeroes with four escorts) on October 25, he came upon the beleaguered escort carriers off Samar. All five bomb-laden Zeros plunged upon the American fleet, and insofar as it is possible to know, Seki's Zero may have been the first kamikaze plane to score a hit upon an American carrier—the *Saint Lo*. Also hit were three other of the baby flattops, but the *Saint Lo,* struck by another kamikaze, ruptured and sank.

Thus on the climactic day of the Battle of Leyte Gulf, the Special Attack Corps had achieved its first victory. At the same time it also reported its first exaggerated account of that victory, and that would lead to the fatal decision of expanding the kamikaze. A witness, veteran pilot Hiroyoshi Nishizawa, one of Japan's leading aces, returned to describe Seki's efforts. (Nishizawa, incidentally, was killed a few days later in a transport after a flight to Cebu.) The news of the victory was quickly broadcast via Radio Tokyo: "The *Shikishima* unit of the Kamikaze Special Attack Corps made a successful surprise attack on an enemy task force containing four aircraft carriers at a point thirty miles northeast of Suluan Island at ten forty-five. Two planes hit one carrier, which was definitely sunk. A third plane hit another carrier, setting it aflame. A fourth hit a cruiser, which sank instantly."

A great thrill ran through the corps and Ohnishi could take some pride in the efficacy of his plan. Nishimura's, Shima's, and Kurita's ships had been all but devoured by the American carrier forces and had accomplished little—yet single men in a frail aircraft had actually sunk ships of the American fleet, carriers at that (the Japanese had not yet discerned the difference between a fleet carrier and an escort carrier).

The following day the Cebu-based *Yamato* unit had its chance. An early morning mission (two kamikazes with a single Zero escort) simply vanished off the face of the earth. But the second, airborne shortly after noon and consisting of three kamikazes with two escorts, struck to the east of Surigao, where Nishimura had fared so badly. One of the escort Zeros returned (the other having been destroyed by a wall of Hellcats) to claim another carrier definitely sunk and another seriously damaged. Here again exaggeration entered. On October 26 only the escort carrier *Suwanee* (of Taffy 1) was hit, and damaged, by a kamikaze plane; it did not sink, nor were any other ships damaged.

When the word of the kamikaze "triumphs" reached the Emperor he commented in a curious manner. The ambivalence of the Emperor's reaction, however, was ignored in the excitement of his special concern, and Ohnishi dispatched a message to the surviving pilots.

When told of the special attack, His Majesty said, "Was it necessary to go to this extreme? They certainly did a magnificent job." His Majesty's words suggest that His Majesty is greatly concerned. We must redouble our efforts to relieve His Majesty of this concern. I have pledged our every effort toward that end.

But Ohnishi had been perturbed by the Emperor's words, interpreting them as a form of criticism. Yet he had succeeded where the others had failed; he was determined that Japan must fight to the last man. He must extend the "life" of the kamikaze idea and expand the force with which to strike back at the enemy. And nothing so sustained his point of view as the dismal final outcome of the *Sho*-1 operation.

This was a major point in his argument with Vice-Admiral Shigeru Fukudome, whose Second Air Fleet had flown in from Formosa to make a small effort in the *Sho*-1 operation with its conventional air attacks. Since Ohnishi's smaller kamikaze units had wrought more harm to the American fleet than had Fukudome's large bomber formations, the junior officer (Ohnishi) won the argument and in the small hours of the morning of October 26, 1944, Fukudome reluctantly capitulated. The two air fleets were united as the Combined Land-based Air Force, under Fukudome's command and with Ohnishi as his chief of staff. Certain units were to be set up for kamikaze operations, for Fukudome wished to keep the greater proportions of his still operational air forces for orthodox attacks. But the spirit spread and within hours several new kamikaze squadrons had been formed—enough to establish a second Kamikaze Tokubetsu Kogekitai. The union of the two air fleets increased the supply of aircraft for the special attacks—until they were expended. Besides. the Zero, among the other early kamikaze planes were the single-engined, two-place "Judy" (Aichi D4Y, *Suisei*) and the "Frances" (Yokosuka P1Y, *Ginga*), a twin-engined bomber. The larger craft meant not only larger bomb loads, but also a crew of two rather than the single suicide pilot.

The kamikaze corps survived the failure of *Sho*-1. With the Imperial Navy cut in half, the Philippine battle devolved into a vicious land battle. Ohnishi's mission was changed accordingly and his kamikaze units were assigned sorties that would help the Japanese troops by striking at American transports bringing in reinforcements and supplies. But the very nature of his operation quickly depleted Ohnishi's limited supply of aircraft. In November he flew to Tokyo to present his case before the High Command, demanding that he be given three hundred planes for his Special Attack Corps. About half that number was finally granted, and these were scraped up from several training centers. If the aircraft were not in top condition, neither were the not fully trained young pilots. These youths were sent to Formosa for special training in how to experience a spectacular death.

The special indoctrination took only a week: two days on takeoff procedures, two days on formation flying, and the final three days on how to approach and attack a target. As quickly as this period was over the young pilots were rushed to the Philippines, where it was obvious that the Americans planned to move up the islands to Luzon. That the kamikaze volunteers were exceedingly young and ill trained meant little to their destruction-bent leaders. The poorly trained pilots were regarded as liabilities, even if only subconsciously. One of the critics of the kamikaze tactics, Rear Admiral Toshiyuki Yokoi, revealed this attitude when he observed of his own Fifth Air Fleet during the Okinawa campaign: "I knew that two of the eight units were practically untrained and *so were not fit for anything but suicide duty.*" (Italics added.) Obviously Yokoi did not venerate the kamikaze volunteers as Ohnishi did.

At the same time Japanese ground reinforcements were being slipped into the Philippines and the promise of an impending, even larger-scaled Guadalcanal loomed forbiddingly. The threat of another Tokyo Express, prolonging the fighting and intensifying the casualty toll, was ominously considered by the Americans. Nor did the Leyte airstrips provide Kenney with facilities from which he could operate very effectively. Tacloban, the principal airfield, was little more than a bog which defied Army engineers; the heavy-bomber strip at Tanauan was not operational until mid-December. Air cover, therefore, for the hard-fighting ground troops was provided mainly by the Navy.

During the air strikes upon Luzon to interfere

*A Japanese suicide plane aimed at the* Essex *near Luzon in the Philippines, November 25, 1944, when the first kamikaze planes began operations.*
(NAVY DEPT., NATIONAL ARCHIVES)

with Japanese reinforcement operations and in preparation for the proposed return to Luzon, Halsey's carriers came under powerful kamikaze attacks. On November 25 planes from the carrier *Ticonderoga* sank the heavy cruiser *Kumano* and smashed two coastal convoys, but a swarm of kamikaze planes came out—thirteen suicide planes with a nine-plane escort in two waves—and slashed into Halsey's carriers. The *Intrepid,* which had been hit so often it earned the nickname "Evil I," the *Cabot,* the *Hancock,* and the *Essex* were all hit, with severe damages and casualties. The *Intrepid,* crashed into by two planes, suffered a hundred dead. Once again, at the cost of men and machines, the Special Attack Corps "proved" itself to Ohnishi's satisfaction, but what he failed or preferred not to see was that it did not stop the Americans.

When American landings began (December 15, 1944) on Mindoro Island—a military steppingstone between unlovely Leyte and pivotal Luzon—about forty Japanese planes were still operational in the Philippines. And to these had been added the last thirteen suicide Zeros, which had been flown in from Formosa. The final phase of the Philippine kamikaze attacks was aimed at the Luzon landings in Lingayen Gulf. During these landings the U. S.

*A kamikaze strikes the* Intrepid, *Luzon, November 25.* (NAVY DEPT., NATIONAL ARCHIVES)

*Crew fights the fire on the* Intrepid *after being crashed by a kamikaze. Sixty men died in the crash and fire; the* Intrepid *was hit so often by kamikazes that it was nicknamed the "Evil I."*

(NAVY DEPT., NATIONAL ARCHIVES)

Navy was to realize for the first time the full implications of the kamikazes. This was brought home with force during the prelanding bombardment and minesweeping operations on January 6. A large force under Admiral J. B. Oldendorf (six battleships, six cruisers, nineteen destroyers, a dozen escort carriers which, in turn, were screened by twenty destroyers with escorts, minesweepers, transports, and gunboats) was headed for Luzon. A portent flew in on January 3 and smashed into the escort carrier *Ommaney Bay* (which sank the following day with a hundred dead). Curiously no Japanese claim was made for this sinking—the pilot

*A burning "Frances, "a Nakajima land-based bomber, dispatched from Luzon, passes over the deck of escort carrier* Ommaney Bay *during landings on Mindoro island, about three hundred miles northwest of Leyte.*

*Taking Mindoro was essential to the planned campaign for Luzon to begin early in 1945. The* Ommaney Bay *survived the air attacks at Mindoro, but was sunk by a kamikaze in Lingayen Gulf on January 4, 1945.*
(NAVY DEPT., NATIONAL ARCHIVES)

who sank the carrier may not have been a kamikaze. The next day several attacks originating from Mabalacat, Luzon, spread flame, casualties, and foreboding through the American ships. No ships were sunk but two escort carriers, *Manila Bay* and *Savo,* an Australian ship, H.M.A.S. *Australia,* and six other ships were struck. The future appeared chilling to the Americans—who did shoot down some of the attackers. Still their determination carried some through the heavy antiaircraft fire and the fighter screen.

Vice-Admiral C. R. Brown expressed some of the emotions of the men aboard the targets of the kamikazes, to whom the very conception was inconceivable. "We watched each plunging kamikaze with the detached horror of one witnessing a terrible spectacle rather than as the intended victim. We forgot self for the moment as we groped hopelessly for the thoughts of that other man up there. And dominating it all was a strange admixture of respect and pity—respect for any person who offers the supreme sacrifice to the things he stands for, and pity for the utter frustration which was epitomized by the suicidal act. For whatever the gesture meant to that

central actor out there in space, and however painful might be the consequences to ourselves, no one of us questioned the outcome of the war now rushing to its conclusion."

The morning of the sixth brought a surprise to

*Anxious carrier crewmen scan the horizon for kamikaze planes.* (U. S. NAVY)

Commander Nakajima. He had fallen into an exhausted sleep certain that the last of the First Air Fleet's kamikazes had been expended the day before. But through the night ground crews had worked until they had patched together five Zeros, ready to fly and armed with the suicide bombs (three with the full five-hundred-pound bomb and two with lighter bombs). Thirty pilots remained, so it was a serious crisis in command, for all fought for the privilege of flying the barely airworthy Zeros. Nakajima silenced the squabbling with "Everyone wants to go. Don't be so selfish!"

The final choice was made by Nakajima in consultation with the commander of the group. Selected to lead the attack was a Lieutenant Nakano, only recently released from the hospital after an attack of tuberculosis. Nakano had begged to be given the chance to make a mission before a return of the illness deprived him of the honor of serving. "Remembering his plea," Nakajima wrote, "I kept him in mind for some short-range mission that would not tax his strength."

As the planes were preparing to take off, Nakano raised himself in his cockpit and shouted to Nakajima. "Fearing that something had gone wrong, I ran to the side of his plane to learn what troubled him. His face was wreathed in smiles as he called, 'Thank you, Commander. Thank you very much!'" As each of the remaining four planes poised in the takeoff position for a moment, the pilot waved and through the engine's roar Nakajima heard "his shrieked farewell: 'Thank you for choosing me!'"

A sudden fury descended upon the American fleet standing off Lingayen bombarding the invasion beaches. It began at noon when a flaming Zero (not one of Nakano's, which appeared later in the day) enveloped the navigating bridge of the battleship *New Mexico,* killing the commanding officer, Captain R. W. Fleming, Churchill's liaison officer to MacArthur, Lieutenant General Herbert Lumsden, a *Time* correspondent, William Chickering, and twenty-six other men; in addition eighty-seven were wounded. The destroyer *Walkde* nearby downed two approaching Zeros but a third broke through the curtain of fire and rammed into the bridge. Commander George F. Davis became a human torch until his men as quickly and as gently as possible smothered the flames. Meanwhile a fourth Zero had been destroyed by the *Walkde*'s gun crews. Commander Davis, too terribly burned to survive, died later in the day.

About that time Nakano's Zeros swept in on Lingayen. An escort-observer claimed that the five patched-up Zeros struck a battleship, a cruiser, and three transports. The cruiser may well have been the *Louisville,* which received a Zero in the bridge. Flaming fuel drenched Rear Admiral Theodore E. Chandler, who nonetheless assisted in putting out the flames by manhandling a firehose with his men and only then took his place in line for treatment in sick bay. He died the next day because of severe damage to his lungs. More than thirty others died with him.

The day's toll was high: the minesweeper *Long* had been sunk, and besides the ships already mentioned, seven others plus the *Australia* (for the second time) were also damaged. And, if the ships did not sink, the injuries of the survivors were often frightful. Aboard the transport *Harris* Lieutenant G. R. Cassels-Smith observed in his diary (the date does not matter): "Two more burials at sea this evening—that makes four who have died so far and there are several more who may die. They are so badly burned or mangled that they are really better off dead."

But for all their appalling ferocity the kamikazes had not stopped the Luzon landings, which began on January 9, 1945. The following day Ohnishi and his staff flew out of the Philippines to Tainan, Formosa, where he would reorganize his Special Attack Corps for its final round of glory. Meanwhile, however, those Japanese Air Force men for whom no transportation could be found were left to serve as ground troops in the hills of the Philippines. Fukudome fled to Singapore by flying boat some days later. Tominaga, of the Army's ill-fated air forces, took to the hills as an infantryman.

Attacks from Formosa could still be mounted and were, but such missions were sporadic. One such mission on January 11—a Betty bomber with a dozen fighters as escorts—encountered the two P-51s of Captain William A. Shomo and Lieutenant Paul M. Lipscomb, themselves on an armed reconnaissance mission. The Americans' objectives were the Aparri and Laoag airdromes, which by that date presumably housed only wrecked Japanese aircraft and a few airmen destined for the infantry. The Betty, which they sighted when it was about

*Mustangs of the 35th Fighter Group (Fifth Air Force) prepare for takeoff from Luzon airstrip to bomb and* *strafe pockets of Japanese resistance in the northern section of the island.* (U. S. AIR FORCE)

2500 feet above them, may have actually been an evacuation plane carrying valuable aircrews out of the Philippines to Formosa. Thus the single twin-engined bomber and the rather large escort.

Neither Shomo, who commanded the 82nd Tactical Reconnaissance Squadron, nor Lipscomb had ever been in combat before. With the odds at thirteen to two, the green Kenney boys in their only recently arrived Mustangs climbed to the attack. Whatever the mission of the Japanese, they appeared to be more inexperienced than their attackers, for as the two Mustangs approached no attempt was made to challenge them. The formation flew blithely on its way. Kenney later suggested that the Japanese pilots mistook the new Mustang for the Tony and thought that reinforcements had arrived and did not expect an attack.

Shomo scored first: he came in under the third element and picked off the leading Zeke, which detonated in mid-air. Sweeping away from the debris and flame, Shomo ripped past the second element and shattered one of the fighters in that.

The Japanese realized then that they were under attack and formed into battle stations; even as they fluttered around to do this, Shomo careened around and subtracted one more from their number. This plane, his third victim, blew up also. This brought

Shomo's Mustang beneath the Betty; he raised the nose of the P-51, got the wing root of the Japanese bomber in his sight, and fired. The Betty dropped out of the formation, nosed down into the jungle of Luzon, and crashed. Orange flame and thick black

*Ennis C. Whitehead, commander of the Fifth Air Force, with William A. Shomo, who became a fighter ace in his first air battle.* (U. S. AIR FORCE)

smoke shot out of the thick, lush greenness of the jungle.

One of the escort Zekes came down with the bomber to challenge Shomo, but instead was dealt with: as he pulled up from watching the fall of the Betty, Shomo found himself looking into the nose of an oncoming Zeke. He pressed his gun button and the Zeke flipped out of his path and downward to join the blazing Betty. This had brought him up above the remaining Zekes. Shomo dived upon the lead fighter and with a short burst sent it down. Another Zeke slipped by diving and Shomo raced after it. When they were within three hundred feet of the jungle, Shomo caught the Zeke in his guns and it simply continued its dive into the treetops.

While Shomo was thus engaged, Lipscomb too had been busy. He accounted for three Zekes during the battle. With these three added to the seven Shomo had destroyed, the brief battle had eliminated ten aircraft from the already diminished Japanese

Air Force. The surviving three Zekes found refuge in a cloud bank and managed to get away.

When they returned to the Fifth Air Force base on Mindoro Island (directly south of Luzon), the elated Shomo—who had become an ace on his very first mission—made the traditional "victory roll" over the field. He would roar over the field, twist and turn, then come back again and repeat the maneuver. The first couple of rolls were greeted with cheers, but then when the number reached five, then six, and finally seven, the cheering stopped. Obviously some hot-shot stick-jockey was making sport of the honored victory roll. This was a decided breach of etiquette and must be reprimanded officially. The brass jumped into jeeps and drove out to the strips.

Lipscomb had already landed and stood near his Mustang awaiting Shomo's landing. The loaded jeep pulled up alongside the lanky Texan. He being the nearest target, a colonel began reaming him for

*Luzon from the air. Marine Dauntless in foreground is seeking a Japanese position on which to drop the five-* *hundred-pound bomb it is carrying.*
(DEFENSE DEPT., MARINE CORPS)

Shomo's abuse of the symbol of victory. Lipscomb, in a lazy drawl, explained that Shomo was indeed legitimately exercising the honored privilege.

"Sir," Lipscomb said, "he got seven Japs." He then added, "And I got three."

It was a bit difficult to believe (but gun cameras proved it to be true). Then one of the brass suddenly realized another anomaly.

"Lieutenant," he asked, "if you got three planes, why didn't you make any victory rolls?"

"Well, sir," Lipscomb replied, taking his time with each southern-inflected syllable, "I just checked out on this airplane and I ain't sure I know how."

Kenney was of course delighted with the performance of his kids. Although they had had no previous combat experience, obviously their training had been greatly superior to that of the hapless Japanese pilots they had come upon that day. Jokingly he inquired, "Why'd you let the others get away?"

"To tell the truth, General," Shomo answered, "we ran out of bullets." Lipscomb, apparently having used up his syllables for the day, merely nodded. Kenney promoted both men on the spot and saw to it that Shomo received the Medal of Honor and Lipscomb the Distinguished Service Cross. With characteristic curiosity Kenney inquired about the prewar occupations of the two men. "Lipscomb was a Texas cowboy," Kenney learned, "Shomo—believe it or not—was a licensed embalmer. Poor Nips."

IV

On Formosa Ohnishi, a man now determined to establish an air force on a death wish, set to work on the reorganization of his First Air Fleet kamikazes for the predicted invasion of Okinawa.

The reorganization was completed by the first week in February and the new Special Attack Corps activated even earlier—on January 18—was named the Niitaka Unit (after the mountain on Formosa). Even this carried its special full-circle irony, alluding as it did to the Pearl Harbor attack message, "Climb Mount Niitaka." Within the month yet another Special Attack Unit was formed: the 601st Air Group of the Third Air Fleet (based in Japan in the Kanto Plain area around Tokyo). This unit consisted of thirty-two aircraft, a conglomeration of Zekes and Judys—fighters, bombers, and torpedo planes—organized into five elements ranging from

four to eight aircraft each. This unit first saw action during the invasion of what appeared to be the insignificant island of Iwo Jima.

Less than eight hundred miles from the Japanese homeland, Iwo Jima was a threat to LeMay's Twentieth Air Force B-29s because of a radar warning station on the island and the Japanese fighters stationed there. But there was an even more important function in mind for the roughly five-by-three-miles pork-chop-shaped dot in the Pacific, which lay halfway between the Marianas and Tokyo: in American hands Iwo could serve as an emergency landing field for distressed B-29s, navigational aids could be set up, fighters could be based there to provide escort for the Marianas-based Superfortresses, and it could be used as an Air-Sea Rescue base. Of especial interest were the three Japanese airfields, two of which were actually operational.

The battle for Iwo Jima in February of 1945 was primarily a land battle, one of the costliest in the history of the U. S. Marines in terms of land taken divided by lives lost.

Iwo, however, was but a portent of things to come. The island's commander, Lieutenant General

*The first flag on Iwo Jima: Marines dug around an antiaircraft gun with Mount Suribachi in the background. When the flag (in a famous staged ceremony) was put atop Suribachi the island would become a B-29 base from which to strike Japan. All this was done, but at great cost.* (U. S. MARINE CORPS)

*Iwo Jima as an American air base. More than a hundred Mustangs and a couple of B-29s parked on what had once been a Japanese airstrip.*

(U. S. AIR FORCE)

My Girl *gets the go-sign for a B-29 escort mission. Iwo-based Mustangs rendezvoused with Marianas-based B-29s for bombing missions.* (U. S. AIR FORCE)

Tadamichi Kuribayashi, had developed the island's natural defense system by digging under the volcanic ash and into caves until he transformed it, as his orders had read, "into a fortress." Despite the heavy aerial bombardment by the Seventh Air Force's B-24s and the 313th Bombardment Wing's B-29s, plus a heavy naval bombardment followed by carrier plane attacks, the Japanese troops were generally unhurt. Nor did they come out to meet the invaders head on, as once they might have; instead, the Japanese waited in their caves and dugouts to render the taking of Iwo Jima a foot-by-foot nightmare. Instead of the planned-for two weeks, the securing of Iwo Jima required twice that time (and even after that, Marines and Army soldiers continued to flush out—and kill—the more recalcitrant of Kuribayashi's men). Nearly five thousand American lives were exchanged for that small island, and the wounded numbered well over twenty thousand. Japanese dead reached an estimated total of twenty-one thousand; about two hundred were taken prisoner. The savage fighting, deadly, resolute, and for the Japanese, to the death, was a devastating foreshadowing of what lay in the future.

As the casualties mounted the question was asked in stateside papers, "Is Iwo Jima worth the price?" —an insignificant little volcanic dot of no apparent strategic value. But even before the fighting had reached its full fury and the landing strips were fully readied by the Seabees and Air Force aviation engineers, the first B-29 landed on Iwo on March 4. Lieutenant Raymond Malo, whose plane had developed fuel problems, had to make a choice between ditching and violating orders: they were, not to land at Iwo Jima, which was not yet ready for them.

It was a relatively simple choice: Malo set course for Iwo. He first quizzed the crew, warning them that finding Iwo without radar (that too had malfunctioned) would be its own little problem; in addition, the war was still going on there, the runways were probably too short for the B-29 (the Tinian strip was eighty-five hundred feet, the Iwo strip four thousand feet), and there might be other problems. The crew voted for Iwo Jima.

Navigator Bernard Bennison, despite the poor weather and with no radar, found the island, and Malo, with copilot Edward Mochler, brought the big, sixty-ton aircraft onto the short runway with a squeal of brakes, the stench of burning rubber, and the information from the tower that the strip was under Japanese mortar fire. The landing was extremely delicate, for Malo and Mochler, in deference to the short and narrow runway, had to bring the plane in at near-stall air speed. With the crew at crash positions the pilots throttled back until the great plane all but dropped the few final feet to the runway. They were on land, but would they stay there? As they careened down the strip it seemed to contract with each fraction of a moment. With Mochler applying full brakes, with full flaps down, Malo attempted to keep the racing monster under control. Finally he kicked full left rudder, a telephone pole snapped as one wing flicked against it, and the plane came to a halt.

The Japanese immediately increased mortar fire on the strip, hoping to destroy the prize. But four hours later, after two thousand gallons of fuel had been poured into the B-29 by hand, Malo managed to take off from the strip using up only twenty-five hundred feet of runway. His plane and its eleven-man crew returned safely to Tinian (and no official reprimand, for he had already proved the value of taking Iwo Jima). Malo's B-29 was the first of twenty-four hundred Superfortresses that would land in distress upon Iwo Jima's two strips. Thus about twenty-five thousand men, a fraction at least of which might have been lost if they had been forced to ditch, landed safely on the ugly little island. Its importance to the final surrender of Japan is unquestionable. It would be impossible—and pointless —to attempt to compare the lives lost in taking the island with those saved after it was taken. Perhaps the best tribute was that of an anonymous B-29 pilot who said, "Whenever I land on this island, I thank God and the men who fought for it."

Certain Air Force commanders, among them Spaatz and LeMay, believed that Japan could be bombed into submission by the B-29s, but the Army commanders did not share that belief. The next step then was to take another island close to Japan, one large enough to serve as a staging area for the proposed invasion of the home islands. Formosa (Taiwan) had been bypassed in favor of the Philippine invasion; besides, it was heavily fortified and garrisoned. It was decided that next on the central Pacific schedule, therefore, should be one of the Ryukyu Islands, Okinawa, which lay about 350

miles south of Kyushu, the southernmost of the home islands of Japan.

And it was at Okinawa that the divine wind consummated its most lethal frenzy.

Following the abandonment of the Philippines the surviving naval air fleets were regrouped or combined with untried units into four air fleets—the First (at Formosa), the Third (in the Kanto Plain

*Iwo as a hazardous haven: a damaged B-29, unable to make it all the way back to Saipan, made an emergency landing on Iwo. With brakes locked, the bomber turned into a line-up of Mustangs and crushed four before coming to a stop and bursting into flame. Only two members of the crew were injured seriously enough to require hospitalization.* (U. S. AIR FORCE)

area), the Fifth (on Kyushu), and the Tenth, which was still, around the beginning of 1945, undergoing basic training and stationed on the main island of Honshu. Like the Tenth, the Fifth Air Fleet had not completed its training, so that the Imperial High Command saw nothing in the future for these two air fleets (of about a thousand planes) except special attacks. The more advanced Fifth would be expended upon enemy task forces and the unskilled Tenth on transports and lesser craft.

The Army air forces too were expected to participate in the special attacks, although never with quite

*The invasion of Okinawa begins and the* Franklin *is hit by bombs of a Japanese dive bomber.*
(NAVY DEPT., NATIONAL ARCHIVES)

the dedication as the Navy. In fact, only the Navy special attack pilots were called kamikaze pilots; the Army used the term *Tokko Tai,* an abbreviation of the official *Tokubetsu Kogekitai* (Special Attack Unit).

From the time Ohnishi had fled the Philippines in January until the invasion of Okinawa on Easter Sunday (April 1, 1945), the kamikaze concept spread and the organization solidified—as did the belief that suicide attacks would be the only means of stopping the enemy. The Imperial Navy was all but non-existent—only the great battleship *Yamato* remained of the superbattleships; the *Haruna,* the last remaining battleship of the *Kongo* class, was under repair. The decisive battle must take place in the air above and around Okinawa.

The opening action of the Okinawa campaign was carried out by carrier planes of Mitscher's Task Force 58, which during the period March 18–21 lashed out at airfields at Kyushu and shipping targets in the Inland Sea at Kure and Kobe. During these strikes, particularly those upon Kure Harbor, Japanese antiaircraft proved most effective and thirteen U. S. Navy planes were lost. Also the carrier *Franklin* became the victim of a lone single-engined Japanese plane, which placed two bombs upon the deck. The resulting fires, as well as the initial explosions, took a heavy toll in lives: more than 700 (and 265 wounded). The *Franklin,* although badly damaged, was towed out of the battle by the heavy cruiser *Pittsburgh.* Heavy air cover protected the

*The* Franklin, *burning and listing, and out of the battle for Okinawa.* (NAVY DEPT., NATIONAL ARCHIVES)

stricken carrier from further Japanese attack and the *Franklin* eventually arrived (after a twelve-thousand-mile voyage and only one stop between) in New York for repairs.

On the final day of the preliminary strikes, March 21, a large number of bogies were detected upon the radar screens and an equally large force of Hellcats (about 150) was scrambled to intercept. Two dozen Hellcats from the *Hornet, Bennington, Wasp,* and *Belleau Wood* were the first to meet the Japanese force of Betty bombers with Zeke escort. The first elements of Bettys and Zekes were disposed of in a brief, ferocious encounter, during which two of the Hellcats were lost.

The Navy pilots were especially surprised at how vulnerable some of the Bettys appeared to be—slower and less maneuverable than normally. Some even appeared to have a curious additional wing beneath the main wing. Unknown to the Hellcat pilots, they had broken up the first attempt at an *Ohka* bombing of the U.S. fleet.

The *Ohka* ("cherry blossom") bomb was a small glider, twenty feet long with a sixteen-foot wing span, with rocket boosters in the tail and a ton of explosives in the nose. It was literally a flying bomb with one exception: a pilot who guided it. The *Ohka* was carried under the fuselage of a Betty to the general target area, where the kamikaze pilot would transfer from the mother ship (through the bomb bay) into the tiny cockpit of the flying bomb. About twenty or thirty miles from the target, the *Ohka* was released and alternately gliding and rocketing would attain a speed of more than five hundred miles an hour by the time it was within striking distance of American ships. The *Ohka,* brain child of one Ensign Mitsuo Ohta, was a hard-luck design. An early shipment of fifty, for example, was lost when the battleship-turned-carrier carrying them, the *Shinano,* was sent to the bottom by a submarine early in November.

Likewise, the initial *Ohka* mission, which had consisted of eighteen Bettys (sixteen carrying the *Ohka*) and thirty fighters (of the fifty-five originally assigned), fared poorly. The Japanese formation got no closer than fifty or sixty miles to the American warships before it clashed with the Hellcats. Most of the Bettys managed to jettison their encumbering *Ohkas* (the suicide pilots, of course, remained in the bombers), but of the eighteen that had taken off

*Japanese-manned flying torpedo, the* Ohka *("cherry blossom") bomb, which was carried to its objectives by a bomber and released near the target. The small wooden craft carried more than a ton of explosives in its nose.* (NAVY DEPT., NATIONAL ARCHIVES)

*A pre-kamikaze flight ceremony. Before taking off, the pilots went through a formal ceremony of a religious nature. It was a solemn rite, much like a funeral, which, in effect, it was.* (U. S. AIR FORCE)

only three escaped destruction under the guns of the Hellcats. These three, one of them carrying the leader of the mission, Lieutenant Commander Goro Nonaka, slipped into a cloud bank. Even so, they were never heard from again. The fighter escort too was heavily decimated, and the first mission of the "cherry blossoms" was an abject failure.

When the *Ohka* appeared in the Okinawa area itself its name was quickly changed from the poetic cherry blossom by the U.S. sailors to a more blunt, precise *Baka* ("stupid"). It was not an inappropriate designation, considering the ultimate performance of the *Baka:* of the eight hundred manufactured fifty were used in suicide missions and three actually exploded on target. While the concept was *baka,* indeed, the devotion and courage of the *Ohka* pilots were exceptional.

## v

When U. S. Army and Marine troops swarmed across the beaches on the East China Sea side of Okinawa on Easter Sunday morning, 1945, it appeared that the Japanese, unaccountably, had complied on this occasion with the treaty wrested from the Okinawans by Commodore Matthew C. Perry in 1854 (a quarter of a century before the Japanese annexed the Ryukyus).

"Hereafter," the treaty read, "whenever citizens of the United States come to Lew Chew [the original name of the Ryukyus], they shall be treated with great courtesy and friendship." And so it seemed to the citizens of the United States—about fifty thousand strong—who splashed ashore on "L-Day"—"L" for Landing. Resistance was so feeble that the Marines referred to it as "Love Day."

They had not expected this as they moved ashore taking two airfields and spread over a beachhead roughly eight miles wide and three to four miles deep. Okinawa, even those most ignorant of strategy realized, would be the prelude to the Last Battle—and it would have to be deadly and vicious. When an eager young Marine lieutenant attempted to explicate the taking of Okinawa into the Grand Strategy, he told his men, "From Okinawa we can bomb the Japs anywhere—Japan, China, Formosa . . ."

"Yeah," was the characteristic comment by the typical tough, realistic sergeant, "and vice versa."

It was food for thought and worry. Besides, as the ships stood off the beaches Tokyo Rose had promised them ill. "This is the Zero Hour, boys. It is broadcast for all you men in the Pacific, particularly those standing off the shores of Okinawa—because many of you will never hear another program. . . .

"Here's a good number," she purred, " 'Going

Home' . . . nice work if you can get it. . . . You boys off Okinawa listen and enjoy it while you can, because when you're dead you're a long time dead. . . ."

Later she would broadcast some of the latest hit records from the States—Miller, Dorsey, James. "Let's have a little jukebox music for the boys and make it hot. The boys are going to catch hell soon, and they might as well get used to the heat. . . ."

"Love Day" had not been hot at all and they went in "standing up," not as at Tarawa, Guadalcanal, or Iwo at all. Only skirmishes marred the calm. By the second day Major General Pedro del Valle, commanding the 1st Marine Division, called a press conference and said, "I don't know where the Japs are, and I can't offer you any good reason why they let us come ashore so easily. We're pushing on across the island as fast as we can move the men and equipment." The anticipated "most fanatical" resistance had simply not materialized.

Not yet and not for some days. ". . . Love Day turned into Honeymoon Week at Okinawa," Marine historian Robert Leckie observed. But then the honeymoon ended.

Okinawa was visualized by the Japanese High Command as a kind of massive sponge which would absorb American blood, ships, and aircraft, a tropical Stalingrad, perhaps. The island commander, capable, quiet Lieutenant General Mitsuru Ushijima, deployed his Thirty-second Army through the hills, cliffs, and caves of the southern third of the long (about sixty miles), narrow (ranging from two to eighteen miles) island. The bulk of Ushijima's roughly hundred thousand troops (about a fifth of whom were reluctant Okinawans) were concentrated in the southern third of the island; another, smaller, concentration was dug in to the north, on the Motobu Peninsula, off which lay the tiny Ie Shima (on which the beloved war correspondent Ernie Pyle was to be killed by a sniper on L plus 17).

The plan was to hold out as long as possible, killing the American invader, and to keep the American fleet within striking distance of the kamikazes. Okinawa would be the great proving ground for Ohnishi's Divine Wind. Ushijima's men would engage the ground troops while the kamikaze pilots—and suicide boats on the surface—eliminated the

American fleet. This accomplished, there would be no invasion—or else the Americans would be so badly torn up that their invasion attempt of Japan (finally set for November 1, 1945) would be weakened. Once again a kind of grim optimism emboldened the Japanese. Major General Isamu Cho, Ushijima's chief of staff, had traveled to the homeland from Okinawa to present Ushijima's plan for the defense of Okinawa to the High Command and returned not only with approval of the static defense plan but also with a high regard for the promise of the reorganized and augmented Special Attack Corps. Cho, hard-bitten, driving, and not very popular as Ushijima's tough right arm, returned to Okinawa in an expectant state, informing the commanders of the Thirty-second Army of the promise: "The brave ruddy-faced warriors with the white silken scarves tied about their heads, at peace in their favorite planes, dash out spiritedly to the attack. The skies are brightening."

In reality it was the glow of the setting sun; the brightness was the glare of sudden, violent, meaningless, and prodigal death. The major thrust of the kamikaze operations came from bases in southern Kyushu. The Formosa-based Special Attack Corps contributed little to the Okinawa campaign and Ohnishi himself was transferred to Japan to serve as vice-chief of the Naval General Staff. His forceful, outspoken devotion to an absolute Japanese-American Armageddon only added to his already tarnished popularity in Tokyo. So, with pervasive asperity, a sense of frustration and humiliation, Ohnishi—who had blueprinted Yamamoto's Hawaii Operation, which, despite his own doubts, had proved extravagantly successful—was forced to await the end in an office in Tokyo.

Yamamoto's chief of staff at the time of the Hawaii Operation, Vice-Admiral Matome Ugaki (who had escaped death when his chief was killed in the attack by the P-38s over Ballale) was given command of the Fifth Air Fleet, which, in turn, was placed under operational control of the Third and Tenth Air Fleets. Direction of the kamikaze attacks during the Okinawa campaign devolved upon Ugaki. When he had assumed his new post before the Pearl Harbor attack Ugaki had said in an impassioned speech to flag officers at naval headquarters in Tokyo that the "success of our surprise attack on Pearl Harbor will prove to be the Waterloo of the war to follow."

But whose Waterloo? Ugaki had falsified the results of the Midway war games, making it appear that Japan must be the victor in that battle—and the actual outcome was its own Waterloo. Ugaki, like Ohnishi, had been in on events from the glorious inception and was destined to play his role to the bitter end. His three air fleets could muster a combined strength of about 1815 aircraft, of which 540 were set aside for special attacks. The Sixth Army Air Force was ordered to co-operate with Ugaki's naval planes in annihilating the enemy in and around Okinawa. Besides the aircraft there remained also a fraction of the once proudly numerous Combined Fleet. Only one battleship, the superb *Yamato,* was operational at the time of the Okinawa invasion. There was, too, the light cruiser *Yahagi* and a handful (eight) of destroyers. This pitiable remnant was called the Second Fleet and placed under the command of Vice-Admiral Seiichi Ito; captain of the formidable *Yamato* was Kosaku Aruga. When this force sortied from the Inland Sea on April 6, 1945, the name had been changed to "Special Surface Attack Force."

The 10-ship fleet, without air cover, was intended to challenge Admiral Spruance's Fifth Fleet, which consisted of some 1500 ships. Among these, which included transports of the amphibious forces, minesweepers, salvage ships, and repair vessels, there were more than 40 carriers, 18 battleships, and 200 destroyers. Task Force 58, the Fast Carrier Force under Mitscher, itself was made up of over 100 ships, 10 of them heavy carriers and 6 escort carriers. Co-operating with the Americans was Task Force 57, 22 British ships under the command of Vice-Admiral H. B. Rawlings. Aboard the British carriers were 244 aircraft, while the American carriers could put up 919 planes, fighters, dive bombers, and torpedo planes. To augment the carrier air forces, the Okinawa invasion plan called for the establishment of a Tactical Air Force on the island itself as soon as possible. This would consist of Marine units as well as U. S. Army Air Force fighter, medium and heavy bomber groups; these forces would be under the command of a Marine, Major General Francis P. Mulcahy.

The invasion of Okinawa, code-named "Opera-

*Navy 40-mm. guns firing at kamikaze planes.*
(NAVY DEPT., NATIONAL ARCHIVES)

aiding the troops already ashore, where Ushijima's men would wipe them out.

In every aspect the *Kikusui* plan was suicidal; it was not even a gamble. It began with the early morning attack launched from Kanoya and Formosa, both kamikaze and conventional attackers taking part. Although the exact numbers that participated in this first, largest *Kikusui* attack cannot be determined with any accuracy, at least 198 suicide planes attacked the American fleet on April 6 (the attack, continued into the next day, is believed to have consisted of about 355 kamikaze planes alone, with perhaps an equal number of conventional planes participating).

The air filled with unreasoning death as hundreds of kamikazes swept in upon the concentration of American ships. This concentration was capable of ripping the very air to shreds with its antiaircraft guns, numbering literally in the thousands. Despera-

tion Iceberg," was the "most audacious and complex enterprise yet undertaken by the American amphibious forces," according to British observers. And, indeed, it was. It was also the bloodiest battle of the war; the spirit of "Love Day" had not persisted.

The Japanese name for the hellish reaction to the Okinawa invasion was beautiful, *Kikusui* ("floating chrysanthemum," obviously inspired by the banner of a fourteenth-century warrior patriot, Masashige Kusunoki, who led his men to certain death in the Battle of Minatogawa). The first *Kikusui* attack was scheduled to take place on April 6 and 7 and would be a mass, combined Navy and Army suicide plane attack in which the Second Fleet—the "Special Surface Attack Force" spearheaded by the *Yamato*—would participate. It was hoped that the *Yamato* and the nine other ships in the fleet would lure the American carrier planes away from Okinawa while the kamikaze planes, Navy and Army, dealt with the American fleet. Thus off balance, the Americans might not be capable of

*A Judy falls to the guns of the* Wasp *near Okinawa.*
(NAVY DEPT., NATIONAL ARCHIVES)

tion inspired the men aboard the ships to feats of remarkable endurance and firepower. Din and clatter, shouts and curses, the sound of a thousand rapid-firing guns, the cry of straining engines as a Zeke attempted to break through the myriad of black puffs: all these merged into a jungle of sound.

When word had come of large groups of bogies on the ship's radars, torpedo planes and bombers were struck below decks, their bombs removed and their fuel tanks emptied. Hellcats were quickly readied and the fighters of Task Force 58 were launched to meet the enemy. Combat Air Patrol planes met the first attackers midway between Kyushu and Okinawa and began shooting them out of the sky. But they came on like a swarm of hornets, singly and in large groups of thirty or more. The Japanese planes ranged from the most recent Zeke or Tony to ancient fabric-covered biplanes; few if any experienced pilots guided these planes, for the Task Force 58 airmen were amazed at the easy mark they made. By sheer weight of numbers, however, some of the suicide planes broke through the CAP, only to be met by the guns of the radar picket ships—destroyers which had been set out around the major ship concentration at Okinawa.

Antiaircraft fire stopped 39 of the kamikazes, which splashed and cartwheeled into the Pacific; escort carrier planes accounted for another 55 and the fighters of Task Force 58 destroyed 233 before they could do any damage. But 22 kamikaze planes dashed through the curtain of fire and spread havoc among the ships. As it would develop through the remaining nine major *Kikusui* attacks (from April 6 through June 22), the radar pickets suffered the worst of the attacks. The picket ships were not only bombed, but also took the brunt of the "floating chrysanthemums." On April 6 Radar Stations No. 1 (destroyer *Bush*) and No. 2 (destroyer *Calhoun*) were both sunk under the fury of the mass attacks. By the next day, when the attacks diminished, twenty-two other ships had taken kamikaze hits. Another destroyer, the *Emmons,* was sunk; 466 men were dead and 568 horribly wounded by fire. *Kikusui* No. 1, though heavily sacrificial, had hurt the American fleet. Reports, in fact, from the Thirty-second Army on Okinawa claimed that thirty American ships were seen sinking and an additional twenty or more burning. Because of the smoke-blackened skies, Japanese reconnaissance planes

*A twin-engined suicide plane falls short of an escort carrier after being attacked by a Marine Corsair and finished off by a Navy gun crew.*
(NAVY DEPT., NATIONAL ARCHIVES)

were unable to check the Army's extravagant report.

But *Kikusui* No. 1 had one more act to go: the drama of the Second Fleet. Before setting out Admiral Ito sent a message to the crews of the ten ships in his force in which he said that the "fate of the homeland rests on this operation. Our ships have been organized as a surface special attack corps. . . . Every unit participating in this operation, whether or not it has been assigned for a special attack, is expected to fight to the bitter end. Thereby the enemy will be annihilated and the eternal foundations of our motherland will be secured."

The *Yamato,* which had fuel enough to get to Okinawa only, was to shell the American positions with its giant 18.1 guns (which outranged any gun in the American or British fleets), while closer in the light cruiser *Yahagi* and the eight destroyers would do the same. The *Yamato* was the last survivor of the once great battleship array of the Japanese fleet (the *Haruna* was then under repair and was in fact the last surviving Japanese battleship; the *Yamato* was the last of the giants). American planes had contended with the big battleship on three other occasions: Midway, the Marianas, and Leyte Gulf, but the mammoth had escaped despite hits.

In the evening of April 6 the American submarines *Hackleback* and *Threadfin* reported the emergence of the Surface Special Attack Force from the Inland Sea through the Bungo Strait. There was literally no air cover, for the few planes which provided it were land-based and were forced to leave as soon as they had reached their maximum range. The one-way navy continued on through the night.

Word having reached Spruance and Mitscher of the approaching Japanese force, Mitscher immediately sent three of his task groups north to intercept. At dawn of April 7 forty Hellcats fanned out to the north and west searching for the *Yamato* and company. An *Essex* plane sighted the ships passing through Van Diemen Strait just south of Kyushu at eight twenty-three in the morning. The force seemed to be heading into the East China Sea away from Okinawa. Ito, however, was hoping to

elude the carrier planes by taking a course beyond their range. If lucky, he could approach Okinawa from the west and open up with his big guns—guns that hurled a projectile of more than a ton over a distance exceeding twenty miles. In the hold there were a thousand of these missiles.

The weather was not ideal: a low cloud ceiling (three thousand feet) with visibility from five to eight miles, hampered by rain squalls. As Ito watched from his bridge on the *Yamato,* the American planes gathered in the distance, first a few, then many. About half past twelve the first attack came. Although antiaircraft fire was intense it was not accurate and the Helldivers and Avengers swooped down upon the Japanese ships. Within ten minutes two bombs had struck the *Yamato* and an additional rent opened up its side as an Avenger placed a torpedo in its path. The *Yahagi* too had been hurt and for the next two hours scores of Avengers, Hellcats, and Helldivers slashed and ripped at the hapless ships. The *Yahagi* was the first to go, its deck a shambles and a slaughterhouse under the blows of a dozen bombs and seven torpedoes. The destroyers too suffered heavily, although they were not the major objectives: but the carrier planes sent four—the *Isokaze, Hamakaze,*

*A kamikaze falls short of an escort carrier off Okinawa.* (NAVY DEPT., NATIONAL ARCHIVES)

*Kasumi,* and *Asashimo*—to the bottom before the battle was over.

It was the *Yamato* that was the prize, however. After the first attack the big ship took a list to port but continued on course at a good speed and remained very active with antiaircraft fire. Desperately, Captain Aruga ordered the ship on a zigzag course, hoping to throw off the aim of the attackers. But there were too many of them. *Intrepid* planes swarmed around the ship with bombs and torpedoes, adding further to the battlewagon's distress. Then six *Yorktown* Avengers appeared on the scene. Because of the list to port, the starboard side had lifted from the water, exposing the thinner underplating of the "invincible" *Yamato.* The Avengers circled around to the starboard; torpedoes were set for a depth of from ten to twenty feet—and the Grummans dropped down for the run on the *Yamato.* The upper decks, as with the *Yahagi,* had been reduced to twisted wreckage, and the once formidable gun batteries were either silent or desultory, so that the Avengers made perfect runs; all six fish pierced the exposed underbelly.

A series of explosions shook the gigantic ship as if it were a child's toy in a bathtub. A thousand men below decks were trapped and had no chance to get out. On the bridge a typical argument ensued. Captain Aruga had ordered his executive officer to tie him to the remains of the bridge. He was afraid that if he once got into the water he would instinctively save himself. As the waves washed around him and the deck assumed an acute slant, Aruga spoke to Admiral Ito, commander of the no longer existing Second Fleet.

"You are indispensable," Aruga said. "Please leave the ship."

But Ito chose to remain; there would be no world for him in which Japan was vanquished and in which aircraft had written the final chapter in the history of the proud battleship.

The ship tipped and below decks the big shells rolled across the deck of the ammunition room. More explosions followed and the ship, 863 feet in length, turned over and churned to the bottom of the East China Sea, exploding and detonating as its compartments burst under air pressure and exploding ammunition. At two twenty-three in the afternoon of April 7, 1945, the world's greatest battleship no longer existed. And, for that matter,

neither did the Japanese Imperial Fleet (the last battleship, the *Haruna,* originally announced sunk by Captain Colin Kelly's B-17 attack early in the war, was sunk by carrier planes in its own dock at Kure Harbor on July 28, 1945). The death toll on the *Yamato* alone was 2488; the cost to the Navy attackers was four Helldivers, three Avengers, and three Hellcats (four pilots and eight aircrews were lost). During the battle the carrier *Hancock* was crashed by kamikaze planes twice with a toll of about seventy seamen killed.

*Kikusui* No. 1 had, like *Sho*-1, succeeded in its predicted Japanese losses, but it had decided nothing. Japan's military future now lay in the systematic, inconclusive pursuit of death.

This pursuit continued for the following several months, literally until the August surrender. In between the *Kikusui* mass raids, small groups or individual attacks also took place, so that from April through August it was impossible for the men in the

*The* Bunker Hill *shortly after being hit by a kamikaze during the sixth* Kikusui, *May 11, 1945.*

(NAVY DEPT., NATIONAL ARCHIVES)

*Flight deck of the* Bunker Hill, *with the fire nearly under control but with aircraft destroyed and men dead and guns not manned.*

ships in the Okinawa area to relax. The ten *Kikusui* assaults opened with the climax, during the April 6-7 raid, when six American ships were sunk and seventeen damaged (ten seriously enough to be out of the war for the duration). The other *Kikusui* attacks, with American losses from U. S. Navy sources, were:

|      |            |                     |
|------|------------|---------------------|
| *2.* | April 12-13 | 2 sunk; 9 damaged  |
| *3.* | April 15-16 | 1 sunk; 6 damaged  |
| *4.* | April 27-28 | 1 sunk; 4 damaged  |
| *5.* | May 3-4     | 6 sunk; 6 damaged  |
| *6.* | May 10-11   | 0 sunk; 4 damaged  |
| *7.* | May 23-25   | 3 sunk; 6 damaged  |
| *8.* | May 27-28   | 1 sunk; 7 damaged  |
| *9.* | June 3-7    | 0 sunk; 3 damaged  |
| *10.*| June 21-22  | 1 sunk; 4 damaged  |

These were but the major concerted Japanese Army and Navy attacks. Also there were rare lulls, while the Japanese scrounged more aircraft and impressed more young pilots into the Special Attack Corps. Weather too intervened. Even so, to the men on the American ships it was a rare day,

indeed, when they were not under the horror of the lunatic attacks.

During the second *Kikusui* another innovation fell upon them when Lieutenant Saburo Dohi piloted an *Ohka* bomb into the destroyer *Stanley;* Dohi had climbed into his flying bomb assuming that his target was a battleship. Of the eight *Ohka*-carrying bombers that were dispatched on April 12, only one—the one that had transported Dohi to the target area—returned. The others were destroyed before doing any damage. Dohi's *Ohka* did strike, but the *Stanley* was not seriously damaged. On the same day the destroyer *Mannert L. Abele* was crashed by a Zeke kamikaze; after being hit by what may have been an *Ohka,* the ship seemed to dissolve and sank within five minutes, with a loss of seventy-nine of the crew.

The special attacks did not, as the Japanese High Command so fervently believed, alter the course of the war. This must have been obvious even before all the chrysanthemums had fallen, but the mania grew more and more incurable as the situation grew worse. However, if the purpose of going out to battle is to kill, maim, and destroy (once accepting your own destruction as part of the price), then the kamikazes were a great success. The fiery charnel house each plane created when it struck was all but unspeakable.

"The deck near my [gun] mount was covered with blood, guts, brains, tongues, scalps, hearts, arms etc. from the Jap pilots," wrote Seaman First Class James J. Fahey in his *Pacific War Diary* aboard the *Montpelier* (in the Leyte Gulf area). "They had to put the hose on to wash the blood off the deck. The deck ran red with blood. The Japs were spattered all over the place. One of the fellows had a Jap scalp, it looked like you skinned an animal. The hair was black, but very short and the color of the skin was yellow, real Japanese. I do not think he was very old. I picked up a tin pie plate with a tongue on it. The pilots tooth mark was into it very deep. It was very big and long, it looked like part of his tonsils were attached to it. . . . This was the first time I ever saw a person's brains, what a mess. . . ."

Throughout the *Kikusui* attacks, the radar picket ships, stationed around Okinawa in all directions ranging in distances from eighteen to ninety-five miles out, bore the brunt of the devastation. If these ships were eliminated, the Japanese believed, it would be possible to get through to the more important larger ships closer to Okinawa. The pickets then became the most frequently struck victims. One enterprising seaman, after days of attack, put a sign out on his ship: THAT WAY TO THE CARRIERS.

But the only sure method of disrupting a suicide attacker who had slipped past the combat air patrol was to shoot him out of the air before he came in close enough to read the sardonic message. When a heavy raid developed there were simply too many targets to shoot at. During the fifth *Kikusui* (on May 3) the destroyer *Aaron Ward* rang with General Quarters at six twenty-two in the evening. In seven minutes a tiny speck materialized out of the sunset. Another minute, during which there had been a general intake of breath aboard the ship, and the speck became a Val. The guns of the *Aaron Ward* boomed and roared when the Japanese plane was still seven thousand yards dis-

tant. It would have been impossible, what with the massive cone of fire vectored on the lone plane, to have missed. The Val smoked but continued on its path toward the ship. It had already assumed the kamikaze approach dive before, at five hundred yards, a five-inch projectile from the *Aaron Ward*'s No. 53 Mount made a direct hit. The Val blew up, still coming on, and splashed into the water about a hundred yards from the ship. As the gunners watched spellbound, the Japanese pilot was hurled by the impact of the crash over the ship's deck and into the water on the other side. Parts of the wrecked Val smashed into the ship; the engine rammed into No. 53 Mount, putting it out of action for a while. Even when the engine was removed the mount would operate only on difficult manual control.

The Val's propeller whirled across the water and cut its way into the after deckhouse, where it jammed the door of the after passageway. The clean-up crew there found the pilot's boot near the deckhouse; his foot was still in it.

There was no time for speculation, for another Val appeared bearing down from the port bow, but that one splashed twelve hundred yards out, with no damage to the ship. Suddenly a Zeke came in from the port, undetected by radar but spotted by the gun captain of No. 42 Mount. Nothing seemed capable of stopping the Zeke, which magnified in size with alarming speed. When it was within a hundred yards the Zeke had begun to smoke and its bomb fell from underneath the belly—but struck the port side of the ship under No. 44 Gun. The Zeke continued on to wrap its flaming wreckage around the ship's superstructure.

The bomb struck the *Aaron Ward* below the water line, ripping open fifty feet of the hull upon exploding in the after engine room. The rudder jammed and the ship began circling to port as fuel from ruptured lines fed the flames topside. The deck was a shambles and a caldron. All men but two around No. 44 Gun were dead, burned to cinders, blown overboard, or just simply "missing," never to appear again. The wounded, burned and with broken limbs, writhed out of the way of the fire fighters. The horror of the kamikaze attack lay as much in its sensless persistence as in the gruesome details of the aftermath.

Was it the perverse human instinct for harassing

cripples? Despite the obvious fact that the *Aaron Ward* was listing, burning, and running in circles, this did not divert other kamikazes from hitting the ship again and again. The nearby *Little* was stricken too, so badly that it eventually sank (as did two other destroyers, the *Luce* and *Morrison*).

For an hour or more the Japanese aircraft sprinted in on Radar Picket 10—some splashed and others contributed to the misery aboard the mangled destroyers. The still operating gun mounts on the *Aaron Ward* spat out fire and succeeded in knocking down ten kamikazes before they reached the ship. Marine Corsairs from Okinawa strips some seventy miles away bore in to stop the ravaging planes. Even as they swept in to destroy the Zekes, Vals, and Bettys, the Corsairs suffered the hazards of "friendly fire," for the gunners on the beleaguered ships, overwrought, weary, and in pain, hated all things that flew; and there was no time to discriminate between friend and foe.

The fifth aircraft splashed in that flaming twilight was a twin-engined Betty, which burst into flame and went spinning into the water. The geyser of the impact had barely settled before two more Vals appeared; these had Marine Corsairs on their tails and in the near-surface battle one of the Vals erupted burning fragments and crashed into the water. But the other Val came on in a precipitous dive. All guns trained on the lone attacker, who appeared to ride in on the tracers. It capered through the serried air, its nose growing ever larger, its wings widening, reeling and yawing from hits— but coming on nonetheless. Suddenly it jinked, the nose snapped up, a wing dropped, and the Val cleared the bridge, its high wing ripping through the lines of the signal halyards, wrenched out most of the signal antennas, crunched the top of the forward stack, and, in a shower of debris, cartwheeled across the starboard rail into the sea.

The din that followed in the Val's wake was something out of a nightmare. The Val's slashing plunge across the deck had opened up steam lines to the ship's whistle and siren, which now hooted and shrieked in a crescendo of pandemonium. One sailor, a survivor of the sunken *Little* (not understanding the plight of the *Aaron Ward* nor noting the fires aboard), pondered in his own misery the sanity of a ship that, in mid-battle, would do nothing but go around in circles whistling and hooting.

This ludicrous situation was not appreciated by the men of the *Aaron Ward;* there were the wounded to care for, men whose burned flesh dripped from them as they moved, and the dead to identify, if possible. There were raging fires below decks and the word came round that the ship's sinking was imminent. No word to abandon ship came, however.

But another Val came in, the pilot strafing a path before him toward the bridge itself. No. 42 Gun's crew stood its ground in the face of the onslaught until a stream of fire chopped off a wing. But momentum carried the plane forward as the bomb fell short of the ship; the plane struck in a fiery mass onto the main deck and the bomb burst in the water adjacent to the ship. A hammer blow shook the *Aaron Ward,* a hole ripped into the forward fireroom, and the flood which followed drowned the last operating engine.

The *Aaron Ward* lay smoldering dead in the water as out of nowhere an unseen kamikaze added its bomb, fuel, and flame to the agony. Seconds later another unseen attacker smashed into the main deck. To the men aboard the *Aaron Ward* their world, confined to the single ship, had become a fiery bedlam and charnel house; flames lit up the sky, thick smoke choked them, and the decks grew slick with blood. It seemed that they had taken all anyone could be expected to endure.

But that was not to be—a Zeke slashed in and slammed into No. 43 Gun, the crew of which vanished in a ball of flame. Others in the area of impact were seared by the fire, others disappeared in the explosion over the side. There was barely time to attend to the dead and dying before the tenth attacker appeared.

"Here comes another one!" someone shouted.

"God, we can't take another one," the ship's executive officer, Karl Neuport, muttered.

Low on the water, difficult to see in the smoke and darkness, the Japanese plane came at them first from the starboard and then from aft. The remaining guns chopped away at the plane, which whipped down on the *Aaron Ward* and shattered against the base of the after stack. The bomb detonated as the stack, fragments of the plane, a searchlight tower, and guns lifted into the heavens and showered death and dreadful pain onto the decks.

Horror had accumulated upon horror, but it was

The Aaron Ward *after enduring a series of kamikaze attacks.* (NAVY DEPT., NATIONAL ARCHIVES)

the final attack of the day. "The once trim *Aaron Ward* resembled a floating junk pile from the bridge aft," wrote Lieutenant Commander Arnold Lott. "Stacks, guns, searchlight tower, boats, everything was smashed and battered beyond recognition. Fires raged on deck, in the officer's and chief's quarters, in both clipping rooms, and in the after engine room. The main deck was only inches above water, both firerooms flooded, after engine room flooded, after diesel engine room, machine shop, shaft alleys, crew's bunkrooms, all flooded. Dead and wounded littered the wardroom, mess hall, sick bay, fantail and passageways." But the *Aaron Ward* remained afloat.

As rescue ships pulled alongside, it was a relief to realize that the ordeal was over; but for the afflicted it was not over. Forty-five men were ultimately listed as dead (some were never found); forty-nine were wounded, some fatally, many horribly. None of the survivors would ever forget the testing of the *Aaron Ward* during *Kikusui* No. 5.

Not all Japanese operations during the *Kikusui* mass attacks were suicidal. Conventional bombing missions were attempted (generally with poor results, as the bombers were stopped by carrier air-

craft or the Marine and Army fighters based on Okinawa). A steady combat air patrol was maintained over Okinawa at all times. During one of these during the morning of May 10, 1945 (which opened *Kikusui* No. 6), a four-plane (Corsair) division of Marines took off from their base at Kadena, Okinawa. Led by Captain Kenneth L. Reusser, the four planes were flown by members of VMF-312; Reusser's wingman was a Navy and Marine veteran, twenty-eight-year-old Lieutenant Robert L. Klingman of Binger, Oklahoma.

The Corsairs had climbed to about ten thousand feet to patrol over Ie Jima, just west of northern Okinawa, when at an altitude fifteen thousand feet above them they detected the contrails of a twin-engined Japanese plane. Throttling up their engines the four Corsairs set off in pursuit of the lone intruder. As they climbed, so did the Nick (Kawasaki Ki. 45), apparently out on a photographic mission. At thirty-two thousand feet one of the Corsairs had gone as high as it could go—the engine simply refused to lift it higher. Four thousand feet higher and another Corsair left the chase for the same reason. Reusser and Klingman persisted, firing some of their ammunition to lighten the load. Fi-

*Robert R. Klingman and the Corsair with which he chopped off the tail of a Japanese reconnaissance plane.* (WILLIAM BEALL/U. S. MARINE CORPS)

nally, at thirty-eight thousand feet, they reached the Nick's level. The Marine Corsairs closed in. Reusser opened up first and with his remaining ammunition shot up the Nick's left wing and engine. But the Nick continued on its way, with the rear gunner menacing the Corsairs but not firing.

Klingman soon learned why as he moved in to take up where Reusser had been forced to leave off. Hoping to make certain his .50-calibers could finish off the Nick he throttled to within fifty feet of the Japanese plane. But when he pressed the gun switch he found that at the high altitude his guns had frozen. Incensed, Klingman moved ever closer upon the Nick, determined to get the plane one way or the other. The Corsair was equipped with a massive thirteen-foot propeller and a rugged, powerful Pratt and Whitney eighteen-cylinder engine; since his guns had gone dead, Klingman was determined to employ some of his plane's other assets.

He charged the fleeing Nick and with his propel-

ler started hacking away at the tail assembly, biting pieces out of the rudder and nearly into the rear cockpit, in which the Japanese gunner furiously pounded away at his own frozen guns. The Nick flew on—and so did Klingman's Corsair. He brought it around again and this time sheared away the rudder completely and chewed away a piece of the right stabilizer. Still flying, Klingman jammed rudder, turned, and came in for the third time. His buzz saw propeller went to work again on the Nick. The stabilizer fluttered away into the slipstream and the Nick bucked into a spin. By the time it had fallen to fifteen thousand feet the wings had snapped from the fuselage, and the Nick plunged into the water below.

But Klingman had overstayed his patrol. Before he could return to Kadena—with Reusser providing ammunition-less protection—his fuel supply ran out. Even so, he succeeded in bringing the Corsair into VMF-312's strip on Okinawa with a dead stick. Klingman jumped from the plane to inspect the damage and found that a generous portion of propeller tip was missing; wing, engine, and fuselage

*The* Enterprise *loses its No. 1 elevator, blown hundreds of feet into the air after a suicide Zeke crashed into the carrier.* (NAVY DEPT., NATIONAL ARCHIVES)

*Carrier-based Corsairs leaving the* Essex *for a strike upon Formosa. While the fighting continued on Okinawa, carrier strikes upon Formosa as well as the*   *Japanese homeland were made to throw Japanese fighters off balance.* (NAVY DEPT., NATIONAL ARCHIVES)

were pocked and pieces of the Nick were found lodged in the Corsair's capacious cowling.

Klingman's adventure occurred during *Kikusui* No. 6; in the lull which followed sporadic kamikazes harried the invaders. During the early morning CAP on May 14, the *Enterprise,* 150 miles off the island of Kyushu, was alerted to individual or small attacks. One lone, determined Zeke broke through the Hellcats and the heavy 20-mm., 40-mm., and five-inch fire. As the Zeke came in close it appeared that he might overshoot, but at the last moment the pilot—whose name was Tomi Zai— flipped the Zeke onto its back and plunged inverted through the forward elevator. The flame shot out of the deck and the bomb continued through five decks before detonating. The explosion shot flames hundreds of feet into the air and No. 1 elevator ripped skyward four hundred feet above the flight deck of the *Enterprise.*

Tomi Zai had accomplished one of the few effective kamikaze attacks of the war. His crash had killed thirteen men and injured sixty-eight, but he also eliminated the *Enterprise* from battle for the rest of the war. There was, however, the other, eternal but: it did not alter the outcome.

After *Kikusui* No. 10, in late June, the kamikaze attacks waned except for rare, small flutters up to the moment of peace. Okinawa, eighty-two days after "Love Day," was declared secure by Marine Major General Roy S. Geiger, an airman who had led the fighting on Guadalcanal.

Except for skirmishes in isolated areas, or flushing still resisting remnants of the Japanese Thirty-second Army out of the hills and caves (often with napalm bombs lobbed into cave entrances), the fighting on Okinawa was ended. The technique of these mopping-up operations had been developed over more than eighty days of hard fighting. Close-support operations between ground and air men, called by Army Major General James L. Bradley (commander of the 96th Infantry Division) as "superior throughout," brought a scourge of napalm and rockets to the dug-in Japanese. Likewise, strafing runs upon Japanese positions directed by radio from the ground cleared the way for the advance of American ground troops. Especially effective in such operations was the Corsair, which earned the name from Marines of "Sweetheart of Okinawa." The Japanese name was not so affectionate. Because of the aircraft's characteristic sound, the result of the rush of air through the vents on its bent wings, it was feared by the Japanese and called "Whistling Death."

It had been one of the bloodiest campaigns in the history of American arms; for the U. S. Navy it was the costliest battle of the war. Most of the Japanese fought to the death, many dying in the final days of the battle in senseless banzai charges upon Marine and Army positions with no other ammunition but dirt to throw into the faces of the Americans. Great numbers committed suicide in a frenzy of slaughter by throat gashing, holding hand grenades to heads, or leaping from cliffs.

The island's top commanders, Ushijima and Cho, went out in proper style. On the morning of June 22, ceremoniously dressed, the two men were disemboweled in a cave within a hundred feet of advancing Marines. Their deaths added but 2 to the 110,000 Japanese who died on Okinawa (about 10,000 were actually rounded up alive and taken prisoner). American losses too were high: about 12,000 killed; of these about 4000 were Navy men. At least 80 per cent of these deaths (there was an equal number of wounded) could be attributed to the kamikazes. The toll was high, but not determinative. Okinawa only meant that the fight for Japan in the home islands would have to be horrific.

But those who knew realized that the kamikazes failed in their defined mission; they succeeded only in killing, maiming, and destroying equipment. The Japanese people were not aware of this failure, although the general issue of sharpened bamboo stakes with which to meet the expected invader should have inspired at least a glimmer of misgiving. That and the effects of LeMay's B-29 fire raids on city after city.

Following the *Kikusui* No. 3 raid (April 16), Radio Tokyo informed the Japanese people that:

393 American warships have been sunk or damaged by the divine wind attackers since March 23. This includes 21 carriers, 19 battleships, 16 battleships or large cruisers, 26 large-type warships, 55 cruisers, and 53 destroyers. 217 ships, including 85 of cruiser size or larger, have definitely been sunk. 60 per cent of the Allied fleet in the Okinawa area have either been sunk or damaged.

*Marines on Okinawa. As the fighting drew closer to Japan itself, it became more vicious than ever and required killing without mercy. This team—flame thrower and B.A.R. rifleman—stalks through the mist to clear caves of fanatical Japanese.*

(DEFENSE DEPT., MARINE CORPS)

The truth was that at that time, 14, not 217, ships had been sunk. Throughout the entire Okinawa campaign a total of 17 American ships (including one baby flattop) were actually sunk; observers of the kamikaze flights (those that returned) claimed 44. Claims were put forth for 99 ships damaged; actually 198 American ships were damaged. (It might be noted that no British carrier was seriously damaged during the Okinawa campaign, because of the armored flight decks.) To sink those 17 and damage the 198 ships kamikazes were dispatched 1809 times; of these 879 returned and 930 planes were expended. Nearly an equal number of Army suicide planes were sortied, besides conventional aircraft. During the Okinawa fighting nearly 8000 Japanese aircraft—and pilots—were lost of all types. But Okinawa had fallen and the enemy was camped within 350 miles of Japan—the tactics of desperation had not worked. (All kamikaze operations beginning with Leyte Gulf and ending at Okinawa had actually sunk 34 American ships, although official claims were made for 81; 288 had been damaged, claims were made for 195. These "triumphs" had been gained at the cost of 1228 aircraft, a fraction of which carried two men.)

It was during the Okinawa *Kikusui* missions that

*"Whistling Death" on Okinawa. A rocket-equipped Corsair provides close support for Marines clearing the hills of dug-in Japanese.*

(DAVID DUNCAN/MARINE CORPS)

*Marine airfield on Okinawa under a Japanese night attack; heavy American antiaircraft fire laces the sky.*

(DEFENSE DEPT., MARINE CORPS)

*The remains of what had once been a Japanese airfield on Okinawa. Bulldozed away, they made room for U. S. Marine and Navy aircraft.*
(DEFENSE DEPT., U. S. MARINE CORPS)

American airmen of the Twentieth Air Force incinerated Japanese in the homeland in vaster numbers than the falling chrysanthemums could ever achieve. For a time, from mid-April to May 11, LeMay's fire-spreading B-29s were diverted for the most part from their primary mission to attacks upon airfields on Kyushu and Shikoku. The objective of these diversions was to cripple the kamikaze effort

*Signal to close bomb bay doors. A B-29 being readied for a mission to Japan on Guam.* (U. S. AIR FORCE)

an obvious disenchantment with the kamikaze emerged. Rear Admiral Toshiyuki Yokoi, chief of staff of Fifth Air Fleet during the Okinawa campaign, noted that ". . . toward the last, the doomed pilots had good reason for doubting the validity of the cause in which they were told to die. The difficulties became especially apparent when men in aviation training were peremptorily ordered to the front and to death.

"When it came time for their takeoff, the pilots' attitude ranged from the despair of sheep headed for slaughter to open expressions of contempt for their superior officers. There were frequent and obvious cases of pilots returning from sorties claiming that they could not locate any enemy ships, and one pilot even strafed his commanding officer's quarters when he took off."

And to what purpose were they ordered to take off? Like Nicolai Rostov in *War and Peace,* the youthful Japanese pilots, sacrifices to the blindness and vanity of their elders, asked, "For what, then, those severed arms and legs, why those dead men?" When no reasonable answer was forthcoming, the shrieking horror of the divine wind became a whisper.

### VI

Even as the young Japanese kamikaze pilots incinerated young American seamen around Okinawa,

*Long lines of Superforts rumble on the runway to take off in massed attacks upon Japan.* (U. S. AIR FORCE)

*B-29s of the 73rd Bomb Wing skirt Fujiyama over Japan.* (U. S. AIR FORCE)

of Ukaki's units, besides destroying air installations and drawing off some of the aerial opposition from Okinawa.

Another diversion was the mining of Japanese waters, particularly in the Shimonoseki Strait between Kyushu and Honshu. Japanese shipping soon came to a practical standstill; in fact, the work of American submarines had nearly put it there even before the final blow was struck by Brigadier General John H. Davies' 313th Wing. It was because of this mining that the *Yamato* was forced to leave the Inland Sea via the Bungo Strait into the sights of U. S. Navy submarines and the bombs of carrier aircraft.

When he was released from the support of the Okinawa campaign, LeMay turned again to the desolation by fire of Japan's major industrial cities. Within a month—just before *Kikusui* No. 10—the campaign against the major cities—Tokyo, Nagoya, Kobe, Osaka, Yokohama, and Kawasaki—was over. One by one the cities were scratched off the target list. Not only had the industries of these cities been

destroyed, so had their people and vast areas of the cities. A third of Yokohama was burned in a single raid. On May 25 the second and last—and worst —fire raid was made upon Tokyo itself. Over five hundred B-29s appeared over the city at night and dropped their incendiaries, which burned sixteen

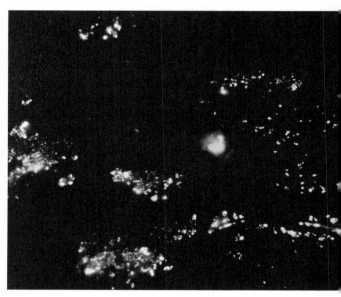

*The last fire raid on Tokyo, May 26, 1945: the first fires begin to flicker (left) and then spread widely over the city in the most destructive raid of all.*

(U. S. AIR FORCE)

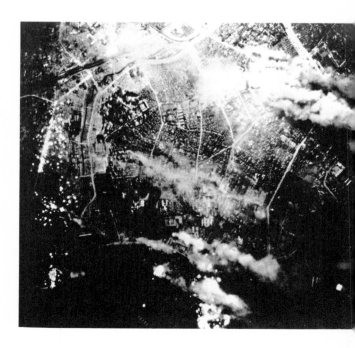

square miles out of the heart of the city. Antiaircraft fire that night was intense and twenty-six Superfortresses fell and a hundred returned to the Marianas with damages of varied seriousness. But when they had returned one half of Tokyo no longer existed. Even portions of the Emperor's sacred palace burned that night when the fires ran wild. The Emperor took this as a sign to his people that even he was not immune to attack and had no special dispensation from the gods.

The Emperor wrongly assumed that the palace had been deliberately bombed. But that was not the intent, for orders had long been in force to spare the Emperor. As Arnold had written to LeMay, "the Emperor of Japan is not at present a liability and may later become an asset." The fire in the palace raged for fourteen hours before it was brought under control. Twenty-eight members of the palace staff died in the fire, including twelve firemen who, because they had no orders to do otherwise, remained at their post in the path of the flames and burned.

The incendiary missions were supplemented by precision attacks, which included bombings of oil targets. These became the specialty of the 315th Wing, commanded by Brigadier General Frank A. Armstrong, a veteran of early Eighth Air Force strategic bombing over Europe.

LeMay turned his incendiary attacks upon the smaller cities after the middle of June. Between June 17 and August 14 some fifty of these secondary industrial-population centers were bombed with frequently devastating results. Several missions occurred simultaneously, which confused Japanese fighter defenses, but most of the secondary cities were practically defenseless, without antiaircraft guns or fighter protection.

At this time LeMay took yet another chance: he began dropping warning leaflets upon target cities in advance of B-29 raids. On the face of the leaflet the statement was simple and direct: "CIVILIANS! EVACUATE AT ONCE!" it warned. On the reverse face it read:

These leaflets are being dropped to notify you that your city has been listed for destruction by our powerful air force. The bombing will occur within 72 hours. This advance notice will give your military authorities ample time to take necessary defensive measures to protect you from our inevitable attack. Watch and see how powerless they are to protect you.

We give the military clique this notification of our plans because we know there is nothing they can do to stop our overwhelming power and our iron determination. We want you to see how powerless the military is to protect you. Systematic destruction of city after city will continue as long as you blindly follow your military leaders, whose blunders have placed you on the very brink of oblivion. It is your responsibility to overthrow the military government now and save what is left of your beautiful country.

"There wasn't any mass exodus until we knocked hell out of the first three towns," LeMay later learned. The Japanese took the warning as typical wartime propaganda; their only precaution was to fill the warned cities with fire engines, instead of massive concentrations of antiaircraft guns, as LeMay feared. As for the fire engines, which were lined up about a hundred feet apart along the streets, they "burned up with everything else."

The first three cities, Tsu, Aomori, and Ichinomiya (actually a total of six were struck on July 28), were, respectively, 57 per cent, 64 per cent, and 75 per cent destroyed. On August 1 the city of Toyama (population: 127,860) was all but totally eliminated out of existence; 99.5 per cent of it was nothing but a dark patch of earth.

The problem confronting the Emperor by this time was not how to win the war, not even how to lose it as gracefully as possible, but how to get out of it. Standing between him and this solution were his military leaders, chiefly his Minister of War, General Korechika Anami, and Army Chief of Staff General Yoshijiro Umezu; the Imperial Navy's chief advocates of a fight to the finish were Admiral Toyoda and Ohnishi. Nor was the newly appointed Premier, Admiral Kantaro Suzuki (the cabinet of Kuniaki Kioso had fallen a week after the invasion of Okinawa), of much help, although he was selected to find a means of an honorable peace. Old, nearly deaf, Suzuki rose up in a meeting of the Japanese Diet and cried out for a desperate last-ditch fight. If he were to die in the service of his Emperor, Suzuki said that he expected "the hundred million people of this glorious Empire to swell forward over my prostrate body and form themselves into a shield to protect the Emperor and this Imperial land from the invader!"

Soon there was an announcement of the formation

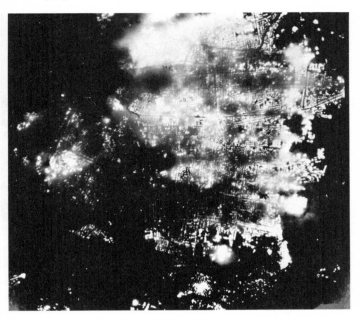

*A fire bombing in full fury: Toyama, August 1, 1945. More than 95 per cent of the city was destroyed.*
(U. S. AIR FORCE)

of a Japanese Peoples Vounteer Corps, whose "volunteers" were liable to defense duties, most undoubtedly with the sharpened bamboo poles. All men between the ages of fifteen and sixty and all women from seventeen to forty were expected to meet the invaders at the beaches. By July 21 Fifth Air Force Intelligence issued the statement: "There are no civilians in Japan. We are making War and making it in the all-out fashion which saves American lives, shortens the agony which War is and seeks to bring about an enduring Peace. We intend to seek out and destroy the enemy wherever he or she is, in the greatest possible numbers, in the shortest possible time."

At the same time plans were being drawn up for Operation Olympic, the invasion of southern Kyushu on November 1, 1945, to be followed by Coronet, the invasion of the main island, Honshu, on March 1, 1946. Predicted and expected losses ranged from 250,000 casualties to a million on each side.

There was every reason for Japan to surrender by July; in May Germany, Japan's only ally, was finished. The Soviet Union in April renounced its neutrality pact with Japan—and there had been

Leyte Gulf, Iwo Jima, and Okinawa. In June, with the Emperor's urging, attempts were made through the Russians to bring the war to a close. But the Russians were not very helpful; they were, in fact, often devious, apparently waiting for the moment to pounce. Stalin had promised that three months after Germany surrendered Russia would declare war upon Japan.

On July 26 the Allies, with Churchill, President Harry Truman, and Chiang Kai-shek as signatories, issued the Potsdam Declaration demanding the unconditional surrender of Japan. The alternative, the document warned, for Japan was "prompt and utter destruction." The offer was rejected in Tokyo, although the Emperor and the peace group, which now included the wavering Premier Suzuki, favored immediate acceptance. The war party—Anami, Umezu, and Toyoda—found the Declaration a threat to the entire Japanese way of life and to the Emperor—not to mention the fate of "war criminals." In the light of this argument, Suzuki decided it was best to postpone an immediate formal reply, although his statement to the press was interpreted by the Allies as an outright rejection.

In fact, the terms of the Potsdam Declaration were not regarded as particularly odious to many

*Aftermath: the aspect of a burned-out city after a fire bombing. One propeller plant as well as 66 per cent of Shizuoka went up in smoke.* (U. S. AIR FORCE)

*The massive aerial concentration on Saipan creates a traffic problem. James B. Lazar acts as traffic director while Thunderbolts take off. Truck belongs to 805th Aviation Engineer Battalion.* (U. S. AIR FORCE)

*A conventional daylight B-29 mission, rather than a night fire bombing, struck at Tokuyama naval station by no less than 400 B-29s.* (U. S. AIR FORCE)

of the Japanese cabinet. It was even considered as less severe than they expected: there was no direct threat to the Emperor, nor to the Japanese way of life. But as released to the press by the military leaders, the Potsdam Declaration was edited so that the people would not see the more attractive sections. Suzuki's blunder and the obtuse stupidity of the military faction sealed the fate of two Japanese cities, Hiroshima and Nagasaki.

VII

Of the 1767 men who made up the oddly structured 509th Composite Group, only one, its commander, Colonel Paul W. Tibbets, Jr., was aware of what the mission of the group was to be. Consisting of a single combat squadron, the 393rd Bom-

*While the special B-29 squadron trained, the other Marianas-based B-29s continued bombing Japan with Mustang escort. The escorts frequently, as in the last days of the war in Germany, then went down on the deck to strafe.* (U. S. AIR FORCE)

bardment Squadron (VH), the 509th was a self-sufficient unit with its own engineering and ordnance section, its own transports, and even its own Military Police Company. Fifteen modified B-29s were set aside for the 509th and its men; aircrews as well as ground crews were given special training for a very special mission. One of the maneuvers learned by the pilots was a steep diving turn of 158 degrees that enabled the plane to travel a distance of eight miles (presumably from the point it released its bomb) in forty-three seconds. For some strange reason formation flying, previously so critical in all bomber training, was not part of the program. High-altitude bombing and long over-water flights, on the other hand, were extremely important.

After several months of intensive training the 509th Composite Group began moving into North Field, Tinian, at the end of May 1945. By early July the complete group had settled into North Field as part of, yet separate from, the 313th Bombardment Wing. On July 20 the 393rd Squadron began flying its first combat missions, as part of preparation for its ultimate mission.

Still no one on the base knew what that mission was except Tibbets and a few scientists. The standoffish demeanor of the men of the 509th, their seeming preferential treatment, their odd missions (small formations of three aircraft which, although the other men on Tinian did not know, dropped a single oddly shaped bomb which was called a "pumpkin"); and their planes were strange too: the bomb bay was different and there were no guns in the turrets excepting the twin .50s in the tails.

While the other units in the Marianas were burning up Japanese cities, destroying its aircraft industries, or mining the harbors, it appeared that the 509th was, in the folk idiom of the time, "goofing off." Men in the other units began composing satirical verses about the mysterious 509th:

*Into the air the secret rose,*
*Where they're going nobody knows;*
*But we'll never know where they've been.*
*Don't ask about results or such*
*Unless you want to get in Dutch;*
*But take it from one who is sure of the score,*
*The 509th is winning the war.*

A second stanza repeated the taunting "The 509th is winning the war." It was true, of course, for the

*"Little Boy," the bomb carried to Hiroshima in the single B-29* Enola Gay *on August 6, 1945.*

(U. S. AIR FORCE)

509th had been selected to drop a new bomb based upon the principal of atomic fission (and originally suggested to President Roosevelt by Dr. Albert Einstein in August 1939). Under the direction of Dr. J. R. Oppenheimer, such a bomb was actually perfected beginning in the spring of 1943, and the first so-called "atomic bomb" was detonated on July 16, 1945, during the Potsdam Conference. On the day of the Potsdam Declaration, July 26, the cruiser *Indianapolis* delivered materials, including uranium-235, for use in the atomic bomb. If the Japanese accepted the terms of the Potsdam Declaration the bomb would not be used (meanwhile a second and third were on the way, more powerful and efficient than the first). Ultimate decision lay with President Truman.

When it appeared that Suzuki had rejected the surrender ultimatum, using the word *mokusatsu* in his press release (the word implied that he would treat the ultimatum with "silent contempt," when he actually meant a simple "no comment"), Truman ordered the bomb to be used. He was at the time aboard ship in mid-Atlantic on the return trip from Potsdam.

The first bomb, called "Little Boy," was 120 inches in length and 28 inches in diameter and weighed nine thousand pounds. Its explosive yield was equal to about twenty thousand tons of conventional high explosives. Its assembly, in a well-guarded North Field bomb hut, where temperature and humidity were carefully controlled, was completed the first of August. On that same date General Carl A. Spaatz assumed command of the United States Army Strategic Air Forces, Pacific, on Guam. LeMay became his chief of staff, while Lieutenant General Nathan F. Twining took over the Twentieth Air Force; the Eighth Air Force, under Lieutenant General James H. Doolittle, had begun moving into the Pacific by the middle of July; it would be based on Okinawa. In effect, these preparations were directed toward the mounting Olympic, the invasion of Japan.

Spaatz, like LeMay, believed that Japan could be beaten into surrender without an invasion. This became a critical point in the light of the fighting on Iwo Jima and Okinawa. Once the President gave the word, Spaatz could use the atomic bombs; the word came that the bomb could be dropped after August 3 on the first possible day when weather made visual bombing feasible.

That day came on August 6, 1945. The city of Hiroshima was selected as the primary target. Other cities mentioned in the orders to Spaatz were Kokura, Niigata, and Nagasaki. Weather aircraft which had preceded the striking force (one bomb-laden plane plus two observation aircraft) radioed near-perfect weather over Hiroshima. Had it not been favorable, Hiroshima might have been spared and one of the other cities bombed.

Hiroshima, from which, ironically, Yamamoto had directed the Hawaii Operation, was the home of the Second Army as well as several war industries; it was an important transport base, site of a shipbuilding yard, electrical works, and a railroad yard. Hiroshima had suffered very little bomb damage because it had been reserved as a target for the 509th Group. The populace had grown lax in their precautions. Even so, it is unlikely that, in view of the type of bombardment they suffered, it would have made any difference had the Hiroshimans sought shelter.

They had grown accustomed to seeing small formations of B-29s passing over harmlessly on reconnaissance flights. The three aircraft which passed over Hiroshima on that fateful day were the *Enola Gay,* carrying the single "Little Boy" and piloted by Colonel Tibbets; *Great Artiste* (pilot: Major Charles W. Sweeney); and aircraft number 44-27291, flown by Captain George W. Marquardt. The latter two planes carried scientific and military observers, cameras, and various measuring instruments.

At 8:15 A.M. (Hiroshima time) from an altitude of 31,600 feet, in perfect weather, the *Enola Gay* released the "Little Boy." Curious Japanese on their

*The* Enola Gay, *named for the mother of pilot Colonel Paul Tibbets, Jr., first aircraft to transport an atomic* weapon, *to deliver the* "flame that burns to the bone." *With this delivery war from the air took on a new, deadlier, meaning.* (U. S. AIR FORCE)

*The Atomic Age is born with a blast of power and massive birth pains—and eighty thousand dead.*
                                                      (U. S. AIR FORCE)

way to work or in their gardens watched the descent of the lone object as it fell into a heavily built-up residential, commercial, military, and industrial area just south of Second Army headquarters.

"Suddenly," an eyewitness Japanese newspaperman later told Marcel Junod of the International Red Cross, "a glaring whitish pinkish light appeared in the sky accompanied by an unnatural tremor which was followed almost immediately by a wave of suffocating heat and wind which swept everything in its path.

"Within a few seconds the thousands of people in the streets and the gardens in the center of the town were scorched by a wave of searing heat. Many were killed instantly, others lay writhing on the ground screaming in agony from the intolerable pain of their burns. Everything standing upright in the way of the blast—walls, houses, factories and other buildings—was annihilated and the debris spun round in a whirlwind and was carried up into the air. Trams were picked up and tossed aside as though they had neither weight nor solidity. Trains were flung off the rails as though they were toys. Horses, dogs and cattle suffered the same fate as

human beings. Every living thing was petrified in an attitude of indescribable suffering. Even the vegetation did not escape. Trees went up in flames, the rice plants lost their greenness, the grass burned on the ground like dry straw."

A violent fire was swept by powerful, unnatural winds. "By evening the fire began to die down and then went out. There was nothing left to burn. Hiroshima had ceased to exist."

As soon as bombardier Major Thomas W. Ferebee had toggled "Little Boy," Tibbets gripped the control column, turned the *Enola Gay* sharply around, and pushed the nose down to gain speed. In fifty seconds, when the plane and the two observation B-29s were about fifteen miles from Hiroshima, a great flash illuminated the interiors of the planes and powerful shocks convulsed the Superfortresses. After gazing with wonder and horror upon the disaster they had brought to Hiroshima, the men in the three planes returned to Tinian, twelve hours and thirteen minutes after they had taken off.

The war of the twenty-first century had arrived at Hiroshima. Eighty per cent of its buildings were totally destroyed. According to official figures 71,379 people were dead or missing, with an equal number injured. The death toll figure may be too

*Hiroshima, 1945. A drainpipe on the Chugoku Power Company tells its own story of the profane wind.*
(U. S. AIR FORCE)

the war according to the terms of the Potsdam Declaration.

Consequently, while conventional bombing missions continued, another bomb, this one using plutonium, was assembled at Tinian. Sixty inches in diameter and 128 inches long, the bulbous bomb was called "Fat Man." Three days after the destruction of Hiroshima, "Fat Man" was cranked into the bomb bay of the B-29 named *Bockscar* and with Major Sweeney as pilot set out for Kokura. (Sweeney's own plane, *Great Artiste* was flown by Captain Frederick C. Bock, with whom he had switched planes.) Bock accompanied the mission, along with another aircraft, Major James I. Hopkins, pilot, as observers.

Unlike the Hiroshima mission, the second atomic bombing mission did not proceed smoothly. Weather closed in and Sweeney lost contact in the heavy clouds with Hopkins' plane. Three bomb runs were made upon Kokura without any sighting of the target. This consumed fuel and appeared to be getting nowhere. *Bockscar* was then set for the secondary target, Nagasaki, with the decision that one run would be made and the bomb dropped by radar if necessary.

Cloud covered Nagaski also, but at 10:58 A.M. (Nagasaki time) bombardier Captain Kermit K. Beahan sighted the city in a cloud rent and in a flash

moderate—the number of dead may have reached about 80,000 (still less than the number of casualties of the Tokyo fire raids and the Dresden attacks). All this, however, by one single bomb.

Until President Truman announced that the destruction had been caused by history's first atomic bomb, the Japanese High Command had no idea of the nature of the force that had been unleashed at Hiroshima. Truman again appealed to the Japanese to surrender or "expect a rain of ruin from the air, the like of which has never been seen on this earth."

But no word, not even a *mokusatsu,* came from Tokyo. Nor did any mention of an atomic bomb appear in the Japanese press. The military conceded that some type of new "parachute bomb" had caused extensive devastation at Hiroshima and that it "should not be made light of." But there was no light shed on the situation by the High Command, despite the Emperor's obvious desires to end

*General Carl A. Spaatz (second from right) and staff await the return of the* Enola Gay *from Hiroshima.*
(U. S. AIR FORCE)

*The bomb that fell on Nagasaki, "Fat Man," which subtracted forty thousand people from the population of Japan.* (U. S. AIR FORCE)

—"a light brighter than a thousand suns"—thirty or forty thousand souls simply vanished from the face of the earth.

After taking the shock waves from the blast —"it was as if the B-29 were being beaten by a telephone pole"—Sweeney realized that the fuel expenditure had been high (plus the fact that six hundred gallons were wasted in a bomb bay tank because of malfunction). Instead of turning back for Tinian, he headed south for Okinawa, followed by Bock. After refueling, the B-29s were flown back to Tinian; all three had returned safely.

Even after the second atomic blast the Tokyo die-hard fanatics demanded that the war be continued to the very bitter end. They still had a large army in the home islands, there were perhaps 10,000 aircraft of assorted types (including wood and fabric trainers) and 500 pilots in kamikaze training. There was practically no Imperial Navy left, but there were hundreds of midget submarines, 120 *kaiten* (manned suicide torpedoes), about 2000 *shinyo* (motorboats loaded with explosives), and, of course, a fearful populace armed with their bamboo poles. There were broadcast threats to the "peace agitators" and "defeatists" over Radio Tokyo.

Immediately following the Nagasaki bombing an

Imperial Conference was called in which, at last, the Emperor intervened, announcing to the stunned assemblage that his decision was for an end to the war. Word of the decision was relayed to the Allies through Switzerland and was accepted. This acceptance was not gracefully taken in Tokyo. When the Imperial Conference met again on August 14, War Minister Anami, Army Chief of Staff Umezu, and Navy Chief of Staff Toyoda begged the Emperor that "one last battle" be fought in the home islands to preserve the national honor. But the Emperor was firm and had decided to record an Imperial rescript which would be broadcast to his people the following day, August 15, 1945.

There would be peace. Operation Olympic could be canceled; there would be no invasion. Nor would a third atomic bomb, then being readied, be dropped on the next selected target: Tokyo.

## VIII

On "the 14th Day of the 8th month of the 20th year of Showa" an unprecedented event occurred:

*While the world waited for word from Tokyo and the third atomic bomb was being prepared to be dropped on that city, a vigil was kept. A Wildcat takes off on a dawn patrol—Japan may have been beaten but its samurai and kamikazes were unwilling to accept that.* (U. S. NAVY)

for the first time in history the people of Japan heard the voice of their Emperor. At the sound of it many of the simple folk prostrated themselves before their radios, listening to the high-pitched, sometimes choked voice with foreheads pressed to the floor.

"To our good and loyal subjects," Hirohito began. He spoke in an archaic, royal dialect that was strange to most of his listeners.

"After pondering deeply the general trends of the world and the actual conditions obtaining in Our Empire today, We have decided to effect a settlement of the present situation by resorting to an extraordinary measure." The language was stilted, the delivery nervous, and the auditors had difficulty in grasping the point of the words.

"We, the Emperor, have ordered the Imperial Government to notify the Governments of the United States, Great Britain, China, and the Soviet Union that We accept their Joint Declaration."

He reminded them that the well-being of his subjects was the traditional rule left "Us by the Founder of the Empire of Our Illustrious Imperial Ancestors," who would wish to share "with all the countries of the world the joys of co-prosperity . . ." but that "the military situation can no longer take a favorable turn. . . .

"Moreover, the enemy has begun to employ a new and inhuman bomb, the power of which to do damage is indeed incalculable, taking a toll of many innocent lives. To continue the war under these conditions would not only lead to the annihilation of Our Nation, but to the destruction of human civilization as well."

The Emperor tendered his regrets to "our Allied nations in East Asia, who have consistently co-operated with the Empire toward the emancipation of East Asia." Thoughts of those who had died in the four long years of savagery "pains Our heart night and day. The welfare of the wounded and war-sufferers, and of those who have lost their homes and livelihood, are the objects of Our profound solicitude."

The broadcast drew to a close as Hirohito observed that "it is according to the dictate of time and fate that We have resolved to pave the way for a grand peace for all generations to come by enduring the unendurable and tolerating the intolerable." He was, of course, referring to the impending occupation.

The fanatics were still a problem—five of them

the previous night had tried to seize the recording of the rescript and prevent its broadcast—so Hirohito voiced a warning. "Beware most strictly of any outbursts of emotion which may engender needless complications, or any fraternal contention and strife which may create confusion, lead ye astray and cause ye to lose the confidence of the world."

The Emperor closed the rescript with a plea rather than a royal order. "We ask you, Our subjects," he said, "to be the incarnation of Our will."

A wave of national mourning followed in the wake of the speech, but so did rebelliousness, with cries of continuing the fight until the entire nation was destroyed and every last Japanese was dead. But only a small minority would have dared ignore

*Night vigil: Northrop P-61s—"Black Widows"—the best of the American night fighters on the alert in the Pacific for Japanese surprise night attacks. Even after the Emperor had asked for peace, the possibility of last-ditch attacks by die-hard fanatical pilots was possible.*
(U. S. AIR FORCE)

the Emperor's plea and his will. Such had been the group, led by Major Kenji Hatanaka, who had violated the Imperial palace grounds in search of the broadcast recording. When this failed, and when they could not enlist more men to their cause, four of the five plotters committed suicide.

A wave of high-level suicides followed the Emperor's broadcast, among them War Minister Anami, who had burst into tears when the Emperor had announced his decision for peace. General Hideki Tojo, who as Minister of War had planned the attack upon the United States, attempted suicide, bungled the job, and lived long enough to be hanged as a war criminal. Umezu and Toyoda, though they had urged for "one last battle," chose to live.

Admiral Ohnishi, the father of the kamikaze, dined with friends the evening of August 15, after which he retired to his study on the second floor of his official residence and disemboweled himself.

He had also attempted to cut his own throat but succeeded only in making a ragged wound. Thus he lingered in agony for several hours, refusing all aid and *coup de grâce,* until death came ten hours later. Before committing traditional hara-kari Ohnishi had written a note in which he said, "I wish to express my deep appreciation to the souls of the brave special attackers. They fought and died valiantly with faith in our ultimate victory. In death I wish to atone for my part in the failure to achieve that victory and I apologize to the souls of these dead fliers and their bereaved families. . . ."

The kamikaze spirit continued to burn in some breasts and there were loud boasts among pilots that when the *Missouri* steamed into Tokyo Bay for the surrender ceremonies they would crash into the American ship. This threat was squelched with the arrival of Prince Takamatsu, the Emperor's brother, at Atsugi airfield to put down an incipient re-

*Vigil rewarded: American troops moving into Japan before the official surrender. Building in background* *is part of an aircraft experimental grounds factory at Yokosuka.* (DEFENSE DEPT., MARINE CORPS)

bellion there. Leading it was Navy Captain Ammyo Kosono, who had showered leaflets upon Tokyo reading:

Government officials and senior statesmen who were caught in an enemy trap have enticed the Emperor to issue the message ending the war. It was a terrible thing to do. The Emperor is a God. There is no such thing as surrender in Japan. There is no surrender in the Imperial forces. We, as members of the Air Force, are sure of victory.

This threat expired when Kosono was removed from Atsugi to the Nobi Naval Hospital in a strait jacket.

There was, in fact, one final kamikaze attack after the broadcast of the Emperor's rescript. Vice-Admiral Matome Ugaki, who had commanded the devastating kamikaze attacks during the Okinawa campaign, had decided to lead one final attack upon the enemy at Okinawa despite the Emperor's plea. He ordered three aircraft of the Oita detachment of the 701st Air Group to attack the enemy fleet at Okinawa. "This attack," the order read, "will be led by the commanding admiral."

All attempts to dissuade Ugaki from the mission were fruitless and often tearful. And, in fact, when Ugaki came to the airstrip instead of three bombers he was surprised—and no doubt moved—to see eleven planes and twenty-two men. The unit commander, Lieutenant Tatsuo Nakatsuru, explained that when the commander himself was to lead an attack, a mere three aircraft would not suffice. "Every plane in my command will follow him!"

Deeply touched, Ugaki climbed into Nakatsuru's plane, taking the rear seat of Warrant Officer Akiyoshi Endo. Though Endo objected, Ugaki ordered him out of the plane. The young airmen jumped to the ground and then, determined, clambered back upon the wing to squeeze into the rear cockpit with his admiral. Ugaki, shaking his head in mock dismay at the show of zeal, made room for Endo. Then the eleven aircraft took off from the Oita base and headed for Okinawa.

Four of the dive bombers were forced to return with engine trouble, but Nakatsuru's lead plane continued on for Okinawa. Endo radioed Ugaki's final message to the base: "I alone am to blame for our failure to defend the homeland and to destroy the arrogant enemy," the message began. "I am going to make an attack at Okinawa where my men have

Clyde W. Cooksey, Jackson, Tennessee, cuts away the Japanese surrender flag in preparation of the raising of the Stars and Stripes on the crest of Tahyama, near Sasebo, Kyushu, Japan.

(DEFENSE DEPT., MARINE CORPS)

fallen like cherry blossoms. There I will crash into and destroy the conceited enemy in the true spirit of *Bushido*, with the firm conviction and faith in the eternity of Imperial Japan. . . ."

Why he did not realize that his attack might very well have led to a renewal of hostilities that could have doomed Imperial Japan into eternity is not known. The final words of the message were "Long live His Imperial Majesty the Emperor!"

Another message was flashed at 7:24 P.M. on that August 15, that the admiral's plane was making a plunge upon a target and the six others were following.

There was silence after that. Ironically, and fittingly perhaps, the last kamikaze attack of the Second World War was an utter failure. The fate of the

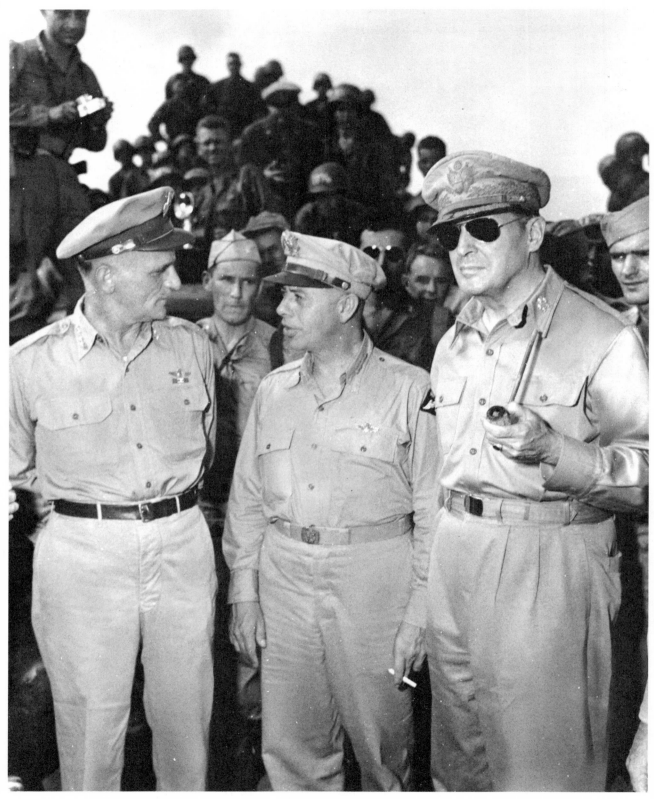

*Carl A. Spaatz, George Kenney, and Douglas MacArthur at Atsugi air base, Japan, for the surrender ceremonies.* (U. S. AIR FORCE)

*U.S.S.* Missouri, *Tokyo Bay, September 2, 1945, the close of the Second World War.*
(NAVY DEPT., NATIONAL ARCHIVES)

seven dive bombers and the fifteen men remains one of the mysteries of the war. Not one of the aircraft hit any Allied ships, nor were they heard from again.

On Sunday, September 2, 1945, the formal surrender ceremonies took place aboard the *Missouri* in Tokyo Bay, without incident, and with General Douglas MacArthur presiding. After the formalities of affixing signatures to the documents were concluded at 9:25 A.M., the sun broke through the morning overcast and a deep rumble pervaded the air. It was as if Hollywood had set the scene: the blue sky, the broken clouds, the sun shafts, and the deep-throated rumble. After so many months of warring the very thought of peace was unreal.

Great armadas of B-29s swept over Tokyo Bay; to the sonority of their engines was added the roar of Air Force fighters, Mustangs and Thunderbolts and more than four hundred Navy Hellcats, Avengers, Helldivers, and the Marine's dreaded "Whistling Death" Corsair.

The war that had begun and closed with an aerial attack was over. In the recognition of the extreme and frightful disparity between those two attacks— a handful of Stukas and one lone B-29—lies the new definition of air war and the destiny of civilization. The Second World War closed, as had no previous major war in history, with all the weapons at hand for the Final World War.

*Man, have pity on man.*

# Acknowledgments

MY DEEPEST DEBT I owe to my editor, Harold Kuebler, from this book's very inception through the long period of conception, and after. Harold is an extraordinary editor who not only knows his subject but has a genuine interest in it. He is blessed, too, with the gift of patience, gentle wit, and a total absence of affectation. Never over the years of our association has it congealed into the typical "editor-writer" relationship, which is roughly comparable to that of the Navy and the Marines.

For the bulk of the photographs I am indebted to Office of the Assistant Secretary of Defense's Magazine and Book Branch, Directorate for Information Services. Not only were these photographs freely supplied; so was certain specific information which I required along the line—from the correct spelling of names to the identification of Air Force units. This was an immense help, and a comforting one, for as the manuscript grew heavier the opportunity for error multiplied. The information I asked for was dug up out of the archives stored near Washington and it was indeed helpful that the digging was so graciously done for me, thus saving time that could be spent trying to conquer the typewriter. Individual names of those who assisted me in a time of need may be found listed after these opening paragraphs.

Another remarkable source of material, courteous service, and co-operation was the National Ar-
chives and Records Service of the General Services Administration in Washington, D.C. My impression is that every worthwhile photograph and document in existence is stored in our National Archives. Several of the beautiful carrier war photographs, many produced under the supervision of the great photographer Edward Steichen during the war, came from the Archives. Although I spent many hours in the National Archives (one easily might spend years there), much of the hard work was done by the U.S. mails, zip code and all. Thus was the often time-consuming and tiring work done for me by the superb staff of the National Archives.

In England I spent several days in the Imperial War Museum doing research through the vast files and picture collections. Here again the attention I received was thoughtful, courteous, and valuable. My guide through the great collections was an ex-RAF crewman, E. C. H. Hine, who could tell by simply looking at a photo of a Spitfire whether it had served during the Battle of Britain or not. Ed Hine is also a musical type—a Harold Arlen fan, in fact—so we did not spend all our time talking about the war. He was also delighted that the weather in England had been so "nice" during my stay. It was March—and true, the sun did shine, but frankly I froze.

Also in London I visited Mr. W. J. Taunton at

the Air Historical Branch, Ministry of Defence, Queen Anne's Chambers. Not only was I offered valuable suggestions (and later prompt replies to frantic queries), but also the best cup of tea I had in England. And I hate tea. Mr. Taunton also told me a fine joke, something to do with cricket balls, but I've only spoiled it ever since.

The Division of Information of the United States Marine Corps has also exceeded the call of duty in finding interesting photographs at the last minute.

Heinz J. Nowarra, the German aviation scholar and archivist, was most generous in making his great photo collection available to me; his own books on the Messerschmitt 109 and Focke-Wulf 190 were invaluable reference sources.

The "hapless designer" who so handsomely "put it all together" (the "all" adding up to more than a thousand pages of manuscript and nearly 800 illustrations) is Doubleday's own Jim Leach.

Nor can the following be overlooked or sufficiently thanked:

Sir Max Aitken, of *The Daily Express,* London, veteran of the Battle of Britain.

Robert R. Allen, Golden, Colorado, for a fund of technical information plus a treasury of tech manuals.

Anya and Harold Arlen for discussions while the work was in progress and refreshing friendship during the lulls between. Harold Arlen's regular line of work has nothing to do with aviation or war, but his several research suggestions were most perceptive.

Douglas R. S. Bader, of Shell Centre, London, and veteran of the Battle of Britain.

R. Baker, Chief Photographer, Home Counties Newspapers, Ltd., Luton Bedfordshire, England.

John F. Bartel, Bay City, Michigan—again.

J. Bax, Head, Press and Information Services, City of Rotterdam, the Netherlands.

John M. Bennett, Jr., Major General, USAF (Res.) and San Antonio, Texas—also again.

Jack Birdsall, Saginaw, Michigan, who is my sister Mary's husband, for helping so unselfishly during the final writing of this book in an especially trying time.

Sissel Bohman, secretary to Harold Kuebler, ever helpful, thoughtful, and understanding—pretty, too.

Robert S. Bolles, artist, an ex-ground crew man; possibly the only man in history who ever lost a DC-3—on the ground at that.

Lt. Col. C. W. Burtyk, Jr., U. S. Army, Office of the Assistant Secretary of Defense.

Col. F. C. Caldwell, Head, Historical Branch, U. S. Marine Corps, Department of the Navy, Washington, D.C.

John Camden, Republic Aviation Corporation, Farmingdale, N.Y.

Mrs. Sylvia Carson, P.S. 87 (Manhattan), for invaluable historical information on the development of the aircraft carrier.

Frank A. Celantano, ex-384th Bombardment Group (H) Eighth Air Force, now an attorney in New York City.

Robert C. Chapin, also ex-384th Bombardment Goup (H), now in public relations in Philadelphia and New York. Bob Chapin's collection of memorabilia, photographs, and technical material, carefully preserved since the war, was invaluable to me.

Alex Chervitz, flier and teacher, N.Y.

C. F. Clark, Librarian, Fox Photos, Ltd., London.

Claire and Peter Clay, Rickmansworth, Herts., England. Peter and I, musical pen pals from the beginning of the Second World War, never met until my research trip to England. Such meetings are always delicate, but I, for one, was thoroughly delighted. Claire and Peter provided me not only with a home for my entire stay but also with the atmosphere of a genuine English pub and meetings with ex-RAF types. Peter, incidentally, served in the RAF during the war; Claire was a nurse. Some of my affection for them is evident, I hope, in the dedication of this book.

Cecil Cohen, ex-34th Bombardment Group, now Flushing, N.Y.

Mrs. Jean Coleman, National Archives, Washington, D.C.

F. Czajkowski, Polish People's Republic Permanent Mission to the United Nations.

Grant Daly, Historian, Grumman Aviation Engineering Corp., Bethpage, N.Y.

Air Commodore Alan C. Deere, DSO, OBE, DFC—RAF.

Michael Farlam, Hawker Siddeley Group, Ltd., London.

Mrs. Virginia Fincik, Air Force Photo Center, Washington, D.C.

Royal D. Frey, Chief, Research Section, Air Force Museum, Wright-Patterson Air Force Base, Ohio. Again and again and again.

Col. Francis S. Gabreski, USAF (Ret.), with thanks for a pleasant visit to Suffolk County Air Force Base, lunch in the officers' mess (my first GI meal since 1945: no comment), and illuminating talks on the fighter pilot and an enlightened attitude toward war.

W. D. Gallavin, *Kent Messenger,* Maidstone, Kent, England, for a copy of *Hell's Corner* and photographs taken during the Battle of Britain.

# ACKNOWLEDGMENTS

M/Sgt. Beresford B. Gilkes, USAF (Ret.), Albuquerque, New Mexico, for excellent suggestions, lively letters, and photographs.

Col. C. V. Glines, USAF, from all parts: Washington, the Alaskan Command, and Virginia; he is the author of fine aviation books, from which I unashamedly cribbed.

Cap. J. M. Gratto, U. S. Marine Corps, Division of Information, Washington, D.C.

Lt/Col. Gene Guerny, USAF, author and friend.

Col. Grover Heiman, Jr., USAF, Office of the Assistant Secretary of Defense, Washington, D.C.

Raymond E. Houseman, Lt. Col. USAF (Ret.), "Pappy" —who kept the faith. Once one of Kenney's Kids, now with Lockheed Aircraft Corporation, N.Y.

Gordon M. Jackson, American Aviation Historical Society, General Dynamics, Convair Division, San Diego, California. As historian at Convair, Gordon Jackson is keeper of the files on the B-24 Liberator and permitted me to go through his collection on this bomber as well as the PBY Catalina.

Albert Jaynes, Bay City, Michigan, ex-Saipan resident, U. S. Army.

Jan Kinast, Press Secretary, Embassy of the Polish People's Republic, Washington, D.C.

Capt. F. Kent Loomis, USN (Ret.), Assistant Director of Naval History, Department of the Navy, Office of the Chief of Naval Operations, Washington, D.C.

William MacNamara, now of Brooklyn, but once one of Kenney's Kids.

Commander Joseph W. Marshall, USNR, Magazine and Book Division, Directorate for Defense Information, Office of the Assistant Secretary of Defense.

Crosby Maynard, Director of Public Relations, Douglas Aircraft Corporation, Santa Monica, California.

N. L. Mead, Curtiss-Wright Corp., Wood-Ridge, New Jersey.

Bill Merklein, formerly of Polk's Hobby Shop, expert on aircraft and markings of the Second World War.

Elliot H. Miller, the Martin Company, Baltimore, Maryland.

Erik Miller, Lockheed-California Company, Burbank, California.

Col. W. Morris, U. S. Marine Corps, Washington, D.C.

Josephine Motylewski, National Archives, Washington, D.C.

Mark E. Nevils, The Boeing Company, New York, N.Y.

J. R. S. Nicholls, Hawker Siddeley Aviation, Ltd., Coventry, England.

Peter Northcote, RAF Association, N.Y.

Joseph Oravec, ex-Eighth Air Force, now of the Scranton *Times,* Scranton, Pa.: for a stream of ideas and suggestions plus the loan of old copies of *Yank* and *Stars and Stripes.*

Ramsay D. Potts, veteran of the Ploesti raid, now an attorney in Washington, D.C.

John F. J. Preston, American Aviation Historical Society, of Brooklyn, N.Y.

Helga Rippka, Lufthansa, New York.

Col. J. Rougevin-Baville, Conservateur du Musée de l'Air, Paris.

Arthur L. Schoeni, American Aviation Historical Society, Ling-Temco Vought, Inc., Dallas, Texas.

Robert H. Scholl, North American Aviation, El Segundo, California.

Ernest Shipman, formerly of the 31st Fighter Group, Fifteenth Air Force, and now with the 9215 Air Reserve Squadron, for assistance with many technical matters from this book's inception. I am especially grateful for the free use of his diary.

Major G. W. Smeltzer, Head, Service Branch, Division of Information, Marine Corps, Washington, D.C.

Winder D. Smith, ex-Fifteenth Air Force, now Hancock, New Hampshire.

Lt. Gerald Somers, USN, Public Relations Office, N.Y.

David Trollope, of Kent and Baker Street, London.

Lt. J. E. Tuthill, U. S. Naval Photographic Center, U. S. Naval Station, Washington, D.C.

Anna C. Urband, Office of the Assistant Secretary of Defense, Washington, D.C.

Stephen H. Vogel, National Archives, Washington, D.C.

John Owen Ward, Manager, Music Department, Oxford University Press, New York; once, however, of Biggin Hill and north Africa.

Lt/Col. Robert A. Webb, USAF, Magazine and Book Branch, Office of the Assistant Secretary of Defense, Washington, D.C.

Fred T. Wells, Pratt & Whitney Aircraft, East Hartford, Connecticut.

Paul White, National Archives, Washington, D.C.

Raymond C. Wier, Wellesley, Massachusetts, for unusual photographs taken by himself during the Ploesti raid.

Ursula Vaughan Williams, London, for permission to quote from her poem, an excerpt from "Noah's Ark" from *Silence and Music* (Essential Books, Fair Lawn, New Jersey, 1959). Thanks too for a wonderful musical afternoon in London, not to mention the fine lunch, the sherry, and the lively talk.

Margaret Yost, Lufthansa, New York.

*Final personal note:* Work on *Airwar* was begun at the home of my parents, William and Isabel Jablonski, in Beaverton, Michigan. It continued and grew in Washington, D.C., in Seattle, Washington, and in Luton and London, England. The final half was started in Santa Ana, California, and finally completed in New York in July 1968, almost three years after its inception. Throughout this extended period I was tendered (and I use the term advisedly, perhaps even in a Gertrude Stein-ish sense) every manner of loving support and understanding by my wife Edith (who, as an editor and columnist, had her own literary problems and deadlines). Without her, the spelling and punctuation, not to say semantics, would have been even stranger than they are. My son David (who is fifteen as this is being completed), was a constant source of enlightenment and information. One of the rare, true scholars, David has provided much instant information and research assistance. His knowledge of the aircraft and battles of the Second World War is impressive. My daughters Carla and Emily only dread war—they make no effort to understand it or to find some redeeming glorification or nostalgia in it. They impress me as being exceedingly wise. If we could all see war through their eyes, simply and realistically, we might yet have a chance of making it into the next century.

# Bibliography

BESIDES personal interviews, contemporary newspapers and magazines, plus some checks into various official archives, the making of this book has depended a good deal upon the many postwar official histories published with the co-operation of various governments. Not only are these works of an imposing scholarship, they are often equally objective; they do not take sides, generally. The English are especially good at this sort of thing. To judge from what little is yet available, the Germans tend to lean the other way. Not so much to place the blame upon their enemies, as much as to attempt to explain away defeat in terms of the great betrayal by Hitler, or to scoff at the idea that Germany went into the war with the most powerful air force in the world.

Certain works, such as the multivolumned official histories or general histories of the war, were referred to throughout the writing of *Airwar*. Since footnotes have always annoyed me, I have refrained from using them. Having read through literally hundreds of works, ranging from those barely above the level of pulp magazines to those of impeccable scholarship, I am not convinced that a half page of footnotes really proves much. As a reader I have always expected an author to do his job to the best of his ability, to be honest, and to know what he's talking about. If he is dishonest, the footnotes make

no difference: I found this to be the case with one of the biographies of Göring.

Unless a book is little more than a listing of facts, it of course cannot be purely objective. We assume the author has a point of view and that the use he makes of facts (even to the point of twisting them: and the more skilled he is, the more subtle the twist) will conform to that point of view. Footnotes to back up the point of view won't undo the twist. The worst type of footnote is the one that compels the reader to turn to the back of the book. As a student, as a reader, and as a writer I have never quite been able to fathom this distracting practice.

Therefore no footnotes.

The facts that make up this book were drawn from the various sources already mentioned; that some of these were not facts I found upon checking several sources against each other. The interpretation of the facts and the "facts" are my own: I have, in other words, added my own of both varieties, no doubt. Needless to say, I have attempted to make the book as factual as humanly possible, and likewise my editor, Harold Kuebler, and Harold Grabau, copy editor at Doubleday (may his tribe increase!), have done all they could to assure the historical accuracy of the book.

The bibliography, for easier handling, has been

subdivided into three major sections. The first contains those books to which I referred throughout—of a synoptic nature, general histories of the war which may have had nothing to say about the aerial aspects, and reference books and anthologies.

The second section is devoted to memoir-histories, many of which are not quite either, but fascinating just the same. They present the views of the actors in the drama, generally after the fact, as if the actor himself is given the chance to revise the script. Curious memory slips, reinterpretation of events, axes to grind, self-justification: all these tend to make these works a bit suspect as pure history. Perhaps the major truth is that history is neither pure nor scientific. The views of the authors are always valuable, even if suspect.

Finally, a separate bibliography germane to each of the major units establishes the chief sources for the chapters within each unit. And for good measure a section entitled "Miscellaneous" is added for certain volumes, mainly pictorial, which were useful as reference and for the location of long-forgotten photographs.

David, my son, assisted in the compilation and arrangement of this bibliography. Many of the books listed, in fact, are from his personal library, which, I am happy to say, is not devoted exclusively to war. His science fiction collection is extensive and his section on paleontology is definitive.

### SYNOPTIC AND GENERAL HISTORIES ANTHOLOGIES AND REFERENCE WORKS

Baldwin, Hanson W.: *Battles Lost and Won,* New York: Harper & Row, 1966.

Bekker, Cajus: *The Luftwaffe War Diaries,* Garden City, N.Y.: Doubleday & Co., Inc., 1968.

Buchanan, A. R., editor: *The Navy's Air War,* New York: Harper & Brothers, 1946.

Carlisle, Norman: *The Air Force Reader,* Indianapolis: Bobbs-Merrill Co., 1944.

Craven, W. F. and Cate, J. L., editors: *The Army Air Forces in World War II* (7 vols.), Chicago: University of Chicago Press, 1948–58.

D'Albas, Andrieu: *Death of a Navy,* New York: Devin-Adair Co., 1957.

Davis, Kenneth S.: *Experience of War,* Garden City, N.Y.: Doubleday & Co., Inc., 1965.

Dupuy, Col. R. Ernest and Bregstein, Lt/Col. Herbert L.: *Soldier's Album,* Boston: Houghton Mifflin Co., 1946.

Emme, Eugene M.: *The Impact of Air Power,* Princeton, N.J.: D. Van Nostrand Co., Inc., 1959.

Esposito, Brig. Gen. Vincent J., editor: *A Concise History of World War II,* New York: Frederick A. Praeger, Publishers, 1964.

Flower, Desmond and Reeves, James, editors: *The Taste of Courage, The War 1939–1945,* New York: Harper & Brothers, 1960.

Goldberg, Alfred, editor: *A History of the United States Air Force,* Princeton, N.J.: D. Van Nostrand Co., Inc., 1957.

Green, William: *Famous Bombers of the Second World War* (2 vols.), Garden City, N.Y.: Doubleday & Co., Inc., 1959, 1960.

———: *Famous Fighters of the Second World War* (2 vols.), Garden City, N.Y.: Doubleday & Co., Inc., 1962.

Greenfield, Kent Roberts, editor: *Command Decisions,* Washington, D.C.: Office of the Chief of Military History, Department of the Army, 1960.

Gurney, Maj. Gene: *The War in the Air,* New York: Crown Publishers, Inc., 1962.

Hinton, Harold B.: *Air Victory,* New York: Harper & Brothers, 1948.

Jacobsen, H. A. and Rohwer, J., editors: *Decisive Battles of World War II: The German View,* New York: G. P. Putnam's Sons, 1964.

Killen, John: *The Luftwaffe: A History,* London: Frederick Muller, 1967.

King, Adm. Ernest J.: *U.S. Navy at War 1941–1945,* Washington, D.C.: United States Navy Dept., 1946.

Leckie, Robert: *Strong Men Armed,* New York: Random House, Inc., 1962.

Lee, Asher: *The German Air Force,* London: Duckworth, 1946.

Loosbrock, J. F. and Skinner, R. M., editors: *The Wild Blue,* New York: G. P. Putnam's Sons, 1961.

Marshall, Gen. George C., Arnold, Gen. H. H., and King, Adm. Ernest J.: *The War Reports,* Philadelphia, Pa.: J. B. Lippincott Co., 1947.

Martin, Ralph G.: *The G. I. War 1941–1945,* Boston: Little, Brown & Co., 1967.

Maurer, Maurer: *Air Force Combat Units of World War II,* New York: Franklin Watts, Inc., 1963.

Morison, Samuel Eliot: *The Two-Ocean War,* Boston: Little, Brown & Co., 1963.

Moyes, Philip: *Bomber Squadrons of the R.A.F.,* London: MacDonald, 1964.

Nowarra, Heinz J.: *The Messerschmitt 109—A Famous*

*German Fighter,* Letchworth, Herts., England: Harleyford Publications, 1963.

————: *The Focke-Wulf 190—A Famous German Fighter,* Letchworth, Herts., England: Harleyford Publications, 1965.

Richards, Denis and Saunders, Hilary St. George: *Royal Air Force* (3 vols.), London: Her Majesty's Stationery Office, 1953–54.

Robertson, Bruce: *Spitfire—The Story of a Famous Fighter,* Letchworth, Herts., England: Harleyford Publications, 1960.

————: *Lancaster—the Story of a Famous Bomber,* Letchworth, Herts., England: Harleyford Publications, 1963.

Sherrod, Robert: *History of Marine Corps Aviation in World War II,* Washington, D.C.: Combat Forces Press, 1952.

Shirer, William L.: *The Rise and Fall of the Third Reich,* New York: Simon & Schuster, 1960.

Smith, S. E., editor: *The United States Navy in World War II,* New York: Wm. Morrow & Co., Inc., 1966.

Snyder, Louis L.: *The War, A Concise History 1939–1945,* New York: Julian Messner, Inc., 1960.

Straubel, James H.: *Air Force Diary,* New York: Simon & Schuster, 1947.

Sulzberger, C. L. and the editors of *American Heritage: The American Heritage Picture History of World War II,* New York: American Heritage Publishing Co., Inc., 1966.

Tourtellot, Arthur B., editor: *Life's Picture History of World War II,* New York: Time, Inc., 1950.

Wagner, Ray: *American Combat Planes,* Garden City, N.Y.: Hanover House, 1968.

Watts, Anthony J.: *Japanese Warships of World War II,* London: Ian Allen, Ltd., 1966.

Webster, Sir Charles and Frankland, Noble: *The Strategic Air Offensive Against Germany* (4 vols.), London: Her Majesty's Stationery Office, 1961.

Weigley, Russell F.: *History of the United States Army,* New York: Macmillan Co., 1967.

## MEMOIR-HISTORIES

Arnold, H. H.: *Global Mission,* New York: Harper & Brothers, 1949.

Baumbach, Werner: *The Life and the Death of the Luftwaffe,* New York: Coward-McCann, 1960.

Brereton, Lewis H.: *The Brereton Diaries,* New York: William Morrow & Co., 1946.

Churchill, Winston: *The Second World War* (6 vols.), Cambridge, Mass.: Houghton Mifflin Co., 1948–53.

Eisenhower, Dwight D.: *Crusade in Europe,* Garden City, N.Y.: Doubleday & Co., Inc., 1948.

Galland, Adolf: *The First and the Last,* New York: Henry Holt & Co., 1954.

Harris, Sir Arthur: *Bomber Offensive,* London: Collins, 1947.

Kenney, George C.: *General Kenney Reports,* New York: Duell, Sloan and Pearce, 1949.

LeMay, Gen. Curtis E. with Kantor, MacKinlay: *Mission with LeMay,* Garden City, N.Y.: Doubleday & Co., Inc., 1965.

Lochner, Louis P., editor: *The Goebbels Diaries,* Garden City, N.Y.: Doubleday & Co., Inc., 1948.

MacArthur, Douglas: *Reminiscences,* New York: McGraw-Hill Book Co., 1964.

Montgomery, Bernard Law: *The Memoirs of Field-Marshal the Viscount Montgomery of Alamein, K.G.,* Cleveland, Ohio: World Publishing Co., 1958.

Sherwood, Robert E.: *Roosevelt and Hopkins,* New York: Harper & Brothers, 1948.

White, Theodore H., editor: *The Stilwell Papers,* New York: William Sloane Associates, Inc., 1948.

## UNIT BIBLIOGRAPHIES

## PROLOGUE: *PAX GERMANICA*

Arps, Lt/Col. Leslie H. and Quigley, Frank V., "The Origin, Development and Organization of the Luftwaffe," paper, dated 1 October 1945; Special File of General Frederick H. Smith, Jr., U. S. Air Force.

Bewley, Charles: *Herman Göring and the Third Reich,* New York: Devin-Adair Co., 1962.

British Air Ministry: "Notes on the German Air Force," April 1943; U. S. Navy reprint.

Bullock, Alan: *Hitler, A Study in Tyranny,* New York: Harper & Brothers, 1960.

Carr, Edward Hallett: *German-Soviet Relations Between the Two World Wars,* Baltimore: Johns Hopkins Press, 1951.

Craig, Gordon A.: *The Politics of the Prussian Army,* New York: Oxford University Press, 1955.

Frischauer, Willi: *The Rise and Fall of Hermann Goering,* Boston: Houghton Mifflin Co., 1951.

Goerlitz, Walter: *History of the German General Staff,* New York: Frederick A. Praeger, 1953.

Hallgarten, George W. F.: "General Hans von Seeckt and Russia, 1920–1922," Chicago: *Journal of Modern History,* March 1949.

Hilger, Gustav and Meyer, Alfred G.: *The Incompatible Allies,* New York: Macmillan Co., 1953.

Manvell, Roger and Fraenkel, Heinrich: *Goering,* New York: Simon & Schuster, 1962.

Melville, Cecil F.: *The Russian Face of Germany,* London: Wishart & Co., 1932.

Wheeler-Bennett, John W.: *The Nemesis of Power,* New York: St. Martin's Press, 1954.


I.  BLITZKRIEG

Benoist-Mechin, Jacques: *Sixty Days That Shook the West,* New York: G. P. Putnam's Sons, 1963.

Bolitho, Hector: *Combat Report,* London: B. T. Batsford, Ltd., 1943.

Divine, David: *The Nine Days of Dunkirk,* New York: W. W. Norton & Co., Inc., 1959.

Garnett, David: *War in the Air,* Garden City, N.Y.: Doubleday, Doran & Co., Inc., 1941.

Gourtard, A.: *The Battle for France,* New York: Ives Washburn, Inc., 1959.

Hagen, Louis, editor: *The Schellenberg Memoirs,* New York: Harper & Brothers, 1957.

Halstead, Ivor: *Wings of Victory,* New York: E. P. Dutton & Co., 1941.

Michaelis, Ralph: *From Bird Cage to Battle Plane,* New York: Thomas Y. Crowell Co., 1943.

Monks, Noel: *Squadrons Up!,* New York: Whittlesey House, McGraw-Hill Book Co., 1941.

Richey, Paul: *Fighter Pilot,* London: B. T. Batsford, Ltd., 1941.

Taylor, Telford: *The March of Conquest,* New York: Simon & Schuster, 1958.

Welles, Sumner: *The Time for Decision,* New York: Harper & Brothers, 1944.


II.  THE BATTLE OF BRITAIN

Anon.: *Coastal Command,* New York: Macmillan Co., 1943.

————: *Front Line 1940–41,* London: His Majesty's Stationery Office, 1942.

————: *Ourselves in Wartime,* London: Odham's Press, Ltd., ca. 1941.

Boorman, H. P. P.: *Hell's Corner 1940,* Maidstone, Kent, England: Kent Messenger, 1941.

Brickhill, Paul: *Reach for the Sky,* New York: W. W. Norton & Co., 1954.

Childers, James Saxon: *War Eagles,* New York: D. Appleton-Century Co., 1943.

Collier, Basil: *The Defence of the United Kingdom,* London: Her Majesty's Stationery Office, 1957.

————: *Leader of the Few,* London: Jarrold's, 1966.

Collier, Richard: *Eagle Day,* New York: E. P. Dutton & Co., Inc., 1966.

Deere, Alan C.: *Nine Lives,* London: Hodder & Stoughton, 1959.

Fitzgibbon, Constantine: *The Winter of the Bombs,* New York: W. W. Norton & Co., Inc., 1957.

Forester, Larry: *Fly for Your Life,* London: Frederick Muller, Ltd., 1956.

Gribble, Leonard R.: *Epics of the Fighting R.A.F.,* London: George G. Harrap & Co., Ltd., 1943.

Kennerly, Byron: *The Eagles Roar!,* New York: Harper & Brothers, 1942.

Lane, B. J.: *Spitfire!,* London: John Murray, 1942.

Lasserre, Jean, editor: "The Battle of Britain," special issue, *Icare, revue des pilotes de ligne,* Orly, France: Automne-Hiver, 1965.

Mason, Francis K.: *Battle over Britain,* Garden City, N.Y.: Doubleday & Co., Inc., 1969.

Masters, David: *So Few,* London: Eyre & Spottiswoode, 1946.

McKee, Alexander: *Strike from the Sky,* London: Souvenir Press, 1960.

Middleton, Drew: *The Sky Suspended,* New York: Longmans, Green & Co., 1960.

Reynolds, James: *Paddy Finucane,* New York: Edmond Byrne Hackett, 1942.

Shores, Christopher and Williams, Clive: *Aces High,* London: Neville Spearman, 1966.

Spaight, J. M.: *The Battle of Britain 1940,* London: Geoffrey Bles, 1941.

Taylor, Telford: *The Breaking Wave,* New York: Simon & Schuster, 1967.

Thompson, Laurence: *1940,* New York: Wm. Morrow & Co., Inc., 1966.

Wood, Derek and Dempster, Derek: *The Narrow Margin,* New York: McGraw-Hill Book Co., Inc., 1961.


III.  GREATER EAST ASIA CO-PROSPERITY SPHERE

Anders, Curt: *Fighting Airmen,* New York: G. P. Putnam's Sons, 1966.

Boyington, Gregory: *Baa Baa Black Sheep,* New York: G. P. Putnam's Sons, 1958.

Chennault, Claire Lee: *Way of a Fighter,* New York: G. P. Putnam's Sons, 1949.

Edmonds, Walter E.: *They Fought with What They Had,* Boston: Little, Brown & Co., 1951.

Fuchida, Mitsuo and Okumiya, Masatake: *Midway, the Battle That Doomed Japan,* Annapolis, Md.: U. S. Naval Institute, 1955.

Fukudome, Vice-Adm. Shigeru: "Hawaii Operation," Annapolis, Md.: *U. S. Naval Institute Proceedings,* December 1955.

Garfield, Brian: *The Thousand-Mile War,* Garden City, N.Y.: Doubleday & Co., Inc., 1969.

Glines, Carroll V.: *Doolittle's Tokyo Raiders,* Princeton, N.J.: D. Van Nostrand Co., Inc., 1964.

Gurney, Gene: *Five Down and Glory,* New York: G. P. Putnam's Sons, 1958.

Ito, Masanori with Pineau, Roger: *The End of the Imperial Japanese Navy,* New York: W. W. Norton & Co., 1962.

Lawson, Ted W. and Considine, Robert: *Thirty Seconds over Tokyo,* New York: Random House, 1943.

Lord, Walter: *Day of Infamy,* New York: Henry Holt & Co., 1957.

———: *Incredible Victory,* New York: Harper & Row, Inc., 1967.

MacDonald, Scot: *Evolution of Aircraft Carriers,* Washington, D.C.: Office of the Chief of Naval Operations, Department of the Navy, 1964.

Mears, Frederick: *Carrier Combat,* Garden City, N.Y.: Doubleday & Co., Inc., 1944.

Merrill, James M.: *Target Tokyo,* New York: Rand McNally & Co., 1964.

Miller, Lt. Max: *Daybreak for Our Carrier,* New York: Whittlesey House, McGraw-Hill Book Co., 1944.

Potter, John Deane: *Yamamoto, The Man Who Menaced America,* New York: Viking Press, 1965.

Reynolds, Quentin: *The Amazing Mr. Doolittle,* New York: Appleton-Century Crofts, Inc., 1953.

Scott, Robert L.: *God Is My Co-Pilot,* New York, Ballantine Books, 1956.

Stafford, Edward P.: *The Big E: The Story of the U.S.S. Enterprise,* New York: Random House, 1962.

Toland, John: *But Not in Shame,* New York: Random House, 1961.

Tuleja, Thaddeus V.: *Climax at Midway,* New York: W. W. Norton & Co., Inc., 1960.

Ulanoff, Stanley M.: *Fighter Pilot,* Garden City, N.Y.: Doubleday & Co., Inc., 1962.

Whelen, Russell: *The Flying Tigers,* New York: Viking Press, 1942.

Wohlstetter, Roberta: *Pearl Harbor: Warning and Decision,* Stanford, Cal.: Stanford University Press, 1962.

## IV. THE BIG LEAGUE

Barker, Ralph: *The Thousand Plan,* London: Chatto & Windus, Ltd., 1965.

Brickhill, Paul: *The Dam Busters,* London: Evans Brothers, Ltd., 1951.

Burke, Edmund: *Guy Gibson, V.C.,* London: Arco Publications, 1961.

Caidin, Martin: *Black Thursday,* New York: E. P. Dutton & Co., 1960.

Dugan, James and Stewart, Carroll: *Ploesti,* New York: Random House, 1962.

Gibson, Guy: *Enemy Coast Ahead,* London: Michael Joseph, 1946.

Jostwick, Jerry J. and Keating, Lawrence A.: *Combat Camera Man,* New York: Chilton Co., 1961.

Morrison, Wilbur H.: *The Incredible 305th,* New York: Duell, Sloan & Pearce, 1962.

Owens, Walter E.: *As briefed, a family history of the 384th Bombardment Group,* copyright by Walter E. Owens, 1946.

Peaslee, Budd J.: *Heritage of Valor,* Philadelphia: J. B. Lippincott Co., 1964.

Rumpf, Hans: *The Bombing of Germany,* New York: Holt, Rinehart & Winston, 1963.

Saundby, Robert: *Air Bombardment,* New York: Harper & Brothers, 1961.

Wolff, Leon: *Low Level Mission,* Garden City, N.Y.: Doubleday & Co., Inc., 1951.

## V. KENNEY'S KIDS, SOME SAILORS, AND A FEW MARINES

Johnston, Stanley: *The Grim Reapers,* Philadelphia: The Blakiston Co., 1943.

Simmons, Walter: *Joe Foss, Flying Marine,* New York: E. P. Dutton & Co., 1943.

## VI. TARGET GERMANY

Collier, Basil: *The Battle of the V-Weapons 1944–45,* New York: Wm. Morrow & Co., 1965.

Devon, Francis: *Flak Bait,* New York: Duell, Sloan & Pearce, 1948.

Hall, Grover C.: *1000 Destroyed,* Dallas: Morgan Aviation Books, 1961.

Irving, David: *The Destruction of Dresden,* New York: Holt, Rinehart and Winston, 1964.

Johnson, Robert S. and Caidin, Martin: *Thunderbolt,* New York: Rinehart & Co., 1958.

Rust, Kenn C.: *The 9th Air Force in World War II,* Fallbrook, Cal.: Aero Publishers, Inc., 1967.

Ryan, Cornelius: *The Last Battle,* New York: Simon & Schuster, 1966.

Toland, John: *Battle, the Story of the Bulge,* New York: Random House, 1959.

———: *The Last 100 Days,* New York: Random House, 1966.

## VII. THE DIVINE WIND

Benedict, Ruth: *The Chrysanthemum and the Sword,* Boston: Houghton Mifflin Co., 1946.

Caidin, Martin: *A Torch to the Enemy,* New York: Ballantine Books, 1960.

Craig, William: *The Fall of Japan,* New York: The Dial Press, 1967.

Fahey, James J.: *Pacific War Diary 1942–1945,* Boston: Houghton Mifflin Co., 1963.

Falk, Stanley L.: *Decision at Leyte,* New York: W. W. Norton & Co., 1966.

Gurney, Gene: *Journey of the Giants,* New York: Coward-McCann, Inc., 1961.

Inoguchi, Rikihei; Nakajima, Tadashi; and Pineau, Roger: *The Divine Wind,* Annapolis, Md.: U. S. Naval Institute, 1958.

Jablonski, David: "The Rise and Fall of the East Asia Co-Prosperity Sphere," New York: Bronx High School of Science, 1968.

Morrison, Wilbur H.: *Hellbirds: The Story of the B-29s in Combat,* New York: Duell, Sloan & Pearce, 1960.

Mosley, Leonard: *Hirohito, Emperor of Japan,* Englewood Cliffs, N.J.: Prentice-Hall, Inc., 1966.

Snyder, Earl: *General Leemy's Circus,* New York: Exposition Press, 1955.

Wehrmeister, R. L.: "Divine Wind over Okinawa," Annapolis, Md.: *U. S. Naval Institute Proceedings,* June 1957.

Woodward, Vann C.: *The Battle for Leyte Gulf,* New York: Macmillan Co., 1947.

Yokoi, Toshiyuki: "Kamikazes and the Okinawa Campaign," Annapolis, Md.: *U. S. Naval Institute Proceedings,* May 1954.

## MISCELLANEOUS

Anon.: *Battle Stations! Your Navy in Action,* New York: Wm. H. Wise & Co., Inc., 1946.

Brandt, Lt. Robert, editor: *Into the Wind: U.S.S. Yorktown in World War II,* unit history of CV 10, undated.

Jensen, Lt. Oliver: *Carrier War,* New York: Simon & Schuster, 1945.

McCahill, Maj. William P., editor: *Hit the Beach! Your Marine Corps in Action,* New York: Wm. H. Wise & Co., Inc., 1948.

Silsbee, Col. Nathaniel F., editor: *Bombs Away! Your Air Force in Action,* New York: Wm. H. Wise & Co., Inc., 1949.

Steichen, Capt. Edward: *Power in the Pacific,* New York: U. S. Camera Publishing Corp., 1945.

# Index OUTRAGED SKIES

*Note:* Page numbers in *italics* indicate illustrations

# INDEX

# INDEX

# INDEX

# INDEX

# INDEX

# Index WINGS OF FIRE

Note: References to illustrations are in *italics*.

# INDEX

# INDEX

# INDEX

# INDEX

# INDEX

# INDEX